TETA, MOTHER, AND ME

TETA, MOTHER, AND ME

Three Generations of Arab Women

Jean Said Makdisi

W. W. Norton & Company
New York • London

Manufacturing by Quebecor World, Fairfield
Production manager: Amanda Morrison

Library of Congress Cataloging-in-Publication Data

Makdisi, Jean Said.
Teta, mother, and me : three generations of Arab women / Jean Said Makdisi.—
1st American ed.
p. cm.
Previously published as Teta, mother and me : an Arab woman's memoir,
London : Saqi, 2005.
Includes bibliographical references.
ISBN 0-393-06156-6 (hardcover)
1. Makdisi, Jean Said—Family. 2. Family—Middle East. 3. Women—
Middle East—Biography. 4. Middle East—Biography. 5. Beirut
(Lebanon)—Biography. I. Title.
DS61.52.M35A3 2006
305.48'89270560922—dc22
2005029991

W. W. Norton & Company, Inc., 500 Fifth Avenue, New York, N.Y. 10110
www.wwnorton.com

W. W. Norton & Company Ltd.,
Castle House, 75/76 Wells Street, London W1T 3QT

1 2 3 4 5 6 7 8 9 0

*In loving memory of my mother, father
and grandmother*

and for

*Rosemarie, Joyce, Grace
and, of course, Edward, though too late*

Contents

MOTHER'S WORLD

WOMEN TOGETHER: MOTHER AND ME

Prelude

I began to think about this book when my maternal grandmother, Munira Badr Musa – or 'Teta' ('Granny'), as we called her in accordance with Arab tradition – was gradually sinking into the mental oblivion that darkened her last days. My mother, Hilda Musa Said, was then in the early years of her widowhood. All her children had grown up and gone away, and she was feeling the emptiness of her nest with a deep bitterness.

I was then a young married woman with young children, teaching at the Beirut College for Women and trying to cope with the often contradictory demands of a professional and a family life. Imbued with the ideas and attitudes of the revolutionary changes I had lived through – Palestine and Egypt in the 1940s and 1950s, America in the 1960s, Lebanon beginning in the 1970s – I felt myself to be overwhelmed and oppressed by my domestic duties, and feared that I was following in the footsteps of Teta and Mother towards what I saw as an inevitable marginality.

Somehow, over the decades, I had absorbed the notion that the new and the modern had brought with them success and happiness, especially for women. Yet now I felt excluded from these improvements, and could not help but wonder, as I compared my life with my mother's and grandmother's, in what way mine was better. I began to see the much-trumpeted advancement of women as a fiction. In this attitude of mine lay hidden deep misapprehensions and misunderstandings of modernity and the social life of women in our part of the world, and even of our personal lives.

I had thought Teta's life had always been imperturbably domestic, as I thought my mother's was, and unrelated to the outside world. Indeed, the idea of a perfected domestic life was as much a part of our feminine existence as the air we breathed. It had been drummed into me from my earliest age that not only did my husband, once I had one – and it was inevitable that I would – have to be catered to, comforted, supported and encouraged; not only did my children have to be well-cared-for, well-dressed, well-fed and well-behaved; not only did my house have to be perfectly clean and my household orderly and well-managed; not only had there always to be food and drink available for chance visitors; not only all that but, in addition, I myself had to be gracious, comforting, polite, friendly, generous, hospitable and always well-dressed. It was up to me to keep the family in its proper place in society by paying visits, condoling with the mourning, congratulating the rejoicing, comforting the sick. I was taught all of this from my youngest days, submitted to these highest standards of domesticated femalehood by Mother and Teta – first as a novice, then as an initiate.

These high standards permeated my life, and I found myself applying them to my professional concerns as well. I felt that for the benefit of my students I had to listen to each set of problems, read every book, see every film, attend every concert and join every university committee. My life was an endless round of duties, and in my heart of hearts I felt that though I might be modern, modernity was not all it was trumped up to be, and I was thoroughly worn out by it.

I resolved that one day, when I had the time, I would write about my grandmother's life, about my mother's and about mine, examining, comparing, reflecting. When Teta died in 1973, my resolve was deepened by sorrow, and when the war in Lebanon began two years later, it deepened further. So intensely did I feel my alienation from the politics of the war, and from all the decisions that had led to it, even while feeling as intensely my attachment to some of the issues it raised, that a great need arose in me to investigate my function as an individual, as a woman, as a mother and as a teacher in its context. I especially felt the need to validate my woman's role in society – for I had felt myself to be an unconnected and redundant object – and therefore my mother's and grandmother's as well.

By the nature of the war, I was thrown into very close contact with Mother; this added to the natural complexities of our relationship. All our emotions were heightened, augmented by the war, and the love and profound empathy we felt for each other were tangled up with anxiety, nervousness, and the doubt that seemed to consume everything in those terrible days. Her last illness, drawn out for months in exile, was a last straw of agony and of mutual, womanly, understanding. When Mother died, writing about her became an even more urgent need.

The war ended a few months after Mother died. Having experienced its shattering effects, I felt a new defensiveness for both Mother and Teta, who had lived through so many wars and upheavals. I felt they had been wronged, and I wished to redress the wrongs done them. We of the younger generation had judged them, and often found them wanting. We thought they lacked strength, or imagination, or gratitude, or willpower, or intellect, or *something*. From my new vantage point as war veteran, I felt that we had minimized the sapping, breaking effect that events had had on them. We did not understand how much strength they had. We did not credit them enough with their survival and ours, with what they had done to make life quite simply continue, nor did we understand the inner price they had paid.

Teta died when I was in my thirties. I had lived with her, talked with her, knew her, I thought, intimately. My memory of her was vivid, and I felt I could still smell the faint scent of eau de cologne that emanated from her. I could feel the softness of her skin and the frailty of her frame.

Yet when I came to write about her, I was shocked to find that I knew hardly anything about her life beyond its basic shape, and had only a vague idea of its relationship to the historical background. I discovered that I knew nothing about what schools she had attended, what clothes she had worn as a child, what songs she had sung, what games she had played. I knew next to nothing about her mother, or her relationship with her.

The many stories Teta had chosen to tell me in my childhood were mostly from the Bible, or about members of the community at large, and almost never about her own individual experiences. I suddenly saw that she had hardly ever talked about herself. She had blotted herself out as much as I was later to find the historians had generally blotted out the lives of women. With her silence and self-effacement she had denied herself and her own private personal story.

With a further shock I realized that I had never asked her about her life. I had collaborated in her self-effacement, as though accepting that the past of old women had no interest. It became part of my task to find out why, as I traced the few marks she had left, holding up the old ink to the light in order to try and read what had been rubbed out.

Later, I discovered that my ignorance of the past encompassed Mother as well, and that I knew little about the particulars of her childhood and youth, about the clothes *she* wore and the songs *she* sang.

I was astonished when I found that to write intelligibly about them, and especially about Teta, who belonged to an earlier, unknown Ottoman era, I would have to do historical research. It had always seemed to me, somehow, that beyond receiving blows from it, Teta, Mother, and I had nothing much to do with history, or it with us. I saw history as a parade of external events that went on entirely independently of us, without our intervention, our consent or even our awareness. Instinctively, I had accepted our outsider status, our separation from politics and history as a natural or at least a social reality, one that was absolute and self-evident. I did not understand history, and I did not understand that they – and I – had had much to do with its inner workings, even while often being alienated from its outer forms.

Teta was born in 1880, a subject of the Ottoman Empire, in the Syrian town of Homs, where her parents, natives of Mount Lebanon, had settled. She died in Beirut in 1973. Her long life spanned an era that saw enormous cultural change and conflict, as well as social and political upheavals, in the area known to Arabs as *bilad al-sham* – that is historic Syria, including Palestine, Syria, Lebanon and Jordan – and in Egypt, where her destiny was also to take her.

Mother was born in Nazareth, Palestine, in 1914. 'I opened my eyes to war!' Mother said to me many times. She closed them to war, too. She died in Washington D.C. in 1990, when the war in Lebanon was in its sixteenth year. Like her mother before her, and like me, Mother witnessed extraordinary and unsettling times. She lived through events that redrew maps, shifted populations, shook confidence in an environment that would not stand still, that created terrifying situations and bewildering changes in expectations, in ways of life, in morals and customs. Yet she had a richly rewarding life, and grew with her changing circumstances.

I too opened my eyes to war. I was born during World War II in Jerusalem, in what was then still Palestine. During my childhood, the Palestine war cut a brutal swath through my family, culture and history, and since that time I have experienced other wars and different forms of upheaval, as well as much happiness, in Egypt, in America and in Lebanon.

As I tried to reconstruct the lives of Teta and Mother and connect them to their surroundings I found that the standard histories by and large ignored the lives of women, and I had to go beyond them. My search was long and difficult. For every clue I found, a hundred new puzzles arose, and for every answer, a hundred questions. Luckily, however, I had a priceless resource at hand.

Ever since this book began to form, however vaguely, in my mind, I had asked Mother to write down memories of her childhood and early youth. She had repeatedly shrugged off my request, which at first was not very serious. I had thought it would be convenient, quite simply, to have a written map of the past to which I could one day easily refer, and had no idea how imperative that map would prove to be. It was only during the Lebanese war, when our world was crashing down on our heads – sometimes literally – that a tangible, permanent memory became a matter of intense and urgent importance to me. I began to plead with her, to pressure her, to write.

At last she agreed to set down her memories on paper. Perhaps she, too, felt the fleetingness of the moment and the need to trap the past in a concrete form for sanity's sake. In those dark days of the war, as confinement became more and more a way of life for her, she wrote and wrote. From the terrible conditions of the present she looked back at her past.

In a few months of fitful writing, during which she repeatedly stopped and started, she filled a notebook with her memories. One day she handed me the notebook and announced gloomily that she would write no more. What was the point of this exercise, she complained. It was depressing her; she was being reminded of the dead, and she had enough problems with the present without remembering the past. After a half-hearted attempt to make her write some more, I took the book from her reluctantly, acknowledging that I could ask no more of her. It was difficult to concentrate during the war, and I only glanced at her notebook when she surrendered it to me in that despair. Then I hid it away with my most precious belongings.

Only when the war ended, a few months after her death, did I read the notebook through. From the first page, Mother came alive for me, just as *her* dead had come alive for her as she wrote: her father, her husband, her brothers, even her younger self and, most of all, I think, her mother.

Mother had always been a maker and teller of stories. Even if she were recounting the smallest incident, she would embellish it with detail and colour, turning it into a matter of social and historic interest. And the reverse was also true: reality was, in her life, so often strange that the more logical and organized narrative of fiction was required to make sense of it. For Mother telling stories fulfilled a need, something like the one her mother's famous little cotton bags had filled, into which messy, confusing history could be neatly placed and tidied up, *snap-snap*.

Teta had made little bags for everything she owned, and always added steel snaps to close them with, *snap-snap*. I can see her now in my memory with some of those bags in her invariable evening ritual. She sits in her bed, propped up by pillows, playing patience on a thin wooden board balanced carefully on her knees. When she finishes she ties a rubber band around the pack of cards; places it in a bag; seals it in, *snap-snap*; puts the board down in its appointed place by her bed – everything Teta owned had its appointed place. She then picks up another cotton bag, which she carefully unsnaps, and takes out her black, leather-bound Arabic Bible. This, too, is bound by a thick rubber band that she must remove before starting her evening prayers, which she always ended with a mumbled '*Ameen*' ('Amen') and a little sigh. Now the rubber band goes back around the Bible, which goes back into the little cotton bag, *snap-snap*, which is then carefully placed on the bedside table. Next, the crocheted shawl and the gloves she has been wearing come off, are folded carefully, then placed neatly over the board. Only then does Teta move down in her bed and turn off the light. In the darkness I can hear her pat the sheets down, so that everything remains perfectly neat and orderly. I think she hardly moved at night, trying even in her sleep to maintain an un-rumpled bed.

She made bags for Mother's silver platters, and when I got married she made some for mine. She made them as part of her wedding present to me, along with some crocheted clothes-hanger covers and doilies. The bags are of soft pink cotton, and most of them have a fine pattern embroidered around the edges in blue. I have sometimes wondered why some of them are not embroidered, and whether even Teta's apparently infinite patience was exhausted by that little pattern. The clothes hangers are in different colours; around the steel centers of some she tied little felt flowers and strawberries, and around others, crocheted ribbons knotted into bows. The doilies are white and beige, in different shapes and sizes.

I have always treasured these things: they are her legacy to me, and from the beginning I tried to understand their meaning, which seemed always to elude me. I was sure there was more to them than mere little bags and doilies, more even than the hours it took to make each one, with failing eyesight and arthritic fingers and a stooped back. From the first, I felt in them some secret and agonizing meaning, if only I could find it, a frantic message I always felt I must decode.

Although I did not understand why, I felt instinctively that her obsessive needlework, her obsessive neatness and her equally obsessive memory were related to one another and, somehow, to me. I had always been aware that Teta was famous for her memory. She would often be consulted on questions of the past. She knew when everyone in the extended family was born, married, died; she could rattle off the dates without hesitation, and she was always right. It was a matter of pride to her that she also had full knowledge of the family of each of her acquaintances, knowing who was married to whom, tracing cousins and in-laws through generations, a formidable feat of memory. Whenever anyone was mentioned in conversation, it would be necessary to pause while she would run the name through her mental system, and then say, 'He is the one who married so-and-so, who was born in such-and-such a year', or 'Yes, she is the first cousin of the brother-in-law of the wife of so-and-so'. She kept a vast database on the subject of who left Palestine when, during, and after the war of 1948 that displaced her and her children. She knew where each acquaintance in her large circle had lived, and where they ended up as refugees.

Dates, names, places, relationships, comings and goings – all were tidied up and put into little mental bags, sealed neatly in her memory, *snap-snap*. It was her way of dealing with the world, tying past and present together, hers and her people's, lest they get away from one another. She wanted no loose ends floating about, adding confusion to the turbulent history she had lived. Her memory was a deliberate construction, an act of creation, a work of art – one could almost call it a work of fiction. She provided an order, a narrative shape, a cohesion, a reorganization of the chaotic arrivals and departures, the scattering of the people and of the world she knew, and all the confusion that adventure, colonization, wars and revolutions had brought. In keeping this record she had become the unofficial chronicler of her time and place, a time and place inordinately susceptible to change, to movement, to the destruction of more permanent forms of records.

In her last years, Teta's physical decline was paralleled by an ever-deepening mental one. She became more and more silent, and her body shrank visibly. Her normally impeccable clothes began to show signs of neglect, with uncharacteristic little spots, stains and rips apparently escaping her attention. She collapsed finally when her memory did. Her mind gradually disintegrated, atrophied, dissolved, and her whole being with it. The vagrant experiences of her long life, held together only by her carefully constructed catalogue of relationships, escaped from her will, and she lost the ability to hold them together. They drifted purposelessly around, colliding with each other at random.

One day, I suddenly realized that she no longer recognized me, and had no idea who I was. I was devastated. My lifeline had been cut, and I had been set loose, adrift. Without her constant and reassuring presence, I felt lost, almost terrified.

I was to experience the same feeling many years later, when Mother died.

As she wrote down memories of her early life, Mother told me much about Teta's as well. Now her natural gift for storytelling created a new magic, and as she spun her enchanted web, I understood both their lives as I never had before. From the threads that made up the realities of my mother and grandmother, I was able to make out the strands that had been spun into mine.

Still, Mother's memoir left many of my questions unanswered, and raised many more that I had never thought of. I turned to her two surviving brothers: Alif, her childhood companion, and Emil, the youngest of the family. Each of them wrote a memoir for me, complementing their sister's. Later I discovered that Mother, who had always been a prolific letter-writer, had preserved many of her own letters; I discovered other family letters as well.

The Teta who emerged from those memoirs and letters was radically different from the woman I had known. She had often appeared to me, especially in my childhood, like a figure in a negative picture, white, ghostlike, insubstantial, upside-down, inside-out. Looking at her again from the perspective of their own advancing age, her three children had, without intending it, written proud tributes to their mother. They wrote of a bustling matriarch, an active and creative member of her society, not the meek and marginal person I knew. When, trying to glean more about the past, I interviewed an ancient relative of ours who had known Teta in her heyday in Palestine, she said to me, beaming, 'Your Teta was *sit al-sittat* ('lady of ladies'). Everybody knew her; everybody loved her. There was no one like her.'

Though I felt a glow when I heard this, I was overwhelmed and drained by the vision of her decline that became clearer and clearer the more I understood of her past, and of the details that constituted her private story and its connections to public history.

Gradually I began to see how she had become the frail, bent, ghostlike Teta I knew. And gradually, as I learned details of my mother's early life about which I had known nothing, I began to see how her towering personality had emerged from the little girl she remembered herself to have been, so touchingly dependent on, and obedient to, her mother.

And once I saw how I was related to both, I began to write this book. We have become a family of storytellers and record-keepers.

For several years now, since I began, I have been jousting with history, with feminism and with received notions about Arab women. As I read and worked, every new discovery and picture confronted a pre-existing image or thought based on my personal experiences, and in the feminist view that I had adopted years ago. I answered some of these questions, but many new ones emerged, and the simplest impression turned out to consist of a hundred possibilities. While I struggled to reconstruct the lives of my mother and grandmother and tie them to my own, I learned that many of my preconceived ideas were wrong, and that my notions of modernity as opposed to tradition, especially in their application to the lives of my mother and grandmother, were irrelevant if not utterly false. The past now mingled with the present, the dead with the living. I had thought I was going to rediscover their lives; I found that what I was doing was *discovering*, a different process entirely. It was like an archeological experience, like searching for one set of relics and finding quite another instead, one I had no idea existed at all.

As I worked, I discovered not only aspects of their lives, historical facts and trends that I knew nothing about, but geography and architecture as well, noting the way one civilization interacts with another. I traveled around the land, searching for places significant to my work, landmarks of my mother's and grandmother's lives; seeing as though for the first time places I thought I knew; going into mosques, churches and monasteries I had passed a hundred times but never entered; visiting old towns, looking for old buildings, examining old books. I looked at pictures from the past, noting the clothes people wore. I discussed food with older people, learned about old menus, when certain dishes were invented and by whom, what people ate, and how they regarded table manners. I noted vegetation and seasonal changes, examined the colors of the countryside and the smells of the land. I developed a sense of continuity with the land and the buildings, as I came to terms with the history they signified.

The history of the region came to life, and with it an era long past, and forgotten by many – when historical Syria was one open space, and the whole region was connected with itself and with its past. This was before the constrictions brought about by modern imperialism, which divided and locked people into new, small countries that became rivals, and even fought each other. I reveled in that sense of wide open space, and freedom from those narrow boundaries which were created by the

British and the French after World War One, and breathed more easily in that mental atmosphere than I do in real life.

As I sorted out the details of Teta's and Mother's lives, tracing my consciousness through theirs, I discovered that we women had made history as much as it had made us, that our lives and our very being were intertwined with it, knotted up in its tangled webs. The result has been for me a complex re-reading of my life, and the lives of other women of my generation.

By the time I finished, Teta's and Mother's past had become mine, and mine theirs. Through my new understanding of their lives, my own became in my eyes less fuzzy, less detached from theirs. I felt less alienated, more attached to the world, more at peace with my mother and grandmother, and with myself and the world in which I live.

The various aspects of my identity, which I had felt had been at war with one another, fell at last into place, not neatly, mind you, not silently or meekly, but at least intelligibly. The modern, the traditional; the Western, the Eastern; the Christian, the Muslim; the rich, the poor; the political, the apolitical; the past, the present: I have learned to see them not as contradictions or as exclusive categories from which I could choose only one, but as a rich background of cultural and historical circumstance to the life I have lived.

Though it has raised many questions, and caused me much perturbation, this work has been one of self-discovery as much as of reconciliation.

IN MY OWN TIME

Jean, c. 1945.

CHAPTER I

Jean

My name is Jean, and in my name lies my history. I was named after my father's mother, Hanneh Shammas, but my name was anglicized. Naming me after his mother was, for my father, an act of devotion and affirmation. Anglicizing her name, however, was an act of repudiation: like so many Arab men of his generation, my father saw the future as lying in Europe or in America, to which he had emigrated in the early years of the twentieth century. He had returned to Jerusalem in the early 1920s to honour his mother's deathbed wish, but never really forgave her for deflecting him from what he had seen as his destiny in the New World. In anglicizing the name that he bestowed on me, he showed his belief that my future lay, hidden, curled up, unborn, in the English language. To him, Jerusalem and all its travails was tied up with the past.

From my earliest childhood I was told that I had been named after Teta (Grandmother) Hanneh. I only saw her picture for the first time a few years ago: in my childhood hardly anything existed of her except her name, and she always seemed an abstraction. Her only legacy to me was indirectly relayed, an admonition to her children not to eat too much cheese 'or else you will get worms'. My father frequently repeated this advice to me when I was young, referring to his mother's wisdom. Mother used to laugh when he said this, and whisper to me that she thought Teta Hanneh used this as a way of controlling the cheese consumption of her numerous progeny, thus saving herself the labour of making more of that delicacy. 'Eat olives,' Daddy used to say. 'They are better for you than cheese.' On the other hand, my brother, who was always ready to tease me when we were children, used to say that an olive tree would grow in my stomach if I accidentally swallowed an olive stone. Whenever I swallowed an olive stone, or any other seed for that matter, I would stare in alarm at my stomach, watching in terror for sprouting leaves.

When I was born during the Second World War, the British were in control of Palestine, as well as Egypt, and their royal family had lost the allure that had previously charmed my parents into naming my brother after Edward, Prince of Wales. I was their fourth child: their firstborn had died during a delivery bungled by a drunken doctor. Romantic films were no longer a satisfactory model, as they had been when my sister was born a few years earlier. She had been named after the lead character in the film *Rose Marie*, starring Jeanette MacDonald and Nelson Eddy. My birth occurred at a particularly unromantic time: the anxiety of the war and events in Palestine and Egypt weighed heavily on my parents. It was a time for retrenchment, for protective solidarity, and so they turned to the name of my father's mother.

My name was not without a certain romantic aura, however. When I was growing up, I had to contend with 'I dream of Jeannie with the light brown hair,' who was, you may remember, 'borne like a vapour on the summer air.' Though when I was young, Stephen Foster's song brought me much grief, especially when sung at me by aunts and uncles and older cousins in the embarrassingly sentimental style of the time, I must admit to a certain nostalgic sense of proprietorship when I think of it today. I was always called 'Jeannie' at home, though Daddy often and inexplicably called me 'Yona' as well. I hear, down the fading corridor of time, his voice affectionately calling me by that name.

Mother sometimes called me 'June', but mostly I was called 'Jeannie', especially by my brother and sisters. Joyce is the only one of my siblings who still uses that name for me, the others having promoted me to a more formal, sterner and less childlike 'Jean'. My sisters too are now addressed by their formal names, instead of the 'Gracie' and 'Joycie' of our childhood. Rosemarie, however, has remained 'Rosie'. Edward always reacted vehemently to any attempt to shorten his name: 'Ed' or 'Eddie' would render him almost speechless with irritation.

I have often been tempted in recent times to change my name back to that good old-fashioned Arabic 'Hanneh', in commemoration not only of my paternal grandmother, whom I never knew, but of an earlier time, when names were more certain and less unsettling. I have had many embarrassing moments with my English name, especially in Lebanon, where it is read like the French masculine *Jean* and puzzles many who hear it for the first time. I have been scolded by Lebanese officials for the unreasonable nature of my name: why, an immigration officer at the airport once asked me petulantly, did your parents give you a man's name? History has affected our sense of irony as much as our linguistic sensitivity: for most people in Lebanon, where I have unexpectedly ended up, French is the natural second language. English, on the other hand, was the second language of mandate Palestine and colonial Egypt. With America, these were all places with which my family was more closely associated. On the other hand, there are those here in Beirut who, much to my distress and annoyance, insist on calling me 'Jane'. I cannot understand why they prefer 'Jane' to 'Jean', which, though it has from the beginning been a thorn in my flesh, is at least my name.

But 'Jean' is not the worst thing about my name, for attached to it is an astonishing 'Rosalind'. The closest I can come to an explanation for this middle name is a nostalgic schooldays memory cherished by Mother of her having played Celia in *As You Like It*. Why Mother found it more attractive to name me 'Rosalind' instead of 'Celia' I do not know, but I suppose I should be grateful that I was not encumbered with the latter name. Each of my sisters is also burdened with an inexplicable middle name. When I married, I exorcised 'Rosalind' from my new official papers, but to my everlasting chagrin and ire, my husband restored it while absent-mindedly filling out a form at some later time. It has remained to irk my children for ever, as their official papers are also saddled with it, and with the various transformations to which it is subject – mostly 'Rosa Lina' – by officials who receive it even less graciously than the offending 'Jean'.

No one seems to have thought of naming any of the grandchildren after Teta Munira.

One of my clearest childhood memories may have been reinforced by a family picture in which the memory is sealed. We used regularly to linger over it when Mother's carefully assembled photograph album was taken out and the whole family pored over it, enthusiastically pointing out names and faces, some long forgotten, or so vastly changed as to be unrecognizable. The album is a relic of our Jerusalem past from which we have been violently torn – a past that might have faded away, like the pictures themselves, had we not devoted ourselves to its preservation.

The photograph is of the wedding in 1946 of my cousin George Said, the middle son of Auntie Nabiha, my father's sister, and I am one of the flower girls at the wedding. I am standing on the stone and marble stairs of the house in Jerusalem, lifting the skirt of my long blue taffeta dress. I well remember the rustle of the taffeta, and the light blue colour that matched that of the bridesmaids' dresses. Joyce is standing a few steps below me. She too is wearing a long taffeta dress, identical to mine. Our dresses are hand-smocked: we had smocks on many of our best dresses, which Mother used to send to the nuns for smocking. Both Joyce and I have the long Victorian-style curls achieved by the use of curling irons. Rosie is standing in the background, similarly dressed. Ribbons are tied around our hair, and fixed into large *fionkas*, or bows, at the top of our heads, a little to the side. Joyce and I are both carrying straw baskets full of rose petals, and the handles of our baskets are decorated with ribbons matching those in our hair.

I remember driving to the Anglican church. The car, decorated with flowers and ribbons, passed through the gates and pulled up under some large trees, cypresses, I think, or ficus. I remember the sensation of coolness as we descended into the shadow of those large trees, and as I listened to the sound of the church bells. I remember the bridal procession into the church, after it had assembled outside while the bells continued to peal, with Joyce and me leading the way into the organ music as the sound of the bells subsided. Our task was to throw petals in the path of the bride, the beautiful Huda, and I remember most earnestly being aware of her beauty, about which everyone commented, and of the importance of my work, which I saw as serving her beauty. Joyce, however, had misunderstood our task and assiduously picked up the petals even as I tossed them from my basket. In that distant memory I can hear the amused murmur of the congregation as we walked down the aisle, Rosie behind us, carrying the bride's train.

Some months later my sisters and I were bridesmaids at the wedding of George's elder brother, Youssef, and his beautiful bride, Aida. Another picture in the family album commemorates this event.

I remember the house in Jerusalem, with its wide marble staircase and its garden, where I used to play with my siblings and cousins. I remember walking home from school in 1946 or 1947, and seeing the English soldiers at the sandbag barricades they had erected in the large empty circle. I believe it was Salameh Square. I did not know its name then, but I have now identified it from one of the many books dedicated to the memory of our Jerusalem as it was then, before the war.

I remember the Old City well, the drives to Bethlehem and to Haifa, where we visited Uncle Alif's family, and to Safad, where Mother's eldest brother, Uncle Munir, lived. I especially remember Uncle Munir's house and playing with my particular companion, my cousin Marwan. I remember walking down Jaffa Street in Jerusalem, holding my father's hand, towards the Palestine Educational Company, the family business. I remember entering it, and the feeling of being embraced by the darkness of the book-lined shelves that covered the walls, as well as its musty smell. Indeed, Jerusalem often comes back to me in a series of scents. I smell Jerusalem in the jasmine and the orange blossom, the smell of a lemon being squeezed, the smell of cinnamon sticks in syrup, the bay leaf and olive oil of the soap from Nablus they used to wash us with.

As I look back on these weddings, at the house, at the streets, at the old shop, and as I smell those old scents, I cannot help thinking yet again of the deep and irreversible transformations that have taken place in our family since the loss of Palestine, and the series of separations and scatterings which have resulted from its loss. An unbreachable chasm separates my time from Teta's, and from Mother's, separates the past from the present, separates my family's life from its heart and soul in Palestine. Things were never the same afterwards. All peace ended then, not just for us personally, but for the entire region, perhaps the entire world, and a deep anxiety has reigned in all our hearts ever since. Somehow the loss of Jerusalem sank deep into my being, though I was a little girl at the time and did not know it.

My memories of Jerusalem tie me to my past, and into the heart of history. To be from Jerusalem, and to have lost it, is to be attached to the struggle for Palestine, and therefore to the heart of Arab history. And since I have often felt left out of the political struggle, I cling to these memories, feeling that in preserving a lost time and place I am after all making a contribution, however infinitesimal.

Until 1948, and the Palestine war, our family moved regularly between Jerusalem and Cairo. For Palestinians, the year 1948 was a time of movement, of scattering, of families breaking up and moving apart. It was a time of breakdown, of entropy. The community broke up, dissolved: only later did it re-form itself, with the political aim of returning and retrieving what had been lost. In 1948 people who had been close lost touch with each other. Many ended up living permanently in places they had never dreamed of visiting; accident and chance had much to do with which Palestinians ended up where.

We were in Cairo during the 1948 war, and among my clearest – and saddest – childhood memories are those surrounding the various and sudden arrivals of all those confused and anxious relations, and the palpable panic in the air. Auntie Nabiha, widowed for some years, came with her children, by now grown men and women. I learned little directly from Mother herself about this tumultuous period in Palestinian history, or of what she did during her various sojourns in Palestine. I never spoke to Auntie Nabiha about it either, at least not that I can remember: I did not speak to her about very much at all, because I hardly saw her once I became an adult.

The year 1948 was, for Mother, a time of domestic retrenchment. She was a busy mother of five children – the eldest a teenager, the youngest a toddler – and was running a large household. The plight of those relatives and friends who kept arriving one after the other, and the anxiety for those who did not come and with whom they lost touch, must have brought her to a high level of political awareness. In spite of that, her domestic duties, elevated in her mind to the level of a vocation, must have created a barrier between her and the outside world.

I have been a mother of young children in wartime too, and I know that even – perhaps especially – in the most intense and dangerous crises, young children have to be fed, bathed, changed, comforted, nursed. Sensing the tension around them, they often in their turn become tense and tearful; they misbehave and demand attention. No matter what terrible events might be unfolding, their reality supersedes all others. In addition, all those refugee guests had to be catered for, fed and housed, and their spirits calmed. The political crisis created a domestic emergency, which demanded all Mother's attention and energy.

The role of women in Palestine in the 1940s, however, has been widely documented. The Palestinian Women's Union, founded in Nablus in 1921, and at first mostly involved in charity work, became more directly involved politically, especially in the cities, and occasionally in the villages too. Urban women participated in the Palestinian political struggle by demonstrating, sending telegrams of protest, and organizing women's conferences consisting mostly of members of the national bourgeoisie. The peasant women, on the other hand, enjoyed far greater freedom of movement and were therefore more effectively and directly involved in the battles that pitted the Arab resistance against European Jews and British forces alike. They carried arms and food to the fighters, smuggling these under their ample dresses; they sheltered the men when they were escaping arrest.

Auntie Nabiha's life in those last months in Jerusalem must have been similar to that of Hala Sakakini. A schoolteacher, and daughter of the principal of the Jerusalem Girls' College, Sakakini kept a journal in which she recorded her last months in the city. The Sakakinis lived in the Katamon quarter of Jerusalem, which, like Talbiya, where the Saids lived, was one of the prime modern residential areas. Sakakini describes the women's meetings she attended as well as the Red Cross work at which bandages were wrapped and First Aid learned. At night, the Jerusalem women endured the profound anxiety that accompanied the fighting; when they heard explosions, they wondered where they were, and then listened for more, worrying about their men. They would hear fighters scurrying around in the gardens or streets outside their windows, whispering sometimes, and wonder who they were. Long empty days without work, and then the gradual forced departures, are recorded in countless stories and memoirs similar to those with which I grew up. At one point Sakakini writes: 'I shall be proud to say in the future that I stuck to Jerusalem during the most dangerous period.' I am sure that Auntie Nabiha too must have proudly resisted, but in the end she and her family also moved to Cairo.

As the years passed, some of our relations stayed in Cairo, while others left for Arab cities such as Amman, Baghdad and Beirut. Eventually, as one city of refuge after another was engulfed in war or revolution, these relatives moved further away. My Said cousins, children of Auntie Nabiha, ended up variously in Canada, Switzerland and Jordan. Mother's brothers, all scattered by the 1948 war, ended up in different places as well: Uncle Munir moved from Safad to Ramallah, on the West Bank of the Jordan, which had become part of the Hashemite Kingdom of Jordan. Later, after Ramallah was occupied by the Israelis in 1967, he moved to Amman. Uncle Alif, Mother's closest childhood companion, and Uncle Emil, the youngest of the family, settled first in Egypt and then moved on to Beirut. Uncle Rayik, Teta's middle son, went first to Beirut, but in 1950 he emigrated to the United States with his family, and Teta never saw them again. Today Uncle Alif lives in Seattle, Emil in Miami; we have been scattered to the four corners of the earth.

It took some time for those people who had been forced to leave Palestine to realize that there was to be no return. Usually it was years before they came to this understanding: very few had the prescience to know from the first that Palestine had been irretrievably lost to them and that they were condemned to live as exiles and refugees. Hala Sakakini's journal dramatically illustrates the progress of this dawning realization:

> This is our twentieth day in Cairo and how we long to go back to Jerusalem and our home ... Today we have been exactly one month in Cairo ... I hope we shall not have to stay here

more than a month longer ... We are still refugees in Cairo. It is almost two months since we left our home in Jerusalem ... I hope it won't be long before we go back ... We will have nothing when, or rather if, we go back to Jerusalem ... It is so painful to think that we might never go back ... Now everything seems so hopeless ... Our return to Palestine seems to lie very far in the future ... In a few months we will have spent a whole year in Cairo as refugees and we still cannot tell if we are ever to go back to Jerusalem.

My family was lucky, of course. We had a home and means in Cairo, to which all those relations and friends could turn. Yet, though my father had always complained of Jerusalem's provincialism, though he had claimed to hate its gossip and cemeteries, a light went out of his eyes after 1948. The Old City remained accessible until the Israelis occupied it during the 1967 war, but he refused to go apart from one occasion: to attend the wedding of his nephew, Robert Said, Auntie Nabiha's youngest son, in 1966.

In 1948 the heart of our family was torn out, and the centre of our existence was broken. It was as if the constellation by which our family had navigated through the rough waters of our history was eclipsed. It is only recently that I have come to understand how deeply affected we have all been by the Palestinian experience, how we have lived our lives in its shadow. Most of all, though we have lived well and done well, and accomplished much, though we have made many deep friendships throughout the world, since 1948 we have been outsiders – not only my parents, but their children, and, I fear, their children's children as well.

CHAPTER 2

A Cairo Childhood

From 1948 until the early 1960s we were entrenched in Cairo. As I look back over this time, I see my own development blended in with my mother's, and with Teta's palpable decline. In some of my earliest memories, however, I often see Teta and Mother, mother and daughter, united in their common task of domestic life and child care.

In one particularly vivid set of memories, I see them standing side by side at the edge of the bath-tub in which I struggle as they hold me down to wash my hair on a Sunday night, each with a towel tied around her waist. When I was a child my hair was very thick and curly, and very long. Washing it was an agonizing procedure. They used the square blocks of soap made of olive oil and bay leaf, purchased regularly from Nablus. When we were in Cairo, the soap was brought from Jerusalem by Auntie Nabiha, or by Teta when she came from Palestine to stay with us. Sometimes soapy water would mingle with the tears, my eyes would burn, and I would scream and struggle. After testing for the squeak of cleanliness, they would pour on a conditioning concoction made of *babounij* (camomile). *Babounij,* Mother always claimed – wrongly, as it turned out – would preserve the reddish-golden colour of my hair, but I hated the smell.

After the *babounij* was rinsed off, I would climb out of the high-sided bath-tub into their arms, where I would be engulfed in a warm, towelly embrace before the final and most difficult phase of the operation began. Dressed in my clean pyjamas and, despite my tears, secretly enjoying the lingering scent of the soap, I would sit on the ottoman near Mother's armchair, in the corner of her Cairo bedroom, where the sun used to pour in through the slatted shutters, making lines of light which always fascinated me. My tightly curled hair was dried with towels, and then, as I struggled more than ever, Mother or Teta would untangle it with a big iron brush before combing it with a wide-toothed wooden comb. Eventually it would be tied into plaits, held together with rubber bands.

I can see Mother and Teta standing together near my bedside when I was sick, the mother teaching the daughter how to attach the warm cups to my chest to alleviate the cough: cupping was an integral part of the medical arts practised on us as children. I do not know if it did any good, or indeed any harm, though we all survived. I see Teta urging Mother on with the impossible task of forcing me to swallow a raw egg when I had a cold. I see the nightly sessions in which, just before bedtime, they wrapped swathes of wool around our middles, like warm but clumsy cummerbunds, or a kind of swaddling, as my siblings and I stood on the beds one by one, turning, turning, and then, making a game of it, turning too much and too fast, and being scolded to make us stand still.

Domestic life as I grew up was a work of art, an act of theatre. Mother was the producer, the director, the principal actress and also, in some ways, the critic and the audience. And though it was a construction, a creation, though it was short-lived and a product of its own particular time and place, it worked naturally, spontaneously and very well. Watching my mother establish a vast authority in her domestic role was a formative experience for me. It was also the time during which

I absorbed the lessons of the relationship between her and my father. They idealized this relationship, and we constantly had little lectures and homilies about it, about what it meant to be husband and wife, and what each was supposed to mean for the other.

Their relationship was certainly a construction, a creation of their own, made by history and travel and schooling as much as by their own characters. Mother, who was naturally sociable and outgoing, socialized my father, who was by nature introverted and reticent. She created their social life, presiding over it and enjoying it whereas he tolerated it mostly for her sake. It was she who took credit for his appearance, who made sure his shoes were shined and his suit pressed, who provided him every morning with a clean white linen handkerchief for his trouser pocket, and another one tucked neatly into his chest pocket. Before guests arrived she would look him over, as she did in any case every morning when he went to work, check his tie and collar, make him change, despite his protests, one or the other if she wasn't satisfied, and then dust off his shoulders and proudly check her work as he walked out into the living-room.

It was she who made sure he wore his cologne, and who saw to his meals. It was she who ensured that he saw the doctor when he was ill, and then followed the doctor's instructions. She was his guardian and his lifeline; without her, he would have been isolated and entirely cut off from pleasant society. He would have enjoyed none of the graces of cosmopolitan life, none of the company, none of the prestige that she helped provide him with in that society.

And he was her guardian and her lifeline. He was endowed with a mischievous, boyish sense of humour, with which he countered her tendency towards morbid anxiety. Whereas she provided him with the graces of life, the comfort and the status in society, the hospitality, the neat clothes, the many well-behaved children and the well-looked-after house, he provided her with the means to do all the things that made their lives meaningful. Theirs was a harmonious, symbiotic relationship. His business was to create their place in the world; hers was to define and refine it. There was equality and there was a division of labour: quite simply, he took care of everything outside the house and she took care of everything within it. The house and the family were the focal point of their existence: because they were cut off from political participation, they invented and defined their own particular world.

Marriage, child-bearing and domestic life were regarded by Mother – and I am sure by Daddy as well – not only as women's principal function, but as a valid counterpart to the function of men, which had to do with financial provisions, with protection and in general with dealing with the world outside the house. The female function was in no way regarded as inferior or secondary to its masculine counterpart. The two were seen as necessary, complementary and entirely equal. There was nothing oppressive about the relationship that worked on a social level as a practical, shrewd adaptation to circumstances, and was functionally efficient.

From the early days of my childhood, I remember my parents' jocular discussions with their friends about these roles. If someone called to invite them to dinner or tea, Daddy would respond laughingly: 'I can't answer you until I have discussed this with the Minister of the Interior.' He referred all matters concerning the household to the 'Minister of the Interior'. These jokes were endlessly repeated, and endlessly laughed at: Daddy was, predictably, 'Minister of Finance' and occasionally – when he got into trouble with Mother – 'Minister of Defence'. There were a great many jokes, too, about Adam and Eve, serpents and apples, some of which perhaps had connotations that I did not then understand, *double entendres* too subtle for the children, though I doubt that there were ever any risqué jokes.

A woman was supposed, above all else, to achieve her place in the world by the intelligent exercise of diplomatic power. Any effort to confront a husband directly was doomed to failure, and it was only by using her powers of persuasion that she could get him to do what she wanted. I can hear Daddy repeatedly laughing and saying, pleased with the analogy: 'The man is the head of the family, but the woman is the neck, who turns the head about as she pleases.'

I would sometimes listen to Mother and her women friends as they sat and engaged in earnest discussions on the nature of male–female relationships. Sometimes I would also eavesdrop on gossip: indeed, I think Mother deliberately tolerated this eavesdropping, finding it a convenient teaching device. 'Men are like children,' the women would say wisely to each other. 'You have to know how to treat them.' Or, disapprovingly, of someone's failed marriage: 'She did not know how to handle him,' as though the husband were an over-ripe orange. The most frequent comment, taken as a self-evident, natural truth, was one I heard over and over again as I grew up: 'Marriages are made by women, not men. Women have to sacrifice more. If a marriage is successful, it is because of the woman: if it fails, it is because of the woman.' In Mother's unshakeable view, it was a woman's business to see to it that marriage and the home were comfortable and easy, shady and pleasant oases created to protect the family from the killing sunshine and burning heat of the threatening world outside.

Needless to say, food was central in all of this. Mother was a wonderful cook. Her greatest specialities were dishes that she had learned from her mother, or from members of the *shawwam* community, those who had come from *bilad al-sham* (historic Syria) to Egypt. By a synthesis of Egyptian and Syrian ingredients and tastes, they had developed a distinctive cuisine, inventing, adding to or altering dishes that already existed in one or the other place. Their most famous adaptation is their particular concoction of *mouloukhia*, today a culinary institution in the Levant.

Retaining the soupy consistency of the Egyptian tradition of cooking *mouloukhia,* which resembles spinach, the *shawwam* added fried garlic and coriander with lemon juice. Keeping the Palestinian style of serving it as a stew over rice, they added layers of toasted bread and browned chicken. The dish was topped off with chopped onions marinated in vinegar or lemon juice. *Mouloukhia* was, and still is, traditionally served at long and leisurely Sunday lunches. A member of the community proudly pointed out to me recently that the name of the dish echoes the word *mouloukia*, or 'royal', a food fit for kings.

The full production of *mouloukhia*, served to guests with all its accoutrements, became one of Mother's great culinary accomplishments. In the full flower of her matronhood, in her days as a Cairo, and later a Beirut, hostess, she also mastered another speciality of the *shawwam*: *kenaffe*. Served hot from the oven, it consists of a custard-like filling, flavoured with orange-blossom and rose water, baked between two layers of buttered vermicelli; the whole is topped with a warm syrup flavoured with cinnamon sticks and orange-blossom water. She used to serve it on festive occasions, especially New Year's Day.

Mother also often catered to the culinary tastes my father had acquired in America: scrambled eggs were always served with ketchup, and pancakes and waffles were served sometimes with maple syrup, and sometimes with thick English Golden Syrup. We also ate the Egyptian classic breakfast beans, *foul m'dammas*, though Mother flavoured the *foul* the Syrian way she had learned from her mother, with garlic, lemon juice and olive oil, instead of the cumin that Egyptian taste favours. She served the good strong healthy food of Syrian tradition: *tabbouleh*, *kibbeh*, vine leaves, courgettes and aubergines stuffed with rice and meat; sometimes they were cooked without meat, in olive oil. On Good Friday, Mother always made a point of not serving meat, and our usual Good Friday lunch was the classic lentil dish, *moujaddara*.

At the cosy family parties – especially after church on Sundays, when Auntie Nabiha and her family, or Teta's formidable elder sister Emelia, 'Auntie Melia' as she is known to this day even by members of the family born long after her death, or others would come for lunch – Mother served *mouloukhia* or *kibbeh*, or frequently both. On other occasions, when visiting friends or relations were pressed to stay for what was known in their circle as 'a Protestant supper', they would be served *labneh* (cream cheese made from yoghurt), cheese, sausages, cold cuts, boiled eggs and tea. Mother bought her cheeses and cold cuts from the great Cairo delicatessen, Lappas, and from Simmonds she bought sesame-covered baguettes, known as *simid*, which were always served piping hot. When we broke the thick crust of a loaf, steam would escape from the soft doughy interior, sesame seeds would spill on to our hands and we would lick them up. Chocolates and sweets always came from Groppi's, as did cakes and ice-cream when they were not homemade.

At the large formal dinner parties which became more frequent as time went on, Mother served both European and Arab food. She had collected sets of silver platters and cutlery, as well as fine European china, all of which were laid out on tablecloths often commissioned from and embroidered by nuns in the convents of Palestine, Lebanon and Egypt.

My father's role in the food business in our house was central. He bought the fruit and vegetables, and I remember Mother regularly scolding him as his generous nature induced him to buy too much. She always prepared two sets of dishes, one for him and one for the rest of us. His food was cooked with no fat and very little spice and salt.

He had, she always said, a delicate stomach, but I suspect that she also had a need in this regard – a need to fill up that great hole that began to yawn in her as her children grew up and, one by one, left home. She watched over his health with deep anxiety, and what seemed to be her morbid and unreasonable worry about his health sometimes led them to quarrel when he was guilty of even a minor infringement of his strict regime: the early death of her father hung heavy over our childhood.

As part of her domestic duties, Mother saw it as her business to discipline her large brood. When any of us misbehaved, her punishment for us was 'standing in the corner'. I remember sometimes having to spend what seemed an eternity (but was probably no more than fifteen minutes) in the corner behind the door of her room. When I had been especially naughty, the punishment lasted longer: once I tried to pull up a chair to sit on, but Mother sternly removed this, wanting me to remember the lesson.

Sometimes she got very angry, especially if she had told one of us to clear up our room but found instead an even worse mess. On those occasions, she would show a great propensity to dramatic verbal responses. As we got older, these responses lost all their threatening power and would reduce us – and her – to open laughter. Before pronouncing the punishment, for example, she would declaim the phrase, '*Khreisti sineisti*' as, with much dramatic exaggeration and sweeping movements of her arms, she made an elaborate sign of the Cross. Only recently did I discover that Mother was mispronouncing the '*Christos aneisti*' ('Christ is Risen' in Greek) of the *hajmeh*, the Greek Orthodox Easter service. She must have picked it up from the Orthodox church in Nazareth, to which her family's beloved maid, Halimeh, took her when she was a child, without the knowledge of her father. A Baptist pastor, he would not hear of his children attending what he regarded as the pagan rituals of the Greek Orthodox Church.

Her children's transgressions sometimes called up from her other phrases, though this time in a more comprehensible Arabic: '*Ya fattah, ya alleem; ya razzak, ya kareem*' (O Conqueror, O Knower of all things; O Giver of Treasures, O Generous One), the call to God using some of His divine attributes. Sometimes she pronounced dramatically, '*Ya sater, ya rab*' (O Protector! O Lord!). She had picked up these expressions in Egypt, and said them with the intonation typical of Egypt and in Egyptian dialect, traces of which she continued to use fondly until the end of her days, though she had been out of Egypt for almost thirty years by the time she died.

Mother's most effective expression of displeasure was not a word at all, but a sound emanating from the throat, something like a small gasp but not nearly so sweet – a slow, guttural intake of breath, rasping against the vocal chords, almost a snarl. As she made it, she would slowly dip her head downward, and then from the lowered head her eyes would glare belligerently at the offender. Standing in the corner became a much more severe punishment if it was accompanied by this awe-inspiring performance.

I do not remember that my father ever did the punishing, or the disciplining, at least not of his daughters. My brother had a different memory of this. My father often laughed indulgently at our naughtiness, sometimes undermining Mother's discipline if we were crying. I remember Mother complaining to him: 'You spoil them.' He only became strict if one of us badgered Mother too far, thus challenging her authority: he always saw himself as her protector, and he drew the line – or was made to do so by Mother – at the point at which the dignity of her position was at stake.

My father's boyish sense of humour often made Mother laugh when she threatened tears. This was a skill that Edward picked up from him, and practised on Mother in her last years, but I think none of us girls ever learned how to placate her in this manner: like most mother– daughter disagreements, ours were always much more emotionally charged.

My father enjoyed magic, and learned tricks from books that he carefully studied, and from the magicians who were brought to entertain us and our friends at birthday parties. He mastered only a few of those tricks, however, usually bursting out laughing before the game was done, revealing the secret and destroying the illusion. His greatest triumph was to pull coins out of our ears, or an egg from under his sleeve, and he was quite skilful at the card tricks he repeatedly showed off. He often used his limited magical talent when he played pinochle with Teta. She never understood how he managed to defeat her so consistently, or why we found it so funny that he did. He used to let us in on the joke, so that we could see what she could not: that he was hiding the pinochles and jokers in his slipper only to pull them out at strategic moments. He always teased her outrageously, pretending to show consternation, for instance, at a fictional dip in his supply of wine or whisky: '*Ya mart 'ammi* (O Mother-in-law)', he would say with a completely straight face, 'Have you been drinking?' And she, the Baptist pastor's wife, who thought drink was a great sin, would explode in righteous indignation and self-defence.

Once as a young child I was stricken with trachoma, a common but dangerous eye disease. My parents were under doctor's instructions to keep my eyes open at all costs, and not allow me to sleep. The task of keeping me awake through the night fell to my father: Mother was then occupied with the two younger children, the youngest a suckling infant.

Early in the evening, he sang songs with me and did some of his card tricks. Later, as my normal bedtime passed and I was overcome with a need to sleep, we moved to the living-room, where the large radio stood. All night he and I sat together in a large armchair and listened to the BBC. It is a memory that I have always cherished: my father helping to save my sight by making me listen to the radio all night long. Whenever I became drowsy, he would wake me up with a game, and when I complained and cried, he hushed and comforted me, and pulled a coin out from behind my ear.

CHAPTER 3

Men and Women, Girls and Boys

Our large household was made up principally of women and girls. As I look back, I think that for most of my early childhood I saw the world as through a screen of moving female figures principally engaged in sewing, washing and cooking, but also talking, gossiping, scolding and singing. Together with various domestic helpers such as maids and dressmakers, my mother, grandmother, aunts, sisters and myself formed, it seems to me, a single body, among which the figures of men – the male servants, my father, my brother – were mere punctuations in the all-enveloping femaleness.

Although the male servants, Ahmed and Hassan, did all the heavy housework, they were somehow less visible than the females. When they had finished the day's work, they used to retreat into what I thought – when I thought about it at all, which was not very often – was a kind of black hole from which they could easily be recalled if the need arose. There was an iron staircase leading from the kitchen up to the roof, where the laundry used to be hung, and down to the garage. To this day, I am not sure where the menservants' quarters were, on the roof or in the garage. Perhaps I once knew and have forgotten. Though the kitchen was certainly in my mother's domain, I hardly ever entered it. All that I retain of that most important region of our domestic geography is a very vague picture of high marble counters, a large window, a huge table in the middle, on which vegetables were cut and meat prepared for cooking, the landing outside the door, and the iron staircase of which it was a part.

While my father and brother played an enormously important role in my childhood, and especially in the evolution of my identity and self-image, and the sense of my incipient womanhood – and, I am sure, my sisters' as well – they were so much the exceptions to the female rule in our household that they too seemed to occupy a separate sphere and were, to a large degree, excluded from its intimate workings.

For Mother, there was an essential manliness, as there was an essential femaleness. My siblings and I grew up with the ditty that she often repeated:

> Little boys are made of frogs and snails
> And puppy dogs' tails.
> Little girls are made of sugar and spice
> And everything nice.

And we were meant to act accordingly: though Edward as a boy often got into trouble for being naughty, he was taught, however indirectly, that his mischief was predictable and somehow acceptable, perhaps even admirable. Mother's face would light up as she recounted his latest escapade, though she would try, usually without success, to disguise her laughter. My sisters and I, on the other hand, were encouraged to be 'nice', and many are the books I still occasionally stumble on in my library, presented to me on a birthday or Christmas in my childhood, dedicated to 'My darling little girl' or 'My little angel'. I do not believe I had any angelic qualities whatsoever, but I see in these words an effort by my mother to subtly steer me in their direction. Perhaps, however, they did have an effect, possibly even a powerful one, in encouraging me towards the kind of behaviour that Mother thought proper for a girl.

From the beginning of my life my father was held up to me as the ideal man, and it became clear to me that it was my duty to honour and uphold this manhood. Indeed, what it meant to be 'a man' was a leitmotiv of our moral education. When Daddy died, decades after the time I am writing about, Mother wanted Mark Antony's eulogy of Brutus from *Julius Caesar* read at his funeral. She often quoted the lines and applied them to him:

> His life was gentle, and the elements
> So mix'd in him that Nature might stand up
> And say to all the world 'This was a man!'

At the same time, a generous reciprocity caused him to represent my mother to me, and to my sisters, as the ideal woman, on whose example we would do well to model our lives. If this sort of gender idealism sounds quaintly old-fashioned today, and even faintly amusing, if not downright reprehensible, I am not sure that it was such a totally bad thing. The manhood that my father represented had nothing whatever to do with the emptily macho or the physically brutal or repressive; quite the contrary. The word as it came down to me suggests gentleness, goodness, consideration, thoughtfulness, tenderness, kindness, loyalty, though all of this of course is tied up with force of character, stamina, determination, and above all the physical and moral courage that allows a man to stand up to powerful and wrong-doing oppressors.

My father's generosity of spirit manifested itself most obviously and outwardly in monetary terms, but in a far deeper way it reflected an inner strength that allowed him to give moral support and impart moral strength to others. Over the years we began to recognize this generosity in our parents' attitude towards others. Though they always emphasized the supreme Protestant values of thrift and prudence, which they had learned in their youth, and it was not in their nature to be extravagant or lavish, in their eyes miserliness and meanness were deplorable qualities. There was never any room for the mean and the second-class in their lives. And it was always clear that their special brand of generosity, learned and adopted by Mother (who married at such a young age that she was as much his student as his bride), came originally from my father, and was one of his main characteristics. It had something to do with that love of life, that enthusiasm, which he so enjoyed.

Though I remember many coy references on Mother's part to my father's 'manly' good looks and his athletic abilities, these were perhaps too subtle for me to pick up or understand in my childhood. What she explicitly emphasized in addition, however, as constituting his manliness were most of all his fighting spirit and his strength of character. For his part, the patriarchy in which he believed, and of which he was the embodiment, was manifested mostly in his loyalty towards and pride in his family and children, and his insistence that it was a man's duty to 'protect' as well as provide for them. I grew up with the notion that it was my father's business to protect us from the outside world and later to teach us how to protect ourselves. He saw himself as the last resort, the outer walls of our family fortress, a bastion of moral and political authority.

His brief life in America had left some major impressions on him, which he passed on to us as values. One was his admiration for the latest technology, and we became accustomed to always having the first of the new domestic appliances, of whose existence our friends often had no idea. Another equally important American value was the belief that the individual, rich or poor, old or young, had a God-given right to justice, but that this right had always to be fought for and protected. Whenever we faced an unjust rebuff of whatever sort, he insisted that we go back and try again to win what had been denied us. And it was never any use telling him that someone stronger than us had ruled against us: he saw that as all the more reason to fight back and win.

This lesson applied to matters both great and small. Once, for instance, I set off with a friend – I think it was Josianne – to play tennis at the club. We were perhaps eleven or twelve years old, and, though we had booked our slot, no sooner had our game started than it was aborted by adults who had arrived ready to play and shooed us off the court. I returned home quashed, hurt, my dignity wounded and my sense of injustice awakened. My father was furious. 'Go back', he insisted, 'and tell them: "My daddy says since we booked, we have a right to the court."' I did, most reluctantly, and though I do not remember the outcome of this little experience, the lesson was certainly learned. Many a time did he say to us, first with deadly seriousness, then as we grew older with a twinkle in his eye, 'Tell them: "My daddy says … "'. I think all of us learned this lesson: that people in power had to be challenged if they infringed on our rights, whether over a small matter or a great one.

Many of the moral lessons of our childhood came from him. 'Never give up' was a constant exhortation of his, and Mother characteristically transposed it into the moral ditty she had probably first heard at one of her mission schools: 'If at first you don't succeed, Try, try, try again.' Steadfastness and persistence, directly related to 'Never give up,' were also qualities that my father prided himself on. One afternoon, when I was about twelve-years-old, Rosie accidentally spilled ink on her physics notebook. She sat down to the grim task of copying out every word, graph and diagram into a new book. It took her hours, but she would not stop, not even for supper, until she had finished. For weeks after that – it seemed to me for ever – I was exhorted to behold the wonders of my sister's meritorious behaviour, which was, of course – and this was a major part of the lesson – a reflection of Daddy's noble character. '*Faltahia!* (praise be)', they kept saying over and over again, much to my annoyance, as they recounted her feat, urging me, somewhat hopelessly, to learn the lesson.

My father's journey to America and back was often recounted, with the lesson drawn from it that he was a 'self-made man'. How much of this hagiography had to do with him and his strong character, and how much with the particular virtues of America, which were always hammered into us, it is hard to tell, though it is clear to me now, so many years later, that both were directly involved in the representation of individual success and merit.

Though Edward teased me mercilessly as a child, and even as we advanced into adulthood, he became, like my father – perhaps partly at my parents' behest – a model of manhood for me as well. 'Your brother' was a phrase that resounded throughout my childhood and early adult life, almost invariably as a proud announcement of his achievements or good looks. And he always made me laugh even as he teased, which somehow made me enjoy the teasing. He had a disconcerting habit of springing out at me from behind closed doors, pronouncing a blood-curdling Tarzan's call, which he had long ago adopted as his own. Or he would leap up from under the waves at the beach, or splash me by revolving his hands in the water at the swimming pool until I could hardly catch my breath. He would scare me half to death, but I would never have had it otherwise and always enjoyed his attentions. Throughout my childhood he called me 'Shrimp', and I accepted this as an affectionate appellation, rather than a wounding reference to my short stature.

As we grew older, Edward quietened down from his legendary childhood naughtiness and began to grow into himself. Soon, his vast promise began to manifest itself, and his talents to bud. I began to measure myself against him, and my accomplishments, or lack of them, against his. Perhaps as a reflection of our parents' relationship, I began to see it as my duty to assist him in whatever he was doing: sibling competition did not exist between us then, and was only to emerge much later, on my part sometimes repressed, and sometimes bursting forth in feminist rancour.

At the time, ours was naturally a most unequal relationship: after all, he was five years older than I, and in childhood that is a huge gulf. We took it for granted that he was to be the doer and I the spectator, sympathetic and assisting, applauding and comforting. It was my task to watch him play tennis – in his teens he was a star tennis player – and to be the ball-boy who, never fast enough, had to be repeatedly berated. Adoringly, I applauded his lobs, smashes and ace serves, especially when he proudly relived them in the telling. As his talent at the piano grew, I became his regular page turner, especially when as a teenager he could play the big noisy pieces, the great Beethoven sonatas and the Chopin Polonaises, while I was still painfully working out the small, intricate Scarlatti sonatas and Bach inventions.

I followed him through the woods in Dhour al-Schweir when he went hunting, whispering and tiptoeing so as not to warn away the prey, though I hated both the hunt and my specific task. I carried his equipment and the dead birds, whose tiny necks I had to squeeze on to the iron clips that hung from a belt around my waist. I think he made me carry them because he hated the hunting as much as, if not more than, I did. I don't think he did it very often, perhaps only three or four times.

As time passed, and Edward grew older, he became more and more like Daddy, though I don't think he ever recognized the resemblance himself. He learned the lessons of self-discipline and self-reliance, and most of all perhaps, he learned the lesson of courage, challenging those in power if he thought they were wrong or unjust. He had the same boyish sense of humour and the same love of life. Though over the years we lived on different continents and did not see each other for months at a time, and though we sometimes quarrelled, we always kept in touch. Though his vast accomplishments and his fame sent him spiralling into ever higher spheres of existence, our relationship remained grounded in the intimacy of our shared childhood. For me, he remained, after my father, and together with my husband and sons, the measure of manhood. His death in 2003 broke my heart: it was as though the mirror in which I had grown accustomed to see myself and my unfulfilled potential reflected had been smashed, and there was instead an emptiness, a hole in the wall where the mirror had once hung.

It was in the late 1940s and early '50s that I started to observe and get to know Teta, as well as my Aunts Nabiha and Emelia. Along with Mother, these were my models of womanhood.

When I think of Teta today, her image springs mostly from a well of childhood memories. I see a small, stooped, ghost-like figure dressed in black, moving silently about the house. Occasionally, in my memory perhaps of an earlier time when she was sometimes left in charge of the household as my parents were on their travels away from home, she bursts into action. In this memory, she bustles about the house, jingling the bunch of keys in her hand. The two thick gold wedding rings that she always wore on the fourth finger of her left hand also jiggle, clicking against each other with her every movement. Her elbows are turned outwards, and I see the palms of her hands moving back and forth, like a pair of paddles, helping her navigate her way around the house. A sharp *click-clack* made by her slippers slapping against her feet announces her purposeful advance on the kitchen, or the laundry room, or wherever she is heading so busily. The *click-clack* recedes rapidly as she turns a corner and disappears from my sight and hearing.

In one of the clearest and most persistent of my childhood memories, I see Teta standing in front of the full-length mirror in the room I shared with her in Dhour al-Schweir, high up in the mountains of Lebanon to which my family came every summer from Jerusalem or

Cairo. My father loved the village for its informality and the total break it gave him from the gravity of his business responsibilities; my mother hated it for its inefficiency, having to manage her large household with the water shortage that was her perennial complaint. A little below Dhour al-Schweir, protected from the harsh mountain winters, is the village of Schweir, Teta's father's ancestral home.

On the chest of drawers near the mirror stood the large bottle of 4711 eau de cologne that she always wore, and that still, to this day, evokes her presence. Sometimes she used lavender water instead, when she received it as a gift. I think most of the gifts she received were of that type: sweet natural products, *aramiche bi fustuq* (sugared pistachios), which she loved, eau de cologne and lavender water. Perhaps that had to do with the natural sweetness of her character, which everyone who came in contact with her instinctively recognized. No one ever gave her French perfume, though she wore fine clothes and a black velvet turban when she went out.

In that childhood vision, as persistent as the faint, lingering scent of eau de cologne, Teta is combing her long, white hair, wearing a little cape over her shoulders. She ties her hair into a plait, which she twists into a coil on the back of her head, and fixes it with two large horn pins. When she finishes, she undoes the snaps that hold the cape together around her throat with a rapid movement – *snap snap* – then, with a little flourish, she swings the cape off her shoulders, exactly reversing the movement with which she had put it on. She replaces her brush and comb in the bag which she has made for the purpose, and which has a thin white crochet cover, with her initial, *M*, crocheted into the delicate pattern. She made a bag like that for my combs and brushes, and for each of her granddaughters. I still cherish mine, though I never use it except to remember her by.

Though by this time other-worldly, and withdrawn from a reality now dominated by her daughter, Teta was nevertheless a powerful and central force in my childhood. It was mostly the aura of sadness and abstraction surrounding her that, along with her obsessive, ritualistic neatness, impressed itself on me in that time of seething political developments. Her grandchildren, including myself, used sometimes to tease her about her bags and her obsessive neatness. It was often tempting, especially on those long summer days in Dhour al-Schweir, to entertain ourselves by jumping on her bed and then running away and watching from a safe distance as she hastened to put it back into perfect order again, pulling this and patting that until all the elements once again formed harmonious straight lines and equal heights and depths.

When we were children, Teta often used to read to us from the Bible. Indeed, she didn't so much read as recite, having memorized it over a lifetime of study. She found in the Old Testament an endless stock of stories, which she would offer us on all occasions. I particularly remember her reading to me from the Book of Esther. I do not know why: it is foolish to try and put together all the pieces of a puzzle when so many of them are missing or undecipherable. From the New Testament she gave us an intense notion of goodness. She had a literal belief in Christ and His miracles, and an absolute faith in forgiveness, charity and, in spite of everything, hope. Teta took all the standards of goodness and piety laid down in the Sermon on the Mount literally, as absolute demands. She was thoroughly unphilosophical and unquestioning in her piety, which gave her a mysterious strength.

My cousin Marwan remarked recently on Teta's enormous, though subtle and indirect, impact on all our lives: I remember recognizing with a little shock how right he was in this observation. Perhaps her influence had to do with the Bible sessions, and the prayers and traditions which our parents left to her to pass on to us, and which we never realized we had taken seriously. Or perhaps it had to do with her mere presence, and the profound anguish that we sensed in her. She never talked about her past suffering, and yet we felt it intensely. Somehow she seemed to transcend it, pinning her faith always in Jesus. Yet her piety was not obnoxious, not the sort which leads to cant, self-righteousness, hypocrisy and cruelty. Rather, it seemed to provide her with a kind of shelter, an alternate space in which to exist, and thus she had about her an air of serenity and an other-worldly calm. Strangely, she was always palpably and really there, and yet at the same time not there at all.

Though she was meek and mild, as she taught us Jesus was ('Gentle Jesus, meek and mild' we learned to sing from our earliest childhood), there was one area of her life in which Teta showed an uncompromising pride. She always said of herself that she was 'highly educated'. I remember being puzzled by this assertion of hers, so old-fashioned did she seem. This was, of course, long before I had learned her history. I suppose I did not take her claim seriously because I could not imagine her doing algebra, fractions or logarithms, or learning French grammar, or drawing maps of Europe with all the rivers and towns written in, or any of the other things that I had to do at school, and so somehow I could not understand – or believe – that she was indeed highly educated, especially by the standards of her time.

On the rare occasions when Teta got angry with us, she had a distinct vocabulary that caused us much hilarity. We used occasionally to tease her when she said something in English which was unidiomatic or, to our ears at least, quaint. She had, for instance, the most unaccountably Scottish accent for certain words, saying 'gehrl' for 'girl', and 'yehr' for 'year'. She pronounced white '*h*wite', and which '*h*wich'. When we challenged her pronunciation, she would respond with an indignant exclamation: 'My little *toe* knows more English than you!' As a riposte to this extraordinary claim, we often used to question that toe's ability, and its history. This was before the days when we became aware of the ambiguity and complexity of our own education – let alone hers – and before we questioned the relative roles of English and Arabic in both our personal and public history, and their relationship to imperial realities.

In her use of language, which I found so oddly amusing at the time, there was something strangely resistant to what I then perceived as an open field of opportunity. She was in many ways what today would be called fundamentalist, and reacted with horror if she ever heard a coarse word or an oath. 'Do not take the Lord's name in vain,' I can hear her chiding me in consternation, as in those days I took it in vain rather often, especially as a teenager dazzled by the endless possibilities of language.

It was only while researching this book that I discovered the links between Teta's story and the political and economic events in Palestine: before that I had always thought of her as totally unconnected to the violent real world, as though she had an abstract existence. When my siblings and I were children, we thought of her as a most unworldly woman, whose travels were limited to Palestine, Syria, Lebanon and Egypt. Yet she thought of herself as widely travelled, which, by the standards of her time, she surely was. Her frequent remark, '*safart al-hind w'al-sind* (I have travelled to India and Sind)', usually uttered in rebuke to some impertinence offered by one of her grandchildren, was for us merely a reminder of her archaic vision of reality. For us, wide travel was to become a way of life, as it already was for our parents. Not only did Teta never set foot outside historic Syria and Egypt, but her expression also recalled a time when the Arabs looked east to India and beyond for geographic reference, instead of westward, as they usually do in my time.

Teta seemed to me particularly old-fashioned in the way she dressed. I did not know it then, though my older sister and cousins did, but she was in fact a fastidious dresser and insisted on the finest fabrics and the best cuts. Because she eschewed the changing styles assiduously followed by her worldly daughter, she always seemed to me to wear the same style, always in dark colours, black, dark green or navy blue. Her skirts were always of ankle length, and under them she wore long white petticoats; in winter she wore long johns underneath, which I found amusing. Near the hem of the petticoats she sewed in pockets with steel snaps into which she always neatly placed a handkerchief and some sweets. When she went out, she invariably wore a turban, usually of black velvet. I don't think she ever went out without one.

I can still see her walking arm-in-arm with her sister Emelia, both of them wearing their velvet turbans, sharing a parasol which they hold up between them against the hot midday sun, and proceeding slowly down the main street of Dhour al-Schweir, their father's ancestral town. People stop to turn and stare at them, these relics of the past, though they do not notice. In spite of their visible frailty and the familial stoop in their backs, there is something extraordinary about them, perhaps something regal, their beauty striking even in their old age.

Unlike Teta, who played such a singular role in my life, it was Auntie Nabiha and Auntie Melia who, along with Mother, provided me with the clear impression of absolute and formidable matriarchal and feminine power.

Auntie Nabiha's propensity to produce twins was almost mythical, and she counted several sets of twins among her progeny. She also represented a protocol of an ideal brother–sister relationship, for that is often how she was presented to us. My father adored her. He used to boast that her youthful beauty was such that people called her *nabahet al-jamal*, roughly translated as 'one famous for her beauty'. We found this rather unconvincing as, however fond we were of her, none of us ever saw her as a great beauty, and could not imagine her as such even in her far-distant youth. His insistence on this phrase, however, pointed to another, more convincing reality: that he believed a brother's business was to protect and support his sister, just as it was her business to protect and support him. Men support their sisters financially and stand by them legally, thus protecting them from the world, and if necessary from oppressive husbands and mothers-in-law; but they also support them by praising their beauty. Sisters support brothers by giving them a sense (however illusory) of their own importance, by adding to the comforts of their domestic life, thus protecting their standing, and comforting them from the ravages of their lives in the outside world. As I researched the lives of my parents, I discovered how close this special relationship between my father and his sister really was, and how influential, especially in the formation of his ties with my mother in the months leading up to their marriage.

Mother, too, used often to talk to me of an ideal fraternal relationship: Islamic law, she would often explain in its defence, gave a brother double his sister's inheritance because a brother had an obligation to look after his single, divorced or widowed sister – and his widowed mother, for that matter – when they needed him. The fact that she knew of several sets of brothers who did not care a straw for their sisters' welfare did not seem to alter her faith in the wisdom of this provision.

Two sets of images of Auntie Nabiha linger in my memory. One is of her bustling around the large and gracious house in Jerusalem. I see her, short and round, but exuding the most intense energy, in and out of the house, her hands always busy with something she is preparing for lunch, stuffing vine leaves or eggplants, working the dough of the *sfiha*, those wonderful Jerusalem meat pies, or standing, giving directions, chatting with her many visitors and with my mother and father, chiding my cousins, on the wide stone staircase lined with potted plants. This sense of her perpetual motion, however, is fixed firmly in Jerusalem and mingles in my memory with the smell of cooking, and with the perfume of jasmine and bay leaf and olive oil and the famous soap from Nablus.

The other image is of a later time, after 1948 and the Palestine war, the loss of her home in Jerusalem and her traumatic move to Cairo. She is transformed, preoccupied and exhausted, with an eternally sad look on her face. I see her at our dining table, nodding absent-mindedly at questions and comments alike, clearly not paying the slightest attention to the conversation around her. Occasionally, she dozes off, and then, starting at an unexpectedly loud noise, she jolts herself into an upright position, and makes a game effort to rejoin the group and be sociable. She would obligingly produce a vague smile to show that she was with us, though it was always such a sad smile. We children found her tendency to nod in her chair hilarious. It was only much later that we understood how exhausted she must have been, and how sad.

After 1948, Auntie Nabiha dedicated her life entirely to the pursuit of justice – or at least survival – for her fellow Palestinian refugees in Egypt. She seems always to have had a vocation for social work. I have heard many stories of her helping this or that family in their time of need, in Jerusalem, long before 1948. Now the condition of the Palestinian refugees gave her ample opportunity to exercise her vocation. Though she too was a refugee, she was well-off; she kept her own home and wanted for nothing.

Soon after her arrival in Egypt, she embarked on an informal career, though one more binding than that of many professionals, as a volunteer social worker. Day after day she would take up the case of one after another hapless individual or family with the Egyptian authorities, or with some school or business, or with the church.

On those evening visits as we sat around the table, she would enter an animated state only when talking about her latest case. So full would she be of the misery she had seen and tried to alleviate that day, the exasperating and cruel impassivity and pitilessness of the Egyptian bureaucracy, that she would be unable to leave it behind or shake it off. She described her attempts to save someone's job, provide this person with the right papers, that one with a job interview, this one with a doctor for his sick child, that one with the money to buy a school uniform for his children, and so on. She convinced Mother to employ some refugee women to assist her in the house, sewing, mending, ironing and cooking.

I think of Auntie Nabiha as quintessentially Palestinian, not only in a nationalist sense, but in another more mysterious and even mystical way. For I have ever heard the names of Palestinian towns and villages in her voice; the geography of our ancestral land sings in my memory in her voice. Places I have never known, or have forgotten, are preserved in my heart in the way she pronounced them. She spoke those names in a loving, soft voice, the voice of a mourner, one who marked every passing day with her broken heart and her lost land. '*beit lahem*', I hear in her voice, '*ramallah, riha, al-khalil, bir zeit, tulkarm, beit jalla*', and, further away, '*yaffa, haifa, akka, tabariyya, al-nasreh ...*' And, most musical of all sounds, to her and to me, '*al-quds*', Jerusalem.

When my parents were on their travels, leaving Teta in charge of us, Auntie Nabiha would often interrupt her busy schedule and drop by to see if Teta needed help. One occasion marked my younger sisters and me for life. I was perhaps twelve or thirteen, Joyce ten or so, and Grace eight. We were enjoying a ferocious free-for-all fight, biting, kicking, punching each other, pulling each other's hair and yelling. It was, as these things tend to be, a half-joking kind of fight, quite capable of evaporating if something more interesting had intervened to occupy our energy. After many valiant attempts, poor Teta had given up trying to stop the mêlée and Auntie Nabiha had volunteered – or had been commissioned by Teta – to see what she could do. She opened the door, took one look at us, and then slowly withdrew, murmuring sadly, though audibly, with a little sigh: 'Ladies, simply ladies'.

Our distinctly unladylike behaviour stopped immediately, as we collapsed into laughter. Her incongruous comment, which, though it seemed to have been pronounced in a whisper, somehow carried over the din that we were producing, proved far more effective than any amount of cajoling and scolding of the sort Teta had tried earlier. Much later, from conversations with cousins and acquaintances, I realized that she had habitually used this astounding talent to bend people to her iron will.

Once, when she arrived unexpectedly at her son Albert's house for a visit, her two young granddaughters had a great fight as to which one would have to sacrifice her bedroom for their grandmother. While they bickered furiously, and while their parents tried to recall them to propriety, scolding them for their rudeness and reminding them of their duties as grandchildren, nobody noticed that Auntie Nabiha had silently withdrawn from the room. Quietly, not uttering a word, she put on her nightgown, carried a blanket and pillows on to the balcony, and there settled down to sleep on a sofa. When they finally discovered this, the girls were overcome with shame and contrition, and now vied tearfully with each other to offer her their beds. Lessons taught in this manner are never forgotten.

At Easter, Auntie Nabiha would join Mother, Teta and other female friends and relations from Palestine as they sat around a table for the ritual making of *ma'mul* and *ka'k*. Later, when the family and the ritual moved to Beirut, there was a spacious, airy kitchen. But in Cairo the dining table would be carefully carried to one side of the room, and a round table set up in its place, covered with a tablecloth fit for the messy work to be undertaken. My sisters and I would have to help, too, though we always tried to escape. Sometimes we would be required to help with the *ka'k*, holding the delicate rings of dough stuffed with the *ajwa* (pounded dates flavoured with nutmeg, cinnamon and cloves) in one hand, and, in the other, the special pincers to pinch the traditional design all around the edges. At other times we would be required to help with the *ma'mul*, taking the balls of dough stuffed with walnuts, sugar, cinnamon and orange-blossom water, and pressing them into the wooden mould until the pattern took, and then knocking them out and admiring the result – if our efforts hadn't broken the *ma'mul* in the meantime.

Easter was always the big event in our lives. For my father, Easter brought memories of the celebrations in Jerusalem when he was a child, and he always exasperatingly woke us up at dawn on Easter Sunday, chanting 'Christ is risen!' in a loud voice. He would not leave us alone until he heard the sleepy and reluctant response: 'Truly, He is risen!' Declaration and response had to be repeated three times, and then finally he would retreat, close the door behind him and leave us in peace. Later we would get up to search for the coloured eggs that he and Mother had hidden around the house, while they sat laughing, sipping their coffee and applauding every triumphant find. Then it would be time to dress for church, in new clothes, of course. We spent the morning of Holy Saturday colouring the eggs.

Memories of Auntie Nabiha at Easter celebrations blend with memories of our ecumenical experiences. Like my parents, Auntie Nabiha went to church every Sunday, and always wore a hat. Occasionally, and with great reluctance, she joined my parents at the American Presbyterian Church in Cairo, though she was full of contempt for the Presbyterian communion service: 'Does the Body and Blood of Christ come to you as you sit in your place?', she asked, full of indignation. And then she added scornfully, in a most exercised tone: 'Next they will be offering cigarettes and candy with it!' She remained ferociously loyal to the Anglican Church, and to bowing at the altar, sipping from the communal chalice, despite what the British had done in Palestine. By the early 1950s, Cairo had enough Anglicans from Palestine to constitute an Arab Anglican community in addition to the English one focused especially on All Saints Cathedral. Of course, Auntie Nabiha attended the Arabic service, and rarely went to the English one.

Physically tiny, Auntie Melia was a monumental presence in our lives, though, for me at least, a more remote one. She had come to Cairo early in the century, after a quarrel over the discriminatory practices of the American Protestant missionaries at whose Beirut school she had been teaching. In Cairo, with an American colleague from the mission school to which she had come, she had helped found the American College for Girls; she remained one of the principal authorities of that institution until she retired. It was only much later, as I worked on this book, that I discovered the details of her life and came to realize the full measure of her authority over her students and the school in general, and her influence on generations of Egyptian girls, not to mention her influence on my mother and her cousins. I shall write more about her later. At this point in my childhood, however, she was to me, and indeed to all of us, merely a great figure, one who inspired awe, fear and immense respect. She was as unlike Teta as it is possible for two sisters to be.

Auntie Melia used to come to our house frequently, for tea or for supper, or Sunday lunch, but I would beat a hasty retreat into my room whenever she came, careful not to do anything naughty that would require a scolding from Mother in her presence. Her air of authority and distance was augmented by her references to 'Miss Malloy' or 'Miss Martin', two of the American principals of the school. I never heard her call them by their Christian names, as I am sure they never called her by hers, and that created in my mind a kind of mystic shroud around her social circle, adding distance to distance. At the College, she was always referred to as 'Miss Badr', a title, I discovered later, that she had fought hard to attain.

Mother sometimes used to take me with her when she visited her in her rooms at the College. Holding Mother's hand, I would climb the stairs in some trepidation, knowing that I would have to be on my best behaviour. I remember the room well, especially the warm colours of the Persian carpets that seem in my memory to cover every surface. Auntie Melia would sit as though enthroned on the inevitable Morris chair – I shall for ever associate these Morris chairs with Lebanon, our summers in Dhour al-Schweir and Auntie Melia. She had a little bell by her side, which she would ring to summon the *suffragi* (manservant). When he appeared, obediently standing at the door, she ordered tea. He would bring in the tea things on a large silver tray, passing the cups around once they were filled, stooping after that to offer the plate of biscuits. I was never offered tea, though the biscuit plate would come my way, as I willed so desperately that it would. I would take my prize with relief, mumble my thanks after Mother's prodding, and then sit on the edge of the little sofa to which I had been relegated, gingerly nibbling away. Every now and then, however, when I thought nobody would notice, I escaped into the corridor outside the room. There I would pace the floor, staring at the various school notices and the drab and faded pictures that lined the walls, and wishing that we could go home.

I always recoiled a little from the chill I felt emanating from Auntie Melia. I remember also being chilled by the sharp look from her penetrating blue eyes. I felt there was no way to keep secrets from her, that she could see right into me. I never warmed to her as I did to Auntie Nabiha, never identified with her. Perhaps this was because she was so different from Teta; perhaps because she died when I was young, and I never had a chance to know her as a woman; perhaps because she did not relate well to small girls. I do not know why, but though I admire her memory and honour her deeply for her accomplishments, I do not warm at the memory of her person.

Like Auntie Nabiha, like Teta, like Mother, like Mother's friends Renée Dirlik, Emma Fahoum, Madeleine Ghorra, Elaine Gindy and her sister Yvonne Tewfik – all the women who formed the background to my restricted social life – Auntie Melia was a 'lady'. Like her mother before her, Mother too was often referred to as *sitt al-sittat* ('the lady of ladies'). As I think about this business of being a 'lady', I see my sisters and myself, sometimes desperately struggling against the ideal, and yet at the same time surrendering to it. And, strangely enough, I see in it a kind of power.

The lesson of 'ladylike' behaviour that my sisters and I and all our friends were taught was no doubt diminishing and isolating, a kind of social retaining wall holding back passions, hatreds and the dense and muddy waters of personal, social and political life. But those who taught us, those who built that wall, stone by carefully chiselled stone, were teaching us how to hold back the landslides of history that might otherwise have engulfed us. I have learned since then, since the long-ago days of my childhood, especially during the long war in Lebanon, that convention is a powerful glue that holds things together even when society is in danger of coming unstuck.

From the women who surrounded me in childhood, I never had the slightest sense of fragility or weakness. Even the washerwomen who came in to help Mother cope with the mountains of laundry produced by her large family seemed tough, powerful and independent: their oppression was a result of their poverty, not their femaleness – that seemed quite clear to me. The notion of the shy, retiring Eastern woman crept into my mind later, and probably had to do with my own self-image. It was an image constructed for me, perhaps by me. I am not sure I understand it fully today, though I am trying hard to do so. I know now that it is a myth, and that this creature does not exist.

Outside of her domestic instruction, the most powerful, most lingering and most explicit of the many lessons in womanhood that Mother taught us was a repeated warning to her daughters: 'Be strong,' or its variation, 'Do not be weak.' As I look back on it, I think it meant:

'Do not let yourself be broken by history. Do not be defeated.' And I think for Mother it meant at the time: 'Do not be like her, do not be defeated by events as she was.' I think it was a warning not to become like Teta, who was now thoroughly worn out and had apparently been sidestepped by history. When I was a child it was clear to me that Mother had an uneasy relationship with her own mother. That was before Mother had rethought that relationship, before she rediscovered her mother, understood her suffering, understood her strength. That rediscovery happened when she wrote about her in her journal, so many decades after the time I am writing about.

I think that I knew, child though I was, that she was wrong about Teta. Even then, I knew, I sensed, though I could certainly not articulate the thought, that there was a kind of strangely ethereal strength in Teta. It was not the strength of status – how could it have been? – or of a massive personality reinforced by wealth or a sharp tongue. I think the strength I sensed lay in her unflappable belief that what she had done in her life was good; it lay in her unshakeable faith in all she had believed in, though it had so obviously betrayed her. She was in many ways in the core of her existence an immovable object. As she grew older, I had the feeling that her body was so fragile that one could pick her up, snap her bones, break her into pieces. Yet at the same time I felt that even if she were broken into pieces, nothing about her would change, and she would be implacably there, absolutely unconvinced, unmoved, refusing to budge. I could certainly not have articulated these thoughts then, when I was only ten or twelve years old. Only now do I understand Teta, when I am almost as old as she was then, and not nearly so strong or immovable.

Thus, inevitably, I was taught by Mother and her friends, by Teta and my aunts, that in order to face what had to be faced, and to withstand the outside forces always threatening the interior, women had to have a very deep courage. Indeed, stoicism and courage were an essential part of their definition of womanhood. 'Never whine,' my sisters and I were constantly chided by Mother. 'She whines' was one of her most ferocious put-downs of a suffering woman.

Many years later, as, with my husband and children, I stubbornly stuck out the war in Lebanon, two fixed visions kept me there. One was the memory of Palestine, of those who left and never returned, of those who lost everything, of all those people with their sad and futile stories, the homes they never saw again, the pots left simmering on the stove, and the photograph albums that became the symbols of their lost lives. The other was the image of Teta, of Auntie Nabiha, of Auntie Melia, and of the sound of Mother's voice saying: 'Be strong. Do not be weak. Do not allow yourself to be overcome.' Women, I had been so well taught, were to be towers of strength, bulwarks of the common defence. I felt it would have been a betrayal of my female role to complain, to nag, to show the slightest weakness in the face of the terrors that beset us.

CHAPTER 4

A Kind of Education

During her childhood, Mother used to take long walks with
her father in the Galilean countryside, near her home town
of Nazareth; she attended village weddings, which went on
for days at a time; some of her relations, including her father, played the
oud (Arab lute). Having establishing herself in Cairo society, Mother
had come a long way from those idyllic experiences that she would
later remember with such fondness. She was now a member of a class
of people who knew nothing of these things.

I grew up almost entirely cut off from them. The closest I came
to the earth was on trips into the Egyptian desert and the Lebanese
mountains, when as children we were taken for jolly family picnics.
On those trips, we were strangers to the intimate workings and the life
of the land. I did not know the names of the plants I tore up in Dhour
al-Schweir for the bonfires for *eid al-salib* (the Feast of the Cross) in
September, nor of the grasses and herbs that we ate in the salads served
in glass bowls, nor of the great flocks of migratory birds that flew

overhead in spring and autumn. We used to ride the elephants and feed the ducks and monkeys in Cairo zoo, but that was the extent of our relationship with animals.

My most intimate childhood connection with flowers remains an indelible part of my memory of domestic apprenticeship at Mother's hands, and had little to do with nature, only with art. Once a week, or on special occasions, she used to buy a mass of flowers from the florist near our house in Cairo. This was followed by a long flower-arranging session in the spacious bathroom as she organized the blooms into her antique Chinese porcelain bowls, and the long crystal vases bought on her trips to Italy and France. I would sit at her feet and watch her arrange them or, sometimes, if she had over-indulged, she would give me a small bunch of my own to arrange and put in my room. Once they were all taken care of, the flowers were then distributed throughout the flat.

Political awareness, not to mention involvement, was almost entirely absent from our domestic existence. The intimacy that existed between the female generations in our house was exclusively applied to the training of the young: we were taught the craft of womanhood by our mother and grandmother, and this had nothing to do with politics. It was nevertheless – though perhaps not intentionally – an exercise in self-containment, in turning inwards, in self-absorption. With their backs to the wall after the loss of Palestine, my parents' primary concern was to provide their children with a security based on relationships, morals and education rather than on more tangible material goods. Our lives, we were constantly told, would depend on ourselves, on the skills that our parents would provide us with through the education in which they always believed, and not on any material circumstance that we might happen to enjoy.

Though sewing and embroidery never played the role in my life or schooldays that they did in Teta's, they were part of the school curriculum and of my family's domestic life. My sisters and I had to practise these arts, which we always protested were devastatingly 'boring', throughout our growing-up years. I am not sure what the boys did when the girls were in embroidery class. During the long summers in Dhour al-Schweir, Mother used to assign us embroidery, 'to keep the girls busy', she would say wearily to her friends. Little tablecloths, runners, cushions, tea cosies and other useless objects flowed, or rather were eked out of those tortured afternoons when we were obliged to be 'ladies'. Sitting quietly, if not in a ladylike manner, we made flowers, leaves and even medieval castles out of needle and thread, cross stitch, long stitch, round stitch and chain stitch.

As we grew older, Mother made sure we knew how to sew on buttons, how to hem and how to knit. When there was a skirt to be hemmed and a lesson to be made of it, I had to do the excruciatingly boring task over again if the stitch was not fine enough to pass Mother's close inspection. 'This stitch is too loose, too big,' she would say, much to my chagrin. 'Do it again,' she would say sternly, mercilessly, as she pulled out the poor stitches in spite of my protests. I still have the wooden darning egg she used to make me use. 'Every girl should know how to darn stockings,' she used to say. 'Wait till you have a husband and children of your own. What will you do then? Throw away stockings that have holes in them?' Yes, Mother, I am sorry to say that is precisely what I do now, although there was a time, a very brief time, when I felt enormous guilt at doing this. I never use the darning egg, although I must admit that, true to the traditions of my family, I have gone so far as to illustrate lectures on thrift to my sons by brandishing this once useful object and suggesting, though without much enthusiasm, that they should consider using it.

The table manners I was taught were a far cry from those that Teta eliminated from her household as she made her cultural transition into the modern urban professional middle class from the far-away world of the Ottoman empire into which she was born. I was taught how to handle and differentiate between the myriad mysteries and nuances of modern cosmopolitan, middle-class domestic life, to which was added the broad and binding inheritance of Arab hospitality. Perhaps the most important lesson drummed into me was the absolute necessity of hospitality. Having heard the lesson about the life-giving reciprocity of hospitality in the desert from Mother a thousand times, how could I not have absorbed it? I learned that my home was not a shelter for my exclusive use, nor my family's, but a place of pleasant rest, in which restorative food and drink were offered to anyone who might come by.

The household was to be like a cocoon, a protecting, sheltering place.

The more dangerous the world outside became, the more thoroughly was it shut out. Home was, self-consciously and deliberately, a place for comfort, for the dressing of wounds, for peace. Home was also the place of female power, female expression: femaleness, women, wives, mothers and housekeepers were all cultivated here, like bees in a hive. It was dominated by a Queen Bee whose function was, yes, to produce and train other queens, but also to care for the community, to offer tranquillity, happiness, sanity, hospitality, in a ferocious world which was barred from entering this place.

This vision of home makes it an agreeable, emotionally rooted place, but also a burden. It gives me a never-ending duty to be always prepared for guests. I think that if I were to choose one function in my complex existence that could be considered its essence, it would be the duty to provide a pleasant place and sustenance for family and friends. It is a duty that supersedes all others, and it is a duty that can never be relegated to a secondary place, no matter what the circumstances.

In all of this apprenticeship nobody ever taught me how to deal with the outside world, or how to understand it. Never in my young years was a political or historical event represented to me in terms that I had to deal with intellectually; never was it explained, never explicitly discussed and argued over. When my parents had friends over for tea, lunch or dinner or for an evening's entertainment, the company would naturally, and without any ideological intention, split into two. The men would gravitate towards each other and sit alone, no doubt discussing finance and politics; the women would sit together gossiping and discussing homes, children and each other's personal problems. It was, naturally, to my mother's circle that I was drawn, and I therefore missed the political discussions.

When, by the sheer force of their violent manifestations, political events penetrated the safe shell of domestic serenity, they were presented to me as vicissitudes that interrupted the natural course of things and had to be dealt with domestically. Packing under stress, leaving behind what had to be left and taking with you what was necessary; taking care of the younger children, silencing their fears and wiping their tears; finding food under curfew, cooking with what was left in the pantry when you couldn't go out, and so on – all this was part of my feminine heritage, and it was a useful heritage indeed.

I was taught that the world outside the ken of domestic life did not belong to me, or I to it. The world was not mine to create or shape. Somehow, I do not know exactly how, I was taught that I was outside history. My function, I was taught, was merely to deal, graciously and without complaints, with whatever happened; to provide shelter, comfort and hospitality no matter what the circumstances. But the normal function of the outside world remained a mystery, and a terrible separation and alienation from it grew up within me.

Covering all other memories, like a gauze curtain draped over the window through which the world is seen, is the memory of being protected, watched over – lovingly, always lovingly. Coming and going, to school and on picnics, to the cinema and to the beach, someone was always watching me – my mother, my father, my brother, my cousin, my uncle, my aunt, the family driver, someone was always hovering nearby.

When we were young, we used to be taken to the sandy beaches of Beirut and Alexandria, and earlier, in a time I barely remember, of Haifa and Tiberias. My greatest joy was to leap into the waves, challenging the sea, laughing, crying and screaming as the strongest waves came crashing over me. I knew I would not drown as I was so near the shore and an adult was always at hand. I remember screaming especially loudly when Edward teased me as usual, until Mother or Daddy would come and put a stop to the teasing and the screaming, and I would be disappointed as they made him swim away and leave me alone.

As I grew older, a new kind of pleasure was afforded by those white sandy beaches: I remember lying in the sun, reading, absent-mindedly staring at the waves or dreamily drawing patterns in the sand. And then suddenly some older member of the family would be there, and I would be called out of my reverie and back into the protective circle. Years later, a chance remark by my brother made me understand that it had been passing oglers who had precipitated the defensive flurries.

The threats against which my sisters and I were so overtly protected were vague and basically harmless: I do not for a moment believe that it ever entered my parents' heads that we might really be hurt or in any way violated. We did not live in that kind of world. The worst that could happen to a girl in our social circle was a hand on the knee in the darkness of the cinema, a middle-aged man ogling her from a distance, a humorous young man calling out a racy and flattering remark, or even, on a crowded street, a pinched bottom or a persistent elbow in a gently maturing breast as the mischief-maker disappeared into the crowd. Indeed, I have many memories of situations like these, and the ensuing flutter of activity to protect me. This protectiveness had more to do with the family's sphere of influence, and with the pervasive sense that a girl was a precious thing, to be looked after and protected at all costs, than any realistic sense of danger. We were a valuable cargo carried on a tempestuous ocean.

Another imperative, this one derived from the puritanical Protestant tradition, was the need for modesty, humility and shyness. Christian humility was hammered into us at all those church services, and to the Christian requirement of self-effacement ('Let not your right hand know what your left hand giveth' and 'Blessed are the pure in heart for theirs is the Kingdom of Heaven; Blessed are the meek in spirit for they shall inherit the earth') was added the female requirement of sexual modesty. I was taught not to raise my voice, not to argue, not to interrupt, not to be naughty or noisy. I was taught, or at least I learned, though perhaps I was not taught it directly, to look down when my eyes caught a man's, to avert my gaze, to avoid an immodest invitation, to withdraw from confrontation. I learned to turn compliments away modestly, to guard against the temptation of conceit. I learned to veil my inner self and my impulses with a veil far darker and more impenetrable, and far more durable, than that outer cloth which covered the faces of some Muslim girls of my age. The protection that surrounded me became a habit, a way of life. Our world became ever more ethereal as the violent real world was increasingly locked out and denied entrance into the inner sanctum of our home.

On a recent visit to Cairo, I suddenly realized that I did not know the city's downtown streets properly because I had never walked them in my childhood. Though my sisters and I rode our bicycles around our own quarter, residential Zamalek, with its quiet, tree-lined streets, its embassies, its private schools and clubs, and though, as teenagers, we even went on long bicycle rides with our friends into the desert and to the Pyramids at Giza and Saqqara, downtown Cairo was more restricted.

Always driven, always accompanied, I had never explored the city, never stumbled on its mysteries, its hidden stories, its cruel poverty and the repressed violence lurking beneath the surface of urban social life.

And yet I do not want to give the impression that my sisters, my friends and I grew up blind, deaf and dumb to the world around us. We were clever girls, and the world has a way of imposing itself on even the most sheltered of childhoods.

Though I was too young at the time to understand what had happened in Palestine, the Palestinian tragedy, with its sense of loss, anxiety and foreboding, hung palpably over my childhood in the form of all our displaced relatives and friends, especially Teta and her sons, and Auntie Nabiha with her endless stories of the refugees. And though I remained thoroughly uninstructed in their theoretical and historical background, I could not help but gradually become aware of the bitter realities, the social inequalities and injustices, and the imperial relationship between Egypt and Britain.

I was growing up while Cairo was seething with post-Palestinian war, anti-British, anti-royalist, pre-revolutionary fervour, and reality was right there in front of me, outside the windows of the cars and buses in which I travelled around Cairo, especially to and from my English school in Heliopolis. The periodic riots and attacks on British establishments form an integral part of my childhood memories, and many is the time our school bus was attacked by an angry crowd, until finally the school authorities painted out the name of the school from the side of the bus. I remember many mornings watching in breathless anticipation as Mother called the school to ask if it were opening that day, or if the situation had forced a suspension of classes. So often my silent prayers were answered, and I can still see Mother looking disappointed as she told us to go to our rooms and do something useful. No school today.

In Jerusalem we were sent to mission schools, my brother to St George's, where my father had been before him, and Rosie and I to the Franciscan nuns at St Joseph's and to the Sisters of Zion. Joyce and Grace were too young then to be sent to school at all. In Cairo, Edward, Rosie and I were sent for a short time to the American school in Maadi. I do not know precisely why my parents moved us out of this school and into the English lay system. Many of their friends sent their children to the mission schools that still flourished in those days, especially the English Mission College and the French Mère de Dieu girls' school, but our parents, for one reason or another, had had enough of them. But for a brief spell during which Joyce and Grace were sent to the Franciscan nursery school near our home in Zamalek, they sent us all to lay schools. Surprisingly, they even eschewed the American College for Girls, where Auntie Melia governed. I have often wondered why.

Once, many years after the time I am describing, and when I felt bitter at being isolated from my surroundings, I berated Mother for having sent us to foreign schools and asked her why they hadn't, for instance, placed us in an Egyptian state school. Her response was swift and certain: 'Don't be silly,' she said, impatiently. Insuperable barriers divided the social classes in Egypt at that time: crossing them was unthinkable.

After the American school, I was sent to the elementary Gezira Preparatory School, located just a block away from our home. Edward had already gone on to the famous Victoria College, and my sisters and I were eventually to attend the English School, Cairo. The education offered by the English schools (which I have described at some length elsewhere) was quite different from that provided by the foreign mission schools that my mother and grandmother attended. The mission schools were intended to 'improve' the 'natives', both morally and intellectually, and often to convert them as well – if not religiously, then certainly culturally. The majority of the students, especially in the early days, came not from the wealthy or sophisticated urban class, but from the rural areas or from the rising urban middle class. The mission schools were mostly segregated by gender, and a puritanical attitude towards all sexual matters was inevitably nourished, if only by their exclusion.

The foreign lay schools that we attended, on the other hand, were intended principally for the children of the cosmopolitan elite of the urban centres which had been converted from Ottoman cities to meet the requirements and tastes of the new imperial powers, Britain and France. In Egypt, of course, the British had been in control since the 1880s, though they were in their final days there when we went to school.

Victoria College catered to the sons of the ruling classes of the Arab world, including members of various royal families, and has always stood as a symbol of British imperial training. The English School, Cairo, catered mostly to British expatriates in Egypt, especially those employed in the Canal Zone and other imperial, and often military, outposts. I remember several classmates whose parents served Britain in Suez, Cyprus and Malta. The Egyptian and diplomatic elite clamoured for places at this school: Mother told me that the headmaster had once expressed his surprise at this. He could not understand, he confided to her, why there was such pressure on him to admit more and more students from this class of people. Why, he asked her quizzically, did they think this school so important? It was, after all, only a normal English school to ensure that the children of those serving the empire abroad enjoyed the same education they would have had at home.

These English imperial schools, like their missionary counterparts, separated the students from their cultural surroundings. Unlike the mission schools, however, they helped shape a master class that bowed its head to no one, including, ultimately, the British themselves. Though the mission schools also produced nationalists, they were perhaps less sure of themselves, less arrogant, than those who came from the secular schools. The latter spoke to their teachers as equals. They spoke the same language, knew the same things. Furthermore, rather than teach an antagonistic and adversarial view of local culture and customs, as at the mission schools, which were, after all, subversive institutions in their origins, the English imperial schools simply ignored these topics altogether.

Arabic was taught merely as one of several languages from which students could choose, including, of course, Latin and French. As far as I can remember, Arab history, literature and culture were scarcely ever mentioned at school, other than from a skewed angle, such as when we read T. E. Lawrence's *Seven Pillars of Wisdom*. European geography and British history, on the other hand, were explored in great detail. If my parents had not been fascinated by the monuments of Egyptian history, taken us regularly to pay homage to the Pyramids at Saqqara and Giza, to the Cairo museum and all the other historical sites, and insisted on private Arabic lessons at home, we would have remained ignorant of our cultural surroundings.

At school, over the years, we read the English poets, especially Shakespeare, Wordsworth, Shelley, Keats and Byron. From them as well as from the English novelists – pre-eminently Dickens, but also Jane Austen, George Eliot, Thackeray and others – we learned their vision of life, their culture, their laws, their history and their language. If there were any non-idiomatic quirks left in our use of the English language, they were certainly not caused by any interference from Arabic, and they were easily ironed out by the daily and continuous references to the King James Bible, the Book of Common Prayer, and through them and the English hymnal, which was also part of our daily life at early-morning school assemblies, to all the sonorities and cadences of the English Church.

Unlike the mission schools attended by my mother and grandmother, the lay schools did not teach morality, good conduct or comportment as part of the curriculum. Great stress, however, was laid on an elaborate code of honour filtering throughout the school, especially at the morning assemblies, in the system of 'houses', and, above all, in the teaching of sport. Team spirit; school loyalty; good sportsmanship; 'It's not whether you win or lose that counts, but how you play the game'; learning to win or lose with equal grace and equanimity; not to indulge in enthusiastic displays of support for your favourite team or player, but to honourably applaud the honourable opponent; to acknowledge mistakes when you made them, even if the referee had not seen them – all these and other rules of the game were taught. Though we were often reminded that the patron of our school was, after all, 'Her Majesty, Queen Mary', the team spirit encouraged nationalist tendencies, especially as it was fed by the growing, and increasingly obtrusive, events in the real world.

Our school reading was elaborated and expanded on at home. My parents had a large library which included leather-bound versions of all the English classics, including the works of Dickens, Shakespeare, George Eliot and Donne, as well as many books on current affairs, the Quran and the complete works of Khalil Jibran. Intellectual endeavour was thus constantly presented to us as not directly, or even necessarily, confined to schoolwork.

Our house was filled with music and song. Both my parents had a great love of music, and partly because of his business my father had an enormous collection of records. It was from this collection that we were all introduced to a wide range of Western music, especially opera, the symphonies of Beethoven and the songs of Schubert. My father would have preferred to spend his evenings at home than in company. Mother writes of their early life together that they spent many evenings at home, listening to operas and symphonies and reading the classics – all books and records at that time came from the Palestine Educational Company in Jerusalem.

Both my parents loved to sing, and some of my earliest memories are of driving into the desert as they sang some of the songs that my father had picked up in America early in the century:

> Daisy, Daisy, give me an answer, do;
> I'm half crazy, all for the love of you.
> It won't be a stylish marriage:
> I can't afford a carriage:
> But you'll look sweet,
> Upon the seat,
> Of a bicycle built for two!

Another favourite was: 'Me and my shadow, walking down the avenue …' My father also taught us songs from his army days in the First World War: 'It's a long way to Tipperary' and the family favourite, 'Pack up your troubles in your old kit bag/And smile, smile, smile.'

Mother used to love singing British and American folk songs that she had picked up at the various schools she attended as a girl: I remember especially her singing 'Loch Lomond', 'Danny Boy' and the Stephen Foster songs. I can also see her in church fervently singing hymns. Her clear soprano was distinctly audible above the others, and, like the rest of the congregation, she always swooped into the high notes, which gave the hymns a peculiarly melancholy sound. She had no doubt picked up this style of singing, not only from her parents, but also from her American teachers in the days of her youth, when it was fashionable even in the West, but I always felt it added an Arabic touch to those Protestant hymns.

My favourite musical picture of Mother was on the occasions when Uncle Emil brought his *oud* (Arab lute) and she accompanied him on a *derbake* (percussion instrument) as they performed the old Arabic folk songs their father had sung to them. She loved the old songs performed by Fairouz, the great Lebanese singer; some of her pleasure transcended the music itself, and had to do with her childhood memories. During her last illness, as she lay dying in Washington, I brought her some records of Fairouz from Beirut, but when I played one of her favourite songs for her, she turned her head away in disappointment, saying sadly: 'That's not the way I remember it,' and wouldn't have me play it again.

We were given a formal musical education as well. The daily torture of piano lessons and practice was as much part of my apprenticeship in maternal martyrdom as it was of my musical education. Every day, Mother would summon us into the music room one by one, seat us at the Blüthner grand piano and preside over our half-hour practice. She would sit there, knitting to alleviate the excruciating agony of the exercise, making sure each of us served our full half hour, making sure the scales and exercises were painstakingly gone through.

Twice a week, Miss Cheridjian, whom we called 'Cherry' behind her back, came for the lessons. She also taught Nadia and Huda Gindy, our neighbours, and Rosie's and my schoolmates, with whom we shared so much of our childhood. She sat at the side of the piano, using an ingenious, though intensely irritating, system for counting. While eighth notes were a predictable '*un*-et, *deux*-et, *trois*-et', sixteenths were '*ta*-fa-ti-fi, *ta*-fa-ti-fi', and thirds '*ta*-te-ti, *ta*-te-ti'. Occasionally, Cherry would impatiently smack us on the arm with her fan. Once, she rapped Joyce on the knuckles, and Joyce promptly rapped her back, triumphantly exacting revenge on all our behalves. With Nadia and Huda, we talked – and laughed – about this incident for weeks.

Cherry's apparently insatiable appetite for scales and exercises was especially maddening when, famished after a long day at school, we were teased by her lusty chewing and sipping of the cakes and beverages served by Mother, ever the dutiful hostess. I could smell Cherry's breath, heavy with the teasing scent of the fresh vanilla and chocolate cake, moistened by the hot coffee, as it wafted out between the merciless '*Répétez, répétez!*'

At the end of each academic year, Cherry would gather all her students and their mothers at her house for a recital. One by one, beginning with her youngest and newest pupils and ending with her oldest and most advanced, we would go up to the piano, do a *révérence* (bow or curtsey), which she made us practise for weeks before the performance, and then play. The audience would sit patiently, politely applauding each effort. At the end, tea was served with cakes and sandwiches. Short of dire illness no one was ever excused and the excruciating exercise, dreaded for weeks in advance, had to be endured year after year. My brother once ate soap to make himself sick enough to be excused. I tried to emulate his action the following year but found the taste of soap even less palatable than the tea party.

Ballet lessons were as much a part of our lives as the piano. Twice a week, Rosie and I went, together with Claude Dirlik and Linda Fahoum, daughters of Mother's close friends, to a dance school run by a teacher called Miss Sonia. She had flaming red hair and was, we were told, a Russian trained at the Bolshoi: Mother later discovered that she was an Armenian from Bourj Hamoud in Beirut. When we were older, we moved to a ballet school in Zamalek run by an Italian woman, Madame de Paolo. That must have been when the troubles were worse, and they wanted us closer to home.

My parents went regularly to the Cairo Opera, taking us with them as we grew older. We heard many of the great European and American singers and orchestras, and saw some of the finest dancers. I probably saw my first opera when I was six or seven, and I was quite taken with it. By the time I left for university, I had seen many classical operas. I remember a performance of *Porgy and Bess* in which, though I am not sure, I believe I heard the incomparable Leontyne Price sing. I have forgotten the names of the other singers whom we heard. My father was a great opera-lover and always had records; he especially admired Caruso, whom he had heard in New York in his first days in America, and I believe that my great love of vocal music comes from him.

The singing of hymns and the saying of prayers at school was reinforced in our family by the strict churchgoing demanded by my parents. Like it or not, there was no escape first from Sunday school, and then, after confirmation, from regular service. I believe that my parents enjoyed the services enormously. They loved to sing the hymns, and Mother especially must have found in churchgoing an anchor to her childhood memories as a pastor's daughter, and a student in the Protestant missionary schools she had attended. In general, even we reluctant children enjoyed Sunday. It was a day for getting dressed up – a welcome change from the boring uniform that one wore, day in and day out, to school – and for good food and family meals.

When my sisters and I were young, getting ready for church was an elaborate procedure. It was only in our teenage years that we were liberated from the long plaits we wore as girls. Every Sunday, Mother would tie bows over the rubber bands that held the plaits together, and often a large bow was pinned on the top of our heads, a little to one side. This bow was known as a *fionka*, one of the many Italian words to have penetrated colloquial Arabic, and part of the linguistic archaeology of the culture. The *fionka* in the hair was often matched by a complementary *fionka* on the dress made by tying the long, ribbony belts at the back. Sometimes, as she prepared us for church or other special occasions, Mother would tie and untie, retie and untie again, the *fionkas* until they came out just right: wide, smooth, perfectly symmetrical bows, like satiny wings, with a perfect knot in the middle. I do not think that Teta had much to do with the *fionkas*: they are very much associated in my mind with the cosmopolitan life of the region.

If the *fionkas* were our principal adornment, they were not the only ones. When I was baptized in Jerusalem, Auntie Nabiha's gift to me was a small sapphire cross encrusted with gold, with a tiny diamond in the middle, hanging from a fine gold chain. Auntie Nabiha gave each of my sisters a similar cross: some of them were made of rubies, and some of sapphires. When my brother was confirmed, she gave him a signet ring that he always wore. Mother would take the crosses out of her cupboard in which they were always locked up. Calling us to her one by one, she would, after adjusting the *fionkas* on each head, turn us around and clasp the chain behind each neck. Sometimes some loose hair would get caught in the clasp of my necklace, and I would squeal, but usually I looked forward to feeling the gold chain, and would finger it and my sapphire cross as I stood. By the time I was a teenager, I wore my cross all the time. It became a talisman and I would finger it whenever I was afraid, or sad, or in pain.

Decades later, during the war in Lebanon, I lost my cross. Never, I think, in my whole life did the loss of an object hurt me as much as the loss of my childhood talisman, my little sapphire cross. I think the trauma lay in the fact that it was wartime, and this loss seemed to represent all the other losses of my life, mostly what was left of stability and order. A part of me was lost with it, something that tied me to Auntie Nabiha, to Mother, to Daddy, to Jerusalem, to Cairo, to my childhood, to my past, to those days when my hair was lovingly washed and plaited, to the smell of the olive oil soap, and to those Sunday mornings when Mother would take out the crosses and my sisters and I, with our *fionkas* and smocked dresses, would stand in a row, waiting for her attention.

Recently I bought a gold cross to replace the one I had lost. I wore it for a while, trying to endow it with a borrowed past and borrowed meanings. My children were horrified: they interpreted my cross in the only way they could, as a statement of narrow religiosity. I tried impatiently to explain why I had bought it; I even told them to mind their own business. But eventually I took it off and put it away. I never wear it. What is past is past, and what is lost is lost.

If my sapphire cross held memories which had nothing much to do with religion, some of my earliest and most persistent memories are tied up with going to church, with Bible stories told me by Teta, with prayers said at night and with religious songs and hymns. I remember particularly a song Mother taught us. We sang it every night, kneeling by the side of the bed, before reciting the Lord's Prayer:

> Gentle Jesus, meek and mild,
> Come to me, your little child;
> Pity my simplicity;
> Suffer me to come to thee. Amen.

When we were little, and Mother taught us this song by singing it with us, we used regularly, perhaps based on her example, to take a breath after the 'sim' of 'simplicity'; we said 'pitymysim', and had no idea what the word meant; nor did we understand 'theeamen', though we felt some relief at having safely reached the end of the song.

Probably because of the musical bent in our family, the singing of hymns played an enormously important part in my childhood and schooling. It had a part in my political as well as my linguistic and moral formation. Early morning assembly at school always included the hymns and prayers of the English church. It now seems to me that the emphasis was far more on the thunder and majesty of the 'Mighty Lord God' of the Old Testament than on the 'meek and mild' Jesus of the New. The former was certainly a more fitting protector of the mighty British empire, which was in those days gradually sliding down the mountain of supremacy and into the ashes of history. The words of such grand and solemn hymns as 'A Mighty Fortress is Our God', 'O God, Our Help in Ages Past', 'Now Thank We All Our God', 'Ye Watchers and Ye Holy Ones', 'Holy, Holy, Holy', and others like them, reinforced by the sonorous melodies to which they were sung, made them and the English language part of the political and moral framework of the system provided by the school.

The hymns we sang at school and at All Saints, the English cathedral of Cairo, were augmented by others that we sang in the American church, to which we were alternatively taken. The American hymns were often directly political in nature, and were particularly associated in my mind with the Thanksgiving Day services to which we were always taken. Far from the imperial assurance of the English songs, the American hymns always trumpeted the words 'brotherhood', 'freedom' and 'liberty'. Not only was there the 'Sweet Land of Liberty', of which we sang, with freedom ringing from every mountainside, but also the melodious 'O Beautiful for Spacious Skies', whose stanzas claimed a path for our feet on 'the thoroughfare of freedom', while heroes proved in 'liberating strife' that they loved their country more than themselves, and 'mercy more than life'. I used especially to enjoy singing the wonderfully sonorous hymn 'God of Our Fathers', each verse of which was preceded by the declamation of organ trumpets. That hymn was sung at Thanksgiving, which I seem to remember we used to celebrate in Auntie Melia's school chapel, before coming home to lunch on turkey, which was always served with cranberry sauce and candied sweet potatoes.

Thus did I receive, through the singing of these various hymns and the moral education that accompanied them, not only a religious, but a political schooling of sorts. For though the intertwining of morality and politics does not necessarily make for a clear understanding of the cynicism that governs world affairs, it does engender impatience with and a rejection of this cynicism, and a real belief in a more perfect, less unjust world. And though I regret not having been taught more about the real world, I have never regretted being taught this kind of morality first.

Indeed, a moral issue was made of the slightest events in our daily lives. A quarrel with a sibling, homework done or left undone, the smallest fib, the least unkindness, an act of generosity or cupidity – each action was analysed for its moral content. And so eventually were the public actions of nations, governments and peoples. I grew up prepared to judge the world rather than to participate in its actions.

Personal morality was also a stabilizing factor in our unstable world. We were on the edge of a great change: in spite of my ignorance and my youth, I had felt the changes brought about by the Palestine experience. Now I felt instinctively that in Egypt also we had reached the end of a world. I remember King Farouq and members of his family passing through the streets of Cairo in their crimson automobiles: only the royal family was allowed red cars in Egypt. The police whistles, the heads turning, the expressions on the faces of the people watching – all spoke of something coming to an end, the last feeble flutter of a butterfly of a species on the verge of extinction, the last flimsy blossom floating down from a dying tree.

I saw not the least flicker of affection or respect, but rather expressions of contempt, on those faces turning to look at the crimson cars. In my parents' circle, I never heard a kind word or a respectful mention of the king: at best, there would be nostalgic references to the promise they had felt when the young Farouq had first become king, a promise which had over the years faded into the corruption and decadence which were to bring about his downfall.

I shall never forget the day in January 1952 known as Black Saturday. The British occupation forces in the Suez Canal Zone had suffered a number of attacks by Egyptian nationalists. They took severe reprisals, and in reaction, angry crowds raged through the streets of Cairo, attacking and burning down mostly foreign enterprises, including hotels, schools, businesses and restaurants. But their rage also expressed a clear frustration brought about by poverty and the injustice of the social system. Black Saturday was not just an uprising against the British and their local political allies, but also a general revolt against the ruling class and against foreign privilege.

I spent much of that day on the balcony, dreamily watching the city burning from across the great River Nile. The sky was red; the air was thick. I coughed occasionally, and rubbed my eyes. There was absolute silence where we were; not a car passed by, not a dog barked, not a child played on the streets. The roar of the flames and the crowds could only be heard in the imagination, but they hung over the city like the red glow of the fire that loomed across the Nile. I stretched out my arm every now and then, trying to catch a blackened fragment of paper or rag as it floated gently by in the quiet breeze. The day passed slowly. One after the other, the names of the ruined companies came over the news bulletins, and from my father's friends downtown, who rang to give him the latest news: Shepheard's Hotel, this bank, that department store, this cinema, that bookshop. Finally came the news that my father's business had been burnt to the ground, along with all those on Sharia al-Malika Farida (Queen Farida Street), named after King Farouq's first wife.

What impressed me that evening was not only the actual event but, even more, the relationship between my parents. I saw and thought about this clearly for the first time that day and it shaped my notion of character, and of an ideal sort of personal comportment. My father was, of course, crushed by the enormous loss he suffered that day: just four years earlier, the family had lost all its possessions and its centre of gravity in Palestine.

After the news arrived, my sisters and I – my brother was by then at boarding school in America – stared quietly at my father as we sat around the dining table for supper: no fire or mob, no catastrophe, was to stop the orderly progress of the household, and meals were served as usual throughout the day. We were filled with trepidation, afraid to see my father collapse in tears or show other signs of weakness. He made a point, however, of not showing his pain, reacting instead with gallant humour. The moment he received the news of the destruction of the business that he had created, he declared his intention of rebuilding it. 'I built it the first time,' he declared, 'and I will build it again.'

Mother herself showed no pain and no anxiety about the future, though she may have felt it: instead she displayed total support, good cheer and her characteristic, almost reassuring, anxiety for his health, though for once she did not overly protest at his heavy smoking, heavier than ever that evening. There was no grimness in their reaction, no quarrelling, no anger, no nervousness, no 'whining'. There was good cheer, and expressions of devotion, and many hugs, and the phrase '*Wala y'himik*' (Don't let it bother you) was repeated throughout the day as they comforted and calmed each other. As usual, I think, and in spite of the great drama unfolding, both of them were conscious of the children watching; they never stopped acting their model roles, self-consciously teaching us at every turn morality and strength of character. 'Be strong,' I seem to remember Mother saying, even at this time.

Later, a great lesson was made out of this 1952 experience, a lesson in stoicism, in character, in loyalty, in marital virtues, in husbandly strength and wifely support. The lesson was made vocally and explicitly over the years by Mother, who often admiringly referred to her husband's courageous reaction. 'This', she would proudly say, 'is a man.' But it was also made more effectively by our own observations. We learned the lesson with our own ears and our own eyes. He was, indeed, a man.

I was to be vividly reminded of this January day many years later, the first time my home in Beirut was shelled and badly damaged during the Lebanon war that began in 1975. As I climbed the stairs to Mother's flat that morning, coming, with my husband and young children, from the terrifying experience, the narrow escape and the wrecked apartment, Mother leaned, beaming, over the balustrade, not even waiting until I got upstairs, and called out: '*Wala y'himik*' – 'Don't worry, it's not worth worrying about objects. The important thing is that none of you were injured.' I felt then that to break down, to cry, to show any but the most stoical reaction would be to betray the norms by which I had been raised.

But no matter how domesticated that Black Saturday in January had become, no matter how politics and public events were in our household transferred to the realm of private life and personal conduct, it was impossible not to take note of the uprising and not to understand that a bell was tolling, a curtain coming down.

We were in Dhour al-Schweir as usual when the Egyptian revolution took place on 23 July 1952. I listened to my parents' reaction, and to those of their friends who had come with them from Cairo to spend the summer in the cool mountains of Lebanon. I listened to the curious inquiries of their Lebanese friends, and the anxious questions of their Palestinian relations. What would happen now? What was next? How would the Free Officers who had led the coup behave? Was Egypt to have a military dictatorship?

Over the next few days my parents and their friends listened to the radio endlessly, and read as many newspapers as were available in that village high up in the mountains, mulling over the news and all the new names. At that point, the spotlight was on the nominal leader, General Mohammed Naguib, while the real leader, Gamal Abdel Nasser, remained in relative obscurity. As usual, my sisters and I were sent out to play and were not drawn into direct discussions over what had happened. Nevertheless I clearly understood that my parents were sympathetic to the revolution. I heard them express no anger, no fear, as others did in those early days.

Even before the revolution, my parents had never been blinded by their immediate surroundings: unlike many members of their circle, they saw beyond the pleasures and charms of their life. Perhaps because of their Palestinian experience, they saw the dangers and they saw the exploitation, the outrage of social injustice. Typically, Mother wrote in her memoir about Fatma, the laundress: 'Can you imagine that at that time we used to pay Fatma and her daughter 15 Egyptian piastres (and they were very happy because most people paid only 10)?' As time passed, it was clear that there was after all to be no bloodbath such as that grimly prophesied since January. The revolution had been a singularly civilized affair: though shorn of their titles and possessions, the king and his family had been safely and even courteously packed off to Europe, and life in Cairo returned to normal, at least as far as I was concerned.

Later, a social revolution gradually took place: major land reforms were undertaken, and the distance between the fabulously wealthy Egyptian upper class and the desperately poor peasants was dramatically reduced. In the meantime, opposition to the British was growing, the great Aswan Dam was being planned, and under the dynamic leadership of Abdel Nasser Arab nationalist fervour was sweeping the region.

Perhaps of all the dramatic actions of the revolution, the one that impressed me most at the time was the abolition of all titles of privilege. Gone suddenly by decree were the titles 'pasha', 'bey', 'effendi', 'king', 'prince' and 'princess'. Suddenly, the *tarbouche*, or fez, so closely associated with the king and his regime and their Turkish origins, disappeared off the streets, never to return. The egalitarianism implied by the decree abolishing titles was reinforced by the opening to the public of the royal palaces. One afternoon, Mother took me to see the Abdine Palace. The grandeur of the place, the voluptuous wealth of the furniture, the excess in the personal ornaments, and the incredible variety and range of the jewellery displayed neatly on glass shelves, was in such shocking contrast to the misery and poverty outside the palace walls that no greater political instruction was needed to awaken me to the meaning of social injustice and political corruption.

CHAPTER 5

'Ladies, Simply Ladies'

Our family's distance from the centre of political life in Egypt meant that we were not at first directly affected by the revolution, and it took time for the great changes to filter down into our home. Except for my awareness of the new political rhetoric, my early teenage years, passed in the shadow of the revolution, continued pretty much as they had before. That at least was my perception of things. No doubt my parents regarded life with much greater anxiety than I: no doubt also, as I think about it now, they must already have been aware of hints as to the future policies of the socialist revolution, the nationalizations and expropriations of property that were to come later. In this, as in everything else, they protected their children from an awareness of the inherent dangers in our situation. Their sympathy for the revolution, and the fact that they were at first distanced from its direct consequences, perhaps made them represent it in less threatening terms.

I remember once being in the lounge at Cairo airport with my father and other members of the family. We were awaiting someone's arrival – perhaps Edward was coming home after his first year away at boarding school. There was a sudden commotion, and in came General Mohammed Naguib and the American Adlai Stevenson. At the time, Naguib was thought of as the leader of the revolution – it was only much later that it became clear that the real leader was Gamal Abdel Nasser. They settled down at a table very near ours, and I was encouraged by my father to ask General Naguib to sign my ubiquitous autograph book, which he did. When he finished, he patted my head and everyone around us beamed.

As I look back at the four years between the revolution and the Suez crisis that ended my childhood, I see myself and my sisters going to school, taking piano and ballet lessons, playing tennis, riding our bicycles on the banks of the Nile, going to the cinema, going on scouting trips and family picnics in the desert and by the Nile, going to church on Sundays and enjoying family dinners and lunches. We regularly picnicked at the Pyramids of Giza and Saqqarra, where we rode camels, horses or donkeys. And though I followed all the events of this tumultuous period from a safe distance and was always directly influenced by the Egyptian revolution, my teenage consciousness was focused elsewhere as well. I was growing up, and was becoming aware of the changes bringing me to womanhood.

As we grew older, Mother sometimes took my sisters and me to the Cairo Women's Club, in downtown Cairo, on Midan Mustafa Kamel, where she and her fellow members attended lectures and drank tea, but also discussed the country's social problems and organized social-work activities. Theirs was one of the first groups, I believe, of well-off urbanites to go to the villages and teach the women there the basic rules of hygiene and health. Though I used to dread going to the club, because I would have to endure being scrutinized by Mother's friends, and then hear judgment pronounced on the state of my appearance, my health and my growth, the women probably did not pay much attention to their daughters as they discussed serious (or not so serious) matters. The club was a kind of escape for Mother, I am sure, but it was also an entry into the larger social life of Cairo. It was an important aspect of my social education, and it taught me something about the civilized interchange of thought.

Some of the other clubs of which we were members were more purely social in nature. My parents had joined first the Maadi and then the Gezira Sporting Club. We also went, though less frequently, to the Tewfikiyya Club, mostly to play tennis. My memory of the Maadi Club centres largely on the swimming pool, with Mother wearing a floral-patterned dress sitting in a deck chair knitting as she watched her brood in the pool. Once a week, the Maadi Club showed children's films, and we attended quite regularly. We saw Tom Mix and the Lone Ranger, Roy Rogers and Trigger, but most of all we saw the old Tarzan films that had such a huge effect on our imagination, especially Edward's.

In those days, membership of the Gezira Club was controlled by the foreign, mostly English, management and was closed to all but a very small, elite group of Egyptians. The staff of trainers and servants, however, was almost entirely Egyptian. In this beautiful place, we swam in a large pool; we played tennis on clay courts, and croquet on the grass; my brother and older sister took riding lessons until one of their friends fell off a horse and was severely injured. My father played golf and tennis, and bridge in the clubhouse. Mother took tea with her friends on the wide and elegant lawns as she watched her younger children play on the swings and seesaws.

Occasionally one or more of us children, depending on our age, were taken by our parents for a special evening at the St James's Hotel, where dinner was served on the spacious terrace while the latest movie was projected on a large open-air screen beyond. By the time I was old enough to be taken out for dinner, the famous Shepheard's Hotel, where my parents often used to dine or take tea on the terrace, had been burned down on Black Saturday. We often went to Groppi's, that most famous of Cairo's culinary institutions, either to the indoor teahouse on Midan Suleiman Pasha, or to Groppi's other open-air location on Queen Farida Street, where we were allowed to run in the garden. Mother used to buy her sweets and cakes for special occasions from the Midan Suleiman Pasha Groppi's. I can still remember looking up from my own height at the huge tables and counters on which sat vast urns full of the chocolates and candies that made the place famous. I especially remember the extraordinary displays at Easter time: chocolate rabbits filled with small chocolate eggs, and egg-shaped candies in a variety of colours. I do not know if these delectable memories come from the period before the revolution, or whether, like so much else in our lives, were carried on somehow by inertia until the final break with this sort of life.

We were frequently taken for tea or lunch to the world-famous Mena House Hotel, at the foot of the Pyramids, where we were allowed to run loose among the antelopes and peacocks as our elders sat and sipped their tea and lemonade on the lawn. When we went there, we would always pay homage to the great Pyramids and sometimes to the Sphinx as well. To this day, I share my parents' admiration for these monuments, instilled in me and my siblings so early in our lives. My parents never seemed to have enough of them; indeed, one of the things I always admired about them was that they never lost their sense of childlike awe at human accomplishments such as the Pyramids.

At school, girls were excused from games if they had 'Willie' (the code name for a menstrual period). Unlike our mothers' generation, we were made aware of our bodies through the vigorous physical education which our mothers had not known, and through the swimming, horse-back riding, bicycling, tennis and ballet, all of which had become not only fashionable, but *de rigueur* for our class of urban girls. It was enormously important, part of one's social accomplishments, to be fit and slim: all the mothers I knew, including my own, exhorted their daughters to follow the slimming diets which formed a major part of our conversation, and eyebrows were raised whenever a girl so much as eyed a chocolate or a piece of cake. Depilation, manicures, pedicures, hairdressers, dressmakers and clothes – all this was a terribly important part of our lives: to be properly, fashionably dressed and groomed, we were taught, was as important as breathing.

Mother had a phrase which, from this time of her maturity and female prowess, she passed on to her daughters, a heavy burden: '*Pour être belle il faut souffrir*' (One must suffer to be beautiful). That *être belle* should be a major goal of a woman's life seemed to Mother beyond dispute, self-evident, irreducibly true. '*Pour être belle il faut souffrir*' was chanted at my sisters and me when we complained of such rituals as the painful depilation to which we were introduced at puberty, the wearing of wired bras and corsets, having to stand on a table and wait for an agony of time as the hem was pinned up centimetre by centimetre on the wide skirts that were fashionable when we were in our teens, learning to walk in high heels, or having our skins scrubbed and our eyebrows plucked.

Once we became teenagers, every other week a woman named Nehmidoh (We praise Him) used to be ushered into our rooms. Nehmidoh was tall and thin, and was dressed in a *millayah*, or all-enveloping cloak, which she removed as soon as she entered the inner sanctum of our house. A door separated the outer, more public rooms of our flat from an inner space, including the bedrooms and bathrooms. This was an almost exclusively female space, where dressmakers, manicurists and Nehmidoh catered to our needs, and we could wander around in varying degrees of undress unseen by the male servants. After all, there were six resident women in the house.

Once Nehmidoh was inside, off would come her *millayah* and then successive layers of her cumbersome costume, except for the gold bangles around her wrist, which jingled and jangled with her every movement. Then she would settle down on a wooden stool in the spacious bathroom, and Mother would call us in, one by one, most reluctant victims. First, Nehmidoh would produce a small saucepan in which she had already prepared a hot sugar paste, boiled to the right consistency with a few drops of lemon juice. She would pour it out on to the cool tiles, and then when it was cold enough to be touched, she would pick it up and knead it, wetting her fingers with water as she did so, until it was ready to be applied to hairy legs and arms. Apply; pat down; pull. Apply; pat down; pull. However much we whimpered or howled, Mother would hear of no excuses. *Pour être belle il faut souffrir.* In fact, as Mother always said, it was not all that painful. 'Don't be silly. Stop whining,' she would say. 'Don't you want to be pretty?'

Lucy, the Armenian dressmaker, was another regular presence in our house and made all our everyday clothes. Mother went to a tailor downtown for her suits, and as we got older she took us there as well. But there was a procession of lesser dressmakers who were an almost constant presence in our house: their job was to mend and darn and sew. These were Auntie Nabiha's protégées among the refugees. I remember one of them especially. She was a thin woman, with long stringy hair and a general air of deep anxiety. I think her name was Maliha.

Lucy had a great sense of humour, which she often expressed in coarse language and facial expressions that served to accentuate her squint and create a comical, almost obscene, effect. Somehow she always managed to sit next to me at lunch, knowing that I was a finicky eater who detested fish and shrimps, which she loved. Mother often served this kind of food and insisted that I eat it. It was part of her discipline that we had to eat food we did not like. I do not know why, but it is a discipline that I practised with my own children. I shall advise them strenuously not to practise it with theirs.

Lucy and I devised a system of collaboration that worked to our mutual advantage. When Mother was not looking, I would scoop up the fish and shrimps from my plate into my napkin and pass it to Lucy under the table. In exchange, she would pass me her clean napkin, and at the end of the meal she would surreptitiously hand the dirty napkin to Ahmed, the *suffragi*, and thus dispose of the evidence of our collusion. These giant shrimps came from the Red Sea: somehow, not only with Lucy's help, but with other forms of subterfuge, I managed never to taste them. I think my phobia was created because of Edward's name for me: 'Shrimp'.

If the bras and corsets my sisters and I were made to wear as teenagers were not as painful or intimidating as their Victorian counterparts, they were uncomfortable enough. Mother had a bra- and girdle-making second cousin, Salimeh Badr, who came every year from Brooklyn to Dhour al-Schweir and we would troop to her house to be measured and fitted for our year's supply. Mother would lead the way, and the rest of us would follow in doleful procession behind her, mother hen and her unhappy chicks. If Edward asked cheekily where we were going, Mother would reply firmly: 'Mind your own business.' He would respond with a broad grin, indicating that he understood very well to which shrine our pious feet were taking us – *Pour être belle il faut souffrir*.

Our bodies were for our clothes, not for us. And certainly not for any sexual matters. Although in our teens we were occasionally allowed to attend the odd dancing party, strict manners still reigned supreme in our household and in our circle. As a young girl, I was totally ignorant of all sexual matters. As I grew older and became familiar with those guessed-at feelings suggested in romantic disguise in the cinema, and in such books as *Wuthering Heights* (required school reading), Mother became progressively more deliberate about which films my sisters and I were allowed to see. She watched our reading carefully and confiscated books that she considered unsuitable for a 'well-brought-up young lady'. One summer we discovered Kathleen Winsor's *Forever Amber*: though today I have not the least memory of that book, I clearly remember our machinations in hiding it from Mother's ken.

Mother's puritanical streak often seemed in sharp contrast to the cosmopolitanism and sophistication she had acquired, with my unpuritanical father's guidance, over the decades since her childhood as a pastor's daughter. Though my father's American attitudes and worldly knowledge influenced Mother, as did the sophisticated circles in which she now moved, puritanism dominated her inner life, and ours. If Mother remembered having being scolded when she had asked about her bed-ridden pregnant aunt ('Little girls do not talk like this'), she never failed to repeat that phrase to me when I was a child.

This puritanism often manifested itself as a refusal, which could sometimes seem comical to us, to tolerate the slightest immodesty of language, which she angrily called 'bad words'. She would refer to prostitutes, of course, as 'bad women'. In general, women were more frequent targets of her moral censoriousness than men, and clearly in her eyes men were allowed greater leeway than women in the practice of their lives. Whenever a rude or coarse word made its way to our lips, she would wash our mouths out with soap; if one of us used a particularly offensive word, we might get a little sprinkling of hot pepper on our tongue.

Along with reading the classics at school, I had been an enthusiastic reader of the classics of English children's literature: *Alice in Wonderland*, *The Wind in the Willows* and others; we were brought up on the stories of the Brothers Grimm and Hans Christian Andersen. But most of all, I read the books of Enid Blyton, borrowing those I did not own from my friends, who read them as obsessively as I did, and lending them those in my library in return. Rosie and I, with Nadia and Huda Gindy, shared books and pictures about the Princesses Elizabeth and Margaret. When the latter began her affair with the dashing group commander, we followed every twist and turn of the sad romance. As far as we were concerned, it was all part of the show-business world that entertained us at the cinema every single Saturday afternoon – I can almost swear to this absolute regularity – of our lives.

We used to go mostly to the Metro and the Radio, and only occasionally to the Diana, whose audience was generally less acceptable to our parents. When we were younger we saw the enchanting Walt Disney cartoons. As we grew older, we were taken to see *The Secret Garden, The Red Shoes, Little Women, National Velvet* and so on. Later we were allowed to see westerns and some mild adventure films: *Lassie*, certainly, and others like it. We saw many historical dramas, especially an endless number of films about Queen Elizabeth I, and pirates. Such war films as we saw were all about heroism, courage and valour, and never showed the slightest details of real war. These films were interspersed with the old Tarzan films, and the Tom Mix that were projected regularly at the Maadi Sporting Club. Of the Cecil B. De Mille films, I remember particularly the Roman films; my steady cinematic diet included the Hollywood musicals of those days.

Mother never permitted us to peep into the world of those dark melodramas featuring Joan Crawford, Barbara Stanwyck and Bette Davis that she herself enjoyed, and which I saw only years later on television. Those films were not considered fit for young girls, for 'ladies' in the making. Girls of our circle – perhaps boys too – were only allowed a sanitized and entirely unreal view of a world that did not exist, had never existed. Not even the sanitized Hollywood versions of adultery, betrayal, sex or violence were allowed to darken that happy view of the world in which we were taught to believe.

But it was not only that kind of unreality that the cinema represented. We hardly ever saw Egyptian films. The one popular entertainment to which we were regularly taken was the Naguib al-Rihani Theatre in one of Cairo's more densely populated neighbourhoods. The theatre itself was small and crowded. People arrived and left during the performance, which went on for hours. The noisy consumption of food – especially that wonderful Cairo staple called *lib*, small roasted and salted melon seeds, the skins spat out loudly – helped to create a mood of vulgar informality that was entirely consistent with the comedy. Drinks, too, were consumed during the performance: young men wearing white caps and aprons walked the aisle calling '*Bibs* (Pepsi), *Bibs; kazouz* (a fizzy drink), *gelati* (ice-cream), *lib.*' Customers would whistle and call for the snacks, and the transaction would be completed without the slightest attempt to lower one's voice or show the least discretion. Children ran up and down the aisle; their parents chased after them, or simply sat in their seats and called.

However chaotic the goings-on in the audience, they could not match the hilarious goings-on on stage. There was little or no attempt at realism: as each actor appeared, the action was interrupted, sometimes for a considerable period of time, as he or she took a long bow, acknowledging the audience's applause. Actors often improvised their lines and invented new twists to the vaguely constructed narratives. Once in a while, an actor would forget his place and pause, smiling broadly in confession, creating even more hilarity in the audience and among his fellow actors. Actors sometimes exchanged comically insulting asides, bringing the house down. The language of the plays was crude, and the voices even cruder. There was a great deal of shouting, a great many vulgar expressions, often with *double entendres*. The themes were predictable: the cuckolded or henpecked husband, the miserly landlord or boss, the rich but disagreeable elderly spinster searching for a husband, confused identities, embezzlements and all the usual stuff of comedy.

We participated in folk festivals, especially Sham al-Nassim, the great spring festival, when all of Egypt would pour outdoors to celebrate the season. We used to picnic with the crowds at the Barrage on the Nile. During the festival of Mawlid al-Nabi (the Prophet's birthday), celebrated with such colourful exhilaration in Egypt – like nowhere else, as far as I know, in the Arab world – we were driven around Cairo to see the famous festival dolls – *arousset al-mawlid* – all gaudy in pink, red and gold, displayed on the wooden carriages and clutched to the bosom of all the small children on the streets. On those occasions my father would buy us cotton candy, though Mother always protested, as it left us with sticky hands and faces, and she worried about the unhygienic manner of its production and sale. These activities were a line into the heart of the society on whose fringe we otherwise lived, and I believe we all cherished them for precisely that reason. Though we were taken regularly to the opera, the ballet, recitals and concerts, our hearts were always at the Naguib al-Rihani, in Sham al-Nassim and the street celebrations of Mawlid al-Nabi.

Summer began early in Cairo, and all defences turned against the burning, searing light of the hot summer sun. The wooden shutters were closed at midday to keep out the sun and create a cool shade in the interior. On all the windows and doors hung long nets, under the curtains, to keep the flies out. On all the balconies, the *tendas*, or awnings, were drawn as soon as the sun appeared on that side of the sky. Fans of all shapes, sizes and speeds were tried out to minimize the discomfort of the ferocious heat of the Cairo summer. When air-conditioning became available, our house, as usual, was one of the first in Cairo to enjoy that luxury.

The ultimate weapon against the heat, however, was our annual pilgrimage to Dhour al-Schweir, and as I look back over these pages, I see that many of my reminiscences are centred in that place. It was a kind of counter-rhythm to our life in Cairo, its antithesis, a totally different lifestyle, and yet at the same time its complement, its completion. Without Dhour al-Schweir, our lives in Cairo would have lost an important reflective dimension, one which allowed us to see it from a different perspective.

We came to Dhour al-Schweir with many other Cairenes. It was also a favourite summer resort for Iraqis, Syrians and of course Beirutis – and for Palestinian visitors before the disaster of 1948. Indeed, my parents had discovered its pleasures long before that date and used to spend part of every summer there, taking the train from Cairo to Jerusalem, and then driving on to Lebanon. Perched on a ridge at a height of around 1,200 metres and surrounded by pine forests, it offered exquisite views, pleasant summer weather, several walking paths, easy access to the many other mountain resort cafes, and in general, an easy life for summer visitors.

In Dhour al-Schweir, Mother had kept up her connection with her mother's family, for they too spent their summers in that village, from which Teta's father had come before he entered the world of the American missionaries, the world that was to shape ours. Teta's brother Uncle Habib and his wife Auntie Hanah – a family favourite, always indulgent and smiling – lived in a house on the main street. I especially remember Uncle Habib for his wry sense of humour and his strong resemblance to my grandmother. He and Auntie Hanah had lived in Sudan for years before retiring to Beirut. Their children also played a role in our summers: Mother's beloved childhood companions, her cousins Eva and Lily, Fouad and Ellen, with their own families, used to come every year. Their children became friends of ours. Lily had married Albert, the son of Teta's other brother, Nassib, who lived in Cairo. His sister Nora, Mother's dearest and closest friend in her youth and early married life, also used to spend time in Dhour al-Schweir with her children. Auntie Melia, too, spent some of each summer in Dhour al-Schweir, and that is where she died.

For Mother's children and her cousins, Dhour al-Schweir played a major role in childhood memories. Many of us have gravitated back there with our own families and children. I am writing these very pages in Dhour al-Schweir, having turned to it for shelter and the warmth of reminiscence and memory after the painful events of the war, and all the deaths and partings of my life, and the scattering of my family.

When we were very young, we played on the dry land surrounding the house that my parents rented year after year in Dhour al-Schweir. As we grew older, we were let loose in the pine woods near the house. We played in the dirt, collecting the fallen pine cones, and later burned them in bonfires, extracting the seeds, pounding them with stones and eating the kernels. We also used to extract gum from the pine trees, not knowing then that it attracted the scorpions that we used to search for in our shoes every morning before putting them on, and every evening before getting into bed. Whenever we caught a scorpion, we would light a little fire and burn it – when we did not run away from it first, screaming. Somehow we had picked up the idea that scorpions only die in fire.

There were several summer festivals, which were celebrated with bonfires and fireworks. The Festival of God in early August followed the Festival of St Elias in late July. The Feast of Our Lady came in mid-August, but the biggest and grandest of these mountain celebrations was *eid al-salib* (the Feast of the Cross), which fell on 14 September. It had the added distinction of marking the end of the summer, for after that the packing began and the melancholic note of things closing down descended on the village. In late September the first rains came, and the cafes took down their summer awnings. Trucks came to carry back to Beirut the furniture brought up for the summer, and windows were boarded up for the winter. Since we were returning to Egypt, Mother would cover the summer furniture with dust cloths and old sheets, and then we would climb into our taxis and drive to the airport.

For the bonfires, we would go out in the woods and collect thorns, dry grasses and pine needles. It is said that the first bonfires were lit hundreds of years ago to spread the news of the return of the True Cross to the Holy Land. The countryside in the Lebanese mountains was bone dry by mid-summer and forest fires were not uncommon, as they are to this day, but this never stopped the bonfires or the fireworks. Crude fireworks, made in China with very few or no safety precautions, were available in the village shop of César Amer. For days beforehand, we would collect Roman candles, and a variety of other devices of which we demanded only that they whistled and went off with a bang. All of us at one point or another singed our hair, and suffered small burns on our fingers, and it is a wonder none of us lost an eye in these dangerous proceedings. The most dangerous of all were the thin rockets that were held at arm's length and then lit from glass bottles; they zigzagged their way shakily up into the sky, producing a little bang at the end, which we applauded enthusiastically. Many times, though, the rockets would not go up at all, and instead fizzled out right there on the ground, where we tried to light them again. We girls were not allowed to light the rockets; only Edward and his friends among the neighbourhood boys were allowed to do so, while we had to stand at a safe distance and watch – ever protected.

As we grew older, we used to take long walks to the neighbouring towns of Bologna, Khunshara, Jwar, Bikfaya or Broumana, where an international tennis tournament took place every summer. We rode our bicycles up and down the hills. We played cards and Monopoly. We did crossword puzzles. We read comic books – *Little Lulu* and *Captain Marvel* were my favourites – and movie magazines. I remember especially *Photoplay* and *Silver Screen*. That is where most of my pocket money went. After doing our morning chores (we always had chores in the morning), we were allowed a few free hours to walk to the *saha*, or village centre, where, not far from the church, a magazine vendor sold these priceless entertainments, many of which hung on strings, like Christmas ornaments.

Freedom of a sort was ours in Dhour al-Schweir, and freedom was a priceless commodity for girls in our day. We could go where we chose, and do pretty much what we chose, as there was not that much to choose from. Let loose, we wandered about the village, never complaining about boredom, as we were never bored. We played tennis, ping-pong and cards. We learned *tawleh* (backgammon) and whist. We peeked through the curtains at Hawi and Nasr, the village cafes, and watched our elders tango and rumba to the tunes played by bands imported from the city. We also watched the *numéros* that we were taken to see at the *thés dansants*, which we were sometimes permitted to attend at Nasr, while Mother sat with her friends. On a tiny stage we watched people dance as we giggled at them, or as we danced with each other. Occasionally, there would be a show: a pair of dancers, he wearing a worn tuxedo and a toupee, she fishnet stockings which seemed very wicked. Occasionally there would be a juggler juggling a dozen oranges, and dishes on a long stick, or a clown on a unicycle, or a singer.

On other occasions we devoured the *chocolats moux* which were the speciality of Hawi. Never were there more delicious *chocolats moux* than those we ate there as children: we used to sit up and wait for the first appearance of the long glasses filled with chocolate ice-cream, topped by mounds of whipped cream, with chocolate sauce poured over the whole thing, quite untroubled by the calories which make a *chocolat mou* impossible to enjoy today.

Though it was summer, and we were relieved from the rigid format of schooldays, we still had to submit to a strict daily routine. Every morning, my father would go to the village to buy the daily stock of fruit and vegetables, and every day, just as inevitably, Mother would have a fit of pique at his having bought too much. There was never enough water to wash the fruit and vegetables if she wanted to do the laundry and then bathe all the dirty children as well. Later he would go and play bridge at the bridge club in the village, and at noon, when lunch was ready, one of us would be dispatched to call him to order and bring him home. In the afternoons he played *tawleh* or more bridge. He often took us for picnics to the many waterfalls and gorges in the mountains of Lebanon.

In the meantime, every morning, we had to do our chores before we were released to play. Though these chores varied in nature, I am sure they were always invented to teach us that the devil makes work for idle hands rather than to accomplish any truly useful purpose. They were also meant to set us girls on our destined paths as accomplished housewives. One of the chores I particularly detested and continuously protested at (which is why, I suppose, I was always assigned it) was cleaning the windows with old newspapers. I had to stand on a stool or ladder, crumple up the papers, dip them in a solution of water and vinegar, and then scrub the windows wet before scrubbing them dry. And they were never clean enough to pass Mother's scrutiny. Her inspection always ended with a scolding, and at least one window invariably had to be done again, however much I grumbled.

Another even more detested chore to which all of us girls were subjected was sewing and darning. Though I have already mentioned this, no amount of writing about it will show how much I hated it. We had to sew our own hems and all our own buttons. If my memory serves me correctly, we had to do Edward's as well – though I will not swear to having to sew on his buttons, I am sure he was exempted from this torment, which was never considered a job fit for a boy. Teta taught me some embroidery stitches beyond those I had been taught at school, though I was a most reluctant student. She even taught me her beloved crochet, which I learned only as a gesture of contrition to her and a sign of respect. I also learned to knit in the summer – another useless skill, as I have hardly ever practised it.

When I was perhaps eleven or twelve, Mother taught me how to bake cakes. The kitchen in Dhour al-Schweir, unlike that in Cairo, was not only accessible; it was part of our lives. First, I was made to don Mother's apron, which made me inordinately proud. Next I spread newspapers on the kitchen table, which had been carried out to the kitchen balcony, and so I enjoyed rather a pleasant view while I worked. A variety of bowls, wooden spoons, measuring cups and spoons, sifters and so on were produced, and I was regularly instructed in their various uses, as I was in the proper way to measure and then blend, beat, fold and turn the ingredients. Eventually I became quite a sophisticated little cake-maker, though that was the extent of my culinary skill until I married and ran my own household.

Every day after lunch, there was an imposed rest time. The adults would withdraw to their bedrooms for two or three hours, and we children were supposed to rest as well. That was the time for reading:

I devoured most of the classics during those long summer afternoons. Dostoevsky, Tolstoy, Balzac, Dickens – I read one long nineteenth-century novel after another, sitting on the balcony swing in the afternoon. Dhour al-Schweir's notorious fog would often rise at around this time, and I loved to watch it, even though it made my hair curl into a tight frizz, which I hated.

And of course, even in Dhour al-Schweir we were never released from our weekly devotions. Sunday meant Sunday school, and then, as we grew older, church. And if church in Cairo was at least entertaining because it was usually Episcopalian and therefore involved a great deal of bowing, kneeling and chanting, the long Arabic Presbyterian service was excruciatingly boring in the summer heat. I did everything I could think of to escape fulfilling my religious duties, but I don't think I ever succeeded – there was a limit to the credibility of an endless series of urgent stomach pains, tooth and headaches, which occurred punctually every Sunday at nine just as we were told to get ready for church.

Summer was a time for dreaming and for fantasizing about the future. A band of gypsies came to Dhour al-Schweir every summer, as surely as we did, and camped just beyond the summit of the hill behind our house. Although we were strictly forbidden to go in their direction, there was no way to stop them from coming in ours. And so there was a steady stream of young women – at least, now they appear young; at the time, they seemed ancient. We would hear a call in the distance: '*Bassara, barraje; bassara, barraje*', a fortune-teller claiming to see what others could not, and to interpret the zodiac.

If Mother was out – for we would never dare do this if she were at home – my sisters and I, and whichever of our friends or cousins were around, would rush out and call for a gypsy to come and tell our fortune. A young gypsy woman wearing long black robes and usually bare-footed, her head covered with a black scarf wound tightly over her forehead and around her chin, would suddenly appear out of the woods, startling us although we were looking for her. Her costume gave her cheekbones height and her face character, all of which was accentuated by the tattoos on her face and hands, and by her eyes heavily lined with kohl. These women always bore themselves with extraordinary grace, as if they should have been carrying a water jug on their head, which they were doubtless used to doing. They swung their hips as they walked, while their upper bodies remained fixed and straight, their necks and heads held high.

The first order of business was always to bargain over how long the session was to last, and therefore how much it would cost. This had to do with our limited resources, which in turn depended on how much of our weekly pocket money had already been squandered on comic books, movie magazines and ice-cream. Sometimes too it relied on a kind of mutual craftiness, each of us trying to get the better of the other. Once the price was settled, the gypsy woman would sit square-legged on the ground, often asking for a drink of water or a soda, or something to eat. Pulling up her robe to reveal neat ankles, also richly tattooed and ornamented with silver anklets, she would produce a dirty little bag from somewhere under all the folds of cloth, which she would then tuck around her legs again. When the contents of the bag were emptied on to the earth, out would tumble a variety of buttons, bones, sea shells and little stones. Once the session was underway, the gypsy would pick them up and throw them down repeatedly, telling the magical meaning of the way they fell. As she worked, her eyes wandered around, perhaps examining the surroundings for future reference. She seemed bored, as though she had said the same words a hundred times before, and would say them a hundred times again. And since we too had heard them a hundred times, and would hear them a hundred more, we were fascinated more by the gypsies than by any future prospects they offered. The gold teeth glimmering in their mouths, the tattoos on their faces and hands, the kohl surrounding their dark eyes, their high cheekbones, the fascinating swing of their hips – all that spoke of a life so different from ours. This, for us, was where the magic lay, not in those buttons, shells and stones.

The fortune promised by the gypsies was always the same. There was to be a road opening before us, and therefore travel. Great good fortune was in the offing. Or bad. Money would be made. Or lost. A great friendship was to be made. Or broken. A bridegroom was waiting in the shadows. But watch out for his wicked mother. Or sister. She hates you. You have a health problem, which will improve. Or worsen, but not to worry. In the end, it will be fine.

The future read in the buttons and stones by the *bassara* was echoed by that read in the coffee dregs. Every time we drank Turkish coffee, the cups were turned over, left to sit on the saucer for a few minutes until the thick dregs ran dry, and then someone – usually an older woman such as one of the maids, washerwomen or dressmakers, someone currying favour – would 'read' the cups. The only difference was that the coffee dregs could be 'white', and therefore meant good news in general, or 'black' and therefore bad, but in the end don't worry, the bad spell will pass, and all will be well. The coffee dregs often contained the warning of a snake: Be careful. You have a friend who seems to be your friend, but she is not. She is really a snake and will bite you. Also there is a bird bringing you a letter from far away ...

I don't know how seriously we took the notion that the road to the future was a magic path, accessible only through mysterious mutterings and the tossing of sea shells and buttons on to the dusty earth, or through peering into upturned cups of coffee. But was the future ever presented to us as a road that we were to plan with our minds and individual will, and forge with our own two hands? I think not.

CHAPTER 6

Suez

I was in my mid-teens when the world in which I was brought up
came to an abrupt end. The nationalization of the Suez Canal
in 1956 was one of the great moments in modern Arab history,
and I am proud to say that I was part of that moment. I have always
felt myself to be, in many ways, a daughter of Suez. The Suez crisis
awakened me to history and politics, and marked the end of my
childhood. At first I was exhilarated by the experience, and reacted to
events with a joy and immediacy that, today, looking back at it, I find
astounding. Later, I would gradually be recalled, restrained, reminded
of my domestic duties; eventually I would re-learn the lesson that I was
not meant to be part of the world which defied power greater than itself,
which vigorously and courageously searched for and pursued justice.
The older I grew, the less directly involved I became in the political
events surrounding me, and the less vocal I became in expressing my
reactions. That remained true until very recently, when, propelled by
the direct and shattering experiences of the Lebanese war, I learned to
speak up on politics.

During the Suez crisis, school was closed and there was nothing to do all day long but follow the news. Because my parents were absorbed in their adult concerns, I was left to my own devices, freed from the exigencies of polite manners and the usual security and affection. In this state of unaccustomed, and totally exhilarating, freedom, I received the world of Suez unedited: no neat explanations intervened between it and me, smoothing out the questions. I was now the oldest child left at home, as Edward and Rosemarie were away at university; I was too patronizing then of my younger sisters to engage with them in any sort of meaningful talk.

I was only a fifteen-year-old schoolgirl, but I shared from my own room the excitement when the Canal was nationalized. Gamal Abdel Nasser was a great orator. He could keep huge crowds spellbound for hours on end, castigating them, telling them stories, making them laugh – he had an extraordinary sense of humour – moving them to a new awareness, not so much of patriotic chauvinism, but of their rightful place in history. His particular oratorical style provided a democratic sense of participation in the events of the day. Later I would become aware of his responsibility in founding a state security system that was typical of the post-independence third world, oppressive, tyrannical and unjust. But at the time, he was just a liberator.

Though we never joined the crowds on the streets – our parents would never have allowed us to, and we never dreamed of asking – my friends and I, especially my neighbours Nadia and Huda Gindy, listened to his speeches on the radio at home. We discussed the issue, especially as our English school remained closed well after the summer had ended. As threats and ultimatums flew between Cairo and London, and the clouds of the tripartite invasion gathered, the mood of excitement and finality grew.

One day in the autumn I was sitting at the piano with Cherry at my side munching away and yelling, '*Répetez, répetez*', when the doorbell rang. My parents were out, and my younger sisters were in their room, playing. I opened the door to find a man from the US embassy who told me to tell my father that he should prepare his family for the immediate evacuation of US citizens from Egypt. When my parents came home an hour or two later and I delivered the message, they went into their bedroom to hold a conference. I stood at the door and listened to them as they debated the matter in low voices.

Clearly, war was imminent. Danger was around the corner. Their primary concern was the safety of the family. But then they started to have doubts. What about their friends? What about the neighbours? What about the employees of the Standard Stationery Company? What about Egypt itself? Were they to abandon their friends, turn their backs on their employees? Were they to leave Egypt in its moment of danger? They had enjoyed life there while all was well: were they to leave now, when it was threatened? And Palestine – Palestine was turning into a lesson for everyone. Palestine weighed heavily on them. If you leave, you do not go back – all you have left are the photograph albums, if you're lucky.

The matter was soon settled: we were staying, not running away. Standing there listening, I was vastly relieved. I was not as aware of the dangers, but I was aware of the excitement, and I did not want to go. Most of all, I was deeply impressed by my parents' feeling of solidarity with Egypt and their friends – I never forgot it. It was one of the things about them that I always admired.

In the meantime, as we waited for the invasion, I was still allowed to go to the cinema with my friends. In the past, the programme had always been preceded by the royal anthem; now it was preceded by stirring nationalist songs and martial music as well. The deep voice of Um Kulthoum was raised as a banner, as was that of Abdel Halim Hafeth, and both came to symbolize the fervently nationalistic mood of the time. As the Suez war began, and the Israelis, British and French invaded Egypt, fever pitch was reached. The marching song '*Allahu akbar*', with its deeply rousing words sung by a vigorous male chorus, still rings in my ears. I was to hear it again during the 1982 Israeli invasion of Lebanon, when once more it became a battle hymn.

The invasion came, and the excitement reached a paroxysm. Though the attacks were mostly on the Canal area, air-raid sirens wailed even in Cairo. At night, we had blackouts. As in those earlier times in my childhood – the Second World War and the Palestine war – we sat in the corridors during air raids, and Joyce, who specialized in this reaction, vomited regularly. This time, however, I was old enough to follow events and understand them.

There is no question in my mind that part of the influence of this event lay precisely in the fact that I was a child of British imperial schooling. The war touched my life and my sensibilities, directly and tangibly. For me the word 'imperialism' was never abstract or polemical. It appeared to me in the guise of the people I knew, the history lessons I had taken, the language I spoke and all the songs and dances I had been taught.

As a result of the war, the English School, along with all British and French interests in Egypt, was nationalized. Our old teachers were ordered out of the country: my friends and I went on a round of farewell visits. We looked at our teachers with new and amazed eyes. Those we visited did not express the slightest regret that Britain, among others, had invaded Egypt, the country in which they had lived and worked all those many years.

What, then, was the meaning of all those hymns, prayers, sermons and rules of behaviour they had taught us with such zeal? What about loyalty, team spirit and all the other rules that comprised the elaborate code of honour we had been taught? Probably only a naive teenager with no knowledge of the world could raise such questions. Perhaps, in spite of my many experiences since then, I have remained a sixteen-year-old girl at heart. Perhaps I have chosen to be this because I preferred my reaction then to the compromises and accommodations that have since overtaken our world. Better, I think, the honour, belief and trust of a sixteen-year-old schoolgirl than the worn-out rationalizations, the passivity and the forgotten pride of the present.

My reaction was not, of course, an individual matter. For once, I was exactly in tune with the world around me. And if the whole Arab world reacted then with the exuberance of unity, the excitement of shared loyalty and pride, the self-assurance of supporting correct actions, those heady days of Suez stand in my personal memory, as well as in the collective memory, as a permanent reprimand to today's general indifference and corruption.

My total freedom was short-lived, however, though my mental freedom continued to the end of the crisis. As the long weeks without school continued, with no end in sight, my mother enrolled me in two sets of activities that were meant, I suppose, to fill my time usefully. She certainly considered them to be part of my education. First I was sent on two or three mornings a week, together with Claude Dirlik and Linda Fahoum, as apprentices to the atelier of one of the great dressmakers of Cairo, Madame Sophie. She was a large pleasant woman, who governed her employees with a rod of iron, while indulging us, the dilettantes, speaking to us sweetly, laughing and spoiling us. We learned how to take measurements correctly, to make patterns, to cut the material – so this was the 'Cutting Out' of Teta's time! – laying it down flat on the table; we learned how to pin it together, sew it and finish it.

On the alternate free mornings, I was sent to study another useful skill: shorthand and typing. 'Let her do something useful,' I overheard my parents say. 'Who knows? Perhaps some day she will have to go out to work.' Here again the Palestine experience, which had forced many exiled families in vastly reduced circumstances to send their daughters out to work, informed their judgement. Among the secretaries my father employed in his business, some at least were from Palestinian families in straitened circumstances.

The war ended, the British, French and Israelis withdrew, the excitement abated and at last school reopened. Like all the other English and French schools in Egypt, it had been nationalized and was now called Madrassat al-Nasr (Victory School). Instead of English teachers, we now had Egyptians, some of them trained at British universities.

The first lesson after Suez was conducted in Arabic. It was short, but utterly spellbinding. The new teacher spread a map of the area, including Palestine, on the board. Though it was probably the first time I had ever seen one, I still looked around at my classmates with a triumphant air of proprietorship and exceptional knowledge. Very simply and briefly, he recounted the story of the British occupation of Egypt, the history of the Suez Canal, the Egyptian labour that went into building it, the benefits denied to Egypt and appropriated by Europe, and the reasons for the nationalization of the Canal. As part of this outline he talked a little about Palestine, tracing some of the events leading to its fall. He told us of the connection with Egypt: that Abdel Nasser had been an officer in the Egyptian army during the Palestine war; how King Farouq had betrayed his own soldiers by sending them faulty weapons; and how Abdel Nasser had come to recognize that both the king and the British had to go for Egypt to become strong and healthy, and to save the Arab world.

I was fascinated. For the first time in my life, I had been made to understand, in however sketchy a manner, the world around me. The experience I had lived through had now acquired a comprehensible framework. Thus, for a brief moment, I felt myself tied directly and consciously into history.

CHAPTER 7

Ringing the Changes

I n the summer before the Suez crisis, I had taken the General
Certificate of Education examinations that were sent out from
England, and then sent back for correction. Like my classmates, I
was being prepared to go on to an English university, but this plan was
interrupted by Suez and the breaking of ties between Egypt and Britain.
Instead, I went to Vassar College in the United States. My brother and
elder sister were already at university there, Edward at Princeton and
Rosemarie at Bryn Mawr. My father was teased a great deal by his friends
over his insistence on higher education for his daughters. To him the
best education meant his children's advancement, independence and
solidity, and he saw no reason to deprive his daughters of what he so
eagerly provided for his son.

Mother was somewhat more ambivalent on the subject. She had
begun to see education as something that stood for all lost dreams,
and in her heart was already rather resentful of the fact that some of
her cousins had completed their education, but, because of her early

marriage, she had not completed her own. Though she was eventually to be very proud of her daughters' education, it came to mean that they had left her behind; it also marked the decline of her maternal domination. In addition, and worst of all for her, it meant separation, losing the family she had worked so hard to establish. I well remember my parents' arguments: she crying and saying he was cruel to make her send her children away; he trying to comfort her, sometimes with tears in his eyes as he felt the same wrenching pain of the separation, telling her: 'Don't be selfish. It's for their good.' He always reminded her of the unjust promise his mother had elicited from him when she lay dying. My father never ceased to tell us – and my mother reinforced this with her own words – that when he went to America he had wanted to study law. Like her, he had never ceased to regret having given up his dream.

I was very young when I left for the US: I celebrated my seventeenth birthday in Poughkeepsie, in upper New York State. I had never been away from home or from my family before, except for two short summer holidays. Edward met me at Idlewild Airport, as Kennedy Airport was then called, and drove me to Poughkeepsie. Having helped me find my way to my dormitory and settled me in with my roommate, he left. On the drive up, he asked me what I planned to major in. I had no idea what that meant, so I asked what he had majored in. 'English', he said. 'Good', I replied, in the easy comfort of those fretless, unselfconscious days of my life. 'I will major in English too.' And so I did. Later Rosie advised me to join the choir as she had done at her university. Obediently, I did that too, and this decision opened up the world of music for me. Thus I spent my four years at Vassar majoring in English, singing in the choir (and later the madrigal group), continuing my piano lessons and in addition taking all the music courses I could.

As I look back at those four years at Vassar, I see one thing very clearly. Perhaps for the last time in my life, I was free: the freedom I had felt during the Suez crisis, which had been briefly interrupted by the resumption of school that year, propelled me forward. I was free of my parents' solicitous watchfulness, which, however loving its methods and motives, was nonetheless entirely constricting, and I was also free of the constrictive manners, clothes and 'ladylike' behaviour of my upbringing. Perhaps most important of all, I was physically free to explore, to roam, to walk, to take trains, to take buses, as I had never been allowed to do in Cairo. I walked around the streets of Poughkeepsie. I wandered around the beautiful college campus to its farthest edges where, above a green hill, beyond Skinner Hall, lay the lake around which I took many walks. Skinner Hall housed the music department, and stood a short distance away from the centre of the campus. I spent most of my time there. To reach it from my dormitory, I had to walk – or bicycle – along a narrow path past the chapel and into the woods, past the lovely little Shakespeare Gardens, over a small footbridge and to the dark building, which, rising behind the surrounding trees, resembled a Gothic castle. Sometimes in the early morning light after a snowfall, it would shimmer in the mist; amidst the hush and whiteness of nature, it appeared otherworldly, reminding me of illustrations of the Sleeping Beauty's castle in the children's books I had left behind.

Nowadays I am amazed at what I did. I was as fearless as I was young. I frequently took the train to New York, staying alone at the Biltmore Hotel with a sense of insouciance and independence I am sure I could not muster now. I wandered the streets of that great city as I had never explored Cairo, went to the opera, the ballet, the theatre and the museums; I took taxis and subways; I went to the Planetarium and to the shops. With friends, I went to Chicago and to Washington. I went to visit my roommate's family in Saginaw, Michigan. I even learned how to smoke, and I had my first drink one evening in a Poughkeepsie bar, quite enjoying the shock I gave myself.

In those four years at Vassar, I explored my interests and tastes as much as I did New York and the countryside. Freed from the disciplines imposed jointly by Cherry and my mother, I discovered my own musical interests, especially singing. Singing in the choir, and then the madrigal group, was a wonderful contrast to the way I had studied music in Cairo; instead of Cherry's tyranny, I enjoyed the democratic practice of choral music. During my years we sang the Brahms and Mozart Requiems, Bach's B Minor Mass and Bruckner's E Minor Mass; we sang works by Gabrieli and Vaughan Williams; we gave Christmas and Easter concerts; and we took turns singing at Sunday chapel services. Along with my continued piano studies, as well as the courses in music history and theory I took, singing opened a new world to me: I spent more time at Skinner Hall and in the chapel than anywhere else.

I have written elsewhere of the enormous impact on my life made by some of the books I was made to read and which utterly changed the way I looked at life, at myself and at society in general. Whether Freud, Ibsen, Bertrand Russell, James Baldwin, or any of the other writers whose work shocked me into a new look at everything I thought I knew, it was not only the material covered but the methods used in covering it that opened new doors for me intellectually.

My political education and experience grew in this period, as did my political isolation. If I had been taught to view the world through lenses provided by British and American political rhetoric about justice, liberty and truth, I had already been undeceived as to the disappointing reality of British politics. Now I was to be disappointed in America. The anti-Arab prejudice that existed then in the eyes of Americans, and is today stronger than ever, not only shocked me; it put me in the place of an outsider condemned to a distant place on the fringe, the place of alienation and unrest in a culture that I might otherwise have embraced.

Had I remained in the Arab world I might have participated, as so many of my generation did, in the strikes and demonstrations of the late 1950s and '60s, particularly those demanding the liberation of Palestine. I might have joined one of the many political parties that were growing in Lebanon, into which young women, especially at the universities, were being recruited. I might have been actively involved in politics in a way that I have always regretted that I was not. Instead, at Vassar, I joined the one major revolt of my time there. Instead of marching for Palestine, against the Baghdad Pact, against unjust social and economic systems, or for or against Abdel Nasser and his various initiatives, I joined a strike against the 'white meals' that were fed us in the cafeteria, of which pork chops smothered in a white sauce, served with mashed potatoes and boiled cauliflower, was a good, and quite revolting, example. I am not sure whether my experience in America was characteristic of middle-class university life, or even of the life of all the elite women's colleges, but it has seemed to me recently that women's isolation from politics is more typical of American than of Arab social life of that time.

Nevertheless I learned the American democratic attitudes that, though new to me as a reality, were in keeping with much of the political ideology I had absorbed from American teachings. I saw people as individuals rather than as members of this or that class. For the first time I was among people whose culture, language and upbringing were in keeping with, rather than in opposition to, their surroundings. This natural and uncomplicated harmony, so uncomplicated that it was almost unconscious, between the individual and her surroundings impressed me deeply.

My last November at Vassar coincided with the Kennedy–Nixon election. The process was utterly new and fascinating to me: I had grown up first in royal and then in revolutionary Egypt, at British schools whose patron was 'Her Majesty, Queen Mary'. We had had no elections even at school, which had been run according to a definite class system, with prefects appointed by the school administration to maintain order. My enthusiasm for the democratic process was dampened only by my new questioning of the magnificent words of American politics: my years at university were, after all, the first years of the black civil rights movement, and the crisis at Little Rock was taking place when I arrived. Still, I shall never forget the excitement of that election. Along with many of my classmates, I stayed up all night as the votes were counted.

During my last year at Vassar, 1960/61, the centennial celebration took place of the founding of the college, the world's first female institution of higher learning specifically founded as such. At the same time, the country was commemorating the centennial of the American Civil War. Several symposia took place on campus: celebrations of the first event brought such women as Hannah Arendt, Mary McCarthy, Susanne Langer and others of that ilk to the campus. I think it was the previous year that Elizabeth Bowen had been Writer in Residence, giving the occasional lecture or reading. A new notion of strong women was added to the one I had imbibed in my childhood from the strong women who surrounded me then.

The Civil War celebrations were more subtly to influence my American experience. The Vassar Madrigal Group, to which I belonged, took an active part, singing, in costume, the songs of both sides in the war. Thus the horrors of that fraternal conflict were much more impressed on me than on others who studied in the United States:

I learned to see that country in its complex reality, with its layers of mythologies and contradictions, rather than as the embodiment of political evil or virtue.

Later, I went on to postgraduate studies and came to be increasingly regarded as 'educated' and 'modern'. And the more 'educated' and 'modern' I became, the more I wondered what those words meant and the more I questioned their significance.

In 1961, following my graduation from Vassar, and during the usual summer holiday in Dhour al-Schweir, my father fell ill and was hospitalized at the American University Medical Center in Beirut. For several weeks he remained in a critical condition, following the removal of a malignant lesion from his leg and several episodes of severe haemorrhaging from a perforated ulcer. My father's illness was an episode of extreme importance to all of us, but especially, I think, to Mother. Memories of the terrible summer of 1928, when her own father and first protector died, came vividly to her mind. Suddenly that special world that she had so carefully constructed and shielded seemed as vulnerable and even flimsy as her mother's had done before her. The nuclear family that my parents had created, partly as a result of the scattering caused by the Palestine war, partly as a result of their upbringing and education, and partly as an aspect of modern urban cosmopolitanism and economic realities, was proving once again to have been a dangerous investment, when all could be lost in a moment.

In a way, Mother's widowhood could be said to have begun then, in the summer of 1961, when she thought that my father was going to die. From that time on, her happiness ended. As it was, he recovered his health and lived for almost a decade more, but she was deeply shaken by his illness and remained overwhelmingly anxious about him. Those weeks of my father's illness marked the end of an important phase in the life of the family, and especially in Mother's life. Her children were almost all grown up: Edward, Rosemarie and I had already graduated from university; Joyce and Grace were seventeen and fifteen respectively, and in their last years at school; and I was engaged to be married. Because of the situation in Egypt, my parents, along with many of their friends, were about to move from Egypt to Lebanon. The transition to Beirut took place in that hospital.

As the crisis passed and my father began his long convalescence, our family congregations around his hospital room, which had been grave and full of stress and sadness, became cheery and attracted many visitors. The tableau of these weeks changes in my memory from the grave silence of the lingering deathbed scene to a lively salon in open session. We were a large and unusual family, new to Beirut and its citizens. Beirutis, always interested in the new and unusual, were drawn to us. Young doctors, interns and residents seemed particularly to enjoy checking on my father – his mischievous sense of humour never abandoned him – and would linger to chat and laugh with us. Baskets of flowers and boxes of sweets filled the room and over-flowed into the corridor, and the torch of hospitality perfected by Mother burned as brightly in the medical centre as it did in her own livingroom.

The outside world pressed on us as we sat by my father's bedside, or in the corridors outside his room. Many of the lively conversations we engaged in revolved around regional and international developments. The war of liberation in Algeria was at its peak; the war in Vietnam was just beginning; the Korean war had not yet been forgotten. In the immediate Arab region it was yet another time of crisis, if not upheaval. The union set up under Abdel Nasser's auspices between Egypt and Syria in the United Arab Republic came to an unhappy end. Egypt was waging a now-forgotten war in Yemen. The dream of Arab unity that Abdel Nasser so eloquently and dramatically expressed, and that he had tried to forge, was shown to be unrealizable at that time and in that manner. And as always, the Palestine question burned in all our hearts.

An elderly Saudi princess occupied the room next to my father's. I believe, though I would not swear to it, that she was the king's sister. She was attended by a large retinue, several members of whom slept in the room with her at night. In the days that she spent in hospital, we established a fleeting though surprisingly warm relationship. Since I found the Saudi dialect unfamiliar and almost incomprehensible, we were separated by an enormous gulf of language and cultural experience, but we were bound together by the common and equalizing anxiety of ill health, and the lay person's bewilderment facing the mysteries of modern medical knowledge and apparatus.

Every morning on arrival at the hospital, and having seen to my father's needs, my sisters and I – my brother, of course, was not permitted to enter her room – would step next door and ask how the princess was feeling. To our polite inquiries she would respond with the obligatory '*Al-hamdu l'illah*' (Praise be to God), followed by a recital of various aches and pains which were graphically illustrated by fingers pointed at the relevant parts of her body. An enormous box of chocolates, so large that I have never forgotten it, would then be presented to us and we would be obliged, whether we felt like it or not, to take one and sometimes two chocolates. We soon learned not to waste time by attempting to thwart her command in regard to the sacred rituals of hospitality.

The princess lay on pink silk sheets and, though our communication was limited, we could see that she was a woman of character and depth. One day, having made our way through the language barrier to the point where she understood that I was engaged, she made me approach her bed. Holding my hand tightly and looking intently into my eyes, she spoke with great enthusiasm and seriousness for some time until, exhausted, she lay back on the pillow in silence, shaking her head in admonition at me. Of this animated speech I could only make out a dire warning as to how to conduct myself in marriage. Whether she was encouraging me to this state or warning me away from it I could not precisely tell, but the undeniable gravity of the marital condition as she saw it was clearly impressed upon me. I have never forgotten this princess, and always think of her and this little episode when I hear discussions about 'the Arab woman': in spite of the myriad contrasts and disparities of class, culture, and situations between us, they speak of us as if there were only one of us, or as though we were all the same.

My impending marriage had been postponed by my father's illness, but no sooner was he discharged from hospital than Mother turned her attention to this first wedding in the family. During my father's illness we had rented a furnished apartment in Beirut, as Dhour al-Schweir was too far away. It was here that he was taken on leaving hospital. While he was recuperating, Mother took charge of the wedding arrangements. In organizing my wedding, she made her final statement on taste and standards. All in all, it was quite a grand affair, and though it took place in Beirut, it was in fact the last act of the family's Cairo play. The next year they were to move to Beirut.

Just before my senior year at university, I had become engaged to Samir Makdisi, son of Anis Makdisi and Salma Khouri. His father was Professor of Arabic at the American University of Beirut (AUB); he had chaired the department for forty years before retiring at around the time of our engagement. The Makdisis, pillars of the Protestant Church in Beirut of which Teta's father, Rev. Youssef Badr, had been the first Arab pastor, were friends of my parents. When they came to Cairo, which they often did because of Prof. Makdisi's work with the Arab Language Academy, they always came to visit us. Like us, they spent their summers in Dhour al-Schweir, where their home was a stone's throw from ours. My parents often had tea and played bridge with them.

Our engagement seemed a natural extension of our lives. Samir had just returned from the US, where he had completed his doctorate in economics at Columbia University. He was now teaching at the American University of Beirut, where his father before him had taught for so long. Samir's mother died the summer we got engaged, after an excruciatingly long struggle against the ovarian cancer that consumed her as it had, like a terrible family curse, consumed her mother and several of her sisters before her.

Unlike my mother and my grandmother, who were deliberately introduced to their husbands by other people with a view to a possible match, I made my own alliance with my husband. Yet, in making my choice, I was certainly bound by that sheltering wall which had been so carefully constructed around my life. Though I had experienced freedom in the US, every summer when I came home from university I was restored to that same enveloping protectiveness and domestic training with which I had grown up, and which I accepted as part of a different reality.

Later – for I was the first of my generation in the family to marry – choices were made from other sources. One of my sisters met her future husband through their professional association; another met hers on a trip abroad. By then, the family was firmly ensconced in Beirut, with its freer, more open society than that in Egypt by which I had been formed. Though my courtship, engagement and marriage took place in Lebanon, where chaperones were a thing of the past, it really belonged to an earlier phase of my life.

Young and inexperienced, I offered no resistance to my mother, as she made preparations for the wedding. One day she said: 'Shall we go and buy the material for your wedding dress?' 'Yes', I replied enthusiastically, embracing the idea as though it were my own. We took a taxi to Souq al-Tawileh. 'Shall we go to Kassatly's?' she asked. 'Yes', said I obediently, pleased that she knew where to go and not having a clue as to the alternatives.

When we arrived, we were greeted warmly by the owner, Mr Kassatly, to whom Mother announced the purpose of our visit. Everyone beamed and we were served lemonade and coffee, though we waved away the proffered cigarettes. 'What kind of material would you like?', Mr Kassatly asked me, and of course I was struck dumb by his question. Much to my relief, however, Mother answered for me. 'What do you think of *satin de soie*?', she asked thoughtfully. Mr Kassatly responded enthusiastically. I had not the faintest idea what *satin de soie* was, though it sounded right, so I nodded my assent. 'Let us see that one,' said Mother, pointing at a roll of cloth among the many she had already surveyed with one eye as she politely carried out the initial greetings and conversation.

The salesman assigned to us brought it down, and then, while Mother tut-tutted and shook her head, he brought down another, and then another, and then yet another. As each roll of material came down and was laid on the long table, Mother fingered it knowingly, and either rejected it or put it aside to be reconsidered later. She authoritatively pronounced her verdict on each cloth before democratically asking my opinion. 'Yes, yes', I said helplessly, or 'No, no', as the occasion demanded, agreeing instantly to everything she said. Finally, after what seemed like hours, and having seen silks, satins and taffetas, in white, cream and ivory, that, in my heart of hearts, I thought all looked alike, we – or, rather, she – settled on a particular silk brocade. '*Mabrouk*' (Congratulations), said the man as he cut the material with a broad smile. 'I hope you will be very happy.'

Later I was dispatched to Mother's friend, Renée Dirlik, in Cairo. She took me under her wing and accompanied me to the same Madame Sophie with whom I had served that brief and reluctant apprenticeship during the Suez crisis, to milliners, to shoe shops, to hairdressers and to beauty parlours, to department stores, to get me and my trousseau organized for the wedding. Mother did not yet feel sufficiently at home in Beirut to undertake these elaborate preparations there. Still, she managed to gather what she regarded as a sufficient collection of embroidered linens, tablecloths and sheets, all of which were commissioned from the famous *rahbat* (nuns) and almost all of which were to remain unused by me.

Teta was hard at work on the little bags for the silver dishes that were coming in as wedding presents. She was also busy making the hanger covers, crocheting them in blue, green, pink and white, and attaching little strawberries and bows cut out from felt. She crocheted a score of doilies in different shapes and sizes.

Once the trousseau had been seen to, attention turned to the wedding itself. Because of all the dramatic moves in my family's life, most recently the move from Cairo to Beirut, I was to know scarcely anybody at my own wedding, except for members of the immediate family and some people from the Dhour al-Schweir summers.

I remember one evening session during which my parents negotiated the guest list with my husband's sister and father. Both sides came armed with their own lists. Mother firmly vetoed some names on theirs. One woman's name in particular was fiercely debated. 'She married two daughters and did not invite us to either wedding,' Mother said firmly. 'I will not have her.' She would not be shaken by the opposing argument of my husband's sister and father: that *they*, on the other hand, *had* been invited to *both* weddings. 'This is *my* daughter's wedding, and I will not have her,' said Mother firmly. The offending lady was not invited.

There were other small arguments over procedure between the two families. I have come to recognize these as a kind of initiation into the state of marriage itself, a preparation for the coming-together: in marriage, it is not only the couple who are being joined, but their families as well, and a certain juggling for position is inevitable.

The wedding was held at the National Evangelical Church in Beirut, over which my great-grandfather Youssef Badr had presided seventy years before. Teta was there, of course, and today I wonder how she felt being in her father's old church: as usual, she never uttered a word to me on the subject. Aside from the ministers of the congregation, my father had insisted on inviting the Arab Anglican bishop of Jerusalem, whom he mischievously insisted on addressing as 'His Lordship', much to the dismay of the puritanical, bishopless Presbyterians. Not only did 'His Lordship' come, but he wore his purple surplice and large gold cross. As he stood at the altar, he offered a colourful contrast to the Presbyterian ministers in their strict black robes. My father was certainly making a point, in this new city to which the family was just moving, of establishing its position as an entity to be reckoned with.

The wedding reception took place at the Carlton, one of the grand seaside hotels of pre-war Beirut. Waiters in black ties carried round silver trays laden with drinks – alcoholic and otherwise – and canapés. Long tables stood the length of the reception hall, covered with white linen cloths and bearing silver dishes full of canapés, small cakes and elegant finger sandwiches of Roquefort cheese, smoked salmon and roast beef. On tall multi-layered dishes were displayed large cocktail shrimps stuck with toothpicks; large silver bowls held the sauce. Tiny spiced sausages and meatballs, chicken livers in wine, delicate pastries, baked or fried, stuffed with spinach, meat and cheese – all these and many other delicacies were served.

Instructed by the *maître d'hôtel*, Samir and I cut the large, multi-tiered wedding cake and fed each other the first bites. Then a bottle of champagne and two long-stemmed crystal glasses were produced. Once again obeying his instructions, Samir and I linked arms and sipped champagne to the applause of the onlookers. It was a pleasant enough event, and I often take out the pictures and look at them while comparing myself to Teta and Mother at the time of their weddings. Unlike them, I had cut no new paths: I was in a fog of directionless, automatic motion, responding to the instructions, the taste, the will of others. I was a feather blowing in the wind. Though Mother always (almost accusingly) referred to me as having been 'educated', I was then an entirely will-less creature.

When I finished university, I could discuss Shakespeare, Shelley, T. S. Eliot and Yeats; I was familiar with Baudelaire, Racine and Corneille, the Wars of the Roses, the Crusades, the causes and developments of the principal wars in our century and in most others. I had studied the music of Mozart, Bach, Machaut and de Pres, of Britten, Prokofiev and Stravinsky; I was as familiar with Schoenberg's *Verklärte Nacht* and *Pierrot Lunaire* as I was with Beethoven's Ninth Symphony. I had read and been moved by many disconcerting texts. I knew about theatre and had seen the latest films by Satyajit Ray, Federico Fellini and Ingmar Bergman, among others. I knew something about politics and had read the classic political speeches of our time. I had been to concerts, operas and ballets. I could play the piano and sing. I had travelled and seen fair chunks of the world. I knew the historic sights and the restaurants, theatres and concert halls of some of the great capital cities. I knew what cultivated cosmopolites of my age everywhere in the world knew.

Yet, despite all this 'education', I felt I knew nothing of significance. I am sure, today, that the reason for this was Mother's confidence in education as a mystery, a miracle, a transforming experience that could change everything wrong in one's life and make it right. Regret, sadness, anxiety about the future, self-doubt – she saw all these as remediable through education. This attitude, based on her own regrets, was represented to me as an unshakeable truth. Since I felt strongly that it did not apply to me, I thought the failure must have been in me rather than in the attitude.

I have often thought that had I chosen to study any of the medical sciences I might have been more truly 'educated' than I was. Had I been made to deal with the reality of sick and smelly bodies, with blood, faeces and urine, with sores and ulcers, with pain and healing, birth and death; had I been forced to stick needles into reluctant buttocks, to administer enemas or to prepare patients for surgery, I would have been more in touch with the real world, and that would have been a truer kind of 'education' than I had had.

I have always felt that less 'educated' girls of my generation knew more than I did, or at least that what they knew was far more relevant to their lives than my knowledge was to mine. *Fallaheen* (peasant) girls knew about nature: they knew the earth, the crops, the animals, the weather; they knew the songs and dances and the ways of their people. Aristocratic girls also knew the ways of their people: they knew about land-ownership; they knew the ways and laws of marriage and divorce, and of familial relationships and how they are classified and stratified as to their relative importance. Girls of the working class and *petit bourgeoisie* knew the cruel realities of the working world, and of class relationships. They knew something about money; they had worked and been paid wages. *Shawwam* girls were supreme princesses of their households;

though we had had the same domestic training, mine had been diluted by that ideal of 'education' which was taken so seriously in my family.

I had been brought up to be something of an intellectual, but there seemed at the time no connection between my newly formed ideas and the world to which I had returned. Indeed, I did not even recognize my ideas as ideas at all: they seemed to be culled from somewhere else and did not belong to me. I did not know then what I am just beginning to know now: that my ideas were indeed mine, that I had reacted and changed and moved, that I had already analysed and synthesized, rejecting some thoughts, adopting others, putting yet others away for a while to be thought on. I did not recognize how mentally active an individual I had become, already divorced from the world through my own thoughts, my own perceptions of right and wrong, of honour and justice, of what mattered and what did not.

Added to my own personal sense of dislocation was my family's. As custom dictated, on the afternoon of the wedding, the groom's family arrived at our house – *beit abuya* (my father's house) – to escort me and my family to church, where Samir was waiting. My mother had prepared the ritual glasses of lemonade and champagne, and sugared almonds were laid out on silver trays. The first round of wedding pictures were taken there, in that furnished apartment to which the family had moved upon my father's discharge from hospital: it was to be several months before my parents made their final move from Cairo and had their own apartment. Some of the photos were taken against a background formed by the curtains of that rented apartment. They were of a style and colour so unlike our taste, and so unconnected to our history, that the pictures are a constant reminder that my father's house was not my father's house at all, but a furnished apartment in a city I did not know. I was an outsider, the alienated daughter of a family dislocated once again by history.

Immediately after our wedding, Samir and I moved to the United States. He had accepted a post at the International Monetary Fund, in Washington, D.C., where we lived for the next ten years. During that time, our three sons were born.

When I first arrived in Washington, I was armed only with a cookbook, a trousseau full of embroidered linens and a wardrobe in the latest fashion. My education, the books I continued to devour, my music studies, belonged to a private inner life, which seemed to have nothing whatever to do with my social existence.

For most middle-class women of my generation, marriage and domestic life had been represented as ends in themselves. Everything I had done so far was to lead up to this grand status. But once I had achieved it, and had set up our home and learned how to cook, however precariously, a great hole, a huge emptiness, seemed to open up in front of me. If I had remained in the Arab world, this hole would doubtless have been filled with visits to and from my mother and her friends, and the gregarious social life of Beirut. Perhaps it would have been filled with political activism: after all, the Palestinian Resistance was just beginning in the early 1960s, and the leftist movement that supported it was strong in Beirut.

Instead I lived the arid, claustrophobic life of prosperous American middle-class women in suburban Washington, where individuals were cloistered in comfortable homes, isolated from even their closest neighbours, whose names they often did not know, with nothing better to do than add comfort to comfort, and object to object. At least at first, the ideology preached by Mother and Teta led me to be entirely alone in my house.

Samir went to the office early in the morning and did not return until evening. He was busy and in touch with the world, while I had long hours with nothing much to do. No woman living under seclusion could have been as secluded as I was then. Later I would make up for this sense of isolation, especially after my return to the Arab world. But during these early months of my adulthood, I learned that the differences between women are dictated more by class and occupation than by the differences between East and West.

I had grown up in a complicated world in which people of many different communities, nations and religions had added cultural wealth and complexity to each other's existence. Though I was given the Christian education that I have described, I lived in the Muslim world, and had not the slightest sense of conflict with it: on the contrary, I identified with it. At school my friends – like everyone else's friends – had been Muslims, Christians and Jews: there were British, Americans, Egyptians, Greeks, Italians, Indonesians, Lebanese, Maltese, Cypriots.

Although we knew these various origins, they had no significance to our friendships or quarrels. We all had to sing the same English hymns at morning assembly, but we never discussed religion, except perhaps to utter impious thoughts or giggle irreverently during prayers.

My two closest friends at school were Leila Ahmed, who had a firm reputation as a leading school athlete and is now a well-known scholar of Islam, and a Jewish girl, Josianne Behar, with whom I entirely lost touch when our world fell apart decades ago. Her family left Egypt a little before mine did. Josianne and I used to whisper our secrets to each other on the long bus rides to and from school. I treasure a photo of the two of us, ungainly thirteen- or fourteen-year-olds, wearing identical Girl Guide uniforms, ties neatly fastened around our necks, berets neatly perched on our heads. Leila and I used to listen to music together: once, we had the bright idea of listening to Beethoven while lying on the lawn of her family home in 'Ain Shams and watching the clouds sail by. Our imprudent effort to transport the record player into the garden led to my being almost fatally electrocuted: to this day, my right hand bears the scars of that accident. Our world was quite simply like that: full of mixtures, full of contrasts, full of variation. We knew each other's differences, but we never thought of each other as differentiated.

The American society to which I now belonged, on the other hand, was a segregated one in which every difference was noted, and this often involved conflict. There were many solid lumps in the famous melting pot, and people of different races, ages and incomes were sharply separated from one another. In the suburb where I lived, everyone was well-off, white, young and healthy. There was no public transport to or from this neighbourhood: this was a deliberate choice by the people of the area to keep their suburb untainted by any of the differences which might have threatened their carefully guarded unity.

I had only been married a few months when this growing sense of isolation and emptiness led me to expand my world and apply to George Washington University for postgraduate work. By the time I received my acceptance, I had almost forgotten that I had applied, and the pleasure of the acceptance was dampened by the uncertainty of my new situation. That part of my character which included ambition had initiated the move to the postgraduate degree; the other part, which included conventionality and ease, though proud, was surprised and confused.

I was the only married woman in my classes, and I never saw another pregnant student on the entire campus – at least not one who was visibly pregnant, as I most certainly was. Though I am not claiming the status of pioneer in this matter, it was certainly not as common then as it is now for a married woman of comfortable means to seek an extension of her life beyond the bounds of domesticity. Today I berate myself for not having done more, for having acquired only a master's degree and not a doctorate. I often wonder why my ambition was aimed at what today seems so middling a target. My sister Rosemarie was working towards her doctorate at around the same time. There was one major difference, however: I was married and she was not. What she took for granted I did not – that one's personal life is one's own. Mine seemed to belong to the community rather than to me.

The first time I returned to Beirut after I started postgraduate work, I had to fight off the charges of eccentricity and of an almost comic misreading of real life. The most encouraging of my mother's friends asked me anxiously: 'Good for you, but can you manage? Isn't it too much for you?', giving me a sense of heroism. Many others laughed at me. 'You're collecting certificates, and then you'll frame them and hang them on the kitchen wall,' joked one. 'You'll soon be peeling potatoes on your MA!', said another. Mother herself was ambivalent about my ambitious move. When I finally completed my MA, she wrote to congratulate me – somewhat ironically, I could not help but feel – on having become 'an MA personality'. She often exhorted me to work less hard, to learn to relax more, to be less driven. At the same time, something in her was very proud of me. I often heard her in her later years boast that I had done more than my share, having produced babies, kept an orderly and stylish household and at the same time continued my education.

Eventually, I had three babies, all boys. As time passed, a veritable war started inside me, as in so many other women of my generation. Part of me was pleasing, submissive, obedient, mild-mannered, polite and happy; but another part was in constant turmoil, resentful, angry, rebellious, ambitious, hemmed-in. As Samir travelled around the world and achieved professional advancement and satisfaction, my domestic and maternal duties, in spite of my MA, drew ever tighter circles around me, defining the shrinking physical boundaries of my life. I took the children on the usual suburban rounds of doctors, supermarkets, drug stores, puppet theatres, public libraries, museums, parks and movies. I entered my eldest son, and later his younger brother (by the time my youngest was of school age, we were back in Beirut), into a Montessori school and proudly showed him off when he learned, so early on, to read and write. I became a gourmet cook, trying my hand at French and Italian cuisine as well as Arabic: that was before the days when Indian, Chinese and Thai cooking became *de rigueur* for an accomplished suburbanite. Edward and Grace were in the US at that time, the one already beginning his academic career, the other acquiring first an undergraduate and then a postgraduate degree. They and the other members of our family who often came to visit expected, and received, the warm welcome of a home away from home, and a mother away from Mother. And though I enjoyed all this and even revelled in it, taking pride in my domestic accomplishments, and in the beauty of my children, the warmth of family life and the reassuring presence of my siblings, I could not help but be aware of the inexorable passage of time and the parallel diminution of possibilities.

I once came very close to quarrelling with Mother as the clash in thought between our generations came to the surface. She was visiting me in Washington. I was still relatively new to the motherhood business and was resenting the claustrophobic confinement that comes with having to care, unassisted, for a young child. I felt some resentment that the burden of domestic life fell entirely on me, that Samir did not sufficiently share in the less edifying duties. I tried, delicately, to complain to Mother, to extract sympathy, making a great effort at the same time not to sound as though I were 'whining'. She cut my complaints short. 'Families are made by women,' she exhorted me in the same words I had heard her use a thousand times before. But this time the simple, direct unfairness of the burden placed on me in her view of family life struck home as never before – not as an abstract, meaningless and faintly amusing cliché, but as an arrow pointed at my heart. I never argued with her about it again.

Defeated, I withdrew into the suburban domestic life, from whose dreariness I was rescued by earth-shaking events. The 1967 June war, and the total defeat of the Arab armies within a few hours, shattered us, as it did an entire generation. What made it even more traumatic, however, was being in the United States and suffering the anti-Arab bias of the press coverage, the jokes of late-night television hosts and even the comments of ordinary people of our acquaintance who glorified Israel, understanding nothing of our history. I know of no Arab in America at that time who did not feel the same way, that the crushing defeat was made more intolerable by the virulently anti-Arab, pro-Israeli sentiment that so bewildered and angered us. It was all so terribly unfair.

The irony was that though I had been brought up in a Palestinian home, though many of my relations had become refugees, though my family had suffered that sense of dislocation and loss that I have described, we never knew anti-semitism or anti-Jewish feeling. It was quite simply not part of our world view, not part of our culture or our history. Israel to us never existed in the mythical, primordial space of anti-semitism: it belonged to the real world of politics, economics, war and dispossession. I tried, probably with little success, to convey these thoughts to those I knew in America at the time: I tried to explain, using maps and datelines, what had actually happened, on the ground, in reality, but the established mythology seemed impermeable on this score, and many of those I addressed were utterly ignorant of world affairs.

Still, the American 1960s was in other ways a most exciting, exuberant time, and it has marked me to this day. I remember with nostalgia the excitement of the civil rights movement, the anti-Vietnam war demonstrations, the war on poverty, the general sense of protest and rebellion. As I sat at home, looked after my children, cooked, ironed and cleaned, I longed to join the crowds yelling anti-Vietnam war slogans; I longed to march with the others in Alabama and Mississippi – indeed, alone at home, I sang 'We Shall Overcome' until I was hoarse; I longed to chain myself to the wire fences around the nuclear bases. Instead, I kept the sacred fire of hospitality blazing. I enjoyed the hard work this entailed. I was happy and unhappy, satisfied and thoroughly dissatisfied. Finally the women's movement exploded on to the scene in the late 1960s, articulating all my privately held dissatisfactions.

I had earnest discussions with my friends – and especially my closest friend, Randi – that evolved into real changes in my personal life. I wonder how many middle-class and professional husbands in those days arrived at their suburban homes and were taken by surprise, as mine was, at being greeted with glares and frowns and angry remarks about prison wardens and prisoners' rights, instead of the dutiful, sycophantic smile and the sympathetic question: 'How was your day?' of former times! How many husbands would ask, as mine did, what they thought was a perfectly natural and utterly harmless question, such as: 'What's for dinner tonight?' only to have the heavens open over their heads, overwhelming them with a deluge of what they saw as unearned abuse and anger: 'Get your own dinner!' or 'I don't know. What do you feel like cooking?'

In articulating in simple, direct and honest terms the feelings of young women like myself, the women's movement of the late 1960s shook the citadel of family life. Yet it made some of the hardest issues palatable by its exuberance and the good humour which seems to have totally disappeared in the years since. It was, I think, precisely that exuberance and humour which attracted so many women to it and which gave us the sense that, while we were part of a universal reaction and were all being swept along by this storm of change, we could keep our heads and not fall apart.

'Woman's work' was one of the principal themes of the consciousness-raising sessions that were so much part of our lives then. We never, in those early days, denied its value: on the contrary, we demanded social and economic recognition of its value. I remember the first time Randi and I discussed a question that at the time seemed utterly shocking and avant-garde: why are women not paid for doing housework or bringing up children? We giggled guiltily like naughty schoolgirls, and whispered the thoughts, feeling that we should not utter the words out loud, so close to unthinkable blasphemy had we come. We raised the question once with an older friend of ours. I can still see her reeling, shocked and unbelieving, not just at our ideas, but at our daring to utter them. 'But', she stammered, 'we do it for love. For our children. For our husbands. We love them.' 'Nothing to do with love,' we answered, enjoying the shock we were causing, 'only exploitation.'

One day, I was fulminating on the issue of women's rights, on history and 'herstory' (though I credit myself with never using that silly word) and on other golden nuggets from the new world of equality that had dawned. I noticed Mother staring at me in alarm. 'Are you,' she asked at last, not believing herself capable of harbouring such an outrageous suspicion, 'are you Women's Lib?' Her question was so loaded with dread, and betrayed such a depth of misunderstanding and astonishment, that my response was to burst into helpless laughter. 'Mother', I gasped, 'Mother, where are you living?' It is difficult today to recapture that sense of turning a world upside down.

CHAPTER 8

Beirut

I n 1972 Samir, I and our boys returned to Beirut, where he rejoined the faculty of the American University (AUB). My hard-earned but hitherto useless MA suddenly stood me in good stead: I got a job teaching English at the Beirut College for Women.

The BCW was the descendant of the American Junior College at which Mother had spent one exhilaratingly happy year, 1931/32. In 1952 it had evolved into a four-year college for women. Part of its attraction for me lay in its connection to Mother and her friends. Mother used to visit the college regularly, attending meetings, and alumnae luncheons and teas. I used to bump into her there, all dressed up, silver-haired and beautiful, and would feel her making, and trying to keep, her connection with her own past.

When I started teaching there, the Beirut College for Women was in its last days as a women's college. The student body included young women from the whole area, including Saudi Arabia, Iraq, Kuwait and the other Gulf countries, Egypt, Sudan, Jordan, Cyprus, as well as, of course, Lebanon and Syria, and the large Palestinian diaspora in all those countries. In addition, European and American residents of Beirut joined the classes, and the result was an interesting and fertile blend of cultural experience. Some of the teachers were American; most were Arabs trained and educated in the US or at American institutions such as the American University of Beirut. The majority of the teachers had PhDs, and most were women.

Socially, an interesting situation prevailed. In the early 1970s Beirut was in its heyday as the region's cosmopolitan centre. An exhilarating atmosphere of freedom of thought was in the air, in which nothing was too sacred to be challenged or discussed, and everything was permissible. Books and newspapers banned elsewhere in the Arab world could be found here; circles of students, political dissidents and exiles from countries far and near, journalists and writers could be seen in cafes and salons, engaged in revolutionary discussion and debate.

Against this background, girls from the most conservative societies and classes mixed with others from the most open and liberal. Thus girls from the revolutionary Palestinian refugee society studied and talked with girls from wealthy and sometimes royal Saudi or Kuwaiti families; American and European girls heard Arab political arguments while offering alternative models of social behaviour. Some of the girls found the situation very challenging. In Beirut, girls from the most conservative Arab countries could go to the beach; they could wear jeans and T-shirts to class; they could discuss and argue over anything and everything; they could even engage in such student activism and lack of respect for authority as was current in those days; they could meet and talk and go out with the male relatives of their classmates. Then they had to go home. I do not know what happened to such girls or how their lives were affected. I can only assume that changes occurred, that there were modulations in the existing patterns of things. Many such transfers of attitudes must have taken place in those years before the war.

The curriculum at the Beirut College for Women, with its emphasis on the arts and the humanities, had a fairly representative, if in some areas rather old-fashioned, American liberal-arts stamp to it. In my day, courses in Domestic Science were sharply on the decline, and Eugenics had come and gone in an earlier generation. The college choir sang such music as would be expected at American college glee clubs and choirs. All instruction, except, of course, Arabic Language and Literature classes, was in English.

The college began to admit male students gradually, for economic reasons. Sarah Gibson Blanding, president of Vassar College when I attended it, famously included in her farewell address when she retired a warning that the private, liberal-arts women's college was no longer economically viable and was sure to become a thing of the past. If that was true in the United States, it was apparently also true in Lebanon.

In the first few years of coeducation, one or two men might be seen, sitting quietly and self-consciously in the back of the classroom. In 1974 the Beirut College for Women became the Beirut University College, and by the time the war began the following year, men formed a large proportion of the student body. As the war took its toll, and foreign students diminished in number until there were scarcely any left, the proportion of men to women grew, until it settled at about 50:50, while the vast majority of students were local.

As I watched this change gradually take place, I felt some dismay and much sadness. A college where women and their concerns were central, where they could study and teach and administer, where they could think together and talk over their problems, where they could debate their future and create their own agenda for change in their lives, all without the aggressive intrusion of a pervading masculine influence to which they had already been taught to bow – the value of such a place was enormous, and its loss incalculable.

The college was gradually reabsorbed into the society from which it had originally emerged and from which it had gradually differentiated the particular role of women. There had not been enough time for the impetus towards a real change in society based on its life and activities: after all, it had only changed from a two-year to a four-year college in the early 1950s, the first of its kind in the immediate area.

Today, the small college has become a large university with a majority of male students, and is merely a reflection of the society outside its gates. The heaviest academic concentration is in business studies. Graduating women students move right back into the outside world, without having had the opportunity to arm themselves with their own thoughts and ideology, even without having had the debates necessary to identify their needs. That mixture of women from all over the region that had dominated the early life of the college, those contacts between women from different nationalities, societies and backgrounds – all this has withered away. Thus was an interesting and important experiment in women's education aborted.

In my early years of teaching, when trying so hard to combine the demands of professional and domestic life according to the high standards that I had been taught, I felt the enormous pressures put on modern women. That was the time when my grandmother's and mother's lives, seen from the standpoint of the questions raised by the women's movement, came so alive to me and when I started to think about writing this book.

When I first started teaching, I felt I was doing something important and new. I told myself, as Mother so often told me, that I was 'modern', a 'modern' wife and mother, one who worked while caring for her family. I did not know then that Teta had been 'modern' long before me, that she had worked decades before I congratulated myself on doing so. It was also very new to me to be known – as I now was on campus – just as myself: nobody's daughter, nobody's wife, nobody's mother, nobody's sister. Just myself. My husband's enormous personality, as well as his high status in society, and the nature of that society, had always made me feel secondary.

As time passed, however, the novelty wore off the pay cheque, such as it was, and the new identity. I began to feel put-upon. I had added new burdens to the ones I had inherited. Professional life had been added on to the domestic; and, though I had a housekeeper to help me with my domestic chores, those chores had themselves increased enormously because of the infinitely more gregarious nature of social life in Lebanon as compared to the United States. And always, though I was working and had a profession, they were not taken seriously: I still felt that my prime existence was for the family. Mother and her friends often commented on my work: 'Oh good, *bititsalee!*' (You will be entertained). And though I smiled sweetly at these remarks and fell docilely in with them, I would feel a deep rage boiling within me that my hard labour was being so trivialized. Mother, who in this as in so much else concerning her daughters was ambivalent, sometimes issued dire warnings to me: 'You are getting too tired … Watch out for those varicose veins … You must rest.' But I knew that even as she was discouraging my hard work, she had an admiration for it, perhaps a certain envy.

When my husband travelled and achieved advancement after advancement, recognition after recognition; when he received more and more professional offers and honours, I was delighted for him and proud. Yet I would be lying if I did not admit to a touch of envy. More than a touch. Much more. I used to feel that he was moving on, while I was standing still; that he was alive and growing, while I had lost my chance; that the train had gone, and left me behind. I felt bitterly that I had paid for his success. Sometimes I even went so far as to say, sourly, sending a poisonous arrow into the heart of his success: 'Well, you couldn't have done it without me,' even when I knew that wasn't true. He could and did do it without me. At times like that, he would lie to me gallantly: 'Of course, I could not have done it without you. Of course, it is you who helped me to do it.' I felt that those gracious lies were easy, a small price for him to pay for the domestic comfort that I had provided.

These thoughts and little resentments were augmented by my almost daily visits to Teta at this time. She was now in her last years. Her life seemed to me so exquisitely old-fashioned, so thoroughly remote from the frantic 'modern' life I was living, that I imagined her past reality irretrievably lost in the mists of ancient time. My great love for her had, I am sorry to say, more than a hint of the patronizing notion that she would not, could not possibly, understand my anguish as a modern woman because she had been so safely ensconced in a carefree, though boring and limited, domestic existence. So arrogant was I then that when I began to think about comparing my life with hers, I thought my assumptions about her life *were* her life. I began my work on this book by taking little mental notes of things she said, and of the manner in which she said them. I began to hoard my knowledge of the shape of her fingers, the sound of her voice, the way she tilted her head a little to the side as she sipped her tea, the expressions she used, the feel of the soft wrinkles in her pink skin, her stooped back, even the faint scent of cologne that still emanated from her. I thought that was Teta, that ancient body: I never thought of her as having a history that I should ask her about.

One of the reasons for that was that her past seemed to embody, instead of actions and thoughts, only sorrows, so that it was kinder not to probe her memory. Once when I was pregnant, she sat on a nearby sofa, staring at me. In a small, distant voice she said:

> Seeing you pregnant reminds me of when I was expecting my first daughter. I was in Safad. Your grandfather had gone to America and the baby was born in his absence. She was beautiful and I named her Ellen. I loved her very much. Then when she was two, she developed cholera and she died. My heart was broken, so I took my other children and went to my parents' house in Marjeyoun.

As she spoke she relived her sorrow, and I could see the pain as she stared into the distance. Drained not only by the sadness of the story, but also by the sadness of the account, I did not know what to say, and sat, frozen and dumb. But a minute later her eyes focused on me again. 'Seeing you like this', she said, 'reminds me of when I was expecting my daughter, Ellen ...' She retold the story, unaware that she had just done so, and the same painful details were repeated with the same pain.

Her physical decline had been apparent for some time, but watching her advancing senility was agonizing. At first the signs were halting, and sometimes difficult to see. Once, I mentioned to her that Samir was going to Damascus. 'Oh, good,' she said pleasantly, 'we have relatives there that he can visit.' 'Who?' I asked, surprised, not knowing that any such relatives existed. 'Oh, there is so-and-so, and so-and-so' – people I had never heard of. Later, I asked Mother about them, and she was surprised to hear their names mentioned. 'Where did you hear about them?' she said. 'I haven't thought about them for decades.' When I told her, Mother laughed sadly. 'They have been dead for fifty years,' she said.

Gradually, Teta became less mobile, and her confusion less subtle. She lived with my Uncle Emil, her youngest son, in Beirut. My own little son Saree used to address her as 'Big Teta' to distinguish her from his own grandmother, who was to him of course 'Teta', but there was hardly anything big about her now. Mother had suggested the name, I suppose translating from Arabic, in which 'big' can also mean 'great' or 'old'. It was traditional to address the female head of a household as *'al-sitt'* (the lady), and her mother or mother-in-law as *'al-sitt al-kabira'* (the old lady), and so from that, I suppose, came 'Big Teta'.

Once when I was sitting quietly with her, towards the end, a woman who was an habitual visitor came in and, addressing her as one does a precocious baby, asked: 'Do you know who this is?', pointing at me. Teta, who was jolted out of a deep reverie by this challenge, obligingly looked at me carefully, and then after a long pause smiled a small and uncertain smile and said graciously: 'Of course. We used to visit each other in Nazareth.' I do not know who she thought I was, but I was shattered. It was not only the wound of not being recognized by Teta. Nor was it the deep anger I felt at the offending woman, who was vastly amused by Teta's confusion: I think she did this sort of thing frequently, baiting the bear of senility, taunting it and watching it perform. I felt discarded, set afloat, alone in the world. I felt lost without Teta, felt that I had lost touch with her memory, and therefore with my roots and my history.

She lay in bed most of the time, although she would struggle up and move around every now and then, especially at night. When asked where she was going, she would look vaguely perturbed, and one had the feeling she did not want to go anywhere in particular, just to get away, to escape from her own immobility. Towards the end, she broke her thigh and had to be hospitalized. It never healed properly, and my uncle had to put up a big sign near her bed: 'My thigh is broken,' to remind her not to get up and walk around unattended. This didn't do much good: she would still get out of bed and stagger to the middle of the room before the pain struck, when she would yell for help. As her voice was now feeble, it would be a while before someone heard her. By the time she was rescued and helped back to bed, she would be crying like a small, wounded child, her face all folded over with pain.

Teta's wandering mind necessitated constant nursing and watching. A series of minders were hired, but one after the other they quit in exasperation. Just before Mother took a trip to visit Joyce, who was living in Switzerland at the time, Teta had to be placed in an old people's home run by Maronite nuns in the Beirut suburb of 'Ain al-Rummaneh. By then she was hopelessly out of touch, and recognized no one around her. She responded only to inner images, and remembered emergencies rose out of her past to torment her. Once, when I went to see her in the home, she was crying, almost whimpering. The nun in attendance that day told me she had been very upset earlier, urgently insisting that it was time to remove the potatoes from the fire, desperately trying to get out of bed to reach a phantom kitchen and save a phantom lunch for her children.

When she returned from her travels, Mother used to go and visit her at odd times, avoiding visiting hours. She wanted to assure herself that Teta was being well treated by the nuns, and would turn up unexpectedly, ready to catch them in any act of cruelty or neglect, however small. She was always reassured, however, and the nuns proved to be very kind. One day she went at lunchtime. A nun was sitting by Teta's bed, holding a bowl full of soft food. For every mouthful she patiently presented on the proffered spoon, she would sing a little ditty, a child's song. Mother came home that day relieved at the nun's kindness, but overwhelmed with sadness, and, I think, guilt.

I have a photograph of Teta taken before her final descent into the irredeemable debasement of her last days: she is staring at the camera, with the merest hint of a smile. Wisps of long white hair peep out from under the black turban; a cameo brooch is neatly pinned on to the collar of the blouse under the black coat, dead centre on the throat. There is a kind of repose in her face: I feel as though she looked on this taking of a picture as a kind of respite, a clear reason, for the moment, for being. The old beauty is still clearly discernible – the clear complexion, the soft skin, the large grey eyes. Mother often said that Teta had been a beauty, '*mitl al-qamar*' (like the moon).

Teta died on 6 June 1973. She was ninety-three. Her children and grandchildren gathered at the nursing home, and followed her coffin in the hearse to the National Evangelical Church, over which her father had presided as pastor almost a century earlier. Her funeral was a big affair: many people came out of courtesy to one or other of her five children, all established members of the community in Beirut or Amman, and of the Palestinian diaspora, or to her nieces and nephews, many of them also well-known members of the Lebanese community. She was the last of her siblings to die: Uncle Habib had died long ago, in 1954; his wife, Auntie Hanah, in 1965. Auntie Melia died in 1954. Two of her sisters who had emigrated to America had also died earlier, as had her other brothers.

Outside the church, as people stood around the courtyard, having passed along the receiving line and presented their condolences, I overheard one woman say impatiently: 'What a big fuss over a senile old woman.' But I heard another, older woman chide her: 'You did not know her in her prime. She deserves this honour and more: Im Munir was a great lady.'

She was buried in the Protestant cemetery at Ras al-Nabeh. Later, during the war, the cemetery, which lies on the Green Line that divided the city, became inaccessible for years. When the war ended, the army had to be called in to remove unexploded shells and in general make sure it was safe to enter. But by then the damage had been done: many of the graves were damaged, and headstones were effaced or broken. The precise spot where Teta was buried is lost and I cannot visit it or tend it with the flowers she deserves, to honour her memory as I would have liked.

When she died, I thought that my dreamed-of book would somehow atone for her suffering, would somehow make amends for her sadness. Throughout my life Teta had been there, homeless, dispossessed, widowed, sad. And I knew (though the implication of this had never sunk in until I came to write, so many years later) that one of those two wedding rings that she always wore, that were too large for her thin fingers and jingled gently whenever she moved them, had belonged to her husband, whose early death had so traumatized my mother. Yet I had never imagined, I never could have imagined her embracing a loving husband, a living breathing man, from whose cold body she had, broken-hearted, removed the wedding ring and placed it on her finger, vowing never to take it off. I had always thought of her as ineluctably old, invariably ancient, shrivelled, so that the idea of her as a young, fertile woman with a life of her own was deeply disorientating. That vision of her only materialized after I actively began my research, when I undertook to investigate a lost time, making connections with a past I knew so little about.

When I first started my research, I felt I was reaching into a thick mist, pulling out a nugget of information here, a nugget there. At last the nuggets seemed to fuse together to form a kind of continuum, and I was able to see, instead of a chaotic series of events, the world out of which mine was formed.

TETA IN HISTORY

Teta around 1927 or 1928.

CHAPTER 9

Teta's Family Origins: The Badrs of Schweir and the Haddads of Abeih

My grandmother, Munira Youssef Badr, was born on 5 July 1880, the fourth child of Leila and Youssef Badr. Her father was born in 1840 in the village of Schweir, in Mount Lebanon. Her mother was Leila Mushreq Haddad from the village of Abeih, also in Mount Lebanon, but quite a distance away. I do not know the date of her birth. Schweir, like many of the villages of Mount Lebanon, dates back at least to the days of the Romans, and may be much older than that. When Youssef was born, however, Lebanon, and the entire area surrounding it, was part of the vast Ottoman empire. Youssef's father was Mikhail Badr al-Kassouf. About his mother I was able to discover nothing, not even her name.

With varying degrees of seriousness, some members of the family claim descent from an Austrian prince, Alexieff, who, they say, came over with the Crusades, married a local girl and stayed on. The legend claims that this Prince Alexieff's name was eventually Arabized and adapted to local pronunciation, hence 'Kassouf'. The sharp blue eyes and reddish blonde hair that appear here and there in the family, mixed with the distinctly semitic features more commonly seen, lend further credibility to the possibility of European blood being mixed in with local, a common enough occurrence in this part of the world. It is more likely, however, that Alexieff, if he existed at all, came at a later time than the Crusades, perhaps during the eighteenth century when there was some interaction between the Austrian empire and the Greek Catholic Church, one of whose principal areas of influence was in Schweir and the surrounding area.

Another possible origin of the family name is more mundane and less romantic, and can be traced to a local species of sweet white grapes grown in Mount Lebanon. Teta's ancestors, after all, were at one point involved in vineyards, either those of the monastery with which they were associated, or on their own lands. The Kassoufs may have originated in the district of Kesrouan, still in Mount Lebanon but further north. Before that, they may have been part of a larger family that lived in 'Ain Halia, near Bloudan, in what is now Syria. Suffice it to say that the family's modern history is directly connected with Schweir, and with the village of Khunshara, a half-hour's walk across the valley.

According to some branches of family lore, Youssef's grandfather was so handsome that he was likened to the full moon (*badr* in Arabic), and his descendants were thereafter known as the children of *badr*, which eventually became the family name. A more scientific account of family history, however, makes no mention of this origin and refers instead to a priest, who may also have been a monk, named 'Badr'. In any case, Youssef's was the last generation to use the Kassouf name: though his tombstone reads 'Youssef Badr al-Kassouf', his children were known only by the family name of 'Badr'.

The Schweiries were renowned for their building skills; indeed, they are still famous today as the builders of some of the most beautiful houses in Lebanon and the surrounding area. The lovely stone palace of the Emir Beshir Shehab, in the town of Beiteddine in Mount Lebanon, was among their accomplishments. Many of the men were absent from the village for months during the spring and summer, leaving their wives and families as they travelled around the area on their building projects.

Among the other principal occupations of the Schweiries were quarrying and stone cutting, and not surprisingly the main cause of death among them was lung disease. Another of their occupations was based on iron, and the Schweiries established a reputation for smithing, especially the making of swords and shields which were sold in their important *souq*. Silk worms were cultivated in the mulberry trees that flourished in the area, and silk factories played an important role in the economic life here as they did elsewhere in Mount Lebanon. Grapes cultivated in abundance were sold, or made into wine or *arak*.

Mikhail himself, however, was a weaver, and made *abayas*, the long cloaks worn in the winter. One of his brothers, whose name has been lost, was a monk in the Greek Catholic monastery of Mar Youhanna (St John) in Khunshara, which is run by the Basilean Schweirite order. The monastery, which was probably established some time after 1648, is famous to this day for housing the first Arabic printing press in the Arab world.

Monastery records show that there had been several monks named Kassouf since 1773, but it is impossible to tell which of them was Mikhail's brother. Legend has it that, starting out with his brothers as a weaver for the monastery, Mikhail's brother acquired a scientific education and became a doctor, or at least a medical practitioner. People called him out at all hours of the day and night to attend their sick, and, despite several warnings from the Superior, so often did he break the curfew that he was finally turned away. Some of his brothers, who worked either in the monastery gardens or as weavers, were turned out with him, and they settled in Schweir.

Teta's first cousin, Faris Badr, son of Youssef's brother Jirjis, told his son Jamil that one day when he was a boy, he and his brothers were playing near their house in Schweir when a monk came by and asked to see their father. The latter was not at home, so the monk turned and, stopping only to drink deeply from a pitcher of wine standing on a nearby table, went away without uttering another word, never to return. Faris thought that that mysterious visitor might have been his father's uncle.

That tantalizing image of the monk drinking from a pitcher as the boys look on, pausing in their game, with the sunlight filtering through the tall oak trees, is one of the few remaining links with a lost past. Another is the house Mikhail built and lived in with his family until his death in 1888. Sold by the last of Mikhail's descendants to own it, it stands to this day, though abandoned and in serious disrepair, at the edge of Schweir.

Saints, archangels, prophets, patriarchs, evangelists, apostles and, in general, scripture provide the bulk of the names of Christian towns in the Lebanese mountains to this day. Thus it was not unusual that Mikhail (Michael) should name his sons Jirjis (George), Youssef (Joseph), Antoun (Anthony) and Hanna (John). There is no record of the names of his daughters, if he had any, which seems doubtful, as no one in the family seems to have any memory, however vague, of the existence of an aunt belonging to that generation. About the women of the family in this generation – cousins, aunts, mothers, grandmothers – there is not a single word, record or memory. I am not surprised: my Uncle Alif made a family tree once, and it had no women in it. There was no room for them, he explained, when I protested. If the editor's art had excised them from his record, what eliminated them so completely from the family memory I do not know.

Thus, with no better way of imagining her, I enjoy conjuring up pictures of my great-great-grandmother around the time her son Youssef was born. Perhaps she and her infants could hear the sounds of war echoing from the battle of Bhersaf, within walking distance of Schweir, and perhaps she had to deal with straggling soldiers escaping from the various armies. In that battle, the Ottoman army, backed by Russian, English and French troops, defeated the Egyptian army of Ibrahim Pasha, son of Mohammed Ali Pasha, bringing to an end his eight-year occupation of Syria.

I think she must have been a tough woman. Schweiries boast that their male ancestors, who were called upon to participate in the battle according to the demands of their feudal duties, were such fierce fighters that all the other soldiers were afraid of them: no sooner did they enter the fray than the battle was instantly won. It was said that Ibrahim Pasha himself repeatedly remarked that Schweir was impossible to capture. Also, Schweiries say, even more boastfully, the women of Schweir were universally dreaded by all intruders and were so tough that they could beat off any army. They were particularly famous for refusing under any circumstances to have anything to do with the English soldiers, which is why, it is said, there are so few blondes in the village, although there are plenty in the surrounding area. I was told this by a Schweirie who is immensely proud of his village and its reputation: I did not wish to offend him by offering the Badrs as the living contradiction to his firmly held beliefs.

Documentation of my great-grandfather Youssef's life begins in 1865, when the records show that he was admitted to a school run by American Presbyterian missionaries in Abeih, a village across the valley from Schweir. Before that, and true to the Schweirie tradition, Youssef had been a mason and had probably been involved in the construction of the school, which was established in 1846. In 1869 the Americans converted the Abeih school into a theological seminary, and Youssef was one of eight men admitted to its first class. As at almost all the mission schools, classes at the seminary were initially conducted in Arabic, as none of the students knew English.

The mission movement was part of an evangelical revival, first in Britain and then in the United States, based on a reaction to the secular trends following the American and French revolutions. American missionaries first arrived in 'the Holy Land' in 1820, and eventually concentrated their efforts on Beirut, Mount Lebanon and the surrounding area. At first, they preached, sold Bibles and other religious books, and tried, with very little or no success, to convert Jews and Muslims and to 'rescue' their fellow Christians of the Eastern sects from the depths of superstition, corruption and error into which they believed them to have fallen. Ultimately, however, and in response to local imperatives, they changed their goals from their early evangelism to education. These and the other Western missionaries who preceded them, principally Roman Catholics, including members of the Franciscan and Jesuit orders, penetrated the densely woven and richly diverse cultural tapestry which constituted the reality of the Ottoman empire, gnawing at its edges and eventually changing it from within, while the military and political arms of the West were engaging it on other levels. By the time the Ottoman empire fell after the First World

War, there was in place a range of people – small in numbers perhaps, but great in influence – who knew the languages, the customs, the clothes and traditions of the Western countries.

The most influential of the network of schools and colleges that was to be the legacy of the American missionaries was the Syrian Protestant College, today the American University of Beirut, founded in 1866. Apparently now keen to focus on their educational rather than their evangelizing work, the missionaries were getting ready to hand over the Protestant church they had founded to a local leadership, hence the need for a theological seminary which would prepare prospective pastors for ordination.

Youssef's eldest brother Jirjis was the first in the family to convert from the Greek Catholic faith: according to the records of the Abeih church, he was a founding member of the Protestant church of Schweir, which was established in 1874. Youssef and his two younger brothers, Antoun and Hanna, both of whom also attended the seminary for short periods, followed suit. Youssef himself was formally admitted to the Protestant church in Abeih on 7 July 1867. In the same year, he started to teach at the mission school, in which he had been enrolled as a student since 1865. Two years later, he joined the first class of the theological seminary, and was to become the first Arab Protestant minister ordained by the American mission.

The early Protestant mission schools often consisted of a single room and were run by a single teacher, probably himself a graduate of one or other mission school, in simple surroundings. One alumnus of the Schweir school, Abraham Rihbany, recalls in his memoirs that each child was required to bring with him or her a piece of wood or charcoal to heat the schoolroom. The older children sat at wooden benches, but the younger ones sat on the floor. The students were taught from a primer, usually a book of Bible stories, and they were also required to memorize from the Presbyterian catechism. Discipline was meted out with sticks of various sizes that were usually — but not always – matched to the size of the offender and the offence. But this was not the only form of punishment. Rihbany remembers being locked in the schoolroom after hours as the penalty for some crime or other. He remained there, accompanied only by spiders and other terrors brought forth from his youthful imagination, until his anxious mother arrived to rescue him from the total darkness in which he had been immured.

As was the custom at all mission schools, foreign missionaries came regularly to examine the students and see what had been accomplished since the last visit. Prizes were offered for progress. A successful recitation of the Beatitudes, for instance, earned Rihbany a penknife. These missionaries were the first Westerners their young pupil had ever seen, and the first people he saw wearing Western costume.

The seminary in Abeih was housed in a property owned by the family of Mushreq Haddad, Youssef's future father-in-law. The Haddad family was originally Maronite, but Mushreq Haddad had become a Protestant. He ran a travel business, renting out his *hantour*, a two-passenger horse-drawn carriage, or victoria, to travellers. This business was probably an offshoot of the vast new network of roads that the Ottomans were building, linking various districts of the area. The Ottomans were in the midst of their major programme of political reform and modernization. Railroads and carriageways were being constructed everywhere, and around them was a growing trade. Not far from Abeih, to which it is connected by a major road, lies the great Beirut–Damascus highway, construction of which began in the middle of the nineteenth century.

When Youssef Badr came from Schweir to Abeih, Mount Lebanon had recently been shaken by terrible events. After a long period of civil disorder and strife in various districts of the mountain, fierce battles had erupted between Christians (mostly of the Maronite sect) and Druze (a minority Muslim sect located almost exclusively in historic Syria) in the summer of 1860, as the culmination of which many Christian villages had been attacked, and hundreds of villagers killed. Abeih, with a mixed Maronite and Druze native population, was one of the villages attacked during the conflagration and many of its people were killed. European intervention, including the dispatching of French troops, led the Ottomans to create a new form of government, the *mutassariffiya* (self-government), which granted a large degree of autonomy to Mount Lebanon.

The Haddads were probably among those hundreds of families who took refuge in Beirut during the troubles. More than a century later, people from Abeih and the surrounding area were to do so again during the civil war in Lebanon. Earlier they had had some experience of the mountain war: somewhere deep in my distant memory of childhood lies a formless, almost inarticulate, impression left by Teta of her mother's memories of this period. But by 1869, when Youssef Badr joined the theological seminary, the Haddads were once again well settled.

Precisely what it was that led the Badrs of Schweir and the Haddads of Abeih to become involved with the American missionaries and to convert to Protestantism is not well documented. It is possible that they had disagreements with the local clergy, and were not obedient to the dictates of those running the ancient churches. A letter from the American Rev. Bird, dated 19 February 1867, notes that Americans 'had often been importuned to open schools' in Schweir. He goes on to recount how 'a mason of our acquaintance' had, after challenging the priest of 'the Greek church', apparently on religious doctrine, received 'a severe drubbing'. That, according to Bird, was 'the opportunity he was waiting for – a good opportunity to abandon that church'. Along with about twenty other similarly inclined young men, he 'took an open stand' and enrolled as a Protestant.

The memoirs of my father-in-law, Anis Khouri al-Makdisi, for decades Professor of Arabic at the American University of Beirut, tell in greater detail, and with less of an ideological slant, how his family, in what is now northern Lebanon, had been attracted to the Americans early on in the nineteenth century and eventually abandoned their Greek Orthodox faith to become Protestants. His story provides an example of the type of social and cultural changes occurring in the nineteenth century.

His paternal grandfather Saba, Makdisi recounts, came from a farming family originally from the Koura district of Mount Lebanon, south-east of Tripoli. While his brothers were attracted to farming, Saba was more interested in trade. He used to buy goods from Tripoli and travel around the area selling them. Later, having noticed that many of the peasants in the area had no ox to assist them in their ploughing, he would buy oxen for them, in return for which he would receive a share of the harvest crop. As time passed, the amount of grain he received was greater than that required for his family's consumption and he began to sell the excess during the winter months. When he built a house for himself in Tripoli, it included a warehouse for storing the accumulated grain.

Now that this enterprising man had a steady income, he yearned to learn to read and write. He went to a village school in the area, and after he had mastered the Psalms and the *Ay Oytoykhos*, the Greek Orthodox book of daily prayers, he himself opened a village school that he ran for some time. After he married the daughter of a prosperous landowner, he returned, in 1837, to Tripoli with the intention of attending to his business. In the same year, however, the Greek Orthodox priest of the district of Duniyyah, near Tripoli, died and the bishop of Tripoli appointed Saba as his successor. Now the *muallim* (teacher) Saba became known as the *khouri* (priest) Saba. Throughout his service as a priest, and until he died of cholera in 1848, he continued his partnerships with the peasants.

Following the death of her husband, the *khouria* (wife of the priest), Elias' mother, took her children to Tripoli, where she continued the business begun by her husband, but, as the family's fortune gradually declined, she moved to Jwar al-Husn. Her son, the writer's father, Elias, was ten years old when his father died. When he completed his elementary education, he was exhorted by the bishop to follow in his father's footsteps and enter the priesthood, but, feeling no inclination for this career, he eventually earned a living as a tax collector. He married a relation of his mother's from Tripoli and settled in the town of Ammar.

At around this time, the mid-nineteenth century, the American missionaries began their evangelizing activities in Tripoli and its environs. Some time earlier, the people of Ammar had asked the Greek Orthodox bishop of Tripoli to open a school in their village, but he had ignored their request. Annoyed with the bishop's indifference, some of the villagers, including Elias, turned to the American missionaries and asked them to open a school, which they proceeded to do. The bishop took umbrage and did everything in his power to thwart the venture, but the people insisted on seeing the project through and, in this battle of wills, finally had their way.

It was Elias' wife, the writer's mother, who was first converted to the new evangelical sect from her Greek Orthodox religion. She was by then around forty years of age, and yearned to read the Bible, as befitted a Protestant. Though Elias himself was attracted to 'the new learning' brought by the Americans, he remained a Greek Orthodox until just before the writer's birth in 1885.

The arrival of the American missionaries came at a time when the rapidly changing social situation, with increasing prosperity and leisure, was leading directly to the desire for learning, and a deaf ear was being turned by the ancient church, and the gigantic bureaucracy of a declining empire, to the needs and aspirations of rising new classes. This coincidence was to prove significant both to the newcomers and to those who welcomed them.

But who were these missionaries? And what was their relationship with those for whom they always reserve the colonial appellation, 'the natives', including my great-grandparents?

The men who came here, who opened and ran the schools, the seminaries and later the university, were no starry-eyed dreamers, as I had previously imagined them to be, no poor outcast priests, no adventurous and barely literate teachers, no ranting and quixotic eccentrics wanting to carry forth the Good Word. The Americans of the Syria Mission, as it was called, the Jessups and Blisses, the Smiths and Calhouns, were men whose background lay in such institutions as Harvard, Yale, Williams and Amherst, and in the Andover, Princeton and Union theological seminaries.

These were well-connected men: when Daniel Bliss, first president of the Syrian Protestant College, went home to the US, he dined with President Lincoln at the White House. He met with his old friend Theodore Roosevelt and was received by the famous hostesses of the period. Henry Seward came to visit him in Beirut, where he also met Kaiser Wilhelm. He was very friendly with Rustum Pasha, the Ottoman governor of Lebanon and a member of the Italian nobility; Jamal Pasha, the Ottoman governor of Syria, called on him at home. Mark Twain visited the college campus and left an autographed portrait of himself, as did Roosevelt; when Bliss went to Britain he was received by Lord and Lady Argyle, in whose house he dined with Lord Shaftesbury.

This was by no means a powerless, naive group of men on the fringe of their society, as I had previously imagined them to be. Nor were they received as such in Lebanon, but were treated as notables:

they were welcomed in the homes of the rich, the powerful and the most sophisticated. Although they sometimes catered to the poor and the unfortunate, they did not live with them, and by no means did they share their lives. The annual salary of an American missionary was generally between $1,000 and $1,500; medical missionaries were paid even more. A 'native', on the other hand, was generally paid between $100 and $200 by the mission. Despite the puritanical nature of their teachings and influence, the Americans lived in spacious, sometimes grand houses, and in the summer moved to gracious summer houses in the cool mountains.

Moreover, there were whole families of missionaries. Daniel and Mrs Bliss and their son Howard; Henry Harris Jessup and his brother Samuel; Eli Smith and his wives – the mission registry is full of the same names: husbands and wives, brothers and sisters, nephews, nieces and cousins. These people formed a closely knit, intimately connected group, which it must have been difficult for strangers to penetrate.

My great-grandparents, and others like them who became involved with the missionaries, were in a difficult position. Few of those Lebanese, or Syrians, as they thought of themselves then, who entered the new American schools which soon developed and taught a modern secular curriculum, or who became Protestants, came from the great or wealthy families of the land. Yet they were proud people with a sense of their own destiny that survives to this day. A photograph of Schweir taken in 1897 shows clearly that it was a prosperous, beautiful town. The stone houses for which it has remained famous are large, elegant structures, with the double- and triple-arched doors, the high pointed windows, which distinguish the local architecture of the time and speak of a comfortable lifestyle. As befits a town in tune with the times, a few of its houses boast the pyramid-shaped terracotta roofs just coming into architectural fashion at the time; the others still had the flat roofs which preceded them.

In the famous village *souq*, to which came people from the entire area, the shops sold grain and the dried pulses that formed the staples of these mountain people's diet. They traded with far-away places and sold fabrics such as wool, silks and cottons. The carpenters made furniture and coffins; the blacksmiths sold swords and shields, the making of which had brought them fame. A particular area of the *souq* was devoted to a gold market: there were twelve jewellers in all, which indicates a degree of prosperity and wealth in the region. The building in Abeih that housed the seminary is still standing. It, too, with its arched and colonnaded balconies and porches surrounding the enclosed courtyard, speaks of a gracious life, of prosperity.

My great-grandparents were part of a new and dynamic movement. They were to inhabit the frontiers, the territorial outposts, of a new cultural map; indeed, they were among the pioneers who helped draw this map. I have often read that the missionaries, with their secular schools, their modern medical knowledge and their new social rules, introduced modernity to this part of the world: they are always referred to as the sole founders of this or that school or university, as though they had done this entirely independently and alone. Not enough credit for the creation of modernity has ever been given to those who pressed them to open schools, sent their children, gave them the land, built the buildings, taught in the schools, and in general participated in the enterprise. Indeed it was often the 'natives' who suggested the next bend in the road, the next step to be taken. Without them, the missionaries could have accomplished nothing.

These 'natives' have sometimes been maligned as having collaborated with the imperial project. That seems to me a shortsighted view of history from an angle skewed to represent the nationalist views of our time. Surely there is a case to be made for their having been, for their own reasons, from their own imperatives, restless, troubled by their world, one way or another dissatisfied with it. As they pursued and embraced what they saw as a new and better world, an enormous gulf grew between them and those on whom they turned their backs – their old church, their old society.

Yet I cannot imagine that my great-grandparents felt at home with the Jessups, the Birds and the Blisses, nor they with them. They could not possibly have been accepted as equals by those Americans, some of whom, at least, felt at home in the company of American presidents, English lords and Turkish pashas. Nor could they have had much kindred feeling for the Americans. The world of missions, conversions, teaching and schools was no more immune to the perils of imperial power politics than the military, political and social world that was its mirror.

Youssef Badr was ordained in Abeih on 8 April 1872, and, apparently in the same ceremony, installed as pastor of the mission church in the Syrian town of Homs, 'ancient Emessa' as the missionary accounts like to call it. He was already well-acquainted with Homs, as he had been there during his studies at the theological seminary, where the students were required to do fieldwork in the outposts. A few days after his ordination, the Rev. William Bird of the American mission married Youssef to Leila Mushreq Haddad in Schweir.

Accounts of wedding customs in Mount Lebanon at the time describe days of festivities, including music and dancing, sword games, weight-lifting contests among the men of both families, and of course much eating and drinking. The bride was usually transported to her new home in her husband's village in a festive procession including members of her family, mostly men on decorated horses or mules, while a mule carrying the all-important and colourful wooden chest in which her trousseau was placed trotted alongside. When she left her father's house, it was customary for the bride to take a long time – sometimes as long as half an hour – to walk from her seat to the door. This slowness would indicate both her reluctance to leave her beloved parents and her unwillingness to appear over-enthusiastic about her new situation.

These were changing times, however, and new and rival influences were being felt. How many of the old customs were observed by my great-grandparents, who were now attached to the puritanical American missionaries, I do not know, nor how much singing and dancing was permitted. What I do know is that soon after their marriage, the couple moved to Homs. Leaving Schweir, they rode mules and horses to the town of Mrouj, a few kilometres to the east. From there, they took the steep mountain track up to Ayntoura and then Tarshish on the peak, from where they rode down to Zahleh in the Bekaa valley, on the other side of the mountain. They would certainly have been riding with a caravan, which would have included other travellers, some walking, some like them riding mules or horses, as well as mules and camels carrying baggage and other goods. From Zahleh they took a carriage to Damascus, and from there to Homs. The journey would have taken them days, not hours, as it would today.

In April, Mount Sannine, towering majestically over Schweir, would still have been covered with snow. On the lower slopes of the mountainside through which they had to make their way, however, spring would have burst forth in its full beauty. Everything would be fresh and green. The pine trees, having shed their dead needles in the winter winds, would be growing new ones – light, intense green. The almond trees would be in full bloom, their branches heavy with pink and white blossom. The cherry, apple and peach trees too would have burst into bloom. Poppies, daisies, anemones and other wild flowers would colour the steep meadows in swatches of red, yellow, pink, purple and white. From the stone walls of the terraced orchards would hang graceful pink and white cyclamens, while wild violets would be growing under the trees. Broom and forsythia would be budding, here and there an early bloom already brilliantly yellow. The air would be crisp and clear, full of the scents of the wild flowers and the new pines, and the sound of the bees. Overhead, waves of migrating birds would soar – herons and storks, eagles and swallows.

As their journey progressed, the extraordinary colour and richness of the spring in Mount Lebanon and the Bekaa valley would eventually fade into the bleak beauty of the anti-Lebanon range, and then the Syrian desert, majestic and awe-inspiring in its vast emptiness.

Approaching Homs, my great-grandmother must have been full of anxiety. Like Teta, who moved to Safad after her marriage; like Mother, who moved to Cairo; like me, who moved to Washington, Leila was starting her married life far away from home, far from her mother, from her family and from that continuity and social tradition that makes a new life somehow less frightening.

CHAPTER 10

Homs

For the next eighteen years, Youssef and Leila Badr lived in Homs. All of their children, including my grandmother, were born during that time. Emelia was born in 1873, Nassib in 1875, Habib in 1877, Munira in 1880, Najla in 1883 and Nabiha in 1886. The youngest son, Rashid, died as a teenager in 1916, though his precise date of birth is not known. Missionary accounts show that Youssef used to return to Schweir occasionally, preaching in the church there and officiating at Holy Communion. Perhaps he went to visit his family, perhaps he went for jovial, or sad, family reunions, when someone married or someone died. We do not know if his wife ever accompanied him, or any of his children. We do know that at least two of their children, Nabiha and Najla, were born in Beirut during the Homs years, but whether all the family accompanied their mother to the city, where she was no doubt attended by one of the American doctors, I cannot tell. I do not remember Teta ever telling me about such journeys: but then, of course, Teta did not tell me much about her early life.

I could not help but feel, as I read Mother's memoirs of a much later time, that Teta and her siblings must have enjoyed a happy family life when they were children. They kept in touch long after they married and were scattered by later events, and always sent their children to each other for holiday visits or safekeeping. Habib was the only one of Teta's siblings, other than the redoubtable Emelia, who was well known to my generation. He and his wife Hanah were to become great favourites in our family. Their children, especially their older daughters, Eva and Lily, were to become Mother's close friends, along with Nassib's daughter, Nora. Habib and Hanah's younger children, Fouad and Ellen, were also to become great family favourites.

Teta and her siblings' early years in Homs were lived against an uncomfortable background. A series of wars during the nineteenth century between Ottoman troops, on the one hand, and bedouin or the Russian army on the other, led to problems of conscription that consistently beset the population. Marauding Bulgarian refugees fleeing the wars in their land were a dreaded part of life in those days. Nature too was not kind: cholera epidemics and plagues of locusts were repeatedly reported by the missionaries and in the various memoirs of the period.

A major theme of the mission accounts concerns the growing enmity of the old churches as the Protestant missions encroached on their territory. The Ottoman authorities were also – understandably – less than friendly, and repeatedly tried to control the activities of the Americans. That the Americans were full of contempt for the Ottomans is made clear from their writings: again and again they show how they sidestepped or disobeyed the authorities. In addition, most of them took an adversarial stand against local customs and traditions.

The adversarial relationship between the American missionaries and local culture is dramatically illustrated by the momentous decision taken in 1878 by the crown jewel of the American missionary movement, the Syrian Protestant College, to stop using Arabic as the language of instruction and to replace it with English. Arabic had been used as a medium of instruction in all the mission schools from the beginning. Henceforth, all the schools feeding into the college would have to use English instead.

The decision to make the change seems to have been taken partly as a practical result of the fact that new teachers were coming from America who knew not a word of Arabic, and of the cumbersome and time-consuming procedures involved in translating textbooks. The most famous chronicler of the mission, Henry Harris Jessup, offers practical explanations for the change. But in the 'Syrian Notes' of the *Missionary Review of the World* (October 1878), the change takes on a different light:

> The Board of Directors of the Syrian Protestant College have shown their appreciation of the new era of British influence in Syria by a recent vote 'that after next year all instruction in the College shall be through the English language', and that in the Arabic shall be taught only the Arabic grammar, etc. – in other words, that Arabic shall be taught like any other language. This remarkable action shows that in the opinion of the most intelligent men in the country, British influence in Syria is hereafter to be not a mere diplomatic flourish of rhetoric, which Turkish evasion may treat as a dead letter, but an all-pervading and controlling power, affecting every interest of society.
>
> Hitherto French Jesuitism, with its wonted sagacity, has striven with much success to make the French language a general medium in Syria, and the international shopping intercourse of Beirut has been conducted in that tongue.
>
> It is language which helps to conquer and assimilate and transform, more, even, than battles and treaties.

It seems quite clear from these words that the decision to switch languages was directly related to political developments, and particularly to the advancement of British imperial interests in the area: Britain had taken over the Suez Canal in 1875, and was becoming the major imperial power of the time. From the days of Mohammed Ali Pasha of Egypt, who, in undertaking a deliberate modernizing process, had placed so much faith in French schools and culture, the influence of French language and culture had been growing dramatically, much to the chagrin of the Protestant missionaries, both American and British, who make many references to their rivals. The use of language had to do with power, and the changing political structure of the world.

Though the American navy was beginning to have a presence in the Mediterranean, America was still a distant and relatively unimportant land. The American missionaries, often referred to by the local people as '*al-Ingliz*' (the English), were protected by the British and took borrowed strength from the great power.

From the time of that fateful decision of the Syrian Protestant College, Arabic, to be taught 'like any other language', was relegated to a secondary position, to be regarded by the foreign schools and most of their pupils as merely the language of poetry, music, song and religion, while English (and French, of course) came to be regarded as the language of knowledge, of science, of medicine – in other words, of modernity. Though there was much resistance to this trend in the modernizing movement in Syria and the rest of the Arab world, it remains firmly entrenched among a certain class of educators and their students.

Tied up inevitably and inextricably with this business of language is the question of authority – political and intellectual – of class distinctions, of the relationship of one culture with another, and of cultural production. But when I think of Teta's and then of my generation, I think particularly of a growing tendency to separation and differentiation, of being at odds with the mainstream of society. Today, command of 'modern' languages is frequently associated not only with knowledge and power, but also with 'modernity' and 'progress'. Like the question of clothes, the question of language as popularly discussed is full of misunderstandings, and foolish conclusions arrived at by thoughtless people – such as those who believe that Arabic is incompatible, for a variety of reasons, with the teaching of science and medicine. Language and its uses is surely one of the great, though insufficiently explored, themes of our time, through which the history of the twentieth century, the comings and goings of empires, can be traced.

Whether she was aware of it or not, my grandmother was partly formed by the mutual hostility between local and missionary cultures. It must have permeated every moment of life, every activity and every decision. It lurked, spoken or unspoken, at mealtimes, in the classroom and from the pulpit. It was the beginning of that alienation from their natural environment that was to dominate not only her life, but also the life of a whole class, a whole segment of the people.

According to her grandchildren, Leila Badr knew little English, and we know from mission references that the same was true of her husband. When I knew her, Teta, though she had a good command of English, used Arabic more frequently: she was more comfortable in it, she enjoyed it for its warmth and beauty. She prayed, read the Bible and told her famous stories in Arabic. When I knew them in their old age, she and her siblings spoke to each other only in Arabic, but at the same time they all prided themselves on their knowledge of English: 'My little toe knows more English than you!'

Mother and her siblings were genuinely bilingual. Their love for the Arabic language and for Arabic poetry formed a tender part of their childhood memories. At the same time, they took their knowledge of English for granted: all of them were educated at English or American mission schools, which by then had established English as the language of instruction. Mother's love of Arabic led her to make sure that we learned not only the language, but a love for it, in spite of the fact that our English schools in Cairo did not do much for us in this regard. It was her first language, the one she thought and dreamed in.

While the Americans made no bones about their contempt for both the Ottoman authorities and the local churches, Youssef had to deal directly with the same clergy and authority, unprotected by British consuls or American naval vessels, and no doubt his job was a difficult one. He handled the problems that arose on the ground with tact and conciliation: he was to establish a reputation as a good, kind man, a peacemaker.

The difficulties faced by the Homs mission station were compensated for by its success. Since 1850 the Ottoman government had recognized the Protestant community as a separate sect, or *millet*, entitled to its own courts, with its own leaders now responsible for its conduct and the collection of its taxes. According to the missionaries, the Homs church was crowded with new Protestants on Sundays. There were regular women's meetings, a girls' school with 130 students in 1878, and a boys' school with 90 students in the same year. The school facilities were crude, however, and the boys were all crowded into one room. Medical missionaries would stop by regularly, holding consultations and sometimes performing surgery.

The pastor and his wife worked hard. She took the ladies of the congregation to her house for Bible lessons; she taught them hymns as they sat together doing their embroidery and sewing. Teta was to do this when she became a pastor's wife. The Badr children, who attended the mission school and were medically attended by the mission doctor, grew up in the security of their parents' success and basking in the respect in which the community held them.

In the 1870s and 1880s, the family's lifestyle offered an interesting and complex blend of customs, clothes, food, furniture and manners, from village and city, Turkish and Arab, from Mount Lebanon and from the coastal lands as well as from the interior. They had by now surely absorbed, not only from the missionaries but also from the general climate, especially from their interaction with Beirut, some Western clothes, manners and habits, yet must as surely have maintained some of their native costumes and habits, themselves under internal pressure of change.

As the nineteenth century progressed, the growing influence of an ever more powerful and pervasive Europe gradually began to manifest itself in changes in style and costume. The architecture of cities and towns, growing because of increased trade, had also begun to change, with a marked Venetian influence. Interiors changed too, as the Western style in furniture and furnishings began to coexist, as it would for many decades, with the Arab style, especially in the homes of the rich and those who travelled to Europe.

As I reconstruct it in my imagination, based on my research, my family's domestic traditions and the homes of others of the same class – because this, like so much else in the family history, is undocumented – the parsonage at Homs was a two-storey stone house. The high exterior walls, unbroken except for small windows at the top, afforded the household total privacy. The windows themselves were covered: a *musharrabiya* (carved wooden screen) let in light and air, while keeping out the prying eyes of passers-by. To enter the house, one had to pass through a low door into a covered passageway from which the interior could not be seen by passers-by or delivery men. This passageway led into an enclosed courtyard, in the middle of which water rippled through an octagonal fountain. The flat roof covered a ceiling made of tightly laid wooden beams all in a line, and was surrounded by a high wall which also shielded the inhabitants from the view of the outside world. In winter, the wooden shutters mounted on the inside of the large inner windows kept out the cold wind and rain, the sleet and hail, while in summer they provided much-valued shade and coolness.

In the courtyard were beds in which grew tomatoes, green beans, cucumbers, courgettes, eggplant, parsley, mint and other herbs and vegetables. In the garden stood trees bearing oranges, lemons, quince, peaches, figs, apples, plums, cherries and other fruit. Near them grew large bushes of rhododendrons, hydrangeas and roses. Dahlias, mostly pink, and iris, purple and white, burst into colour in the spring and summer. A jasmine bush, ripe with its sweet-smelling flowers, crept up the side of the house, by the outer stairs. A large, heavy grapevine covered a favourite spot in the garden, providing a canopy under whose shade the family sat in the summer. In the spring they would pick the vine leaves for stuffing, leaving enough to pickle in brine for the rest of the year. In the late summer, they would pick the green and purple grapes that hung heavy from the vine. As the grapes aged, they were used to make vinegar or dried to become raisins.

Inside the house, rooms opened up from around a large central hall. The inner walls were made of mud-brick, and the doors that punctuated them of polished oak. The house was sparsely furnished. Low wooden divans lined the walls on three sides of the largest room. They were covered with brightly coloured cushions stuffed with straw and wood shavings. Some of them were covered with *kilims*; others were embroidered or appliquéd by Leila and her daughters. Some cushions were made of remnants of materials used for clothes, sewn together in pleasing patterns. Buttons rescued from discarded old clothes were used to decorate the cushions and upholstery, as well as new dresses: nothing was allowed to go to waste in Leila's household.

The floors were covered with carpets, some of them Persian, others woven wool, in the patterns of Syria and Lebanon. Some carpets were purchased from the bedouin, in their characteristic style: made of long and shaggy goat's hair, in black and white, or brown and white, stripes. Carpets purchased from Turkoman peddlers boasted bold patterns of red and black flowers made of knotted wool. Sheepskin rugs lay on the floor in the winter, and the children warmed their feet in them on cold, wet nights. In the summer, the carpets were sunned, beaten and then rolled up and stored; in their place, *hassiras* (straw mats) were laid over the naked tiles, which cooled the house where the carpets had warmed them. The *hassira* was made from the alfalfa plants that grew by the river-banks.

The family slept on mattresses laid out every night on the floor, and every morning folded up and placed in a *youk*, a niche or cupboard especially designed for their storage. Near it were other niches in which the family's clothing lay neatly folded. The mattresses were stuffed with wool, and in winter the family covered themselves with *luhuf* (woollen quilts) to keep warm. The brightly coloured quilt covers were made either of silk or cotton and also provided the girls in the family a chance to practise their embroidery skills. Every summer the itinerate *munajjid* (upholsterer) would come by and install himself in the courtyard. Having first emptied the mattresses of their stuffing, he would fluff it up with an instrument resembling a harp, removing the lumps, airing and sunning the wool; he would then restuff the mattresses and sew them up again. Sometimes an old mattress would be discarded altogether and a new one, with fresh new wool, sewn up. Even in my day, the *munajjid* used to come by and his activities form part of my memory of summer childhood days in Mount Lebanon.

Every morning, when the weather was clear and the sun shone, Leila, her daughters and maidservants would carry the mattresses, pillows and *luhuf* outdoors to be aired and sunned before being stored for the day. This is a habit that I learned from my mother, as she did from hers. Though today's mattresses are too bulky to move, I regularly carry the sheets, pillows, blankets and towels of my household to the balcony to be aired and sunned before making up the beds and getting on with the day.

In the middle of the room stood a large brass brazier in which charcoal was burned on cold winter days. Round brass trays lay on wooden legs carved in the geometric patterns of Arab tradition. A place of honour in the room was given to the wooden bridal chest filled with items of her trousseau that Leila brought with her to her new life. The chest was carved in an elaborate design and appliquéd with coloured velvet and shiny tin cut into arabesque patterns. Low tables carved with the same elaborate designs, or inlaid with mother-of-pearl, stood here and there around the room.

My maternal great-grandmother,
Leila Haddad Badr.

My maternal great-grandfather,
Rev. Youseef Badr.

My paternal grandmother,
Hanneh Shammas Said.

My paternal grandfather,
Ibrahim Assaad Said.

The family of Rev. Shukri Musa, Nazareth, 1924–24;
L to R: Rev. Shukri, Alif, Teta Munira, Hilda and Munir;
seated in front: Rayik and Emil.

Teta Munira as I knew
and remember her.

Mother at Scots College, Safad, Palestine, 1927.

My parents at their wedding, Nazareth, 1932.

Edward, Rosemarie and Jean, c. 1943.

George Said, Auntie Nabiha and Rosie, on the steps of the house in Jerusalem, on their way to George's wedding, 1946.

Jean with Daddy, Cairo, 1949.

Jean in Cairo, mid-1950s, in her Girl Guide uniform.

My parents at a Cairo reception in the 1950s.

Family group in Cairo, c. 1955. Standing in the back row: Robert Said, Sylvia Said (Albert's wife), Albert Said, Lorie Mansour, Hoda Said. Seated: Jean, Teta, Auntie Nabiha, Grace (standing), Mother, Daddy, his cousin and close friend Shafik Mansour. Front row: Samir Said, Boulos Said, Joyce.

Samir and Jean at their wedding.

*The last gathering of the Said family, Dhour el Schweire, 1970. L to R:
standing: Grace, Joyce, Rosie and Samir; seated: Edward, Hilda,
Wadie, Saree, Ussama and Jean (pregnant with Karim).*

L to R: Samir, Karim, Jean, Ussama and Saree, 1971.

L to R: Elora, Ussama, Hala, Karim, Saree and Christina at Hala and Karim's wedding, Dhour el-Schweir, 2000.

In a corner, breaking with tradition, stood a bulky armchair with burgundy upholstery. Its clumsy round legs were ornately sculpted in a design that bore no resemblance to the old Arab style, but was an imitation of the European furniture that had begun to gain popularity in the towns and cities in the 1850s. Another locally made armchair, this one modelled on the English Morris chairs, stood near it: with its adjustable back and matching footstool, it was the favourite chair of the paterfamilias.

In another room stood a large, bulky dining table carved of walnut wood, around which were lined uncomfortably straight-backed chairs with woven cane seats. This business of the dining table and chairs was a great innovation. There were no dining or other specialized rooms in Arab houses: food was served in the main living-room, and diners sat on cushions or on the low divans that lined the walls. The food was placed on trays made of silver, copper, brass or basketry, depending on the family's wealth, and these were laid on low tables or stools. All the diners gathered around the tables ate out of common dishes, usually using bread to scoop up the food. Spoons too were in wide use at this time, though knives and forks were only known in the households of those wealthy Syrians who had had social intercourse with the West. The dining table, with its individual chairs and plates, was certainly brought in by Westerners, or by those Syrians, principally Beiruti traders, who had travelled to Europe and brought back its customs. With it came the need for a dedicated dining-room and a new kind of attitude towards mealtimes, food, family, property and privacy.

In my great-grandparents' Protestant household no religious decoration, no icons or calligraphy, such as hung in their neighbours' houses, would have been tolerated. In their parents' homes in Mount Lebanon only guns or swords were hung on the wall, together with the odd item of clothing and other useful items. The only pictures were photographs of their relations, many of them dead, all of them looking down severely from the walls on which they were hung. In the houses of their Greek Orthodox neighbours would often hang, along with the icons, a picture of the Tsar of Russia, then regarded as the protector of the Orthodox community.

The walls themselves were regularly whitewashed and then decorated with hand-painted geometric friezes that ran in bands around the room. Also on the walls, but not meant as decoration as they are today, were hung round straw basketry trays of various sizes, with coloured patterns woven into them. Leila would use them for serving food or for drying herbs in the shade, or for airing the *burghul* (cracked wheat). She also used them for making *kishk*, the curdled and dried yoghurt mixed with *burghul*, a year's supply of which would be stored in bags hung in the pantry, and then, on cold days, boiled with water and served as a soup, or used to add flavour to some of the winter dishes. An especially fine carpet might also be hung on the wall, or, like a curtain, used to separate two rooms or spaces.

Niches of various sizes were carved out in the walls. On the shelves stood earthenware pots and urns filled with the *munie*, the year's supply of cereals, dried fruit and vegetables, onions, garlic, olives and olive oil. Other niches held ceramic bowls, and bowls made of unglazed earthenware, as well as the dishes and cups, usually made of brass lined with tin, used at mealtimes. There were also niches to hold the oil lamps that lit the house at night.

Brass, iron, wood, glass and earthenware utensils were all used. The itinerant *mubayyid* (whitener) would pass by regularly, and all the brass pots and trays would be given to him to be lined with tin. Like the *munajjid*, he would announce his arrival by calling out his craft – 'Mubayyid, mubayyid' – as he walked down the street. Housewives in need of his services would summon him to their kitchen, as they did the *mujallikh* who sharpened the knives. Even in my days, Mother used regularly to call in the *mubayyid* and hand him the brass cooking trays she had inherited from her mother. He would sit outside her door, or sometimes on the balcony, with his little fire and the other tools of his craft. Child of an industrial age, I used to worry about the quality of this work and always hated those trays of Mother's. I gave them away when she died, the only vestige of her life and possessions with which I parted without regret.

In that changing world of theirs, I do not know if my great-grandparents patronized the public baths, or *hamam*, in Homs. Public baths were unknown in their ancestral Mount Lebanon, and people used always to bathe in their own homes. My great-grandfather, however, would certainly have gone to the *hamam* to meet with people and socialize, as was the custom. The baths in Homs, as in other Arab cities, were open to women from noon to sunset, and then to men from sunset to dawn. Whether in the privacy of their home or in the *hamam*, they would have been scrubbed with coarse *leefas* (loofahs) picked from a vine and then dried in the sun. Squares of soap, home-made with olive or bay oil, were rubbed repeatedly on the *leefa*, which was then rubbed on the skin, acting like a gentle grater. The bathers would smell sweet and their skin would be pink not only with cleanliness, but with the renewed vigour of their stimulated circulation. The toilet was in an outhouse that opened on to the courtyard. I know its name, *beit al-mayy* (water house), from Teta. She always used this name, even for the modern bathrooms with which I grew up.

Large earthenware *jarras* (jars) were filled with drinking water by itinerant *saqqas* (water-carriers), who came by on their donkeys. Unlike most other towns and cities, Homs did not have a central fountain but instead a central reservoir filled by water wheels that dipped into the Orontes, or the Assi, as it is named in Arabic. The full jars were left to stand in the cool shade near the kitchen. Leila would place a piece of cloth over the *jarra*'s mouth to keep out the flies and the dust. Teta would later crochet such caps for Mother's household. I remember them well. She would add a little *oya*, a gaily-coloured fringe like the ones that decorated the *mandeels* (headscarves) that all the women wore at home.

The cool water in the *jarras* would be emptied into a smaller earthenware *ibrik*, or long-spouted drinking jug. Then, holding the jug at arm's length and at an angle from the face, drinkers would skilfully direct the stream of water into their mouths, taking great gulps and never spilling a drop. In our long summer days in Dhour al-Schweir, my siblings and I used to compete as to who could manage this feat best: we always ended up soaked through and choking, as much from laughter as from our inept efforts.

The parish house was lit with oil lamps, as houses in Nazareth were still lit in my mother's day. Small earthenware lamps were placed in the niches, larger ones on tables or stools around the room. In Homs, some, at least, of the oil was imported from America: already at this time, cultural penetration had opened the way to commercial interests. On a month-long trip through the northern zone with Dr Calhoun, the medical missionary, the American missionary Rev. Gerald F. Dale, Jr stopped in Homs, where they visited 'the native pastor'. He writes on 23 June 1883:

We were delighted, too, to find what an influence that far-off
land, which we love, was exerting upon the town. We looked
up to examine the roof of one of the houses, and found there a
portion of a 'Pratt's Astral oil' box from New York – the lettering
in full view! We found the native pastor practicing upon a little
American organ! In one of the shops we found a 'Howe' American
sewing machine; and we noticed too an American medical
missionary taking out an eye with American instruments, using
a 'Mason and Hamlin' organ box as an operating table! In one of
the rooms upon the Mission premises there was a stove plainly
marked 'Wm. Cresson & Co., Philadelphia!' And after ten days
of roughing it, we enjoyed, at Homs, a can of American oysters,
from 'Thomas Kennsett & Co.,' Baltimore, Maryland! If we
add that the church and the houses are lighted with American
oil, and that the only evangelical work is that conducted by our
American Mission, the picture will be complete! [*The Foreign
Missionary*, October 1883]

The 'native pastor and his wife' had things from the East as well as
from America, especially Persia and India: the ancient caravan routes
to those distant lands lay close by. Their connection with Beirut also
allowed them access to the European wares arriving in that growing,
bustling port city. Beirut, which had suffered a deep decline since its
importance in ancient times, had just a few decades earlier begun its
reincarnation as a major seaport, and one of the trading and intellectual
centres of the region.

Most important, most wonderful of all, must have been that Mason
and Hamlin organ! In the Protestant community, the Byzantine chants
from the ancient rites of their rejected mother churches were giving
way to hymns in the Western style imported by the Americans. Mostly
from the revivalist tradition, and often based on American or English
folk tunes, these hymns were gradually translated into Arabic and form
today's Protestant hymnal. With the organ, hymns could now be sung
with tolerable accuracy. The congregation's doubtful attempts at the
new and thoroughly unfamiliar strains and rhythms of the Western
style of church song were now rather more organized and controllable
with the organ accompaniment.

In the evenings, the family no doubt gathered round the organ for their own entertainment – song has played a major role in the life of our family, and it came to us in large part from Mother and from Teta. Teta and her siblings passed on to their children a number of old Lebanese mountain folk songs, some of which Mother loved to sing well into her old age.

Though American and European influence, not only in styles but also in commerce, may have penetrated the area, the ancient domestic rituals were too powerful to be easily swept away, and to this day exert an influence. One of the most powerful was the change dictated by the seasons. Towards the end of summer, usually in September, the ritual preparation for the winter began with the collection of food stores, or *munie*. Beans and herbs harvested in the summer were laid out and dried, and then packed away in specially made calico bags and hung up in the pantry. *Burghul* wheat crushed under two revolving pestles was laid out in the sun to dry, and later also hung up in calico bags in the pantry. Olives were packed in brine in large earthenware jars; other vegetables – cucumbers and eggplants, carrots and cabbage – were pickled in large jars. Already in the summer an extra quantity of every seasonal fruit had been boiled into jams – peaches, apricots, cherries; now the quinces and apples were being boiled as well. Some of the abundant supply of figs was dried in the sun, the rest boiled with sugar, anise and mastic, and poured into jars. Some of the grapes were dried to be eaten later as raisins; the rest was made into vinegar. A year's supply of onions and garlic was laid out in the sun to dry out the moisture, then plaited together in bunches and hung up in the kitchen. Large quantities of goat's milk yoghurt were placed in calico bags to let the water drip out, and then the *labneh*, the soft cheese that was left, was rolled up into balls the size of large marbles, placed in jars and covered in olive oil. In my childhood, this was one of Teta's special tasks in our household. When she became too old to do it any more, Mother started buying the goat *labneh* from the market, as I still do.

It is as though some deep social instinct, like that which governs the migration of birds, has been passed down through the generations. Even today, though I live in the age of supermarkets, food-processing factories, freezers and greenhouses, I think of September as the time for stocking up for winter. Though I do little more than buy a large quantity of onions and garlic, and order my year's supply of olives and olive oil, the feeling that September marks an important beginning is still very present. September is also the time for deep cleaning of the house; walls and curtains are washed, cupboards emptied, scrubbed and reorganized. Then the carpets, which have been taken up and stored for the summer, are laid down again and, though the summer heat continues, a feeling of autumn is conveyed.

The family's clothes were also a mixture of styles: by the middle of the nineteenth century, several foreign observers, as well as Arab writers, were already lamenting the fact that native costume was gradually being abandoned and Western styles adopted, especially in Beirut. No doubt the Rev. Youssef sometimes wore the elegant *qombaz*, the full-length tunic-like garment with long sleeves made of striped, shiny cotton. He would also sometimes have worn the *sherwal*, the wide-legged, wide-seated trousers, tight at the ankles and bound by a silk belt at the waist, worn with a long, wide-sleeved shirt and embroidered waistcoat. When he went out or was in contact with Americans or other foreigners, he dressed like them, wearing a Western-style suit with narrow trousers, and cut lapels on the jacket. In the surviving photograph of him taken when he was a man of advanced years, he is wearing such a jacket, along with what seems to be a clerical collar, or perhaps a Western-style collar with a cravat.

He is also wearing a *tarbouche*, or fez: this was obligatory dress for an urban gentleman. Sometimes in the cold days he may instead have worn a *labbade*, a close-fitting hat made of sheep's wool, which had been soaked in water, then beaten into felt and placed, still wet, on a mould shaped like the head that it was to cover in winter. In the cold, wet winters, he would wear an *abaya*, perhaps one made by his father, over his clothes. The *abayas* of the time were made of camel hair, or thick woven cotton, and were usually decorated with embroidery or appliqué work. He would clutch his *abaya* closely over his chest as the wind blew.

A single surviving photograph of my great-grandmother, Leila, taken when she was quite old, shows her wearing a dress with a severe high neck emphasized by a thin white collar, probably made by herself in the kind of work known as *shughl ibri* (needlework).

There are elements of local Syrian costume in the embroidery, which resembles that decorating the waistcoats and jackets of the time. Her eyes are not made up, not heavily lined with kohl, as were those of her contemporaries. She is wearing the short *mandeel*, or scarf, tied around the head and secured with a knot at the top. Her *mandeel* is decorated with an *oya*, the characteristic coloured fringe that was crocheted around the borders. Head coverings, whether for men or women, have always been an essential part of dress in this part of the world.

Leila may have had an entirely personal and private reason for never going without her *mandeel*. Decades later, Mother mentioned her shock when she caught a glimpse of her grandmother's uncovered head and discovered that she was almost bald, and that the red curls peeping out from under the *mandeel* were sewn on to it. Later still, Mother learned that the hair was in fact Leila's and that she had systematically collected it as it fell out and then attached it to her *mandeel*.

Even if in her youth Leila did not wear entirely Western clothes, she may have abandoned the long, flowing, loose gown of native costume for a tighter, more closely fitting version that resembled the Victorian model of the mission ladies with whom she was in touch. This was a time of flux in fashion and style. The tantalizing reference in Dale's letter to the American sewing machine suggests a connection between the acquisition of the machine and wearing the Westernized clothes that went with it.

Under the influence of the puritanical Americans, Leila eschewed the customary display of prosperity, such as the gold bangles of various widths and weights, earrings and necklaces of silver and gold, and headbands, often composed of gold and silver coins, which formed the principal ornaments of Syrian women, rich and poor. Her picture shows her wearing no earrings, but under the severe, high collar is clearly seen a necklace fastened at the throat from which hangs a pendant. I cannot tell whether it is made of silver or gold: both were fashionable at the time.

When she went to the market, she must have worn the *charchaf*, or the white *izar*, the all-enveloping cloak that was then customary. No doubt she also covered her face. Though it is said that women in the exclusively Christian towns of Mount Lebanon did not veil, women in the districts where Christians and Druze lived together wore

a long white *mandeel* or *tarha* placed over their heads and then wound
around their faces. Those Druze women initiated into the mysteries of
their faith always covered their mouths with their *mandeel*. Christian
women of Mount Lebanon continued to wear the *tarha* well into
my time. Though Schweir today is an almost entirely Christian area,
with only one or two Druze villages in the environs, in the nineteenth
century there were a number of Druze towns, including the village of
Mrouj, on the road to Damascus.

In the cities and towns all women covered their faces. Even
foreigners did so when they went out: it was only decent to do so.
In a letter in the December 1876 issue of *The Foreign Missionary*, the
Rev. S. Jessup describes a journey to Hamath, a town near Homs, with
'the ladies, Misses Everett and Jackson', who 'created a great sensation'
in the market because they were not wearing the *charchaf*, which he
calls 'the great sheet'; 'and yet', he continues, 'the ladies were closely
veiled.' The veiling of Christian and Jewish as well as Muslim women
in the towns of Syria, and especially the hinterland, was common well
into the twentieth century. Though there were many regional and class
differences, Muslims, Christians and Jews dressed, ate and practised
courtesies in much the same way.

Costume had already become an ideological question in Leila's
time: 'the veil' is mentioned by almost all the travellers who wrote
about their journeys to the area. Most of the time it is discussed as
a strange, otherworldly costume and often comes to signify the
backwardness of the area. In Egypt, this perceived backwardness served
the imperialist argument well: the people were to be rescued from their
own civilization by an enlightened West! The same was true in historic
Syria: the American missionaries were as happy as the British to rescue
'the natives' from their own culture.

Many travellers, however, also comment on the beauty and colour
of the local costume and lament its decline. A French Jesuit priest, Père
Badour, who travelled through the area in 1849, writes with admiration
of the democratic, or at least equalizing, nature of the *charchaf* or *izar*;
when wearing it, the wife of a prince or governor was indistinguishable
from that of the simple artisan. He also especially admires the Syrian
women's long, loose-fitting dress and notes its advantages over its
European counterpart, with its adaptability to the climate and its

freedom from what he calls '*l'usage meurtrière*' of stays, corsets and hooks which so tormented European women.

At some point Leila stopped covering her face. None of her grandchildren remembers her otherwise. When she stopped, and why, is not recorded. The public unveiling of prominent upper-class Muslim women in the 1920s has been much discussed, but the quiet transformation that took place earlier is totally neglected or taken for granted, perhaps even forgotten. Nor are the ordinary women, like my great-grandmother and her daughters, credited with earth-shaking social actions.

And yet on this apparently unimportant question: what did she wear? hangs the interpretation of a culture, a history, a civilization. It seems to me, having spent many years thinking about this issue, that it was in the natural evolution of social life that women like Leila Badr quite simply stopped covering their faces. Who knows why? Perhaps she just found it an encumbrance. Perhaps she was in a hurry one morning and could not find the pins needed to keep it in place, and had to rush out anyway, and then discovered it was nicer without it. And when it did not cause a scandal, and thus was apparently acceptable, she did it again and again. Perhaps she was more comfortable, perhaps she stopped wearing it gradually, just as my generation gave up the wearing of girdles and corsets. Perhaps a new informality, like that which occurred in the 1960s, took place. No one, as far as I know, has paid as much attention to masculine costume in this regard and therefore no general trends have been discovered, or even sought.

This is clearly not the place to discuss 'the veil': suffice it to say that the line between national costume and religious habit has become blurred, and little intelligent thought is being addressed to it. The view of Western dress as a symbol of progress, openness, liberal social thought and female emancipation has, most unreasonably and without analysis or class and historical awareness, been adopted by many people, as much in the Arab world as outside it. In reaction, there has been a retrenchment into what is widely and ahistorically regarded as purely religious dress: thousands of young women are adopting this as a 'statement' (almost always regarded as one of religious commitment), without any regard to social or historical imperatives. If the same kind of arguments were applied to the demise of the crinoline, or the return of shoulder pads, for instance, the attempt at rationalizing outside a social context would soon be given up. Here it has become inextricably entangled with both imperial and anti-imperial arguments.

Today, as our area experiences a massive reaction against the West because of its imperial past and its support of Israel, many women have adopted what they call 'Islamic costume' as a way of dissociating themselves from Western ways and values. Donning 'the veil' today is often a political statement, and many young women, claiming their individual right to do so, are as zealous in this regard as their mothers or grandmothers were in removing it. To the degree that both these actions reflect a desire to explicitly express an opinion, and take a stand, both are equally 'modern'. Women in Algeria deliberately veiled themselves during the war of independence as a sign of protest against the French; Iranian women did the same in demonstrations against the Shah and his regime. In both cases, the costume signified revolutionary attitudes, and the direct participation of women in political action. Many other young women, however, and sometimes little girls, are coerced into donning this particular costume, either by political decree or by social pressure, often against their wills, or at least without their voluntary decision. Rarely, in the vehement discussions on 'the veil', is this crucially important distinction made.

Leila's daughter, my grandmother Munira, did not – proudly and self-consciously did not – share the custom of covering herself with the *habara*, the Galilean version of the *izar*, a black cloak worn over the head and reaching the ankles, nor did she veil herself as was still customary among Christian women in Nazareth where she lived. By then, costume had taken on a new meaning, and she used to take pride in her distinction from her fellow Nazarenes. In their memoirs all three of her children comment on her costume, and regard her not wearing the *habara* as a clear sign of her modernity. Yet, until the day she died, Teta never went out without covering her head. To do so would have been to her the height of indecency. Mother apparently never even thought about what kind of clothes she should wear; it was not a question I ever heard her raise. For her, the transformation had been completed long ago and there was no longer any alternative to Western dress.

The strong aversion Teta always displayed to bare feet, an aversion rather like a reverse or negative fetish, makes me think that in her parents' household they had worked at giving up the Syrian habit of removing their shoes at the door. Teta's disgust at bare feet could only have come from a lesson most emphatically taught and learned. Unlike Westerners, Syrians never wore shoes indoors. They left their street shoes at the door of churches, mosques and homes. Indoors, they wore *babouge* (cloth slippers), sometimes embroidered and embellished with ribbons, or they walked in their bare feet, depending on their class and status. On stepping outdoors, men would don leather boots or shoes with pointed, upturned toes. Middle- and upper-class women gradually started to wear the same kind of shoes as the men, though the poorest women and those in the villages went barefoot. Brides, or members of the upper class, wore *qubqabs* (wooden platform sandals with a leather strap) as high as 15 centimetres; they were elaborately decorated, with mother-of-pearl inlaid into the carved patterns. A flat-heeled, basic, wooden *qubqab* was always used in the *hamam,* and even in my day, my sisters and I each had a pair.

A charming image is created by Père Badour as he notes the contrast between the noisy progress of a woman wearing her wooden *qubqabs* and clattering down the street over cobblestones and pebbles, the sequins and gold pieces in her headdress tinkling all the while, the gold and silver bangles on her wrists and ankles adding to the clatter, and the ensuing silence of her movement when she enters her house, and treads on the mats and carpets of the interiors with her feet bare or clad only in the soft *babouge.*

Somehow, as I hear the other women wending their noisy way down the street, their *qubqabs* banging against the cobblestones, the gold pieces tinkling in their hairdos and their bangles jingling away on their wrists, I know, utterly and absolutely, though she never told me, that Teta's mother never clattered down a street like that. The aura of tranquility that so characterized Teta suggests a quieter milieu than one consistent with these descriptions.

And yet, no sooner have I written this than, suddenly, I hear the sound of Teta's slippers slapping against her feet as, an old, bent, frail woman, she bustles about the house – *click-clack, click-clack.*

CHAPTER II

A Nineteenth-Century Syrian Schoolgirl

In the late 1880s, when Teta was nine years old, the family faced a major change in its destiny. The church in Beirut, founded by the American mission, was at last to have a 'native' pastor, and the 'native' congregation had elected Youssef Badr to the post. For more than a year he had been attending the meetings of the elders of the church, which was still led by the Rev. Jessup, and participating in the final discussions leading up to this important moment. Now the whole family was to move to Beirut.

In 1890 Youssef Badr was installed as the first Arab pastor of the National Evangelical Church of Beirut, and the family settled into the parish house that stood by the church. The church itself had been constructed by the Syria Mission in 1865. It was a large, ivy-covered, pseudo-Gothic structure with a red terracotta roof, built in the same style that would later dominate the campus of the Syrian Protestant College three or four kilometres to the west. Across the street from the church stood the Ottoman *serail,* the seat of government. Decades later, Teta used to say proudly that whenever her father, who was tall and bore himself with regal dignity, walked by the *serail,* the soldiers on guard would salute him, mistaking the gentle pastor of the nearby church for the military governor of the city.

In Beirut, Teta embarked on the most significant schooling of her life. Having come from Homs and the mission school there with a good knowledge of Arabic, some English, and a general and keen knowledge of the Bible, she entered, with her sisters, the British evangelical school system. It was at the British Syrian Training College that Teta accomplished her metamorphosis from an ordinary young girl to that archetypal figure in modern Arab cultural history, the Syrian Christian female schoolteacher. The powerful and transforming influence of these women was to be felt not only in the immediate region, in historic Syria, and the countries that are today Palestine, Israel, Jordan, Syria and Lebanon, but as far away as Iraq and Egypt. Under their tutelage, and that of other teachers trained in the many foreign schools mushrooming throughout the area in those days, students were taught new languages and a new way of life, and were trained in an educational style more in harmony with Western ways than with Ottoman. Out of the old society new paths were being carved which were to lead to a cultural schism between these students and those who took a different road to modernity.

At the British Syrian Training College, my grandmother, a daughter of the people, from one of the most ancient of civilizations, bearer of a complex and long history, met with Englishwomen bringing with them from their own complex background an altogether alien notion of reality and history. It was the interaction between these Englishwomen and girls like my grandmother that caused a deceptively quiet but enormously important cultural upheaval, from which many of my mother's and then my generation of middle-class, urban women emerged. Teta's rural origins were by now almost forgotten, and by the time she entered this English school, she firmly belonged to the urban middle class. Gradually she was transformed from a provincial girl from the hinterland to a young woman from the increasingly sophisticated port city of Beirut, with its ancient Mediterranean cultural inheritance and its openness to the world.

When I worked on this period of Teta's life, I could not help being

drawn to the story of the Englishwomen who taught her as I was to
Teta's. As I reconstituted her life, I had also to come to terms with the
story of the English missionary ladies who created the British Syrian
Schools, and especially the Training College. The story of the one is
not complete without the story of the other.

The British Syrian Schools were founded in 1860 by Mrs Elizabeth
Bowen-Thompson, *née* Lloyd. In her biography of Elizabeth, her sister,
Suzette Smith, writes that they came from a genteel background, with
social connections in the colonies. She apologizes for writing without
access to sources, as the family papers were burned in a fire 'that
consumed our brother's mansion at East Coombe'. Their background
was British: they were taught about their ancestry in Lloyd's *History of
Wales*, and there is reference to 'our father's Highland grandmother'
as well as to their grandfather, General Lloyd. Henry Salt, the British
consul in Egypt, was their father's cousin. The family motto was 'Dare
and Persevere,' which was later adopted as the school motto.

Suzette Smith says her sister was much given to prayers of
intercession as a child, and had a great interest in and love of
needlework. As one might expect, the family read the English classics
together, including Goldsmith, Pope, Grey and Milton. The father,
however, would not permit his children to read novels until they were
sixteen, and Mrs Smith says that the first novel they read was 'the
much-coveted' *Ivanhoe*.

Early on in her life, recounts Mrs Smith, Elizabeth began to
manifest signs of her missionary vocation. As a girl she was moved
by a desire to improve the lot of the slaves in British colonial West
Indies. Later she became interested in the Jewish people and Jerusalem,
where she expected the Second Coming to take place, and this focused
her interest on Syria. She married Dr James Bowen-Thompson, who
had founded the British Syria Hospital in Damascus and had run
it from 1843 to 1848. After a few years of married life in London,
the couple moved to Suweidiah, near Antioch, where Dr Thompson
owned some property. It was here that her own missionary inclinations
began to blossom.

In around 1853, writes Mrs Smith, Elizabeth began to teach the
Bible to local women in her house. or, as her sister glowingly puts it,

she 'began her Bible work in Bible lands'. In her letters, she records that women also came to her to learn sewing and needlework, and she went to their houses for this purpose as well. She also taught them Arabic and Armenian: many of the people in the Antioch area were Armenians. She herself had been in the region for only a few months and had had no previous experience of either language. How she managed to convince herself and others that she was qualified to teach these languages I cannot imagine – perhaps it was only a posthumous and entirely apocryphal claim made on her behalf.

Mrs Smith says of her sister's time in Suweidiah: 'Here Elizabeth was initiated into the language and manners of the East; and here her full heart yearned over the darkness and degradation of women.' When the Crimean war began, Dr Thompson felt it incumbent upon himself, as a physician familiar with the diseases of the region, to attend the British troops on the battlefield, but almost as soon as he and his wife arrived at Balaclava, he fell ill, and died a month later. Broken-hearted, Elizabeth returned to England, where her inclination to social work found a new outlet with the Indian revolt of 1857. Her work with the widows and orphans of British soldiers was recognized and patronized by Queen Victoria.

In the meantime, she had become involved with the Bible and Domestic Mission, an offshoot of the Bible Mission Society. She and some likeminded women formed a group known as the 'Bible Women', whose mission was to send women into the slums to sell Bibles to the poor, thus not only evangelizing, but at the same time teaching the poor to redeem themselves by placing, at some sacrifice, monetary value on their renewed faith. Though some of the women were the wives or sisters of clergymen, the group fiercely defended itself from the authority of the clergy. Indeed, in some of their letters they sound quite adamantly anti-clerical. They published regular financial reports, which showed their fund-raising and accounting capabilities, thus declaring their well-deserved independence. This was a feminine – one might almost call it feminist – space carved out by women in a corner of the patriarchal territory of the church.

The 1860 sectarian war in Mount Lebanon was widely reported in Europe, and the heavily publicized plight of the Christian refugees from the mountain areas led to the creation of relief agencies specifically concerned with Syria. Mrs Bowen-Thompson joined in these efforts, and turned her attention to the evangelical social work for which her previous experience in the area seemed to have divinely prepared her. Her sister puts it melodramatically: 'God had work for her in Syria, and she cried out in obedience ... "Here I am; send me!"' She arrived in Beirut in October 1860 with the Syrian Temporal Relief Fund and, like others before her, seems to have been quickly taught an unforgettable lesson.

Her original intention had been to bring to 'the natives', and especially the women and orphans among them, 'the only true remedy', which was of course 'the consolations of the Gospel'. She soon learned that her remedy was not welcome and she 'was seriously advised to return to Europe by the next steamer'. Precisely who it was who thus advised – or threatened – her is not made clear. She stayed on, however, under the protection of Lord Dufferin, the British member of the international commission sent to Beirut to look into the events of 1860. Lord Dufferin, who later became viceroy of India, had received her well from the beginning of her adventure.

Eventually Mrs Bowen-Thompson took a house, in which she began a small mission. Refugee widows, mostly from Hasbaya, came to her door and were given paid work, especially needlework. Later, she started a laundry that only employed women. This became a particularly successful venture when the ships of the British navy began to send their linens whenever they were in port. Her support group in London named itself the 'Ladies' Association for the Moral and Religious Improvement of Syrian Females'. All the officers and members of the group, with the exception of the honorary treasurer, were women, and many of them were titled. Among these female supporters were her three sisters, Suzette Smith, Augusta Mentor Mott and Sophia Lloyd, and the head of the Bible Women group, Ellen Ranyard, to whom many of Elizabeth's letters home were addressed.

Soon after her arrival in Beirut, Elizabeth Bowen-Thompson met a young Damascene, Selim Kassab, who, much later on, was to be Teta's Arabic teacher. Precisely what role he played in the creation of the educational project has never, to my knowledge, been investigated by scholars, whose work always seems to be focused on the missionaries and not their local counterparts. What became clear to me was that he was important to the eventual success of the schools. He became not only the Arabic teacher, and the conductor of the Arabic church services in the schools, but, perhaps more importantly, Mrs Bowen-Thompson's link to the community as translator and interpreter.

Selim Kassab passed on to her the many requests from the community for her to open schools. Mrs Smith's biography and the letters of Mrs Bowen-Thompson are peppered with requests for such schools. Once again it is clear that the impetus for the opening of the schools came from the local people, rather than from the missionaries. Thus began the British Syrian Schools, most of which were, in the beginning at least, designed for the poor, to whom rudimentary lessons in reading and writing were offered.

When upper-class families, eager for their daughters to learn English, started to approach Mrs Bowen-Thompson, the schools were able to become self-supporting. In 1866 there was a flurry of new schools and activities for the 'education of the highest ladies in the land, Druze and Christian, Jew and Mohameddan', including the founding in Beirut of a Normal Training School for girls. It was this training school that Teta would later attend, and which led to her rightful claim of having been 'highly educated'. There was, indeed, in her day no higher institution of learning for a Syrian woman. The success of the venture is probably linked to the fact that it was meant for 'the highest ladies in the land'.

It is surely not by accident that the founding of this new training school coincided with the founding of the Syrian Protestant College. Though at the time the SPC did not take women students – nor indeed was it to do so for more than half a century – it is possible that 'the highest ladies in the land' were already aiming at this distant goal, and that Selim Kassab and Mrs Bowen-Thompson were inspired by it to raise the standards of their schools. It was no doubt necessary to raise the quality of the mission schools whose students would feed into the SPC: the Training College was to remain the main source of teachers for the Protestant mission schools until the middle of the twentieth century.

A mere nine years after her first arrival in Beirut, Mrs Bowen-Thompson took a trip home and died at the house of her sister and biographer, Suzette Smith, at Blackheath College. By then the schools were playing a vital role among the missionary institutions in Syria in their function of cultural transformation. Another sister, Augusta Mentor Mott, who with her husband and yet another sister, Sophia Lloyd, had joined Elizabeth in Lebanon, continued the work. After Mrs Bowen-Thompson's death in 1869, the schools became known in some mission papers as 'Mrs Mott's schools'.

Mrs Bowen-Thompson seems to have been a woman of boundless energy and initiative, truly devoted to her students. In her letters there is less evidence of the kind of contempt for local culture and the Ottomans that mars the letters and utterances of other missionaries, including her sister. Perhaps this was because she was a woman in an extremely patriarchal circle, and had had to struggle with the patriarchal authorities in order to put her own stamp on her work. (Both the mission establishment and the European teaching profession were in those days ferociously patriarchal in outlook.) Thus she felt more sympathy with her students than with her colleagues. Her work with the Bible Women in England had already given her some experience in resisting male authoritarianism. It is interesting to note in contrast that when Mrs Mott took over, her husband was very much involved with the work, especially its financial supervision.

Mrs Bowen-Thompson's attitude towards her students was inevitably patronizing, however, and there is no doubt that she loyally and naturally identified with the efforts of the British empire, and the Protestant culture which, together with the English language, was one of the weapons against its rival in imperial ambition, Catholic France. In 1862 Mrs Bowen-Thompson's school warranted a visit from the Prince of Wales. This colourful event, which says as much about East–West relations at the time as it does about her, her intentions and the nature of the school, is charmingly and rather breathlessly recounted by Mrs Bowen-Thompson herself in a letter home dated 23 May 1862. The school was agog with excitement when the royal procession passed by:

> Flying horsemen passed, and soon the band announced his approach. Next came the mounted guard with their lances, and then the Prince, accompanied by his suite, the Pashas, and other dignitaries, followed by a regiment of cavalry.

As soon as they reached the garden wall, we all struck up 'God Save the Queen'. The women and children had learnt the tune to Arabic words. It evidently took the Prince by surprise. He bowed very graciously, and, as he looked up at the long rows of little children, inquired what place it was. All had a capital view, and went home delighted.

The next day she received a message that the Prince would visit the school:

I received the Prince at the covered archway, under the garden entrance. The children were ranged under the trees along the avenue.

The Prince said it gave him much pleasure to make this visit. He asked if all these children belonged to our schools, looking so pleased at the little things as he passed. When he reached the steps, he made a pause, and looked at the group, and now with one voice they all exclaimed in English, 'God save the Queen,' 'Long live the Queen.' The Prince then asked me to lead the way into the schools ...

The Prince then said he should like them to read a page in Arabic. They read the third of St John, in alternate verses, and he remarked that they read very fluently. They next read English, upon which the Prince inquired whether they understood what they read, or was it merely by rote? and we could assure him they really did understand. The needlework was next inspected ...

He took some of their work [in the women's school] in his hand, and asked why they did not rather do the work of the country than English work. I said there was little demand for any native work, and that our object was to teach them such work as would enable them to earn their bread ...

I told His Royal Highness that many had learnt not only to read in this school, but also to value the Bible, and to know the power of prayer. It was delightful to hear the Prince speak so kindly and courteously. The schools then sang:

Around the throne of God on high,
Thousands of children stand.

After a ceremonial farewell, and the clear expression of royal satisfaction and pleasure at the work of the school, the Prince departed. 'Next day His Royal Highness sent a gift of twenty-five Napoleons, and also a large order for gold embroidery.'

A curious detail emerges from this account of the prince's visit: as Mrs Bowen-Thompson proudly shows off her students' knowledge of English culture to him, he seems on the contrary more interested in their knowledge of Arab culture. When she makes the girls show off their knowledge of English by making them read from the Bible, he asks to hear them read in Arabic instead. When she shows off their efforts at English embroidery, he asks why they do not practise their own traditional craft. She does not comment on his strange resistance to her efforts – but perhaps it is only because I am a child of the post-colonial era that I see more significance in his remarks than is warranted.

Five years later, the Prince of Wales' visit yielded some important results. The Ottoman sultan, on a visit to London, was pressured by the Prince to issue a *firman*, or writ, granting the schools official permission to carry on their work. Thus was the school formally established and its presence legitimized, and it survives to this day, though in a different form.

The old building that housed the school Teta attended still stands in the heart of Beirut, near the '*batrakiyya*', the seat of the patriarchate and principal Beirut school of the Greek Catholic Church. Though today the old mission school has become Hariri High School II, it is still popularly known as *madrasset al-ingliz* (the School of the English). Though *madrasset al-ingliz* is by no means a magnificent building, it is a pleasing one: a modest two-storey house with a slanted roof with red terracotta tiles, attached to what seems to be an older and smaller building similarly constructed. A plain wooden verandah adorns the front of the house: when I first looked at it, for the purposes of this book, I imagined my grandmother as a young girl, her long hair in plaits, wearing a Victorian pinafore and pacing that balcony as she dutifully memorized her lessons for the day.

Over the entrance to the old building is an inscription:

In Memory of
Mrs E. Bowen-Thompson
Founder of the British Syrian School
at Beyrout, Damascus and the Lebanon,
Who came in 1860 in the hour of their deepest affliction
to Bring the Consolation of the Gospel
to the Widows and Orphans of Syria,
and, in the midst of her noble mission
entered her Heavenly rest,
November 14, 1869.

A single old book of records has survived from Teta's time at the school. It is enormous, a kind of massive ledger book, its yellowed pages marked with red vertical lines and faded black horizontal ones, forming little squares for the figures. On the fragile leather binding, which seems originally to have been a dark green with an elaborate design, but is now a nondescript antique brownish colour, is embossed in faded gold letters 'Examination Marks'.

When I first held this marvel, this window into the past, I had no idea what to expect, but I soon discovered that the records covered curricula, the names of students, and the marks they received in the years 1893 to 1912. At first, mysteries and puzzles presented themselves on every page. What, I wondered, did they study in 'Geography'? In what language did they do 'Arithmetic' and what did they learn in it? What was 'Engammon'? What were 'Object Lessons'? What on earth was 'Cutting Out', one of the most persistent subjects?

I set to work to answer these intriguing questions, but first I allowed myself to savour the tone and mood of the book, enjoying the wonderful informality and inconsistency in the records from those long-ago days before the remorseless need for accuracy of modern record-keeping. Teta's family name, for instance, is written variously as Budder, Bedder, Budr and Bedr. In 1903, following the student list of Class VI, this wonderful and totally inexplicable line appears: 'Dolls and Whips and Monkey Sticks'! I made no effort to solve this puzzle, merely enjoying the luxury of allowing the past to keep some of its secrets.

This marvellous book was a map to the lost world of nineteenth-century mission schools, to my grandmother's early life, and to the creation of at least one aspect of Beirut's social fabric as the city grew into a major centre of intellectual life in the Arab East. And at last I was able to answer some of the questions it had raised, and to solve some of the mysteries I had puzzled over.

In 1893, when the record book begins, Teta was thirteen and in the most senior class, Class I; as school practice dictated, she remained in it until 1896. She was also enrolled in the teacher training class. She was by now a boarder: that same year her father resigned as pastor of the Beirut church, and the mission sent him first to Tyre and then to Marjeyoun, in what is today south Lebanon. At the same time, her sister Nabiha, all of seven years old in 1893, was in Class II, the next to most senior class in the school. Their sister Najla appears later on in the registry. Emelia had been sent to the American School for Girls, or had been to the British school before this time. Nabiha's name disappears after 1893. Perhaps her parents decided she was too young for boarding school and took her with them to Tyre.

There were eighteen girls in Teta's class, a total of eighty-four in the preparatory school. Most of her fellow students were Christians, the majority of them Protestants, who belonged to Beirut's growing middle and professional class. Here and there a Druze or Muslim name appears, and a few Jewish names as well: the French Jewish mission, the Alliance Israélite Universelle, had begun its operations in Beirut in 1860 and most Jews sent their children to its schools. Only a pair of Sursocks and a single Trad, members of the wealthy Greek Orthodox trading families that dominated commerce with Europe in nineteenth-century Beirut, and that Mrs Bowen-Thompson refers to as 'the Greek aristocracy', appear in the record. There were only two foreign girls at the school in Teta's time, but a few distinctly regional names suggest that in addition, some girls attended from this or that mountain region.

Two girls whose names leapt up at me from the record were Marie Kassab, daughter of Selim Kassab, later to become famous as the founder of one of the most important national girls' schools in Lebanon, *kuliyat al-banat al-ahliah* (Ahlia Girls' College), and her cousin Adele, who succeeded her as principal. Eventually the Training College was to have a direct influence further afield: the famous Jerusalem Girls' College was also a descendant of this English mission school.

Teachers sometimes wrote in the record book about the progress of their students' work. From this it becomes clear that the classes were composed of students of different ages and levels of competency, who worked at their own pace. Thus, for example, an entry for 1901 sums up the accomplishments of Class VI: 'Arithmetic: 5 know multiplication tables, 5 know subtraction, the rest addition.'

It seems to have been quite common for girls to come to school for only one year, or to leave it and then come back some time later, or, one way or the other, to be irregular in attendance. School administrators in the American system complained of this irregularity and the unexpected numbers who might turn up at any time at the schools. Several sets of sisters started out in the same class; it seems to have been fairly common for an older sister to accompany younger siblings to school. My husband's great-aunt Esther, who was in her nineties when I first met her in 1961, told me that she received her education when she, the eldest daughter in a large family, was required to accompany her youngest brother to school as part of her child-minding duties. Perhaps some older girls, freed of household responsibilities as their younger siblings grew up, were released by sympathetic mothers and came to join younger sisters in the same class, thus acquiring the education of which they had earlier been deprived.

After the final examinations of 1894, Teta was awarded the prize for Scripture. The nature of the prizes provides an ever-changing record of the attitudes towards the girls and their function. For instance, in 1896 when Rosa Mokudsie won the Scripture and Head Girl's Prize, it was, predictably, an Arabic Bible, 'best kind'. Other girls won aprons and scissors for their accomplishments in Cutting Out and Housework, and Nazira Salibi won a prize for Good Conduct. Pencil boxes, work boxes and bags were frequent prizes.

Books were always given as Scripture prizes, including especially the *Spiritual Guide for Students* (*al-MershedIttallabeen*) [*sic*] as well as *The Daily Light*, *Echoes of Bible History*, *Perseverance under Difficulties* and various commentaries on the books of the New Testament. Later on, especially after the turn of the century, more and more secular prizes appear, although of course the Bibles, hymn books, *Daily Lights* and other devotional texts continue to be awarded, as do the pen boxes, scissors and work baskets of yore. *The Swiss Family Robinson* and *Robinson Crusoe* are frequently cited as prizes after 1905. They may have been in Arabic: both these books had been translated and published by the American Press at around this time and were very popular with schoolchildren.

In 1909 and 1910, no doubt reflecting the activities of the feminists in England, such titles as *Women Who Have Worked and Won*, *Four Noble Women*, *Heroines of History and Travel*, *Noble Deeds of the World's Heroines* and *Florence Nightingale* add an altogether new flavour to the prize list. At this point cash prizes were also being offered.

In 1896 Teta's name appears on a list of teachers as 'M. Moneerah Badr', her subject being Arabic. Elsewhere she is listed as 'Assistant History'. When I first saw it, I took the 'M.' that appeared in front of all the Arab teachers' names, including Selim Kassab's, to signify 'Miss' or 'Mr', but I soon realized my mistake. The Arab teachers were all addressed as *Mualim* or *Mualmie* (teacher), usually followed by their first name alone. The English teachers, on the other hand, were addressed as 'Miss' followed by their surname. Thus Teta was known as 'Mualmie Moneerah', and Selim Kassab as 'Mualim Selim', while the English teachers were called 'Miss Cave', 'Miss Harding', 'Miss Thompson' and so on. Between the title *Mualmie* and the title *Miss* lay an unbridgeable gulf that separated the 'natives' from their English counterparts.

The same custom of differentiated address applied in the American mission schools. Teta's sister Emelia rebelled against this differentiation when she taught at the American School for Girls in Beirut. Considering herself to be as educated and as worthy as her American counterparts, she protested at the discriminatory designations and demanded to be addressed as 'Miss Badr'. Her demand was, predictably, rejected. She resigned in a huff and went off to Egypt, where she later achieved fame with several generations of students as 'Miss Badr'.

The subjects that Teta studied in Class I A in 1893 were Old Testament, New Testament, Reading, Writing, Arithmetic, Grammar, History and Composition. All these were apparently taught in Arabic, for, after a short space, marks appear for English Reading, Writing, Grammar and Composition. Geography and Elementary Science are listed, though not everyone seems to have taken these subjects. In later years, other science courses appear in the record, though with some inconsistency; these were Astronomy, Physics and, most frequently, Botany and Physiology. Although there were no marks for Order, Conduct, Needlework or Housework, there were prizes for each of these subjects, as there were for Old Testament, New Testament, Arabic Writing, Arithmetic and Geography.

Teta earned high marks in all these subjects. However, in the Teaching Class of 1893, which was composed of the same girls as Class I A, her marks were not nearly so high. How could they have been, I asked myself, with so much to study, and she only thirteen! The subjects in the teaching class were Criticism Lessons, Singing Drill, Drill, Plain Needlework, Fancy Needlework and Cutting Out. In addition, the students were graded on the ubiquitous Order and Conduct. Marks were given for 'Engannon', or special education for the blind: 'Engannon', I had discovered, was the site of a small school for the blind. It later became the mission's special education headquarters and the blind school, as well as the place where women's meetings were held. What a discovery! My grandmother was being trained in special education in 1893 when she was thirteen, and all along I thought I was the modern one!

In 1895, when Teta was fifteen, her name appears, along with those of four other girls in Class I under the heading 'Monitresses'. Her subjects when a monitress were, in addition to the usual Reading, Writing, Dictation and Composition under the English subjects, English Recitation, Questions, Conversation and Translation. The monitresses seem to have been exempted from Needlework, perhaps because they had already exhausted that subject, though marks appear for them under the inevitable Housework, Conduct and Order.

What precisely was taught in the various classes? In 1906 a scrupulous record appears. Physiology, which was taught in English, included the following: 'Joints, Muscles, Nerves, Skin, Heart and Circulation of the Blood'. In 1908, 'Science' was Geology and included 'Water and Air; Glaciers and Rivers; Structure of the Earth; Kinds of Rocks; Earth Movements'. In 'Drawing', students did 'simple Nature Forms, flowers and leaves (as usual)' and 'Maps' – Palestine and North and South America.

A couple of lists of marks for 'Housework' appear suddenly in 1901. A column listing the tasks involved reads as follows: Visitor's room, Miss Thompson's room, Prayer Hall, Dormitory I, Ladies' Table, Miss Cave's room, Magazine and Hall. The lists go on: Miss Benson's room, Dining Hall, Lavatories, Kitchen, and even Garden, Arcade, Lodge and so on. Clearly the English teachers had their own rooms, which were looked after by their students. There were probably servants to assist in the work, but it seems the girls were in charge. The female 'native' teachers must have lived in the dormitories with the other girls, as there is no note of any other rooms. This is not a surprising arrangement, judging from Teta's experience, as the 'native' teachers rose from the ranks of the students and were, in any case, around the same age.

Tatting, Knitting Stocking, Crochet, Plain Needlework, Gold Work and Embroidery were demanded of students in 1896 as part of their Needlework class. Cutting Out was a subject whose title had intrigued as well as puzzled me when I first encountered it: in 1896 students cut out patterns for Bodices, Chemises, Drawers, Various Dresses, Kumbayes [*sic*], Night Dresses, Shirts and Moslem Dresses. What a 'Moslem Dress' meant I cannot be sure, but can only surmise that it must have meant Beiruti costume, the long loose-fitting gown, or the covering mantle, the *millayah* or *izar*. The use of the appellation 'Moslem Dress', with the dangerous implication of new and artificial divisions between sects, shows the genesis of today's utterly confusing misunderstandings regarding clothes.

A long list of the tasks accomplished in Needlework appears in 1901:

Standard I did:
Thimble Drill
Needle Drill
Position
    a. Work holding
    b. Needle holding
    c. Making stitch
Knitting pin drill
Hemming
Hem folding

Seaming
Knitting Cast On
Knitting Chain Edge
Knitting Cast Off.

Standard II did:
Repeat above with:
Knitting Purling
Sew and Fell
Articles: Cuffs
            Baby's shirt
            Baby's drawers
Crochet.

Standard III did:
Darning a hole
Stitching\Herring bone
Sewing on Tapes
Sewing on Buttons
Fix hems over seams
Pleating
Knitting
Cast on 30 loops
Knit with 4 pins
Shrill ibry [*sic*]
Embroidery
Draw thread.

The list goes on and on, page after page: 'Putting into band, Placquet hole in Petticoat, decrease leg of stocking, Cocoon Work, Rum and Fell Seam, Coral and Feather stitch, Heel & Toe, A Gusset, Whipping and Sewing on Frills, Loops and Eyelet holes, Gold and Silk Work, Aghrabanie [*sic*], Penwipers, Swiss Darn, Grafting, Mantua Maker's Seam, Counter Hem Seam, Double French, Knotting, Sitt Melakie ...'

As I made my way through the lists, I was enthralled, not only by the intensity of the labour involved, nor even by the picture that struck at my heart of Teta, when old and frail, endlessly whiling away the hours bent over her needlework. For if I were to choose one childhood memory above all others of Teta that expresses her essence, it would be of her forever crocheting her little bags, pillow covers, doilies and antimacassars, stitching her embroidery or mending, while the world around us was falling into a shambles and she powerless to do anything about it.

What fascinated me most of all in the lists was the lack of any exterior reality. The real world, the outside world of politics, empire, conflict, resistance, social and economic transformation, was banished from this inner, segregated, rarefied atmosphere inhabited exclusively by highly educated girls. Women's place in life as taught to Teta lay in an alternative, densely constructed and organized space entirely separate from the world. Learning, however elaborate and sophisticated, was not meant to be a liberating path to the outside world, nor a means by which women were to achieve equality with men, but a refinement, an elevation, a kind of exquisite adornment, a way to make them better wives and mothers, and thus only indirectly affect society.

Because of her character, her gentleness, her will to please, Teta seems to have accepted this aspect of the mission teaching. Family and domestic life for her was never to become an enforced state from which she yearned to break out, but the summit of female vocation, an absorbing and demanding craft which had to be painstakingly taught and learned. Eventually Teta perfected this craft, and then she passed it on to her daughter, and she to me. It filled up her life, and, so much energy did she put into it, that it overflowed out of her and her house, to the community around her. Her accomplishments, for which she was to be so admired, though entirely individual and personal in nature, were viewed by herself and everyone else, it seems, as part of an enhanced social fabric, and especially of the modern family, of which she herself was the highest expression and greatest exemplar.

Teta was to suffer terribly because of this attitude. Victorian domesticity was an aspect of the social and economic structure of which it was an integral part: in Palestine, where she was to establish her own family, it was an alien notion, irrelevant to the surrounding social, economic and political realities. From the time of her widowhood, and especially of her withdrawal from the world to which she had been connected – to which indeed she had deliberately connected herself, eschewing all other forms of connection – through her husband and his work, she gradually became redundant. When her husband died and her children were scattered by the events in Palestine, she lost her hard-won place in the world and became increasingly alienated from it.

Throughout the missionary accounts there is a picture drawn of what Mrs Smith calls 'the darkness and degradation of women' in this part of the world, Islam sharing the blame with the 'decadent' ancient Eastern Christian sects. As I read this excessive and self-righteous rhetoric, with its failure to understand the nuances of class and region, two things sprang to my mind. First, there is a total ignorance of local culture and history reflected in these words. The condition of Syrian women, whether Christian, Muslim or Jewish, varied widely, as it did elsewhere, from class to class, and from rural to urban areas. Some upper-class women were indeed literate, and trained in the reading of the Quran and its associated sciences: a few of them were learned. There was even a nascent women's movement as early as the mid-nineteenth century, and Muslim women have a long and honourable place in their own history. Demonstrations by women in the streets of Syrian cities are recorded in the 1820s.

The second thing that kept coming to my mind was the situation of English and American women at the time. Until the Married Women's Property Act of 1870, any money or property earned by an English woman automatically became that of her husband, and it was not until 1882 that women were allowed to keep the property they owned before marriage. By contrast, Muslim women kept control over their own property and managed their own finances. (I am not aware of much research done on Christian women in the area.) The appalling condition of the masses of poor women in London and other urban centres, not to mention the peasants, is well documented, and was compounded by vice and sexual depravity of the worst sort. As for the United States, though the laws governing a married woman's property were reformed in the 1830s, conditions for poor women were not better than those of their sisters in England. One only has to think of the sweat shops and factories of the growing industrial cities; the terrors of the European expansion and the Indian wars, for the women on both sides; and the astounding cruelty of slavery, which flourished at the same time as the mission activities in the Near East were in full swing.

Some, at least, of those foreigners who made damning accusations of Arab, and especially Islamic, culture in their treatment of women, claiming to be their saviours, were themselves thoroughly anti-feminist at home, and had only imperial motives for the position on women they held abroad. The most notable, or at least well studied, of these was Lord Cromer, governor of Egypt, well known for his antipathy as much for English feminism as for Islam.

There is still no reliable and consistent canon of historical writing on Arab women's history that accurately, and without prejudice, delineates the condition of women before the major dose of Westernization entered and distorted the picture – and after it, for that matter. Unfortunately, such nineteenth-century women writers as Aysha Taymoor and Zeinab Fawwaz, with their *hijabs*, their literary salons, their discussions, their adventures and their interactions with their male counterparts, are little known today, and seldom referred to in standard histories. Similarly neglected have been the works of female poets, philosophers, theologians, saints and travellers. Their books are out of print, and their stories almost entirely left out of cultural histories. Whatever influence they may have had on their contemporaries has been stamped out of the public accounts. Until such time as there is an active search for their work, and their poems, essays, novels, memoirs and letters are collected and published, and the work of other unpublished women writers is sought out and brought to light, we will not know how many more such women writers lived, wrote and argued in literary and political circles.

As I searched the past, and talked with women about their ancestresses, I heard many stories of a grandmother, a great-aunt or an elderly neighbour who, in times of hardship, took dramatic and bold steps towards her family's survival, travelling sometimes to far-away places, taking business initiatives, appealing to local tyrants, doing anything that might improve the life of her children. Though some of these women were indeed illiterate, many were not; they were all powerful figures, creating their own history, working out their own destinies. They were certainly not the degraded wretches portrayed by the missionaries.

In any case, the liberation of women, at least as we understand it today, was certainly not the aim of the missionaries: over and over again in their writings, they express the wish to make women better wives and mothers, not free women, a phrase which no doubt would have shocked them profoundly. The nineteenth-century, Anglo-Saxon, Protestant (or, for that matter, French Roman Catholic) public ideal of womanhood was a tight-fitting corset – and I use this phrase literally as well as figuratively – into which women were to be bound. Obedience, not freedom, was the ideal trait of the ideal wife. Her primary duty was to her husband. Mrs Bowen-Thompson herself writes in 1865:

> The long neglected and despised Syrian woman is beginning to rise from her abject ignorance and degradation, and is manifesting in her life and conversation that she is what God made our first mother, a helpmeet for man.

The manner in which Mrs Bowen-Thompson saw her work is all too clear from an article published in England in September 1865. She writes:

> While at Zachleh, we paid a visit to the ladies of the family of an Effendi. They were all reclining on the divan, smoking or idling, except one, a fine young woman, who was seated on the ground with a quantity of white calico beside her, and several paper patterns, fitting and cutting out some garments. She looked up with a sweet smile, exclaiming, 'Ah dear lady, I learnt to work when I was in your schools, and now I am come from Damascus for a few days, and am helping my friends to make some apparel.' I assure you I watched her pretty little fingers adjusting the patterns, and then cutting out so neatly, with perfect admiration and respect. Her little nieces are now in our schools. A respectable young woman, in a plain lilac dress, fastened up to the throat, sat down on the divan beside the ladies. She too had been in the school at Beirut.

I cannot help but see, in the picture she draws of those reclining ladies, a degree of freedom and confidence – a far cry from 'abject

ignorance, degradation, and neglect' – and a kind of contraction, a
diminution, a repression, in those thoroughly domesticated and tamed
mission girls, with their severely buttoned-up long-sleeved dresses,
dutifully plying needle and scissors. Most of all I see the mission girls
as separated, differentiated, even alienated, from their surroundings.

Interestingly, Elizabeth Bowen-Thompson and her friends in the
Bible Women group were adamantly independent and, as I have
dared to call them above, feminist in their interaction with the church
authorities, and in the conduct of their own lives. Yet the course they
and their missionary colleagues preached to the poor in England,
and to the girls in the British Syrian Schools, was conservative and
fundamentally anti-feminist. That is the path they set Teta on, and
that is the path she set her daughter on, and she me. It was a path
that differentiated them from their surroundings, which they also
influenced, and it is a path from which I have spent the better part of
my adult life trying to extricate myself.

An interesting footnote to the lives of Mrs Bowen-Thompson's
sisters illustrates the dichotomy between their vision of themselves
and the manner in which they behaved on the one hand, and what
they preached to the mission girls on the other. This had to do with
their acquaintance with Jane Digby, an English aristocrat who had led
a scandalous life dotted with divorce, adultery, multiple lovers and
children born out of wedlock. She spent the last thirty years of her life
in Damascus, where she married a bedouin sheikh with whom, in Arab
dress, she rode her favourite camel around the desert. She attended
horses and camels during their labour, and claimed to have saved many
a colt or calf in danger of killing itself and its mother.

The diaries of this unusual woman refer to much social intercourse
with various missionaries in Syria, and Mr Mott is specifically mentioned
as a visitor to her home in Damascus. Suzette Smith, Mrs Bowen-
Thompson's sister, visited her just before her death in 1881, and later
wrote a letter to Jane Digby's niece informing her in the kindest possible
words of the last hours of the great lady. It is clear from this story that
what Mr Mott, Mrs Smith and their fellow missionaries allowed in an
Englishwoman of wealth and standing they would certainly not have
tolerated in the girls enrolled in their schools.

Mission activity aimed at girls increased dramatically as the nineteenth century progressed. One of the reasons for this was the constant pressure from the population for more schools: the missionaries, of course, were happy to comply and spread their influence. But they had an entirely practical motive as well: access. That this was so not only in the Arab world, but also in Asia and Africa, becomes clear as one reads through the missionary reports. Every girl taught at a mission school was a potential teacher, a potential mother of a family, and therefore a potential spreader of the new system. In the absence of inns and hotels in outlying areas, and at a time when the missionaries did a great deal of travelling, such a girl was also a potential hostess: this must have been of invaluable assistance to the work of the missionaries.

The European and American mission schools, especially the schools for girls, have been glorified in popular and academic history and political discourse in some circles. This view credits them with having brought in a unilateral modernization of an ancient and decadent society, awakening in its dormant victims a desire to learn and be raised from the abject misery of their existence into a more recognizably human form. This view applies especially to their relationship with women, and in it the missions are seen as liberators of Eastern women, bringing enlightenment, freedom and truth.

An alternative view has emerged, however, especially in the post-colonial political reactions of our time. In this view, the missions are seen as having imposed a form of Westernization that turned a portion of the population – and especially the female part – away from its own cultural tradition. At the very least, there is implicit in this view a profound contempt for the mission schools, based on a rejection of what is seen as the imperial motives of the missionaries.

Implicit in the background to many of today's conflicts lies the clash between these two views. A glorification of the role of the West in modernization, and therefore a glorification of Western clothes, languages, manners, attitudes and viewpoints, clashes with a desire to throw off vestiges of what is seen as Westernized, decadent modernity and a need to return to an older, more authentic, and therefore more moral, existence.

Both these views, it seems to me, contain a major error of vision and judgement, for they lay an almost exclusive emphasis on the missionaries, on their attitudes, motives, lives and work. Much of the received history of the region, after all, including its modernization and transformation, has been based on the writing of the missionaries and other foreigners, consuls, travellers and writers. Their version of the story has eclipsed the role played by the less-documented 'natives' in playing out their own destiny. The Ottoman role in modernization and transformation has been left out of the surviving popular, and almost entirely negative, view of them and their empire.

I have already pointed out that rarely, if ever, in the histories is there a discussion equal in length or consideration of the students themselves, or of the people who sent their sons and daughters to the mission schools, and of their attitudes, motives and lives. It is as though they were entirely without will, mere pawns in the hands of those prime movers, the missionaries, whatever their motives. My grandmother and her parents, and all those like them, are almost totally ignored as much by the histories as by the political rhetoric of our time.

This daughter of the people, as I have called my grandmother, this bearer of one of the most ancient of civilizations, had she had no place in her own history? Had she and her parents no motives, no independent will to change, no need to participate in a new world? Had they no impatience with the forms of their own society that led them to turn to forms brought in by the intruding foreigners? Had the parents of all those who went to the mission schools, the teachers who taught in them, no mission of their own? Were they merely collaborators with the foreigners, blind and dumb instruments of the will of others?

And, at school, had Teta said nothing, done nothing, added nothing, to the intervention of the missionary teachers? Had they entered her consciousness as though it were a *tabula rasa*, with no inheritance from her ancient culture, no resistance to a new one, no refinement, no control, no independence? And at school, though it was run by foreigners, had she no purposeful Arab teachers eager to influence young minds with new ideas or to impress on them the beauties of their own culture? Had the foreign missionaries not learned anything from Arab culture? Had they not taken anything home, anything transformative and widening, anything which changed their cultures and their world views?

My own experience has taught me that all the potent influence of a formal education, with its institutional power, and the political and economic structures of which it is an integral part, can be effectively countered, if not totally undermined, by the gentle admonitions, the telling of stories, the singing of songs, the saying of prayers and the domestic advice of a sweet and elderly grandmother and the direct teaching of a mother. Everything that science can teach and technology demonstrate can be whisked away into doubt and oblivion by the smallest gesture of scepticism, or a withering look of disapproval from a disbelieving relative.

Teta's influence on me – and Mother's, which is not the same thing – has played havoc with the kind of 'modern' education I have had. As a result of the dialectics of these antagonistic influences, I carry within myself a kind of draughtboard of contradictory assertions, doubts, beliefs, practices, morals and scruples.

Teta must, I feel sure, have brought to her teachers influences as contradictory to their world as those they brought to hers. The life of her sister Emelia offers ample proof that a reaction to the absolute vision of the missionaries and their teachings did take place, even within the walls of the mission schools. She vocally and deliberately reacted with proud defiance against the tendency of the foreign missions to invalidate local culture and sweep it cleanly away even while she interacted with them to create a new school. Yet she was as much a product of the mission schools as her sister, my grandmother.

The foreign missionaries did indeed have an enormous influence on education in general, and on the education of women in particular, in this part of the world. Modernity, however, was a new space created partly by an interaction with them, rather than an imposition by them on a people without a will of their own; a synthesis of cultural resources rather than a unilateral initiative by one culture acting on another. Though they certainly had a hand in it, they were part of a complex process that also involved the active participation of the local people of the area as well as the religious and cultural establishments, the governors, bureaucrats and armies of the Ottoman empire. Without the integrating influence of the local people, which gave meaning to the presence of the missionaries by steering them to the schoolroom and thus to the heart of their society, the missionaries might have remained irrelevant, extraneous to any significant change or progress.

This might seem an obvious and even banal conclusion, but so powerful is the mythology surrounding the missionaries that it has taken me many years, and many heated arguments with friends and colleagues, to arrive at it.

CHAPTER 12

Alternative Paths

If Teta's biography cannot be completely understood without
a knowledge of the missionaries who taught her, it is even less
complete without an understanding of her contemporaries among
the 'native' girls, both in the mission schools and outside them. Her
own sister Emelia offers perhaps the most dramatic contrast.

Unlike her sweet-tempered sister Munira, Auntie Melia always had
a rumbustious and rebellious nature. She never got along with her
mother, with whom she quarrelled incessantly even when the latter was
an old lady. Like Teta, Auntie Melia was a great beauty; she had clear
pink skin and blue eyes. Though small of stature, she had an enormous
personality that showed through in her regal bearing.

She studied at the American Girls' College in Tripoli before moving
to the American school in Beirut, where she began her teaching career.
After her quarrel with the Americans there over the discriminatory

forms of address, when she refused a secondary status to the American teachers and demanded to be addressed as 'Miss Badr', she moved to Cairo in 1897. Here she joined another American mission institution, the Ezbekia School for Girls. A failed romance, whispered echoes of which I have heard from family quarters, may also have prompted her move. She may have made the connection with the Cairo school through her father and the missionaries he worked with in Beirut, or through her brother, Nassib, who was in Cairo and part of the network of Syrian journalists and writers, offshoots of the Syrian Protestant College.

At Ezbekia she met an American woman named Ella Kyle. In 1901 the two women started a new school near the centre of Cairo, which became the American College for Girls, and was the first school in Egypt to offer higher education for women. The school was formally opened on 28 March 1910, in the presence of President Roosevelt. A department for teacher training was envisioned from the beginning to be part of the school's function, while the old Ezbekia School was to continue to teach the lower classes, and feed students to the college.

From the beginning of the fifty-odd years of her work at the American College for Girls, Auntie Melia had a place of honour in it. She served as a member of the administrative board and had her own prominently located rooms. But she never became principal; this particular honour was always reserved for the Americans who, one by one during her lifetime, succeeded Ella Kyle, the first principal. And though some of the school literature contains the occasional reference to her as co-founder with Ella Kyle, it is usually the latter who is referred to as the sole founder, while my aunt is called 'friend' and 'associate'. That is the way she is remembered on a memorial plaque that still hangs on the wall at the entrance of the main building of the school, today called Ramses College:

IN MEMORY OF
ELLA O. KYLE
FOUNDER AND BUILDER OF THIS COLLEGE
A WOMAN OF EXCEPTIONAL VISION
UNFALTERING FAITH AND COURAGE
GREAT HEART WHO LIVED

NOT TO BE MINISTERED UNTO
BUT TO MINISTER
IN HONOR OF
EMELIA BADR
ASSOCIATE AND FRIEND OF MISS KYLE
DURING THE BUILDING OF THE COLLEGE
AND OF ITS STUDENTS THROUGHOUT THE YEARS.

Auntie Melia's official title was never clear. Perhaps she was never given official recognition as co-founder because the connections of Miss Kyle, whose father was a Presbyterian minister, lay in America, the principal source of funding. When they began, they had no money, and had to raise it both in Egypt and from church groups in the United States. The money to buy the land came from the First United Presbyterian Church, Allegheny; a pledge of $60,000 from the mission, along with small sums that they had raised independently, were dedicated to the first building. There is no known record of precisely how much Auntie Melia raised from her friends and acquaintances in the Egyptian Syrian community, and therefore I cannot tell whether her inferior status was due to the lesser financial contribution she was able to make to the project.

But perhaps Auntie Melia held a secondary place because that was in the nature of things. In every one of the foreign mission stories known to me, there is a 'native' lurking in the background, without whom the enterprise would not have been accomplished. The success of the Syrian Protestant College is unthinkable without the scholars Butros Bustani and Nassif Yazigi, who form an integral part of modern Arab cultural history, but are never given the same degree of credit in its early history by the institution as their American colleagues. Mrs Bowen-Thompson's work might have remained marginal and unimportant and relegated to some minor evangelizing, or she might even have gone home on the next steamer, had it not been for Selim Kassab. And Miss Kyle might never have founded this new school in Cairo without Emelia Badr. In the histories, the story of these 'natives', if it is mentioned at all, is always secondary to that of the foreign missionaries. The natives are always viewed as 'assistants', 'helpers', 'friends', 'associates', 'links' or 'intermediaries', never as prime movers.

I do not know how close this view is to the truth, or whether there simply has been insufficient historical investigation. I do know that this view of things has taken on a life of its own, and has dictated itself as a tradition from which it is difficult to break away.

Emelia Badr's skills as an administrator and teacher, her huge personality and her relentless iron discipline helped to make her famous. A former student of hers, now in her eighties, told me recently: 'If Miss Badr were to walk into the room now, I would instantly leap to my feet. I know that my knees would be shaking, but at the same time I would make sure that my posture was correct, my clothes in order, and my appearance quite what it should be!' Another former student told me that the school once hired a new janitor who soon heard many stories about Miss Badr, and was cautioned by his fellow-workers not to incur her displeasure. When he first had occasion to see her, he stared in disbelief at her tiny figure. 'That,' he pointed at her, 'that tiny little thing is the "Miss Badr" of whom you are all so afraid? I had thought to see a fearsome giant of a woman – but that little woman … !'

But Auntie Melia's principal function in the school was as the bearer of Arab culture in the American milieu provided by the foreign teachers. This was accomplished not only in her capacity as teacher of Arabic, but as teacher and upholder of the manners, customs and traditions required of Arab women. Even while she encouraged her students to absorb the modern secular education provided by the school, she never allowed them to forget their own heritage. With her gigantic personality, Emelia formed a kind of conduit through which the invading new learning had to pass, altered and adapted to the Arab culture of which she was so proud.

The Americans, also, were continuously reminded by her that they had entered no cultural vacuum, but a living, real world about which they had much to learn. Dr Helen J. Martin, principal of the college from 1923 to 1956, paid tribute to her in a memorial service held on her death in 1957, and then published in a special bilingual memorial issue of *Cartouche*, the school magazine: 'In my almost nightly chats with her … I acquired a useful knowledge of personalities and affairs in Egypt and the Arab world that I could have scarcely secured in any other way.' Sarah Meloy, principal of the school at the time of Auntie

Melia's death, said of her: 'As a member of the administrative committee of the college, Miss Badr served as the link between the East and the West. Her advice was invaluable in interpreting the East to those of us from the West who had much to learn.'

Stubbornly, she kept up the old customs, sang the old songs and ate the old foods. Another American teacher, Miss Robertson, said of her that 'she always had Damascus sweetmeats, fruits and nuts to offer, and when she or they were sad, she could be found by intimate friends reciting her beloved Arabic poetry, or listening to the throbbing strains of Arabic instrumental music or song.'

Her students describe Auntie Melia's role in a similar manner, though, with deeper feeling, they see in her much more than a mere link. Ihsan Sidki Arafa expresses ideas repeatedly brought up by the other Egyptians. Writing of Emelia's 'deep understanding and knowledge of our Eastern customs and a loyal appreciation and love for all our traditions,' she remembers that 'she was ever alert, advising and encouraging us to follow only those Western ways that suited and harmonized with our own.' In doing so, she 'always strove to create a spirit of harmony' between the two sets of teachers.

Suhair al-Qalamawi, who had gone on from the American College for Girls to become a well-known writer and the first woman professor at Cairo University, describes her as 'the axis at which East and West met, at which the ... enthusiasm of the American women, their work, modernity and knowledge, met the eternal spirit of the East, with its noble traditions and its deeply rooted customs.'

In addition to her major role as guardian of Arab culture, and cultural intermediary, Auntie Melia impressed on her students the importance of discipline and intellectual ambition, and inspired in them a sense of morality and justice. Another former student, Eva Habib al-Masri, a well-known journalist and member of the Egyptian Feminist Union, said that Emelia had placed greater value on building 'our personalities and our minds' than on their studies. 'She repeated to us time after time that knowledge, if it is not strengthened with morality, is weakened, and loses its value. She taught us that our success in life would depend more on spiritual and moral values, and strength of character, than on information and knowledge.'

It was she who dealt directly with the students, and according to

the testimonies, she handled the mixture of students coming from
different social classes with tact and intelligence. She protested against
discrimination and segregation in the school. At first the American
teachers had demanded separate sleeping and eating facilities from
their Arab colleagues, claiming that this was required by their different
culinary traditions and tastes. Auntie Melia refused this and, though
sensibly banning the eating of soups, pickles and other vinegary dishes,
because of the difference in the manners required for the eating of
these foods, insisted that the Arab teachers should join the Americans
at mealtimes.

Auntie Melia's proudly nationalist response to the biases of the
foreigners was not new to the women of her generation. In the confines
of the foreign mission girls' schools, and over such issues as mealtimes,
were often echoed the nationalist protests, and the political struggles
within the society being pursued on a larger scale outside the walls. I
was told by former students of several incidents in which Arab teachers
in Lebanon and Palestine fought against discrimination by British or
American missionaries; these struggles had sometimes led to the closing
down of a mission school.

Not all the rebellions were against the Western missionaries. One
story was told to me by a schoolmate of my mother's, the late Rafika
Mikati, and involved her aunt, Ibtihaj Kaddoura, who was to become a
well-known activist in the Lebanese nationalist and feminist movement.
Just before the First World War, Ibtihaj Kaddoura was selected by the
Beirut notables to give a public speech to an audience that included the
dreaded Jamal Pasha, Ottoman governor of Syria at the time. Ibtihaj,
who was then around twenty years of age, and of course wearing a
hijab, stood in front of the company and delivered her speech in
Arabic. After she finished, she was summoned by Omar Beyhum, then
Mayor of the city, to meet Jamal Pasha. Having congratulated her on
her bearing and on the delivery of her speech, which he apparently had
not understood, Jamal Pasha said: 'I have one objection. Why did you
not use the language of your country?', by which, of course, he meant
Turkish. 'I am an Arab and a Muslim,' she said, proudly, 'I am using
my language.' And then, in a tone that made her compatriots tremble,
she asked the Pasha: 'Do you know Arabic?' 'No,' he answered. 'Shame
on you,' she retorted. 'You are a Muslim. If you do not know Arabic,

how can you read your Quran?' By then the company were almost faint with fear at the possible outcome of this impertinence. But Jamal Pasha answered smilingly. 'Next time I come, you will have learned Turkish, and I will have learned Arabic.' Of course he never came back, as very soon after this incident, World War I began.

One of the speakers who paid moving tribute to Emelia Badr at the memorial service was Bahiga Sidki Rashid, who had gone on from the American College for Girls to head the Union of Egyptian Women (*al-ittihad al-nissa'i al-masri*) and it was probably through her and other graduates of the college like Eva Habib al-Masri and Suhair al-Qalamawi that Auntie Emelia established her connection with Huda Shaarawi, founder of the union and the most famous name in the modern Arab feminist movement. Precisely how close the connection was I have not been able to establish, nor do I know how influenced Auntie Melia was by the 1919 revolution against the British, or whether she was one of those women who participated in the famous marches through the streets of Cairo in defiance of the armed British soldiers. Somehow I feel she must have been.

I do know that she took tea at Huda Shaarawi's house and that the latter used occasionally to speak at the meetings organized by alumni of the college, as later on did Amina al-Said and Doriyya Shafik, other luminaries of the Egyptian feminist movement. One speech of Huda Shaarawi, given at the American College for Girls in March 1928, is documented in her memoirs.

Yet, in spite of her enormous impact on her students, and in spite of her influence on Egyptian women, the renaissance of female learning and even on some of these Egyptian feminists, Auntie Melia was not herself a feminist, not, at least, as we understand that word today. The same kind of ambivalence between the life she lived and the one she preached governed her, as had governed the teachers of Teta's mission school.

In her journal, Mother recounts that when my elder sister Rosemarie was born, Auntie Melia expressed deep disappointment that the new arrival was not a male. She was not the only maiden aunt of her generation to dislike the family's production of daughters. In my husband's family, another legend, Aminah Khouri al-Makdisi, sister to Anis al-Makdisi, lived a life not dissimilar to Emelia Badr's. She too was a product of the

American missions. Independently, she founded a primary school in Ras Beirut to which flocked the children of several generations, Muslims, Christians and Jews. She too is remembered to this day with awe by her former students, now elderly men and women. Apparently made of sterner stuff than Emelia, for she was rarely known to smile, and had none of Emelia's beauty or worldly sophistication, she was also known for her sense of justice and her talent with recalcitrant learners.

In the family, however, 'Amti (Auntie) Aminah was known for her bias against the daughters of her brothers and sisters, and, indeed, for her even greater bias towards her brothers' children as opposed to her sisters.' When she witnessed childish quarrels between siblings or cousins, she always sided with the boys against the girls, and the children of her brothers against the children of her sisters.

I do not know how much these powerful maiden schoolteachers, proud of their own cultures, were motivated in their bias by family pride. Perhaps they were also contemptuous of the married, bound and tethered females they knew, including their own sisters. Perhaps they regarded their sisters and their married nieces with derision for not having broken out, as they had done – for both had rejected suitors – from the female conventions, from the inevitable role of wife and mother.

But Auntie Melia was by no means contemptuous of the female vocation as practised and perfected by her sister. She, no less than Teta, was dedicated to the ideal of the well-kept house, the contented husband and the well-looked-after children. Mother writes in her memoir that, when she first arrived in Cairo, her aunt prodded her to make her home and family one 'that she could be proud of'. That she lived in the school and was tended by the school's servants made her no less demanding and judgemental of housework, though it did give her freedom from its practice. She was thus relieved of its tyranny, and was able instead to assume a tyrannical stance towards its practitioners.

At the same time as Teta and her sisters were pursuing their studies at the British and American Protestant mission schools, learning tatting and Scripture, and training to become teachers, other girls – and boys, for that matter – like them were studying more or less in the same way at dozens of American and European Catholic and Jewish mission schools throughout the Levant. They were absorbing European and American languages and cultures, habits and thought.

The majority of the inhabitants, however, took a different path to modernity. In the Christian villages, priests trained in Rome came home to open their own schools. These coexisted with the government schools, as well as with schools run by other sects, including the Russian-backed Greek Orthodox community and the Greek Catholic community.

A network of state, mostly elementary schools existed which underwent major reforms during the *tanzimat*, the great Ottoman reform movement of the nineteenth century. The Ottomans had, from the time of their first contact with the armies of Napoleon, felt that the individual European soldiers were better prepared than theirs. In response, they had opened advanced military academies, known as *askariyyas*, but soon discovered that special schools were needed to prepare students for them. In Syria, where Ibrahim Pasha had opened several *askariyyas*, families of standing often sent their sons to Egypt for education in the new schools opened by Mohammed Ali.

The Islamic *kuttabs*, or Quranic schools, however, carried on the mainstream educational currents of the region. The students of *kuttabs* were mostly but not exclusively boys. The main body of instruction centred on the Quran, which provided the basis not only for religious, but also linguistic, literary and philosophical studies. Mathematics, science – especially astronomy – and the quintessential Islamic art, calligraphy, were also taught, as were history and geography. Islamic tradition dictated that while most children would end their education with the *kuttabs*, particularly talented boys would be sent on to al-Azhar in Cairo or the Sultaniyyah in Istanbul. It was generally understood that one boy from each family would devote his life to Islamic studies. Girls of the wealthy families were generally tutored at home.

In 1878 the Beirut Muslim community, challenged by the burgeoning influence of foreign missions, opened a school for girls which was to be the first in a network of schools. The Makassed Philanthropic and Islamic Association schools were directed mainly at the poorer families of Beirut, and like their foreign counterparts, they still play an important part in the educational life of Lebanon.

Prophetically, the first annual report of the Makassed Association lamented the foreign missions' division of the national community into sects of uneven cultural development, each of which encouraged the use of a different language. They regretted the necessity of behaving like the other communities, having preferred to work towards a universal improvement for the common good of their society. However, because of their limited resources, they were forced to restrict their activities to the Muslim community.

And why start with girls? The report is very clear about this, and fits in neatly with the common assumption among nineteenth-century liberal Arab thinkers that the progress of the nation depended on the progress of women, 'the first educators'. Therefore, the best way to spread education and advance society was by teaching girls how to bring up their children, thus helping them to acquire the knowledge and skills they needed to improve their world.

The Makassed schools were influenced by the Protestant mission schools – the first and one of the most influential of its headmistresses was Julia Tohmeh, herself a Protestant and the product of English mission schools. Later, after a daring cross-religious marriage to Badr Dimishqiyeh, a married man prominent in the Muslim community, she became a well-known writer and journalist. Julia Tohmeh was written about with great affection and admiration in the memoirs of one of her students, Anbara Salam, daughter of Salim Salam. Anbara was born around the turn of the century, and describes in her memoirs her schooling, first at the hands of a *sheikha*, the wife of the sheikh to whom her brothers were sent for their earliest schooling, and later at the Makassed.

The flavour of the school and of Anbara's education was clearly different in many ways from Teta's. For one thing, unlike the foreign mission schools, which were always at odds with the Ottoman establishment, the morning assembly at this Muslim school began with an anthem of prayer and supplication for the Sultan, asking God to protect him. Nor did the school put its students into conflict with local manners and customs. On their arrival at school, for instance, the students all removed their shoes, left them at the door and put on *babooj*.

Academically, the education at the Makassed school in Anbara's time was not dissimilar to that provided by the foreign missions, where the principal had a direct influence. As was the custom in the foreign schools, notable visitors would offer topics on which the girls were invited to write compositions, being rewarded for their efforts with prizes. Once, remembers Anbara, a freshly slaughtered sheep was brought into the room and hung in front of the girls, who were then tested on its anatomy. According to Anbara, hers was one of the first national school for girls to teach Geography, History, Physiology and Botany. The textbooks were translations of American books taught at the Syrian Protestant College. But they were also taught Islamic history and Arabic grammar and morphology in textbooks written by Sheikh Mohieddin al-Khayyat and SPC Professor Jabr Doumit, respectively.

Just as the Protestant schools emphasized Bible studies, the Makassed emphasized the study of the Quran, the rules of chanting it and Islamic principles. By the time she was ten, Anbara had 'sealed' (or perfected her reading and chanting of) the Quran. She describes the celebration organized by the school to mark the occasion. When she reached the age of ten, Anbara entered what she calls 'the iron fence' of the tradition of the *hijab*, and with it the seclusion which was the norm for girls of upper-class urban families. She did not protest, seeing this as a sign of her growing up, and of joining her grandmother and mother in their adult, womanly state. Her only regret at the time, she says, was that she was no longer allowed to play with her brothers in the garden, which was open to the street and could therefore be seen; nor was she any longer allowed to climb trees and eat her evening sandwich in their branches. Anbara stayed at the Makassed for only three years. Her school life was interrupted by the First World War. From then on she was tutored at home. She went on to marry a prominent Palestinian and to play a public role in both Lebanese and Palestinian society and politics.

The story of another Arab girl of the same period is as different from Julia's and Anbara's as it is from Teta's. Huda Shaarawi was born in Cairo in 1879, the year before my grandmother's birth. A daughter of the Egyptian aristocracy – her father was Sultan Pasha, an associate of Orabi Pasha, who led the uprising against the British in 1882 – her upbringing and early education was accomplished in the almost total seclusion required of girls of her class. During her earliest childhood, Huda Shaarawi was educated with her brothers and two young girls, one an Egyptian and the other a Circassian. Their lessons and the tutors who came to the house to teach them were closely watched over by the senior eunuchs of her father's household. Having 'sealed' the Quran, she went on to study Ottoman and modern Turkish, grammar and calligraphy. An Italian woman gave her piano lessons and taught her French.

When she was twelve years old, Huda was married to her cousin, but she soon separated from him and remained in her mother's house for the next seven years. Much of this time was spent in study. The Italian lady came back to continue the French and piano lessons, and Huda was also instructed in drawing and painting. Her great desire to perfect her Arabic was frustrated as a consequence of her seclusion: teachers, even elderly sheikhs, were denied easy access to her presence by the ever-watchful eunuchs, and so she complained that she had a better knowledge of French (taught by the Italian woman) than Arabic.

Both her father and her husband were involved in politics, and Huda Shaarawi later became involved herself. She was one of the founders of the Central Women's Committee of the Wafd Party (the nationalist party that was negotiating independence from the British) and she went on to play a direct role in the Egyptian nationalist revolution of 1919 against British rule under the leadership of Saad Zaghloul Pasha. On the eve of her departure for Rome to attend the Ninth Feminist Congress as the leader of the Egyptian delegation, she founded the Egyptian Feminist Union (*al-ittihad al-nissa'i al-masri*). From then to the end of her life, she was heavily involved both in the national and the international women's movement.

Worlds separate the Egyptian pasha's daughter from the wealthy Beirut merchant's daughter, and both from my grandmother. Even taking into account the differences in individual personalities, and the differences imposed by religion, social situation and geography, some of Teta's characteristics come into sharp contrast with those of the other two women. The principal one is this: in all the years I knew Teta, I scarcely ever heard her comment on politics or public events. Yet the other two girls – one brought up in partial, the other in total seclusion, both from conservative Muslim families – both ended up in public demonstrations not only for the feminist cause, but for nationalist ones as well. Why, I could not help asking myself, was political activity an ordinary part of their daily lives, while apparently totally absent from Teta's?

All three of these girls were taught obedience; all three were given heavy doses of religious instruction; all three were married; and yet two eventually participated in public life and the third did not. Whereas Teta never wrote or spoke much about herself, the other two left memoirs of their lives and times which to this day are widely quoted and referred to.

In the modesty, reticence and delicacy of manner that she was taught and which she absorbed, Teta seems far more repressed than the others. Where they were physically bound and covered, she was domesticated by her education. Her inner soul was covered with a veil of propriety and a fear of disapproval far thicker and more impenetrable than that which covered the faces of the other girls, so much more easily torn off and discarded. Years later, my mother remembered that the words 'What will people say?' were ever on Teta's lips: they were 'the most important thing in the world for her'. Yet in her own private way, Teta marked out a new territory for herself. She created and taught new ways and manners, and left an indelible mark on the world.

No doubt the principal reason for Teta's absence of political participation lies in the fact that both Anbara Salam and Huda Shaarawi came from, and married into, prominent political families, while Teta did not. Their political activity was a continuation of that learned from their fathers, and later their husbands. Julia Tohmeh Dimishqiyeh lived an independent life, travelling, marrying outside her own faith, writing on politics and demanding the emancipation of women, but she too enjoyed some cover from her politically prestigious husband. Other Christian women of the time who became public figures, and wrote and published – Maud Farajallah and Evelyne Bustros, to mention only two from Beirut – also came from prominent families.

Yet neither Teta nor her family were by any means politically unaware, or even unengaged: my uncle Emil remembers that in his childhood lively political discussions regularly took place between his parents and his grandmother, Leila, who read the Palestinian dailies closely, especially *Falastin* and *al-Carmel*, both of which were committed to the Arab Palestinian cause. Aunt Emelia was, however indirectly, politically articulate.

Teta never discussed politics with me as I was growing up because neither she nor any one else in the family believed it to be a suitable topic of conversation for a young girl. But a principal reason for her distance – and my mother's and mine – from active political participation, I believe, had to do with the ideology of maternal vocation that she had absorbed, and to which her sister was less bound.

As I look back at the received history of women in this part of the world, I see it clouded by false assumptions and myths. The complexities of cultural history have been reduced to a few simplistic half-truths. Ordinary women like my great-grandmother, my grandmother and her sisters have been left out of the public account; their contribution to the history of women, to the evolution of costume, education and manners, has gone largely undocumented, and emancipation, such as it is, has been credited instead to their missionary teachers. The missionaries' role in creating a system which repressed, rather than liberated, women is never mentioned, never even understood. On the other hand, the actions of such women as Huda Shaarawi and Anbara Salam, who became public figures, while widely recognized and documented, have often been placed in the context of their religion, rather than their class or personal circumstance and temperament.

The course of women's history is a complex synthesis of regression and advancement, individual and collective action, private and public actions, regional and class differences, alienation and engagement, ideology and mere practicality. The modern age is a construction as much of the small, hidden, processes of everyday life as of the dramatic moments of grand gestures. The wide variety of ways in which modern women conduct their lives today is a reflection of the variety of paths trodden by their predecessors.

I have come to recognize that I have inherited my notion of womanhood as much from Huda Shaarawi, Anbara Salam, Julia Tohmeh and others like them as I have from my grandmother, my aunts and my mother. I have been made as much by the simple schoolroom built by foreign missionaries, and all the contradictions contained in it, as by the great houses in which other women were secluded and from which they broke out. I have absorbed the contributions of Arab and Western women writers and activists, though often I did not know much about them. In addition, a thousand other forms of femalehood, some more important than others, some better known than others, lie tucked away, often unarticulated, somewhere in my background. A complex education, the Palestinian experience and all the wars resulting from it, the women's revolt of the 1960s and 1970s, the long war in Lebanon, the debates on democracy and economic development, my own domestic life – all these together made me what I am. As a result, elements of obedience and restraint inherited from all these sources are woven into my being, together with elements of dissatisfaction and rebellion inherent in the legacy. A kind of cultural conservatism is blended with a kind of cultural adventurousness inexplicable but for my complex ancestry.

CHAPTER 13

Marriage and War

Youssef Badr's resignation as pastor from the Beirut church in 1893 resulted from a dispute within the congregation over the organization of the church and its policy, whether it should follow the Americans as Presbyterians, or take a more independent stand as Congregationalists. Once my grandfather had resigned, he moved with his family first to Tyre and then to Jdeideh, in the district of Marjeyoun, where he remained until his death. On completing her training at the British Syrian Training College, Teta moved to Marjeyoun and taught at the mission school there.

From this time of the Badrs' life in Marjeyoun comes a story that my mother often told me. Indeed, fearing that it might be lost, I often requested it from her. It painfully illustrates the way in which the Badrs and others like them must have been pulled between two rival worlds, the requirements and courtesies of the Arab world pitted against the colder, more calculating and less humane exigencies of an emerging and heartless modern society. It also shows how people from two worlds can misread each other's signs and signals to tragic effect.

In Marjeyoun, Youssef Badr had a helper, a sort of deacon who had a large family. As time passed, this man found it increasingly difficult to live on the meagre salary paid him by the mission, and one day in desperation requested the pastor to intervene urgently with headquarters on his behalf. Seeing the fairness of the man's request, Rev. Youssef agreed to do what he could. He wrote a letter to the mission headquarters in Beirut, explaining his helper's problem. He received a positive response from the mission: on their next trip to Marjeyoun, they would visit the deacon and discuss his financial needs.

Elated, and overcome with anticipation, the deacon insisted that the visitors should lunch at his house on the forthcoming trip. Admonishing his wife to honour the visitors properly, together they made preparations for the traditional hospitality. To make their poor house fit to receive the great men from Beirut, she sold the gold bracelets and earrings that had been her dowry, and with the money bought the necessary furnishings and food. When the time came, they slaughtered the goat from whose milk they made their cheese and yoghurt, and with the meat made *kibbeh* and other delicacies. When the great day arrived, they slaughtered the chickens whose eggs had been a mainstay of their diet. The meal was a triumph of Arab generosity and hospitality; they had sacrificed their living to honour their guests.

The Americans, having eaten and drunk plentifully, and having given the matter some consideration, wrote from Beirut that the man seemed comfortable enough and in no need of financial improvement. 'We should have fed them olives, onions and lentils instead of honouring them as we did,' cried the man, beating his forehead with his fist when he heard the news. 'We should have fed them what we ourselves eat instead of treating them as honoured guests.' I have always remembered this little story as it shows the difference between two world visions, and the boundary between the imperatives of that world in which hospitality defined human relations, and the more practical, but crueller, imperatives of modern economic relationships.

It was in Marjeyoun that Teta became engaged to be married. I have been told two quite contradictory stories about this all-important event. The source of the first version was Auntie Melia, who told it to her nieces and nephews, from whom I received it. According to this version, Teta's future husband, Shukri Musa, whom she had never seen before, arrived one day to visit her father. Having been smitten by her beauty, he came again and asked her father for her hand in marriage. He was invited to lunch and sat at the table with the family. In the evening of that same day, Teta was summoned into her father's presence.

'What do you think of this man?' he asked her. 'He has asked for your hand. Do you wish to marry him?'

She answered her father's question with one of her own: 'What do *you* think of him?'

Her father said: 'He is a very good man and I think highly of him. I think he will make you a good husband.'

'Then I will marry him,' said Teta, simply.

That night, Teta went into her room, laid her head on her pillow and apparently slept soundly. Emelia, on the other hand, could not sleep at all, and spent the night tossing and turning in anxiety and anger. She was astounded and disgusted at her sister's acquiescence, her untroubled acceptance of her father's judgement, the ease with which she accepted her fate.

I received the other version of the story from her son, my Uncle Alif, who had it from Teta herself. It sheds an altogether different light both on Teta and on the process that led to her marriage, and in general I like it better. His father, Uncle Alif recounted, was living and working in Jerusalem when he felt the time had come for him to marry. Neither in Jerusalem nor in his native Safad, however, did he find anyone to please him. At last, a friend of his from Marjeyoun told him he had just the right girl for him. He took him to Marjeyoun and introduced him to Rev. Youssef Badr and his beautiful daughter, Munira. They felt an instant regard for one another. The Rev. Youssef was very impressed with the man, and Munira, who had had many suitors and was at that time being courted by a 'persistent' young minister whom she disliked intensely, was deeply impressed too. She said to her father, 'This is a real man,' and they were married shortly afterwards.

Teta's wedding, over which her father presided, took place in 1905 in Jdeidet Marjeyoun. Among the few things Teta told me about herself was that she was considered very old for a bride: she had, after all, reached the ripe old age of twenty-five. Another thing was a sentence that she often repeated to me: 'On my wedding day, I only washed my face.' I was never quite sure whether her pride in this had to do with the quality of her skin or the purity of her morals, but I used to feel that she projected that image of herself, 'only washing her face' on her wedding day, as a kind of lesson.

Today, her words ring out of the past to haunt my memory of her, and I hear an altogether different message from that which I understood as a teenager. I now believe that she did not mean to lecture me on my use of cosmetics, or to show that she was morally superior to my generation – or my mother's, for that matter – or that she was being puritanical and 'boring', which was the phrase I used to myself then. I hear a woman who had defied local tradition and customs, who had refused the festive henna evenings that precede weddings, especially in Galilee, where she now lived. At these famous Galilean weddings, all the women gather together and surround the bride with songs, dances, food and sweets while they prepare her body for the wedding. The bride's feet and hands are decorated in designs drawn in henna, which she has already used on her hair. Her face is powdered with pounded rice, her lips and cheeks are rouged and her eyes are lined with kohl. The women tending her sing and dance, eat and drink, gossip and laugh, and in general make much festive noise. Finally, the women dance the bride around the room.

In Teta's remark I hear a woman who refused all this, as she refused the other attentions of traditional weddings. I hear a rejection of the past, an announcement that she had clearly chosen a different way of life. Perhaps it was her mother who dominated the wedding preparations, as my mother dominated mine, so the decision may have been her mother's. Still, Teta's pride in the matter, and her insistence decades later on the simplicity of her wedding day, show that she herself had taken a conscious, deliberate stand in this regard.

Why had I not seen or heard all this before? Because it was only after I read Mother's memoir, and her brothers', that I realized how their mother had differentiated herself and her family from their surroundings. Mother herself, perhaps her brothers too, had temporarily reconnected, through their father and his relatives, with the ancient folk traditions that their mother had rejected. I grew up in an urban, cosmopolitan, middle-class world so utterly removed from the folk traditions that I was not even aware of their existence. Teta's participation in the creation of a new way of life has been forgotten. It is only recently that I have come to think of the world I inherited as having been actively made, actively forged from the past, at least in part by her.

My grandfather, Shukri Musa, was born in 1870 in the town of Safad in Galilee, in northern Palestine. According to Uncle Alif's account, his family originated in the village of Furzol near Zahleh, in the Bekaa valley, and was known as Beit al-Abed. The family owned a splendid embroidered waistcoat, or *bisht*. Because it was so exceptionally fine, this waistcoat was regularly borrowed by other families for the bridegroom to wear on his wedding day, and eventually they became known as Beit al-Bisht (the Family of the Waistcoat). But as more and more people in the area learned Turkish, the name became increasingly embarrassing: '*busht*' was an unsavoury Turkish epithet, and so the family abandoned the name. Generations later, they took it up again and adapted it, becoming known as 'Bishuti'. In the meantime, however, each branch of the family took its patriarch's name, as was the custom. My grandfather's father's name being Musa, he became known as Shukri Musa.

One day about 300 years ago, writes Uncle Alif, an ancestor of my grandfather was walking down a street in Furzol a few steps behind a bedouin. From an upstairs window, a woman called to the bedouin: '*Ya badawi! Ya badawi!*' (O bedouin! O bedouin!), and when the man obligingly looked up in response, she threw a bucket of slop at him. 'Our ancestor', as Uncle Alif calls him, was so infuriated that he decided to leave the area. He took his wife and children and rode through the steep and beautiful valley between the Lebanon and anti-Lebanon ranges until they reached Shafa 'Amr in Galilee, where they settled. Later they moved to Safad.

Shukri Musa's father was a member of Safad municipal council, representing the Christian minority. He was a Greek Catholic, the family having converted to that denomination from their native Greek Orthodox faith when they moved to Safad, where there was no other church. He wrote a little book of memoirs, which Uncle Alif claims to have memorized. The book was lost when Teta finally closed her house in 1936. One of his stories tells how one day in the early nineteenth century, when my great-grandfather was in his teens, a great earthquake struck Safad, causing massive destruction. My great-grandfather was out in the fields when the earth opened up all around him, and he survived by leaping over the fissures as they occurred. This story foreshadowed the great Galilean earthquake of 1927.

Another story took place in Shafa 'Amr during the reign of the notorious Jazzar Pasha, pasha of Acre (Akka) at the time of Napoleon's invasion of Palestine in 1798. A member of the family, the story goes, had a wonderful mare renowned as a racer. In the villages of Galilee it was customary to race horses during wedding celebrations, and on one occasion, the mare in question won the wedding race. The following day, she was feeding near the *bayader* (threshing fields) when a man whose horse had been one of the losers came upon her. In a fit of pique he stabbed and killed her. Our relative was so outraged that he resolved to go to Acre and lodge a complaint with Jazzar Pasha.

The latter unreasonably turned on the victim and gave him a choice: either he was to become a Muslim or he was to be hanged. Our perplexed relative asked leave to consult with his brother in Shafa 'Amr, whence he repaired under armed escort. Needless to say, his brother advised him to convert. Accordingly, he converted to Islam and was released, though he never found justice for the killing of his mare. Like so many other stories that I have heard on my journey into the past, this one sounds suspiciously apocryphal. The only detail that can be confirmed is that there is indeed a Muslim branch of the family, or at least another family in Safad which bears the same name, but which happens to be Muslim.

Shukri's mother, Mariam Nakhle, belonged to a large family in the town of Rameh, not far from Safad. She is remembered in Mother's memoirs as Sitti (or Teta) Im Shukri (my grandmother, mother of Shukri). She had so many children that women less fortunate than her would bring their newborn babies to her for a kind of maternal blessing. She used to hold the infant near her body under her robe, thus claiming it as her own, as though adopting it, and giving it long life.

In fact, of Mariam's own numerous progeny, only four survived into adulthood. She herself lived for over a hundred years, the last of which were spent with her son Shukri and his family. Uncle Alif and Mother remembered her as a remote and weird figure, half-blind and living in her own room. Mostly she sat in a wooden chair with a cane seat that was reserved exclusively for her use, but occasionally she would wander out of her room and lose her way in the house. Sometimes the children would hear her pacing the floor, tapping her cane against the stone tiles, singing the hymn, 'Jesus, Saviour, Pilot me,' to a haunting tune of her own composition. One day, they woke up to find her dead in bed.

I was stunned and delighted to learn from my Uncle Alif's memoir that in her youth Teta Mariam had been famous for her horsemanship, and was known as a *farissa* (an accomplished horsewoman). I had had no idea that as a matter of course my great-grandmother had ridden horses, let alone that she had excelled in this sport. No one had ever suggested to me that women did anything but sit demurely at home, looking after their husbands and children, seeing to their welfare and assisting them in their advance towards health, wealth and social standing. I was astounded at the fact that my great-grandmother had enjoyed a degree of freedom that I could not have dreamed of.

What did this discovery say about my inheritance as an Arab woman? What did it say about my lost status, my dispossession, my lost freedom? And what did it say about 'modernness', and about the myths surrounding the genesis of this notion of 'modernness' that have so often led us astray?

Again and again I saw my great-grandmother Mariam Nakhle in a vision. I saw her, young and strong, wearing her loose trousers, leaping on to her horse and galloping through the Galilean countryside, her *mandeel* falling on to her shoulders as her hair flew out behind her, her cheeks reddened by the wind blowing in her face. I saw her racing at weddings, turning her head every now and then, looking back over her shoulder to see which of her countrymen was catching up with her. I saw her arriving at last at her goal, and then, jumping down, panting, making a joke in a loud voice, or even – amazing thought – uttering a loud swear-word at her male rivals, laughing loudly, patting her horse's rump as she prepared to lead him away, back to the stables which she kept for him. There I see her brushing him down, washing him, feeding him. By now she smells of sweat and mud, and of manure. In this vision there is nothing of the delicate scent of eau de cologne, nor of the clear white skin and delicate fingers of her daughter-in-law, my grandmother.

But this is only a vision, and a fictional one at that. I shall be accused of romanticizing the past. The reality is lost in time, buried under the millions of words and pictures of an invented 'tradition' in which my ancestresses have been portrayed as locked up, subdued and silent. Out of the shackles of my own 'modernity' I can look back at the possibility – though I know it is only a possibility – of a different sort of tradition from the one I have been accustomed to imagine.

Following their marriage in 1905, Munira and Shukri settled in Safad. My grandfather worked for the post office in Safad, as he had earlier done in Jerusalem. In 1906 their first child was born. It was, and remains, the custom for the eldest son to name his first-born son after his father. In this case, my grandfather's father's name, Musa, was taken by his brother Constantine for his son, so my grandfather named his first-born 'Munir' after his wife: this was a token of the great love my grandfather had for his wife. And following tradition, she became henceforth known as Im Munir, mother of Munir. On the other hand, and as far as I can tell, my grandfather was later to become known less as Abu Munir, father of Munir, but rather, because of his unusual and unique profession, as *al qassis*, the minister.

Shukri's mother Mariam and his sister Afife lived with them. Both were jealous of Shukri's great love and affection for his wife, and they tormented Teta behind her husband's back. Though she was educated and had been exposed to ideas and other ways of life, and they were less educated and more provincial, her gentleness and sweetness of temperament was probably no match for tough old Mariam and her envious daughter. Always the peacemaker, taking seriously her religious upbringing and her sense of wifely duties, which included loyalty to her husband's family, Teta never told her husband of her suffering, which he only learned about years later. All her children testify to this episode in her life: it must have been impressed upon them on numerous occasions. Even her granddaughters have heard about this, and know that it is a wife's duty to put up with problem in-laws for the love of her husband.

There may have been an explanation for Mariam's behaviour other than sheer unkindness, however. Perhaps she was annoyed with her son for marrying one of the new kind of girls, educated by the foreign missionaries, all tied up in modesty and high-collared dresses; perhaps she saw in her 'modern', ladylike daughter-in-law a shadow of a future which she looked down upon and rejected.

Teta's life was to be made most unhappy by her husband's decision to go to America in 1908. He was one of thousands who, in an effort to improve the family fortunes, made the perilous journey to North and South America in those days. It was not uncommon for families to pool their resources and send one of their number to America as a gamble towards a more prosperous future. A network of agents, known as *samasras*, organized the Syrian emigrants' journeys, helping them leave Ottoman lands and get started in their new lives.

Shukri's nephew Youssef went with him. My grandfather at this time knew no English. On the sea voyage, however, he managed to pick up enough of the language to allow him to get along when he reached the United States. Eventually, he and Youssef made their way to Texas. There they rode horses from house to house and ranch to ranch, selling hardware and cloth. My grandfather later spoke to his sons about his experiences. He and his nephew spent their nights at the last stop of the day, and after dinner engaged in conversation with their hosts. To the Texas ranchers and field hands there had appeared out of nowhere a pair of men who spoke little English but came from the 'Holy Land' and the 'Turkish empire', the land of dreams and poetry, the land of the Bible and Jesus. My grandfather and his nephew too had discovered a whole new world, as unlike the one from which they came as it is possible to imagine. Among other things, they had never eaten so much beef, if indeed they had ever eaten any: the meat eaten in their country was mutton or goat.

Perhaps in those evening conversations they talked about music, and sang and played for each other. My grandfather loved music, though he had had no formal training. He had learned to play the *oud* as a boy by watching the *awwad* (*oud*-player) who played at the coffee house in Safad: he would watch the man's fingers, and then run home and reproduce the tune on his own instrument. Given the size and shape of that most beautiful and characteristic of Arabic instruments, it is unlikely that he carried his *oud* with him, but perhaps he entertained his hosts by playing the *kaman* (violin), which he had also learned as a boy.

Inevitably, those late-night conversations turned to religion. As my grandfather told the others about the rites and beliefs of his Eastern church, he learned about the Baptists who predominated in Texas, and about their beliefs. He was so impressed that he asked to join the Baptist Church. He was referred to a professor at the Baptist seminary in Waco, the Rev. Dr Scarborough, who provided him with the catechism. Eventually, he was baptized and ordained as a minister and became the representative of the first mission of the Southern Baptist Convention in Palestine. Before leaving the United States, he helped set his nephew up in business in Nashville, Tennessee, where he settled down, married and had a family.

My grandfather Shukri returned to Palestine in 1910, transformed by his experiences abroad. He carried with him a little portable organ that was to provide the music for his new church. Much later, when the church he founded had had some success, his parish acquired a real organ. But for the time being, this little black portable organ provided his children with their early and unifying memories of hymn singing.

Teta's life too had been transformed. At the time of her husband's departure, she was pregnant; and during his absence, she gave birth to a daughter, whom she named Ellen. Her daughter's beauty and charm delighted her and warmed her heart. But when the baby was just two, she contracted cholera and died. Unable to bear the pain of her loss alone, or to continue living in her husband's absence with his family, whom she found uncongenial, she left Safad. Taking her surviving child, Munir, she returned to her parents' house in Marjeyoun. This is the story I had heard from Teta that afternoon in Beirut, when her mind had begun to fail her, but her memory of this traumatic event, together with the pain it had caused her, remained mercilessly vivid.

Her husband's return soon afterwards must have lifted her spirits, but I never heard her say what she or her parents felt when they heard about his conversion and new plans. I do know however that, forever faithful, she was his first convert to the Baptist sect. The second was his brother Constantine, and the third was his mother. He chose as the site of his ministry Nazareth, where Christ himself had grown up. Nazareth was not far from Safad. In 1911 he rented a small house for his family there, and a room for his church. His brother moved with him to Nazareth, where he set up shop selling cloth. His mother Mariam moved in with him and Teta, living with them in Nazareth as she had in Safad. Thus began the First Baptist Church of Nazareth, of the Southern Baptist Convention Near East Mission, with only three members.

At first, the dominant Christian community of Nazareth, the Greek Orthodox, was resentful of this man coming to their town with his strange and even heretical ideas. The foreign missionaries at least were rich. Usually British (mainly Scots in this particular area) or Germans, they came with the power and wealth of their countries behind them; they opened schools and brought with them medical benefits, clinics and doctors. The Russians at least sent church bells. This man, on the other hand, was a local intruder from no farther than Safad. Most of all, the local community mocked him, finding his preaching and ways ludicrous rather than dangerous, but nonetheless unacceptable.

Eventually, however, the pastor established a name and reputation for himself as a good, kind man and a local personality. By the time he died, boys who had earlier taunted him became, in Uncle Alif's words, 'his staunchest supporters', insisting on carrying his coffin on their shoulders from his house to the grave, 'crying all the time'. In his work, my grandfather was strengthened not only by his own power of will and character, but by his wife. The young schoolteacher was now to become known as the 'lady of ladies', *sit al-sittat*.

At least partly through Teta's efforts, then, and people's general admiration for her, the congregation grew slowly. But in 1912 Teta had another great sorrow to contend with: the death of her father, a weighty figure in the Protestant community. I do not know whether he had disapproved of his son-in-law's new church and his daughter's conversion; as usual, I never heard Teta discuss this. Teta, now heavily pregnant with another child, went with her husband from Nazareth to Jdeideh to attend her father's funeral, and to be with her mother and siblings as they received the condolences of the people of the district of Marjeyoun. Youssef Badr al-Kassouf was buried in the grounds of the Protestant church in Jdeidet Marjeyoun.

Slowly life resumed its course, and the family grew. Alif was born in 1912, my mother, Hilda, in March 1914, Rayik in 1916 and Emil in

1920. The 1920s were to bring them much success and happiness, and ultimately tragedy. But before that came the First World War.

On 5 November 1914 the Ottoman empire entered the war on the side of Germany against Britain, France and Russia. The war brought terrible suffering to the region of *bilad al-sham*, or historic Syria. The cruel famine of 1917 haunts the collective memory to this day, and though, once again, I do not remember Teta ever telling me about her experiences at this time, I hear the word *al-maja'a* (the famine) in her voice. In response to the British blockade of the eastern Mediterranean, and the consequent hardships for the Turkish armies, Jamal Pasha, Ottoman governor of Syria, ordered the confiscation of all grain and other food from the people of the area. This food was used to feed the Turkish army. Because the British army proceeded northwards, the war ended in Palestine a whole year before it did in Lebanon, and it was during that year that the famine reached its peak. It never reached the proportions in Palestine that it did further north, but food supplies were still very short in Nazareth.

Most of the men of the area were conscripted into the Turkish army; many others were sent into exile for their political activities, and it was the women who had to deal directly with the terrible suffering brought about by the famine, the battles and the serial occupations, trying to provide for their children at a time when there was little or nothing to eat.

Aside from the general suffering, my grandparents had special problems to deal with. When the United States entered the fray and became, as far as the Ottomans were concerned, an enemy power, my grandfather's salary from the Baptists in Texas was cut off. He had not yet been able to achieve for the Baptist community, and therefore for himself as its head, official recognition from the Ottoman government. Had he done so, his congregation would have been allowed the same status as the other Christian and Jewish communities as far as courts and taxes were concerned. He did not even wear the clerical collar that might have brought him the special status of religious leader, and some personal protection during the war, as it did the other Protestant priests, the Anglicans. Among other things, he would have been exempted from conscription.

As it turned out, he was conscripted into the Ottoman army and sent off to Riyak in the Bekaa valley. There, he became friendly with the garrison's pharmacist, a fellow Palestinian Christian who took him under his wing and requested my grandfather's assistance in the pharmacy. As this request was granted, my grandfather spent his service in the relatively comfortable post of assistant pharmacist and was spared the bloody business of the battlefield.

Teta was left with three young children, a mother-in-law, a maid and herself to feed, and once more she found herself expecting a baby while her husband was away. The baby was born in July 1916. She named him Rayik: the calm one. But his name also echoed the name of the town in which her absent husband was now serving.

Alone, Teta faced food shortages, plagues of locusts, epidemics, wandering soldiers, and especially, financial hardship. Out of respect to the family that had earned his regard, her landlord had sympathetically agreed that he would postpone collecting the rent due until after the war was over or, at least, until her husband returned. Her maidservant, Halimeh, who was to play a major role in Mother's memory of her childhood, also agreed to stay on without pay and collect her wages later. Still, there was not enough money to buy the food that was rapidly becoming scarcer and more expensive, and Teta had to borrow from whomever she could to keep her family going. At first she borrowed from her brother-in-law, who for some reason had not been drafted into the army.

Later, she had to sell some of her jewellery. Her husband loved jewellery, and had over the years bought her a number of pieces, including rings, gold chains and, her favourite (Mother later called it 'one of the loveliest pieces of jewellery I've ever seen'), a brooch in the shape of a bow, with small seed pearls, rubies and sapphires. This is the one piece of jewellery that she did not sell, and later she promised to give it to her daughter on her wedding day. But selling the jewellery was not enough, and later she had to borrow still more money.

Her children's memory of this time includes several pictures of interactions with the Turks before their defeat and withdrawal from the area. Mother particularly remembered one of their neighbours, the wife of a Turkish officer. She used sometimes to give Teta sugar as a gift for the children. Otherwise for sweetening they used only molasses, which Mother loved till the end of her days. Uncle Alif had a different sort of memory. At the end of 1916 a Turkish general visited Nazareth. Uncle Alif remembers being taken to meet him, and being instructed to recite some Arabic poetry. 'I was tutored to say "I want my father back" if the general liked my poetry and asked me what I wanted.'

The family were very short of food and had to make do with substitutes. They used millet flour instead of wheat for baking, and olive oil instead of kerosene for lighting the lamps. But even the fruit of the national tree was scarce: only the smallest and bitterest of olives were available for the local population, the largest and juiciest being taken by the army.

The war ended in 1918 with the defeat of the Ottomans. Eventually the conscripts of the defeated Ottoman armies, abandoned by their leaders, straggled home, wending their way back as best they could. Villages and urban neighbourhoods celebrated the return of each of the men as their families joyfully received them.

The political transformations that occurred in *bilad al-sham* as a result of the war and the demise of the Ottoman empire brought changes of almost unimaginable magnitude to the lives of the people. Arab nationalist leaders had placed their trust in the British and the French and formed an alliance with them against the Turks. Intellectuals had also been seduced by the sweet words of American political rhetoric of the time, especially by Woodrow Wilson's promise of a new age of self-determination, democracy and freedom. The Turks responded to what they saw as treason with a ferocious repression, mostly carried out by the hated Jamal Pasha, whose name, to this day, carries about it an aura of dread.

But betrayal was the name of the day. Having wooed the Arabs into fighting on their side with a promise of supporting their claim to independence, at the end of the war the British and French instead divided up the Arab spoils of the defeated Ottomans between them. They carved new countries out of the carcass of Ottoman Syria, created new borders and declared their own mandate over them. The countries that are now Syria and Lebanon became French mandates, while Iraq, Palestine and Transjordan came under British mandate. Under British auspices, and based on the Balfour Declaration of 1917, there was a massive influx of European Jews into Palestine. This culminated in the creation of the state of Israel, the mass exile of the Palestinian population, and the endless and bloody crisis that has followed since.

Disappointment and anger at the breaking of the promises made by the Western powers, and disappointment in the Western powers themselves (and in their political rhetoric, which had turned out to be a sham), is a major theme not only in some of the memoirs that deal with the period, but in today's political and social climate. Many contemporary memoirs describe the war and its aftermath in terms of dreams and poems permeated by a profound sense of loss. This was, of course, to be compounded by the loss of Palestine. Indeed, loss, together with its inevitable counterpart, a proud and defiant resistance, is a major theme of our time in the Arab Mashreq (East), and specifically, *bilad al-sham*.

The first sign of betrayal appeared in Jerusalem, when General Allenby's army took control of the city on 19 December 1917. The British soldiers raised the British, French and Italian flags throughout Jerusalem. Though the Arab army of Hijaz had been of vital importance in the victory (soon to be total) over the Turks, Palestinians noted bitterly that not a single Arab flag was allowed in sight.

The Arab flag, however, was raised in Beirut during a ceremony at the old Ottoman *serail* when the Ottoman governor evacuated it. The person chosen for the honour of raising the flag was a young woman, Fatma Mahmasani, whose two brothers had been executed not far from the spot by the Ottomans for their nationalist activities. The raising of the flag was accompanied by joyful celebrations throughout the city. Decorations were hung everywhere; poems and speeches were received with the same enthusiasm as they were written and delivered.

The joy was short-lived, however. Rumours of the approaching French occupation spread rapidly, and the British soldiers who had arrived in Beirut began to act as occupiers. The final blow came a few days after the celebrations, when the same flag that had been raised over the *serail* with such delight was lowered on 9 February 1919. The episode which finally snuffed out any lingering hope of independence came in 1920 at the battle of Maysaloun, near Damascus: the French finally defeated the Arab army of Prince Faisal, son of Sharif Hussein of Mecca and leader of the Arab armies in Syria.

My grandparents' inner thoughts, their visceral reactions, as the drama unfolded were no doubt similar to those expressed by so many of the Arab memoirists and poets of the time. In one of his last letters, written in 1928, and preserved by his son Munir to whom it is addressed, it is clear that the Rev. Shukri shared the Arab nationalist feeling. He discusses the Jewish immigration, and refers with bitter irony to 'our lords, the English', and their mischievous attempts to divide Arab ranks in Palestine.

Everything changed with the coming of the British, even the details of everyday life. Decades later, Teta told my cousin Lulu, daughter of Uncle Munir, that it was only when the British entered Nazareth that she saw her very first motor vehicle. Others remember that Australian troops brought with them, and distributed among the population, Australian flour, which had an unfamiliar, unpleasant taste and texture. Even the rice changed, coming now from India instead of Egypt. Unlike the subtle cultural changes of the previous century, the rupture with the past brought about by the First World War was violent, dramatic and irreversible.

CHAPTER 14

Happiness

The period from the end of the First World War and up to 1928 was the golden age of Teta's life, and of her family's. Even the political developments in Palestine that were eventually to play havoc with their lives had not yet managed to spoil it. During the decades following the Great War and until the creation of Israel in 1948, there was a continuous torrent of popular political activity, both organized and spontaneous, including demonstrations and strikes. With increasing urgency and sometimes violence, these confronted the British and the Zionists in Palestine. Women participated fully in these activities. Many of them led strikes and meetings to protest the growing power of the Jewish immigrants, the vast majority of whom were European; social and charity work associations sprang up, as well as groups demanding further education for women; and women were especially involved in the political activity leading up to the great Palestinian Arab revolt, or revolution, of 1936–39. When the military confrontations with the Jews began, peasant women were actively involved in carrying arms and food to the Arab fighters.

Teta herself, however, did not participate in any of these activities. She was too involved with her domestic and pastoral duties, too busy being the ultimate wife and mother to spare any time to the public domain. The only political comment I remember her making was when she recounted how she had boycotted a European Jewish dressmaker, whom she had earlier patronized, when she became aware of Jewish intentions in Palestine.

In spite of the new uncertainties and dangers surrounding them, my grandparents were enjoying their reunion and their safe delivery from the war. The Baptist minister's personal ambitions were being fulfilled, with his wife at his side, and their family growing. The couple had an extraordinarily happy relationship. In their children's memories, this is one of their most striking characteristics. As my mother and her two brothers write about their parents, they see them enjoying a kind of marital happiness that, from the standpoint of their own advancing age and experience, they recognize as exceedingly rare. Mother writes in her memoir:

> He loved her so much and they both depended on each other ... He admitted that without her he'd be lost. To her, he was a solid rock, on which she relied. It was marital love and accord that one hears about and is rarely found.

A new sense of prosperity reigned after the hardships of the past. My grandfather's salary was restored, and the arrears were fully paid up. They rented a spacious new home on the third floor of a large building. This apartment had a large hall called a *baykeh* (large storage area), and this became the church. They installed in it the little black portable organ that my grandfather had brought with him from America, and Teta played it during services. On 20 June 1920 their youngest child was born. He was named Emil, in honour of Aunt Emelia.

Their home was simply furnished. Low wooden-framed divans lined the living-room, their upholstered seats covered with patterned cotton material that was regularly washed and pressed, and with *kilims*. Bolsters stuffed with straw lay on the divans and leant against the walls. Large cushions, embroidered or appliquéd by Teta, provided a merciful softness for visitors' backs from the hard bolsters against which they lay. Two or three large Morris chairs punctuated the circular effect of the divans. Teta proudly displayed her crocheted antimacassars on the bolsters and armchairs, and her embroidered runners on the tables. There was little other decoration in the room, and everything, no matter how colourful, served a useful purpose. Large photographs of long-dead relations hung high on the walls and presided over all the household activities that took place under their severe gaze.

The distinctive characteristic of my grandmother's house was the inclusion of a dining-room, complete with dining table and individual chairs. The family sat at the table, eating out of individual plates and using forks and knives, while in most other households, the family still sat around a low table and ate out of a common dish, using bread or spoons as implements. And though the traditional mattresses filled the *youk* (storage niche), rolled up and waiting for the frequent house guests, each member of the family regularly slept in his or her own bedroom, with a bed – or 'bedstead', as both Mother and Uncle Alif quaintly referred to them – instead of the usual mattresses laid out on the floor at night and folded up during the day as was the custom then. Mother writes that as a child she was uncomfortably aware of the difference in lifestyle between them and other families of their acquaintance in Nazareth. 'We were different,' she writes over and over again in her memoir.

The family lived well. The relatively generous salary paid by the mission was augmented by the sale of olive oil from their land. According to Mother, after the war 'Papa wanted to buy back the jewellery, but Mama refused and told him "You are my jewellery,"' so instead he bought some olive trees in Rameh, his mother's town, which produced the best olive oil in Galilee. He also kept goats as an investment, hiring a goatherd with whom he shared the yield of meat, milk and wool. Later, and in spite of her protests, he did buy Teta some jewellery.

They regularly invested the money saved from my grandfather's salary in olive trees, which were entrusted to the care of Grandfather's cousin Jamil. Every autumn, after the harvest, 'Ami (Uncle) Jamil, as the children called him, would turn up with three camel loads of olives and olive oil. The best olives and oil would be kept for the family's use, and the rest sold. People would come to the pastor's house carrying jugs, jars and bottles, which they would fill up from the oil stored in great urns in the larder, or *munie* room.

From this period emerged a picture of Teta, based on the memories of her children, and of a few very old people of her acquaintance with whom I talked about her, which took my breath away. She was tough, energetic, bustling and authoritative. She was a feared and respected matriarch, disciplining, teaching, forming and instructing. She ran a household that included her husband and their five children, her mother and her mother-in-law, her widowed sister-in-law and, for a time at least, her younger sister and two maidservants. As I investigated her life, I saw a large, strong body, embracing a loving husband, giving birth, suckling her many infants, walking long distances, carrying heavy loads, presiding over a large household, working as hard as only the mother of a large family can work, baking, cooking, stocking her larder with jams and pickles that she made in the harvest season, with the olives and olive oil from their trees, and with the *burghul*, lentils, beans and herbs that she dried for storage.

She was the ultimate helpmate, the perfect pastor's wife. She assisted him at church services, not only playing the organ and leading the singing, but conducting children's Sunday school classes, and Bible study classes for the women of the congregation. She also conducted school classes for the children of the congregation, teaching them reading, writing and arithmetic. She helped her husband in his pastoral duties, visiting the sick, condoling with those in mourning and celebrating with those newly married, newly returned from their travels or recovering from an illness.

Teta was also a highly respected member of her community. She was the perfect hostess who always, despite her busy schedule and modest means, kept an immaculately clean house and provided notable entertainment for the guests. The great distinction between the family and their surroundings of which Mother as a child was excruciatingly – and proudly – aware was in part a function of class, as well as education: many of the members of her father's congregation were poor and uneducated. But many of the family's friends came from the merchant and professional class. From all of them Teta was, in her daughter's eyes at least, quite distinct:

> Mama of course ... was much more educated than any other woman I knew at the time. She was always very tidily dressed

and dressed us neatly too. She knew English well, and played the piano but she never made fun of the neighbours or relatives. She was so helpful to all of them and used her knowledge to help them and mixed so well as one of them, and they all loved her.

The family enjoyed high status and a lively social life in the down-to-earth style of the time. Mother writes:

> Both my parents were very much liked by everyone and we were constantly visited. The custom was that every lady had a special day, known as *istiqbal* [reception], that is, when she was sure to be at home, and the ladies came and visited her and had lemonade, coffee, sweets and cookies which we were all so fond of. Mother's day was usually a Wednesday. There were some really beautiful women who came and, of course, whichever of us kids was home had to come in and shake hands … Naturally, Mother paid return visits to all those ladies, and so she was rarely home in the early afternoon.

Teta insisted on an iron routine of hygiene. Bathing, washing clothes, mopping floors – cleanliness in general was an obsession with her. Even when I knew her as an old woman, when Mother was away and Teta was put in charge of our household, there was a most rigorous use of a wide assortment of specialized cloths, buckets, brushes and brooms. 'This floor-cloth', I can hear her say with determined gravity, 'is for the kitchen, this for the bathroom. This one we use only on the balcony, this one in the bedrooms. This pot is for boiling kitchen towels, this one is for soaking dirty socks.' It would never do to use the wrong cloth or bucket for the wrong function: Teta would show signs of horror if such a mistake were made. Mother herself was later to be captive, though perhaps to a lesser degree, to those same cloths, buckets, brushes and brooms. It was only with a great effort of will that I freed myself of them in my early married life and took up the housekeeping habits of the modern age, complete with dishwashers, vacuum cleaners and self-cleaning ovens. Hygiene was not only a tool to deal with an increased and almost paranoid awareness of germs that came with modern medical knowledge, but also a mark of modernity itself, and of advancement: both Mother and Teta were attached to it as such.

Teta was especially renowned for her bookkeeping, and for the fact that it was she, rather than her husband, who handled the family's daily finances: this was unusual in those days, and marked her in the eyes of the community. 'She had the money, she spent it and she drew up our own accounts and the church ones,' writes Mother. 'Everyone looked up to her.' If her beauty, refinement and education gave her such high standing in the community, another reason was her fecundity, her having had so many healthy children, especially four boys. Her daughter writes proudly: 'My mother was not only beautiful but had four boys as well.'

Perhaps it was because of all these qualities, combined with her prodigious memory and that extraordinary capacity for cataloguing names, dates and relationships of every sort, that Teta became the community's unofficial chronicler at this time. She soon became famous for this role, and whenever there was an argument in town over dates or relationships someone would say: '*is'alo Im Munir, is'alo mart al-qassis*' (Ask Im Munir, ask the minister's wife). Only after proper consultation with her would the argument be resolved.

Teta was marked out from the community in which she lived in other ways as well. She never wore the traditional *habara* of Galilee, the long black cloak that was worn over the head and covered the whole body. Mother remembers that 'If the [other] women were to go down to the market, they dressed in the *millayah* and covered their faces with a thick black veil.' She continues proudly: 'Now Mama was completely different … and never put a veil on no matter where she went.' Yet the habit of head-covering, which everyone shared – men as well as women – lingered on. For many years, Teta wore a black silk scarf over her head, and a woollen shawl over that on cold winter days. In the 1930s, at the insistence of the worldly Emelia and my mother, she began to wear a hat. Later still, when she went out she always wore that black velvet turban that was so familiar to me.

My grandfather Shukri maintained his connections with the earth and with the local folk customs. He was a great animal- and nature-lover,

and tutored his children in the flora and fauna of Palestine. He had a
mare which he loved deeply, and which apparently loved him in return.
She would whinny enthusiastically at his approach, and later when
he died and they had to sell her, she recognized the children one day
as they walked by her in the market, and whinnied madly at them,
stamping her legs and shaking her head.

Through their father and his relations, the family kept their ties to
the folk traditions. Though Shukri had been to America, which Teta
never had, and though today one associates the Baptist persuasion of
which he was so ardent a practitioner with American life and politics,
American culture seems to have had very little, if any, effect on him. He
remained attached to the land and culture of his country in a way that
Teta did not. Mother writes in her memoirs that he often used to mock
the new, elaborate and needless domestic procedures that Teta insisted
on, joking about them and not taking them seriously:

> Mama was very careful about our table manners, so much so,
> that Papa made fun of her, because he didn't really care, and
> only when she noticed and scolded him did he revert to her
> manners.

In this, as in so many ways, he showed the love and regard he had
for his wife. I have been told that the custom in Nazareth in those
days was that when a couple went out, the wife walked a respectful
distance behind her husband. Others have denied this, saying that it
was merely natural that, as men walk faster than women, wives would
inevitably fall behind their husbands. This latter interpretation seems
to me quite sensible, as I often find myself walking several paces behind
my husband, with no ideological intent, I hope, on either of our parts!
In any case, whether it was a dictated practice or not, my grandparents
did not observe it. Uncle Emil remembers that his father insisted that
Teta walk by his side, saying proudly to those who chided him: 'She
is not only my wife, but my most trusted friend and guide. For her
merits, she deserves to walk in front of me!'

If Teta and her children were proud of her high place in her
husband's esteem, and in Nazarene society, they assumed that this was
a function of her 'refinement', her being 'highly educated', and most of

all her being 'modern'. Yet, in a strange way, the high place of women in their household seemed to be part of the past, rather than the future. Teta was never to enjoy the influence in her children's households that her mother and mother-in-law enjoyed in hers. It seems to have been quite natural in that society for matriarchs to behave with an assertive authority quite unthinkable later, when they would be viewed as dependents who were expected to behave with fitting discretion.

The harmony that existed between my grandparents extended to include their wider families. The time I write of was filled with music and laughter and good food, and with a constant bustle of visitors. Shukri's many relations in Rameh and Safad often used to come and stay, and Teta's family used to come too, from Cairo, Beirut and Sudan.

One day in 1920, the family came home from an outing and found Teta's widowed mother, Leila Badr, in their house, along with her sister Najla, 'looking', Mother recalled, 'haggard, pale and miserable'. There had been 'trouble' in the Marjeyoun area, so they had fled to Nazareth. The 'trouble' was probably the nationalist uprising against the French mandate led by the Druze leader, Sultan Pasha al-Atrash. Leila lived with Teta until the end of her days, but she died while on a visit to her son Habib's family in Beirut.

Though Mother concludes her comment on their arrival with the words, 'Poor ladies, we all felt so sorry for them,' neither Leila nor her youngest daughter were very popular in the household. Mother writes of her maternal grandmother: 'She was dry, humourless and never hugged or kissed us.' Mother always refers to her as Sitti or Teta Im Nassib (my grandmother, mother of Nassib).

Uncle Emil remembers his grandmother Leila with some awe, writing that she was 'greatly respected by all'. Like their other grandmother, Sitti or Teta Im Shukri, she had her own room in the house, and her every wish and need was catered to. 'Woe betide any one of us children who dared utter a word or show a gesture of disrespect to her,' he writes. Yet Mother and her brother Alif, inseparable friends and companions as children, used to tease her mercilessly. When they knew she was taking a nap after lunch, they would deliberately make a din just outside her window, yelling mischievously at each other: 'Alif!' (or 'Hilda!'), 'Don't make a sound: you'll wake up Teta!' In spite of Mother's denial, the old lady seems to have had a touch of humour after all. She used to call Hilda and Alif 'France' and 'England' because they sometimes quarrelled and sometimes were good friends.

Leila was as cultivated as her daughter, and an ardent reader of the Palestinian dailies, *Falastin* and *al-Carmel*. 'She used to engage with my parents in serious discussions of the political and social issues of the day,' writes Uncle Emil, 'and was a grand lady in every meaning of the word.'

All the children testify to their father's great love for his own mother and sister, and his respectful, devoted treatment of them. When his sister Afife died, Mother recalls, 'It broke my father's heart, he cried like a little boy.' He shared in caring for his mother, even when she was in her final days, blind, bedridden and incontinent. Mother writes of both her parents' devotion to this cantankerous old lady. Teta patiently put up with her imperious behaviour:

> Teta Im Shukri couldn't come and sit with us at the table very often, so from about 11 a.m. we would hear her shouting to ask Mother what the lunch would be. I also remember very distinctly that as soon as she'd finished, she'd shout out, 'What's for dessert?'

Teta's sister Emelia was now living in Egypt, building up her role as the *grande dame* of the American College for Girls in Cairo. Every summer she would come to Nazareth for a few days. Uncle Emil, her namesake, remembers that a week before her arrival, 'Our home began to simmer.' Teta would rent a room from the neighbours, as her own house was too crowded with children and visitors for the grand lady's taste. Her bed was fitted with a mosquito net that hung from the ceiling.

My grandparents would go to Haifa to meet her, and she would always hire a six-seater car for the return journey, imperiously ordering the driver about. During her brief stays, the children would be admonished not to disturb the august person of their dreaded but generous aunt, who always came bearing gifts from the great city of Cairo, but who never had the capacity for warmth and affection that they took for granted in their mother. Emil, who loved to whistle, was forbidden from this noisy activity. Even the neighbours held her in some awe, remembers Emil, and it was 'Sitt Melia this and Sitt Melia that' for the duration of her stay.

Though the children were always relieved when she left, there were some advantages to her visits. Their aunt's relative munificence, part of her Cairo culture, brought them much pleasure. She always 'brought us lots of beautiful gifts, especially for me,' writes Mother, and continues: 'Aunt Emelia also brought gifts for all the neighbours, the maids and friends of my parents, so much so that Aunt Hanah [Habib's wife] laughed saying, "When anyone tells her good morning she immediately gives him a gift."'

The household routine was broken, and many of the strict rules put aside during her stay. Mother remembers:

> The only time Papa played the *oud* and sang was when Aunt Emelia came. He had a lovely soft voice, but since he became pastor he only sang hymns. He'd put one of us on his lap and play the *oud*, singing some old folk songs that I loved.

After a few days in Nazareth, Emelia would go on to Beirut. She always spent her summer holidays with her brother Habib and his family, and while she was there it was she who decided where they went, what food was to be consumed and how each evening was to be spent.

Teta's other sister, Najla, was hardly as charming, and certainly not as beloved of her niece and nephews as Emelia. Mother writes:

> She believed in hand-reading and discovered that she would always be unlucky and miserable. She was not half as pretty as Mama and I still remember how much my father tried to coax her into marriage with men he knew in Nazareth, and how distressed Mama was that she refused.

Much to Mother's relief, Najla finally moved away. She spent some time in Cairo with her sister Emelia, teaching Arabic at the American College for Girls, and then she emigrated to the United States, where she joined her other sister Nabiha in Texas. Both Nabiha and Najla eventually married brothers of Hanah, Uncle Habib's wife, from Deir Mimas. In Texas, Najla became known as Nellie and studied pharmacy. Nabiha became known as Mabel. Teta never saw either of these sisters again, though they remained very dear to her heart.

Teta's two elder brothers, Nassib and Habib, had gone to Sudan after completing their studies at the Syrian Protestant College: the British colonial administration was an important employer in those days, and young graduates of the SPC, with their excellent knowledge of English, were very much in demand. They too used to come by in the summers, and often sent their children to Nazareth for the holidays. Later Nassib, who had married Afife Haddad from Abeih, moved with his family to Cairo, where he worked as a journalist. I do not remember Teta ever mentioning her youngest brother, Rashid, who had died as a teenager in 1916.

Halimeh, the maid, remained a beloved figure in the memories of my mother and her brothers even in their advanced years. She was illiterate, and though Teta made repeated efforts to teach her how to read, she was unsuccessful. Halimeh learned to count only to ten, so that on baking day, when she carried the loaves to the baker, she would report to Teta that, for instance, 'two tens and three', or 'three tens and four' loaves had been baked. She came from a Muslim peasant family who, when she was in her fifties, became belatedly alarmed at what they thought were signs of her imminent conversion to Christianity at the hands of her employer. They packed her off on a *hajj*, and when she returned, they married her to a deaf mute. After the *hajj*, she always wore a *hijab*, but otherwise her relationship with the Musa family remained unchanged, and they shared an extraordinary affection. She kept in close touch with the family even after they moved away from Nazareth. They finally lost touch with her during the 1948 war.

Once Halimeh had married, and no longer lived with them, other maids were hired. Mother recalls the arrival of two sisters, Fatmi and Sabha, one summer when she came home from boarding school for the summer holidays. Fatmi became a servant in the house of the American Baptist pastor in Jerusalem, Mr Watts, while Sabha stayed with the Musas. Teta taught her to read and write, and she joined in the family singing of hymns. Eventually, she learned to read the Bible and asked my grandfather to baptize her. This he did, but her conversion remained a close secret lest her family find out. Sabha remained with the family until she too married.

After short stints at government schools, the children were sent to the missions for their education. Munir, the eldest, was the first of the boys to be sent to the American Friends' School in Ramallah. Mother and Alif were sent to the Scots College in Safad, and later to Beirut. The two youngest boys studied in Nazareth, and later Haifa.

Annual festivities, remembered fondly by the children as a great family affair, with father, mother, servants and children joining in the labour, accompanied the grinding and boiling of the wheat to make the annual supply of *burghul*. Uncle Alif writes:

> It was a great occasion for us and a wonderful celebration. We would try and help but mainly get in the way. Then the best part came when we ate the boiled wheat with sugar, pomegranates and nuts strewn on top.

Early on in her married life, Teta used to cook on a coal stove; later she used a Primus, its flames fed by gas pumped through the nozzle by hand. My grandfather used often to help Teta with the cooking: in particular, he helped her pound the meat for *kibbeh* and the chickpeas for *hoummos* in the stone mortar.

Everyone came to breakfast together, and the day would start with a prayer said either by the patriarch or, if he asked, one of his children. At noontime, the family gathered again, and again prayer preceded the noon meal, a noisy, jovial affair, as was the evening meal. On Wednesday evenings the family went to church. On Sundays, the day started with everyone meeting in the large sleeping room. Each child had his or her own Bible, and had to read it and say individual prayers before going on to family prayers and breakfast. After Sunday service in the church came Sunday school, and then a meeting of the Baptist Young People's Union, and only after that, lunch, preceded, as usual, by prayers. On Sunday evenings there was a church service as well, and usually on Thursday evenings a special prayer meeting at the home of one or another member of the congregation.

When he was old enough, Alif played the organ at church, alternating with Teta. He and his father would agree on the hymns to be sung at that day's service, but he could never be sure that his father would not change his mind during the service, and take him by surprise by announcing a different hymn from the one agreed upon. If the pastor noticed a newcomer to the church he would change the hymn accordingly, and also change the sermon, which he used to read from notes jotted down on bits of paper. His voice, says Uncle Alif, was very beautiful, 'very musical and forceful'. When he spoke, remembers his son, every person in the church felt that he or she was being addressed individually.

The church grew and prospered. In the mid-1920s a group of American Baptists came to visit from Texas, led by the same men, Dr Armstrong and Dr Truett, who had been among my grandfather's religious instructors in Texas. Donations were raised from this group to build a new church. My grandfather bought land near the Tiberias highway, not far from Nazareth's most famous site, the Virgin's Well, where the Annunciation is said to have taken place. My grandfather solicited more donations directly from the United States. One Texas lady's contribution was large enough to finance the building of the new church. Another substantial contribution allowed him to buy a large bell for the church: indeed, so large and heavy was it that when they raised it to the roof, the entire building almost collapsed. They had to build a belfry to hold it up, more than 20 metres away from the church door.

There is a photograph of Teta dating from this time. She is holding a book in her hands. Perhaps that was her symbol: the book, the learned woman. It is an English-language book, although it is impossible to tell its title. She is wearing a satisfied smile. Everything was going well for her now. You can see that on her face, in her posture, in the general sense of matriarchal, almost smug, satisfaction that the picture expresses.

MOTHER'S WORLD

*Mother and Dad on their honeymoon
in London, 1933.*

CHAPTER 15

A Palestinian Girlhood

Mother's journal records the development of her consciousness during her earliest childhood. Written many decades later, during the bitter loneliness and despair of the war in Lebanon, and so many years after the deaths of her father, husband, mother and two of her brothers, this was a sorrowful but at the same time an extraordinarily important experience for her.

For Mother, writing about her own mother as she knew her in her childhood was unquestionably an act of reconciliation and contrition. As she reconstructed the past, she rediscovered her mother. She found in her qualities to admire that she had forgotten or never seen; she noted how widely admired Teta had been in her community in her youth; she remembered with deep nostalgia the maternal love that she and her brothers had enjoyed, and the wifely love which became her model. She saw Teta's trials anew, and as she did so, she developed a profound sympathy for her: recounting what her mother had endured, she wondered where Teta had found the necessary strength. Over the years, she had lost that childish link with her mother that had bound them together; now she rediscovered it.

But it was not only with her own mother that Mother became reconciled as she wrote. Her first mention of her father is almost unsympathetic. He was very strict with the boys, she writes. As she brings him back to life, however, the picture changes utterly and he emerges from the shadows, a loving, kind, thoughtful, beloved figure, taking her on long walks and picnics in the country and teaching her about the land.

As she wrote, Mother also became reconciled with her native Nazareth, with Tiberias and Safad, with Palestine generally, with Egypt, with Lebanon. With all these places she had, for different reasons, developed an ambivalence, caught between the great love she held for them and a deep anger. From each of them, though for different reasons, she had felt alienated. Each of them had, one way or another, rejected her, sent her on her way, kicked her out. She had paid a personal price for the historical developments each had undergone. As she wrote about these places, however, they came back to her in a rush of happy memories, and her love for them was restored. Even the landscapes of these places changed in her memory, becoming more beautiful and sweet with every look backwards, with every page. Streams and hills, lakes and mountains, flowers and herbs, desert and seashore, all came back to her as vividly as the foods and festivals of her childhood.

As I read her account of herself, I discovered someone I had never known, a wide-eyed, naive, innocent girl from a provincial town in Palestine. But I saw that the sophisticated, widely travelled, immaculately dressed and groomed urban cosmopolite that she became (and that I knew) had nevertheless kept something of the naive innocence, the sweet modesty, of her youth. As I read, I saw the history of our society as it affected, sometimes unbeknownst to her, her private and individual story.

Her earliest memories naturally focus around her parents and the extraordinary warmth of their relationship. She writes that she frequently saw them 'kissing and hugging', and remembers that their rare disagreements, usually over domestic manners, would always end with a kiss. Yet, in spite of their open affection, sexuality was forbidden as a subject of Mother's childish curiosity. Once she inquisitively asked as to the mysteries surrounding her pregnant aunt, who was, she writes, ordered to bed by the family doctor. The response to her question was categorical: 'They would all look so angrily at me and tell me little girls shouldn't talk like that.' It was her father who cleared up the mystery: 'Then one day Papa answered all my questions ...' He explained to her not only the nature of his sister's physical problem, but its social content as well, 'that she [her aunt] worked very hard with her husband to make money, and if he dies and has no children all the money goes to his relatives.' On another occasion, she writes:

> I noticed Mama getting bigger and bigger, especially her stomach, and when I asked Halimeh, she hushed me and said that little girls shouldn't ask questions. My youngest brother, Emil, was born in June of 1920.

Both her parents dispensed social puritanism. Her mother presided over daily life and manners, always admonishing the children to behave in what she considered was a proper way. '*Shou bi qoulou al-nass?*' (What will people say?) was the phrase most frequently on her lips. Her father took his Baptist principles so seriously that Mother was not allowed to cut her hair or wear short sleeves, until one day her Uncle Habib, Teta's favourite brother, came from Sudan with his wife, Hanah, and their daughters:

> My cousins Eva and Lily, Eva, my age, Lily about one and a half years younger, seemed so fashionable compared to me ... They wore short pretty dresses and had bobbed hair. Papa loved Uncle Habib and his wife, Aunt Hanah, and really admired and respected them, so when Aunt Hanah decided that it was a shame for me to dress so reserved and have long hair, she was able to convince him to cut my hair, and oh how happy I felt. She cut my hair for me, and Papa allowed me to wear the beautiful dress she sewed for me, a very slightly shorter sleeve and shorter hem than I usually wore.

Mother was deeply conscious of having been raised in a religious household. Not only were meals always preceded by prayers, but as they ate, the children were often reminded of their moral and spiritual responsibilities, and of their good fortune: 'Papa preached to us about the poor people who eat only bread and *zaatar* (thyme) or bread and salt.' Apparently, he did so regularly when they complained of the monotony of their morning and evening meals, which always consisted of *labneh* and white cheese, olives, homemade jam, and the staple *zaatar* in olive oil. The monotony would be broken only after one of his trips to Haifa, 'our dreamland', from which he would always bring back a chunk of *kashkavan* cheese, a family favourite. His admonitions were not always stern, however; sometimes they were comforting:

> I'll never forget one evening when I asked Papa why we weren't as rich as the J's, because [their daughter] was making a lot of fancy dresses which we couldn't afford, and I'll never forget too what he told me then: 'If you continue to look up, your neck will hurt you. Why should you? Keep looking right ahead of you.' Then he explained to me that he was wealthy spiritually!

Her father showered her with warmth, kindness and a wonderful kind of companionship. He taught her and her siblings a game that they often remembered later, through which he instilled in them his love of Arabic – for though he had learned some English, his great love was the Arabic language and its poetry. He would recite a line of Arabic poetry, and the next player would have to search his or her memory to find another line of poetry beginning with the last word of the previous one. I remember watching Mother and her brothers play this word game in my own childhood.

From her father she learned the secrets of the countryside, the names of flowers and plants. Emphatically, this was not a passion his wife shared with him, for she, the modern woman, was separated not only from the customs and clothes of her people, but also from the land itself:

> The spring was beautiful in Nazareth. Papa took us all for lovely walks, where we gathered wild flowers, wild salad like chicory, *hindbi, zaatar, khobeizeh* and *korsamani*. He told us a lot about each flower and plant, and he really loved flowers and always regretted that Mama didn't care for them.

For his children, it was a great treat to be taken on his family or pastoral journeys to Safad and Rameh, where there were jovial family reunions, with much eating, drinking and talking:

> Another big treat for us children was our yearly trip to Safad with Father ... when we made a stop at Tiberias, where Elias Eid Bishuti lived with his father, 'Ami [Uncle] Khalil, and his mother, and we always stopped and spent the night and had a delicious dish of their special *musht* fish.

On these trips, Mother learned of a different kind of Christianity from the restrictive set of rules and repeated prayers that so bored her. Now, on these journeys through his beloved Galilee, her father brought her to a Christianity that was exhilaratingly alive, and gave it a tangible, direct association with the earth and natural life that she maintained to her dying day. There was in her faith as she grew older an astonishingly naive and direct, almost childlike, quality. She maintained an association of religion more with the earth, the fields, the flowers and fruits, and with those charmed walks with her father, than with the dull lessons recited at Sunday school and the obligatory prayers before mealtime:

> Papa always made a point of showing me all the places that had anything to do with the life of Christ, the mountain of the Sermon on the Mount, the lilies of the field that Christ referred to in his parable, and, loveliest of all, Lake Galilee ... Even before we got to Tiberias we would always stop at Cana of Galilee [Kafr Cana], where Jesus performed his first miracle, and where they had lovely *ruman* [pomegranates].

Of her outings with her father, she remembers that the biggest treat was when he took her with him to Haifa: the worst punishment of all was being deprived of this trip. In spite of the great love of the country Mother learned from her father, she was, it seems, from the beginning a city girl at heart. Haifa stands through her memories, large and exciting, sophisticated, beckoning, tempting. The journey from Nazareth would take four or five hours by carriage: later, when they began to go by automobile, the drive would take only forty-five minutes.

Haifa was at least three or four times as large as Nazareth, and to us it seemed fantastic. For weeks on end, we'd wait to get our turn to go to Haifa, and that, of course, was only during the summer. Usually Alif and I went together, unless one of us was being punished at that time. We went by carriage and on the way, about half-way, we stopped at an inn, where the horses were fed and Papa bought us some *simismiyyeh* and *korshelleh*, which we found delicious. In Haifa, when we first arrived, we went to the big square where we were given the most delicious fresh lemonade with big chunks of ice. Then we usually went to a big shop, Zahlan's, where Papa bought us what we needed, like shoes, and for me pretty ribbons for my hair and some other things that I cannot recall. We went and visited Papa's friend Rashid Nassar, who had a pharmacy, and his brother, who owned a hotel with a big terrace, and we looked forward to the different kinds of bon-bons all those people offered us. Papa usually took us to visit and sometimes have lunch at his cousin's, 'Amti [Auntie] Shafika's.

Later Mother would express some guilt and even anger at the place Haifa had played in her life, and in the life of other Palestinians and Arabs, at its fatal seductiveness. For Haifa, like all port cities, was a cosmopolitan centre and was already being settled by the Jews flocking in from European cities. Their shops, displaying the latest and most glittering fashions from Europe, were enticing dens of political iniquity to the Arab middle classes, contributing to their taste for the imported, the grand and the wasteful. Money spent in these shops was to contribute to the demise of Arab Palestine. Much later, political awareness led to a boycott of the Jewish shops, but the damage to the national cause had already been done. However, the pre-war Haifa to which my grandfather Shukri took his children was still very much an Arab Haifa, and he clearly had not the slightest interest in the colonizing Europeans or their fashions.

On those memorable childhood trips with her father to Safad, Rameh and Haifa, Mother would be released from the strict domestic manners and rules that Teta imposed, and would savour the utter delight of 'belonging' that she missed so much in her own domestic context:

My few trips to Safad delighted me. The whole trip and where we stopped was fantastic, and then Safad itself was quaint, and I loved it. I was made so much of; every family was an aunt, uncle or cousin, and we were invited for breakfast, lunch and supper. I felt somehow that I belonged and was part of a large clan. I don't remember Papa talking religion there. The Bishuti cousins Michel Habib and 'Ami Jubran, their uncle, would gather every night, play the *oud* and sing, and they would drink their delicious *arak* and eat *kibbeh nayyi*, and *safsouf* as they called *tabbouleh* – it was delightful.

But Mother had another connection with the land and the culture of her people other than that offered by her father. This bond was provided by the maid, 'our beloved Halimeh'. Mother used to go with Halimeh to draw water from the Virgin's Well in Nazareth, where, of course, the women would meet to gossip:

> The *'ain* [fountain] was the same place where the Virgin Mary used to draw water, and it was the only source of drinking water for the people of Nazareth. People would carry the long black or brown earthenware *jarra* very gracefully on their heads, and take it home where it would be emptied into smaller jars, and once again would be filled at the fountain, sometimes daily, or else two or three times a week.

She draws a careful line between those activities that she undertook 'but only with Halimeh', and those accomplished with her mother:

> I was never allowed to go alone [to draw the water from the well]. Halimeh was our constant companion except when going to church. She took me, Rayik and Emil to the Greek Orthodox church on their feasts – our feasts were nothing. I cried and coaxed my father so much that he allowed us to go to the different feasts – Easter morning, and the funeral of Christ as we called it [the Good Friday service], where all the Orthodox children displayed their new clothes and had money to buy *simismiyyeh* [sugared sesame seeds] and *qaramish* [sugared pistachios] and

hard sugar done in different gaudy colours, especially bright pink. Papa hated the idea and I often heard him arguing with Mama that this was not the way we the Baptists believed, but she kept on coaxing until we did what all the neighbours did, but we went with Halimeh, never with our parents.

Halimeh also took her on long walks in the country:

> Every summer we rented some fig trees and some prickly pear bushes [*sobeir*] ... Halimeh would take me, and whoever of the boys wanted to go, for a long walk up the hill, where those trees were, and we'd pick lots of figs and prickly pears, and take them home for breakfast. She, Halimeh, always carried a loaf of bread with her, so that I wouldn't eat figs on an empty stomach! I'll never forget those lovely walks, and the excitement of picking figs off the trees very early in the morning.

The baking of bread at home was a ritual which Teta supervised, but which Mother clearly associates with Halimeh:

> Of course, we made our bread at home and that is something I remember very distinctly: Halimeh on her knees kneading the bread then cutting it up, rolling it on a special low table with the rolling pin, then spreading it out in classroom order on a sofa, covered by special sheets and blankets. Every half-hour they'd test it to see if it had risen enough, and then Halimeh would put it in order on a straw *tabaq* [tray] and carry it to the bakery. And I'll never forget the smell of that bread! We didn't get butter too often: the bedouin sold it at the door, and when we had it, it was the biggest treat to spread it on that delicious hot bread and watch it melt and eat it.

Indeed, Halimeh's place in Mother's life was almost that of an alternative, unmodern mother. Some of the village customs automatically excluded her father. The famous Galilee weddings, for instance, were celebrated by men and women separately. Teta, it seems, never attended those weddings:

When I was very young, Halimeh used to take me to weddings in Nazareth – I attended many henna evenings, and the night before the wedding, when the bride was held on either side by her two closest young relatives, holding long candles, *jalwat al-arous*.

She describes the wedding of one of their relations in Rameh:

Mama allowed me and Alif to go along for the whole week of the [double] wedding. Up to today, forty-nine years later, I cannot forget that lovely week. A real village wedding with singing, dancing and a night of henna, especially for the two brides. There were all sorts of old traditions, old songs and the *dabke* [a traditional dance]. It was the first time in my life that I had slept on the floor and every night I stayed up till 2 or 3 in the morning. It was also the first time I saw so many lambs [*kharouf mehshi*] cooked and eaten in the real village way, by hand, and so many different kinds of rich foods served ... No wedding or dancing or *jalwat al-arous* was ever like those two brides and grooms in Rameh.

Growing up, Mother was aware that she had a special place in the household: 'I was one girl with four brothers ... Papa was very strict, it seems to me, with the boys, though he was kind and loving to Mama and myself.' From the beginning she seems to have acquired that self-confidence and assertiveness which could only be bred into an individual. Rev. Shukri's attitude was instrumental in this. Going against established custom, he joyfully celebrated the birth of his daughter as though she were a son. No doubt he was painfully aware of Teta's anguish at the death of their first daughter:

I was told by Halimeh and our neighbours that when I was born in March 1914, my father was so happy that everyone who knew him in Nazareth was surprised. No one in Nazareth, not even if they had ten boys, was happy to have a baby girl. Special kind of sweets called *'asida*, a mixture of flour, butter and syrup, were prepared when a boy was born, and also a special kind of cinnamon tea with nuts, but very rarely did Nazareth people offer anything when a baby girl was born – on the contrary, it was a sad occasion. But when I was born, Papa insisted on offering cinnamon tea loaded with nuts for six weeks on end. At that time they didn't know about the special treat of 'asida.

This happily married man, it seems, had a penchant for unusual celebrations: always the animal-lover, when his beloved mare foaled, he also joyfully demanded that 'asida be prepared to celebrate that birth!

When she was born, Mother was given the name Shifa' (Healing). Her brother Munir, however, all of seven years old at the time, soon thought to invert the name and, despite his parents' angry remonstrations, called her Fisa' (Fart). Eventually, in exasperation, her parents changed her name to Hilda. Why they chose this German name I do not know: perhaps the missionary community included a lady of that name whom they wished to honour. There are an inordinate number of Hildas in Palestine, and I have never understood why.

If their father was his children's connection to the earth, the old, the traditional, and if his large family in the Palestinian provinces cushioned their existence with its warmth and its deeply felt roots, Teta, with the 'modern' and alienating social forms that she taught them, seems to have had a more complex, and more enduring effect on them: in the end, it was her mother's way, not her father's, that Mother followed and set her children on.

The alienating influence of Teta and the new culture that she created, practised and taught is clear throughout Mother's notes. Repeatedly, she is struck by the degree to which she and her family were different. 'I cannot forget how lonely I felt most of the time.' Their fellow Nazarenes 'laughed at us'. 'People found us very strange in Nazareth.'

Certainly, some of the alienation had to do with her father's profession. But, as time passed, and as her parents gained the affection and respect of their community, the religious difference became less and less problematic. It was Teta's lifestyle, on the other hand, that marked them as irredeemably different. At one point in her memoir, Mother thoughtfully writes: 'One thing I remember well: all of these men and women loved my father a lot, but looked up to and admired my mother.'

When I read of Mother's intimate, lived knowledge of the country, of its flora and fauna, of the folk songs, the *oud*-playing, and especially the village weddings, I was stunned. I was amazed at the cultural spaces over which she had leapt in her lifetime. I was devastated at my ignorance of her cultural make-up, of her complex identity, and therefore of mine. I had never had any idea that Mother was once so connected.

Teta was ignorant of – or at least ignored – the countryside, and the trees and plants that grew there. She was ignorant of – or at least turned her back on – the customs, weddings and funerals and other celebrations of the native Orthodox Church. She was, in short, partly by an accident of birth, geography and fate, and partly by a deliberate act of will, inwardly estranged from much that was going on about her, even while participating fully in the social life of her town.

Mother was later to follow her mother's lead and move increasingly towards a refinement and restatement of the choices her mother had made. These choices led her farther into the domesticity and general lifestyle of the urban bourgeoisie, and to the strongly felt boundaries of the nuclear family. This lifestyle was in turn to lead her farther and farther away from the earth, from her own people, from their customs and politics, into that never-never land occupied by the global middle class.

By the time I came to consciousness, the separating process, the alienation, which was so painful to her as a child had been completed, and a new kind of culture had been born. This was the culture I knew, the urban, middle-class, cosmopolitan, universalized culture, created by the synthesis between the specialized, the particular, the local, and that other more universal quality which today we call globalization. It was probably during Mother's early youth that the parting of the ways between the 'traditional' and the 'modern' begun in Teta's time was accomplished. And it seems to me true that, even as I write, none of us really understands clearly the meaning of these words, or their implications.

Of all the uncles, aunts and cousins who formed the social background of their lives, Mother had a special love for her father's brother, Constantine, who had moved from Safad to Nazareth when the newly ordained pastor returned from America. He always spoiled her, bringing her presents and playing games with her. His death when she was nine 'brought a great sorrow upon us'. He had only one son, Musa, who was to remain a family favourite until his death in London in 1980. He had emigrated to the UK, where he worked for the Arabic Service of the BBC. Mother and Alif were also especially friendly with Eva and Lily Badr, closest of all the cousins to them in age, and daughters of their favourite uncle, Habib, and his wife, Hanah. Later, Fouad and Ellen, Habib and Hanah's youngest children, were to become close friends of the family as well.

The cousin Mother saw most of and loved best, however, was Nora, her Uncle Nassib's daughter. Nora and her elder sister Wadad were regularly sent from Cairo by Uncle Nassib to stay with his sister's family in Nazareth. Sometimes Nora went to school in Nazareth with Mother. 'Nora', she remembers, 'made me feel that our local government school to which she went with me was very poor.' No doubt Mother – and Nora – were among those children who have been described pacing the grounds of the old Ottoman schools while repeatedly reciting, in chorus, lessons which they were trying to memorize and which had been dictated by the poorly prepared teacher, himself trying to cope with the desperately confusing new situation brought about by the British mandate in Palestine.

It was after one of those idyllic summer visits by her cousins and uncles in 1925 that Mother started begging her parents to be sent to boarding school. Earlier that same year, 'on one of those lovely Safad visits' with her father, she had heard that a Scots College had just opened in the town. There were two schools, one for boys and the other for girls; they were owned by the Scottish Presbyterian mission, and run by a Mr Semple. Her parents finally took the decision to allow her to go. Her brother Alif, as ever her inseparable companion, was to be sent too. To complete her happiness, her best friend, Johara Jiryis, pressed her father, a prosperous businessman, to let her go as well. Johara's father, writes Mother, 'was delighted at the idea that his daughter would become a lady like Im Munir, preparing faultless accounts, playing the piano and talking English so fluently.'

'I still can't remember how Papa was convinced,' Mother muses. His decision may have been due to political factors of which she could not have been aware at such a young age. In the mid-1920s, there was much dissatisfaction in the Palestinian towns with the state of the government schools, not only academically, but also administratively and politically. Furious debates surrounded the schools, which gradually became the focal point of Palestinian nationalism, and played a very active role in the Arab revolt of 1936–39.

In 1925, the year Mother was sent to Safad, the state school system was in a chaotic state of flux, as it had been for several years. When Mother was six, the standard age of entry into state schools, it was 1920 and the British occupation of Palestine was in its third year. The Ottoman schools, elementary and others, were being transformed by the British authorities to satisfy their interests as occupiers. The mandate government became official only in 1922, and the Ottoman laws governing education remained technically in effect until 1933, when the new laws on education were passed. A first draft of a British mandate education law was drawn up in 1927; it was bitterly rejected both by the Zionists, whose growing influence was already being felt, and by the European powers, especially France, Italy and the Vatican. By 1933 the new law had passed through several drafts more conciliatory to these bodies. It made little effort to please the Palestinians.

In the meantime, however, and from the very beginning of the British occupation, new curricula and syllabi were drawn up for the state schools, though not necessarily adhered to, and an entirely new cultural situation was being created *de facto*. Administratively, for instance, whereas the Ottoman elementary schools had been under the direct control of local councils – the more advanced schools being governed more directly by the Ministry of Education – the British placed them under direct state control. Local education officials answered directly to a state inspector, who himself was responsible to the British; local officials were no longer in any way answerable to their fellow townsfolk, nor had they any influence on the decisions being taken elsewhere.

Article 15 of the Mandate, which became official in 1922, was clearly designed to protect both the Zionists, who at this time were being cultivated by the British, and the private mission schools. The Jewish private schools, organized and financed by the Zionist organizations, were on their way to achieving official recognition as a separate state system, known as the Hebrew Public System. The Hebrew Public

System was to be given a generous chunk of the state education budget, while its schools maintained their total independence and pursued their own interests.

The private mission schools, of many nationalities, were given special independent status, and were left more or less to their own devices, their private interests protected. Those foreign mission schools closed by the Turks at the beginning of the First World War as enemy interests had been reopened by the British. Even the German schools, though they were watched carefully by the new authorities, were reopened. Only the schools of the Russian mission were permanently closed, as a result of the Bolshevik revolution.

In short, it was specifically and only the Arab Palestinian government school system that was to be at a disadvantage under the new British government of Palestine. The curricula imposed by the British, especially in subjects like History and Geography, were to come under great attack from Arab nationalists not only for the way they dealt with Palestine, but also because these curricula were viewed as designed to discourage an independent and flourishing class of thinkers while creating a class of artisans and clerks. Later, the nationalists were to demand higher and better education, especially for the peasants, seeing there a crucial element in the battle against the Zionist farmers who were colonizing the land.

There was also, as there had been from the beginning of the modern age, a persistent demand on the part of the public for more schools for girls. The British actively discouraged the advancement of women during the mandate. Whether this was part of their deliberate effort at undermining political activity in the country, or merely the natural result of their own attitudes towards women, they followed it through into the repressive education policy that was one of the major instruments of their power. Thus when Palestinians demanded more schools for girls, the mandate authority insisted on an even greater emphasis on domestic education rather than what they called 'the literacy side', as cited by Elise Young.

As a member of the politically conscious middle class, who shared its nationalist aspirations, it was not surprising that the Rev. Shukri should have chosen the mid-1920s to move his children, Hilda and Alif, to a private mission school, out of reach of the mandate authority. I have heard of several Palestinian families, Muslims as well as Christians, who decided to do the same at this time. Munir, Mother's eldest brother, was already enrolled at the Friends' School in Ramallah, which had the added advantage of being American, rather than British. The decision to send the younger two to Safad may have had something to do with its being their father's home town, with plenty of relatives to look after the children, and with its proximity, for Teta had protested that they were too young to be sent away. In addition, the school had offered the pastor a special discount off his children's fees.

In October 1925, pastor and prospective students piled into an ancient car that started with a *manuella*, a manual crank. They had to stop several times to cool it down with water. So excited were the children that they could not later recall whether they had made their usual ritual stops at Kafr Cana, Tiberias and Tabgha, to visit their old friends and relations.

The principal of the girls' school, 'a really lovely-looking woman of twenty-five or twenty-six', was called Miss Ina Mackintosh. Her assistant was a Miss Henry. These women, though remembered with great fondness by Mother, struck her even as a child as being rather inept. The most important person in the school, she wrote, was the cook, an enormously fat Safad woman named Warde, whose loud voice seemed always to echo around the grounds. 'It seemed to us,' Mother writes in her journal, 'that she ran the school and not Miss Mackintosh. Everyone was scared of her.'

There were thirty boarders at the school and, on the whole Mother's memories of it are summarized in her reflection: 'We enjoyed ourselves immensely and I don't remember anyone working too hard!' Most of her memories of this happy time seem to centre on picnics, with 'delicious sandwiches, scones and cakes', made especially memorable by the setting: 'Safad and its surroundings was a beautiful place. There were lots of streams and small waterfalls and scenic places to hike to.' Safad was cold in winter, and it would snow once or twice a year. And though 'we had absolutely no heat and we all had chilblains', the girls seemed none the worse for this.

Every Saturday evening they enjoyed a social event:

We would dress up and go to Miss Mackintosh's apartment and have a social evening of games and songs. She had a lovely voice and played the piano beautifully. I learned a lot of songs from her, especially Scottish ones and oh! how I loved to sing.

Her father had requested piano lessons for his daughter, and these brought Mother as much delight as her singing lessons.

Living conditions at the school were rather bleak, though that does not seem to have marred the girls' happiness:

We had large cold dormitories, of course no carpets and no running hot water. We had baths once a week ... Warde, the formidable cook, used to heat water and we bathed two at a time, even when it was bitter cold.

Some of Mother's happiness at the Scots College seems to have been due to the easy-going temperament of the British teachers, especially Miss Mackintosh: 'All the girls in the Scots College loved her, and we'd do anything to please her.' The Scotswomen seem to have been rather accomplished and, though lacking the experience and discipline required to run a school, instilled their love of literature and music into their students:

Miss Mackintosh was teaching us Shakespeare and insisted on producing one of his plays in the garden. *Hamlet* was chosen, and Ida Kunzler played the Ghost. It was the first time in my life that I'd seen a play, and when I was asked to play Rosencrantz I was so happy! We also acted *As You Like It*, and I was Celia. I really enjoyed the English classes. I was an ardent reader and Miss Mackintosh was delighted with the way I read Dickens, Thackeray and all the rest. I always had the highest grades, and spent a lot of time explaining Shakespeare etc. to Johara, Souad Nassar and some of the others ... Miss Mackintosh, who chose all the books in the library, was always surprised at how much I was reading. It was a new world for me. I learned so many poems and memorized them.

In addition, these teachers created a deep interest in Britain in the girls. A kind of eager fascination with far-away lands, a longing to see them, is perhaps an inevitable corollary of this kind of education. This longing seems to be a ubiquitous aspect of the foreign schools in this region, and I have had many occasions to wonder at its effectiveness in making the students' real surroundings feel dull and uninteresting:

> Both Miss Mackintosh and Miss Henry talked to us for hours on end about the British Isles, especially Scotland. I always wondered if ever in my life I'd see England. I would sit dazed with wonder and delight in their pretty sitting-room listening to all sorts of descriptions.

In Mother's last year at the school a new teacher arrived, a Miss Lascelles, whom Mother describes as 'a plump Highland girl':

> I'll never forget how she'd tell us all about her home in the Highlands and how beautiful it was, but oh! how cold ... Miss Lascelles gave me all sorts of books and pictures on Scotland ... and created in me lots of dreams and I kept on reading and reading.

So dazzled were the girls with their Scottish teachers, and so greatly did they appeal to their imagination, that the Palestinian teachers, representing dull reality, did not leave much of an impression: 'The only one I remember is Miss Amini Abou Rahmi, who taught us Arabic.' Another Arabic teacher, Mr Elias Haddad, preached in Arabic and occasionally conducted the obligatory Sunday services, though these were usually conducted in English by Mr Semple, the head of the boys' school.

Mother was kept in touch with the real world through her weekly visits to her father's relations, who, always warm and welcoming, fed her the same copious meals that she used to enjoy with her father. She kept abreast of developments in the country through one of her best friends at school, Souad Nassar, daughter of the famous Palestinian journalist, Najib Nassar, owner of the newspaper *al-Carmel*. It was at

least partly because of her friendship with Souad that Mother was able
to claim later that she had some political awareness and knew what was
happening in Palestine.

Another kind of awareness was starting to be awakened in her at
this time. The boys' school was entirely separate from the girls'. 'We
hardly ever talked to them,' Mother remembers. They only mixed at
church, and then 'We would look at each other all through the service.'
Mother records: 'I began to notice that some of the boys at the boys'
college were staring at me.' One of her friends whispered to her that
several of them were in love with her, and for the first time in her life,
she received a compliment about her looks. Mother never regarded
herself as having been as beautiful as her mother.

At last, however, this idyllic period in Mother's life came to an end.
By 1928, the ineptitude of the administrating ladies had bankrupted
the school and the Scottish mission was unable, or unwilling, to bail
out the girls' college. The boys' school, however, was to continue in
Haifa, and Alif moved there with it. Mother's Badr cousins, Eva and
Lily, were by now studying at the American School for Girls in Beirut.
By the time she arrived home that summer of 1928, her father had
already contacted the ASG in the hope that, 'being a pastor with a large
family', he might procure a discount for his daughter and be able to
send her there.

In fact, the previous summer was the time the Baptist community
he had worked so hard to establish was at last housed in a real church.
The dedication ceremony, though joyful and triumphant, was moving:
'My father, when he prayed that day, was all in tears, actually weeping.'
The party, led by Dr Truett, which had come from Texas for the
dedication, included an elderly woman, a Mrs Bottoms, 'who seemed
very important'. She was, it turned out, the wealthiest member of the
group. Having lost her only child, a daughter, she took a great liking to
Mother and offered to pay her way at an American school. At the time,
of course, Mother was still at the Scots College, but once he heard
of the school's impending demise, her father contacted Mrs Bottoms,
who, sure enough, 'sent a considerable sum which helped me through
a couple of years at the ASG'.

As she waited for the time when she was to go to her new school, an episode took place which deeply hurt her feelings and which she recounted to me many times:

> That vacation, I was so unhappy that I kept on singing all the beautiful songs Miss Mackintosh taught me. I had learnt a new one there, the *Ave Maria* of Schubert. I loved the words and the tune and sang it constantly until one day Papa heard me and stood still listening to the words! All hell broke loose when he heard them. He told me he started a new mission in Nazareth, the Baptist, to which he is devoting all his life, and I should not sing the opposite of what he is preaching: that the Virgin Mary is not someone we pray for, we go directly to Christ, we're not Orthodox or Catholics, etc, etc. Useless trying to explain to him that I wasn't being religious in singing it, but he was furious and asked me never to sing it again.

Luckily, the mutual anger generated by this incident was cleared up, and the quarrel between father and teenage daughter healed. In the early summer of 1928, he told her that she was old enough to join the church. Already by then her two older brothers had been baptized, as well as her grandmother, Sitti Im Nassib. Her father, keeping a watchful eye on his daughter's moral development, watched for signs of her religious maturing. 'Papa was so serious about it, and any time he saw me alone and doing nothing special, he'd call me and ask me questions, and discuss things with me.' At last, the baptism ritual was undertaken, and a peaceful memory lingers:

> I had a new white nightgown made, and Father and myself went into the water; he prayed, then immersed me one, two and three times, then told me very proudly, 'Welcome to the body of the Church.'

CHAPTER 16

Partings

In 1925 the family's eldest son, Munir, sailed for America to study at Baylor University in Texas. He was to study medicine and would eventually return to Palestine as a physician. In her memoir, Mother remembers her parents' reactions as they saw him off:

> Papa, though he wept easily, didn't shed a tear, but Mama, poor Mama, I thought her heart would break. For days on end she cried and cried and would hardly eat anything (Munir was certainly her favourite) and I'd see Papa hugging and kissing her.

Six of my grandfather's letters to Munir in the United States survive. Dated June, July and August of 1928, they are written in Arabic on a letterhead that announces in English: 'The Near East Mission of The Southern Baptist Convention, Nazareth Station', with his name, The Rev. S. Mosa [*sic*], Nazareth, Palestine. Near 'Nazareth', he had written on one of the letters, in English, 'The Lord's home city'.

The letters, the following excerpts from which I have translated into English, reveal much, not only about father and son, but the general climate and the family's special concerns. The elaborate and leisurely greetings and endings of the letters offer a delightful contrast to the hurried correspondence of our time:

> Beloved of your father and mother, beloved of the Lord, may your days be safe ... I wished on this beautiful morning to talk with you, so I start my conversation with many kisses and the sweetest of greetings, asking God to grant you more success ... Mother sends you thousands of kisses, and so do I, and each of your siblings, and in closing all of us ask God to grant you success. A special *salaam* from your father, and may God protect you for your parents, Shukri and Munira.

One letter closes thus:

> *Salaams* from your grandmother and your cousins and your brothers and sister. You do not say anything about your going to church, and hearing the Prince of Sermons, as they call him in some newspapers. Are you praying regularly? And reading the New Testament? Please, my dear, love God and live for Him. *Salaams* from your father and your mother.

The letters speak of intense warmth, a sense of humour, and a close and happy relationship. They also speak of a deep longing, and of the terrible distance that separated travellers from home in those days. A fond father speaks to his eldest son, missing him, chatting with him, joking with him, inquiring into his studies, asking about his grades and examinations, sharing his worries, occasionally chiding him, constantly wishing the time of his absence would pass and they would embrace once again. Mischievously, he whispers the latest Nazareth gossip across the oceans; he confides in his son about a business venture in which he has bought some goats; he tells him of his flock, of the services, of how the church is progressing. Fatherly advice about money is a frequent theme:

Money goes, and a man does not know where it went. The wise man is one who counts and knows, and who does not wake up when he needs money but finds it there. God be with you and grant you wisdom so that you should know how to manage your affairs. And miserliness is not the answer; it is like being a spendthrift, and both are bad.

Throughout this remnant of a long correspondence, the nature of the family relationships is revealed. Much of one of the letters is taken up with the antics of not-quite-eight-year-old Emil, clearly the apple of his father's eye: 'When we went to Haifa, Master Emil was constantly demanding "I want syrup, I want cake, I want ice-cream."'

Later on in the same letter, he writes affectionately about 'this little dog that is giving himself such importance'. It was Emil's birthday, and he kept making demands – 'Do this for me' and 'Do that for me' all day. That evening, much to his parents' surprise and embarrassment, people turned up at their house for the birthday celebration. It seems 'the little dog' had long before told everyone it was his birthday, and solicited the required attention for this important event. In the end, however, everyone had a good time. They played the piano and sang, and all the guests joined in, singing around the piano. 'Then we invited them to see the new organ, and to play it, and we went together and the church was full.'

A note of worry creeps into one letter. That week they were expecting Hilda and Alif home for the summer holidays from the Scots College in Safad:

> The matter of the closing of the girls' school in Safad has been worrying us a great deal. We want to send Hilda to Beirut, but we found out that the school costs 40 pounds without piano, and when we add to that the cost of a passport, and boarding, books and expenses, it will amount to around 60 pounds, and this is more than we can afford. We do not know what to do.

But he ends this vexing deliberation on a hopeful note: 'God will provide a way to pay for her.'

His daughter's future is a recurrent theme, as is the progress of her inseparable companion, Alif. The political changes after the fall of the Ottomans have implications for education and, as usual, language:

> Hilda and Alif will take French lessons during the two months of their holiday this summer. In the first place, this is because Alif has to take French at school, and so we thought we would help him along this summer, and second of all, because the American School in Beirut is strong in French, because this has become the language of Syria and Lebanon, and so we hope that Hilda will not be behind her class there.

The letters make clear that her parents believed that their daughter's destiny was to be a teacher like her mother and her aunts before her.

In only one letter, the first of the series, dated 15 June 1928, does he specifically discuss the political situation in Palestine. He is not overly pessimistic about the Jewish immigration to the country: 'Some Jews will remain in Palestine, in spite of the low standard of living, and other Jews will go back to their [modern] countries.' He adds a fatalistic note: 'God will provide for us.' After summarizing the recent splinters in Palestinian political ranks, engineered by 'our lords, the English', he writes: 'I think – no, I am sure – that these divisions are English policy, to divert the factions and busy them with each other. God protect us from them [the English]!'

The last letter of all is dated 7 August. Prophetically, the form of address is even more intense than usual: 'Beloved of my soul, delight of my liver, my beloved Munir, may God protect you.' It begins with a supplication and a prayer: 'I kiss you the kisses of a father, and I give you sweet greetings. I ask God the Almighty to be a support for you, in all times and situations, for He alone is Almighty. Amen.'

He writes of the visit to Nazareth of Dr Armstrong, who had come with Dr Truett from Texas to attend the consecration of the new church that my grandfather had worked so hard to build. He had known Dr Armstrong from his days in Texas, and Munir was also acquainted with him:

> Today they left [for the US] and we sent with them for you some *arameesh bi fustuq* [sugared pistachios], *lukum* [Turkish

delight], nougat, *mlabbas* [sugar-coated almonds] and *ghuraybeh* [butter biscuits]. Today I went back to the hotel to bid them farewell, and came back wishing I were going with them to see my beloved son.

He interrupts his own complaints:

> All right: God is generous. The next three years will pass as the last three have done.

To one of her husband's letters Teta had added a note, the only words other than her name that I have ever seen written by her. Her note is warm and sure, though short. Her words are full of feeling for her son's physical presence, his smell and his touch. She is in a hurry and very busy; she will write soon at length and tell him all the news:

> My dear and light of my eyes:
>   I press you to my heart that yearns to see you and to smell your sweet and delicious scent. I wish I could kiss you a motherly kiss, and pray to Our Lord to protect you and keep you. This time I cannot write for long, but, God willing, next week I will write a longer letter. My prayers are with you and I miss you very much; may God protect you and return you safely to your loving parents.

How could she know that the final curtain was descending on her happiness, that the thoughtless rush of her domestic work, the making of jams and the boiling of syrups, the laundry, the cooking, the Bible classes and Sunday schools, the gracious hospitality – that all of this that was making her too busy to write just now would suddenly become meaningless?

Three weeks after he wrote the last letter, and probably before it or the pistachios and sugared almonds reached his son, the pastor was dead.

Mother had been haunted by a terrible premonition in that summer of 1928. She was very sad that the Scots College was closing, and though she was looking forward to her impending move to Beirut she also viewed this with great trepidation. That same summer Halimeh had married, and though she and her new husband lived next door, things had inevitably changed. Partings were in the air. Pausing in her memories, she writes: 'I was so scared of the month of August.' In August 1926 her Aunt Afife, her father's sister, had died, causing him such sorrow that 'he wept like a boy'. In that same month, her other Aunt Afife, the wife of her Uncle Nassib, Teta's brother, had also died. In August 1927 a terrible earthquake had struck Galilee.

'I'll never forget that terrible August. The heat was unbearable, not a breath of air.' She relives the experience, the house shaking at 3 in the afternoon, the ceiling beams falling, the instinctive scramble to rush out of doors. 'In some rooms,' writes Uncle Alif of the same traumatic experience, 'you could see the sky in the corner. In fact, I saw one of the walls open up and close as we all ran down to the street.' Rayik and Emil both had measles at the time. When the earthquake struck, Teta scooped them both up in her arms and ran down the stairs with them. Later she expressed amazement at her own feat. 'I don't know how I ever got the strength!', she exclaimed.

The house was so severely damaged that the family had to move. Mother describes the search for a new home, and the remorseless irony of the family's happiness when at last they found 'a very beautiful house, *beit* Raja al-Rayis, one of the newest and best houses in Nazareth'. It was a bargain, and they were pleased with their good fortune. In fact, no one else would have it because of its reputation as a *beit mash'um*, a cursed house. It was said that several people had died in this house after they moved in. But, writes Mother, 'Both Mama and Papa made fun of everyone, and said they didn't believe in superstition.'

More than half a century later, three of the pastor's children wrote down their memories of the most terrible event in their lives, the death of their father. Each of them has memorized particular details, and each goes over these details, as though, almost sixty years later, it had just happened, and they are all bewildered and horrified children once again. As Mother wrote, she found herself shaking with emotion: 'Even as I write this after fifty-two years, my pen fails ...'

Uncle Alif describes every moment of the unfolding drama in clinical detail. The children had gone for a picnic with their father. Teta was in the kitchen when her husband came home that evening, sweating profusely from his exertions in the sweltering heat. He went into their bedroom to change his clothes. Always watchful for her husband's well-being, she would normally have shut the window to prevent him catching a cold. On this occasion, she did not see him come in, and sure enough he caught a chill, which rapidly developed into pleurisy and then pneumonia. Mother takes up the story:

> Dr Farah came three times a day, and certainly looked terribly worried as the fever got higher and higher. Then to my surprise, our barber, Salim Asfour, came with a jar full of black worms (they were leeches) and he put them on Papa's face near the ears, where they sucked some of his blood. That was their way then, for lowering the temperature.

His family kept an anxious watch by his bedside as, ever the faithful pastor, 'he delivered sermon after sermon while unconscious of his surroundings.' Finally, early in the morning of 28 August 1928, he died.

Mother records her own mother's despair:

> She just sat there and stared vacantly and when I came in to see what had happened, she looked at me and said: 'You're an orphan, my child.' Father was only fifty-eight, and she was forty-eight. It was as if her world had fallen around her.

Mother describes the period immediately after her father's death:

> Word spread. It seemed to me that all Nazareth came over that night. Word was sent to Safad, Haifa, Rameh, Tiberias and Lebanon, where my Uncle Habib and his family and Auntie Emelia were spending the summer.
>
> Oh! What a nightmare those days were. The Nazareth way of death was terrible. They put the body in the middle of a large room and the family and friends sat around wailing and

crying. I'll never forget that long miserable day. I was so scared for Mama, tired and worn out, but still, I refused to go to the funeral. It seems it was very sad and very well attended. Papa was very popular, and a very straightforward man whom everyone liked and respected. The Baptist congregation with Mr Watts were able to convince the district governor to bury him in the church that he loved so much, and through his great effort was able to build.

All our family from Safad and Rameh came. Uncle Jamil Nakhle, who loved my father, was crying like a child, and he took over all the ceremonies of the funeral, before and after.

Uncle Emil's most terrible memory centres around his mother. He was only eight at the time:

I will never for one moment forget how she seriously attempted to throw herself into the grave as the coffin was being lowered. I took hold of her dress and the others held her back. She was crying bitterly and saying: '*Lameen tarikna, ya Shukri, lameen?*' [To whom have you left us, Shukri, to whom?]

Then he reflects: 'These two people were really like one, even after twenty-three years of marriage and five children.'

Though Sitti Im Nassib, Leila Badr, was there, of course, Mother was surprised that none of Teta's siblings came to be with her. Uncle Habib was still in Sudan, and cabled his sister that he would pass by Nazareth on his way to Beirut, to which he was retiring permanently. Nassib did not come from Cairo though his two daughters, Wadad and Nora, were staying in Nazareth at the time. But Teta was especially surprised – and, in retrospect, hurt – at her Aunt Emelia's absence:

Aunt Emelia was in Lebanon, and was going back to Cairo but instead of passing through Nazareth, as she usually did, she sent us some money and told Mother that she just couldn't face so much sorrow.

Teta suffered a major depression. She stopped eating and lost 20 kilograms in a few weeks. She had neither the energy nor the will to look after her children: she wanted, quite simply, to die. Eventually, she was hospitalized under the care of the Scottish Dr Bathgate. She was brought back to life through a desperate charade created by her own mother. Mother records her grandmother's ruse, which I had already heard from Uncle Rayik himself in America:

> Sitti Im Nassib told Emil and Rayik to go and complain to Teta in hospital that they were being neglected, and not being fed and taken care of. This made her feel so sad. Emil was only eight and Rayick ten years old. She felt so bad for them that she pulled herself together and started to take more interest in life. Eventually she gathered up her strength and went home to look after her children.

The leading members of the congregation also visited Teta at the CMS Hospital. They told her that her husband would have wanted her to continue with his work, which would be lost without her. This thought also helped to restore her.

At last, she came home and resumed her life, doing what was necessary to bring up her children. Gallantly, she insisted that Mother go on to boarding school in Beirut as originally planned. Equally gallantly, she insisted that Munir continue with his medical studies in Texas. On hearing of his father's death, he had wanted to interrupt his work to come home and help share the burden of the family, but she would not hear of this. For a short time she carried on the work of the church, receiving half her husband's pay from the mission. The former assistant to her husband conducted the church services, but it was she who held things together. She continued the Bible studies, the women's prayer meetings and the pastoral visits. Mother writes sadly in her memoir: 'So the hard work my parents had started dwindled, and only Mama's work with the women and Sunday school went on.'

Eventually the Southern Baptist Convention appointed her husband's nephew, the Rev. Louis Hanna, to succeed him. This was the same nephew who had accompanied my grandfather to America in 1908. From having been the pastor's wife, Teta now became the new pastor's assistant, continuing the work she had done before. The congregation felt more at home with her than with Louis' less sweet-tempered American wife, Velora.

Teta was forty-eight years old when her husband died. She owned next to nothing, only the olive trees, the goats, and some pieces of jewellery lovingly given to her by her husband. She managed to hang on to her home until 1936, when the revolution in Palestine brought all economic activity to a standstill. That she spent the rest of her life with her children would in an earlier time not have been a terrible fate; it had been the customary and expected life for a woman in her situation. After all, both her mother and her mother-in-law had lived with her. Indeed, in the old extended family, the matriarch reigned supreme.

With the new forms of society, however, and the coming of the modern nation-state, with its bureaucracy and capitalist structure, property and marital status became all-important. The death of Teta's husband was not just a private, personal sorrow. My grandfather, though kind and generous, had not sufficiently noted that the time for simple Christian charity and jovial family reunions had passed, and a new and merciless era had arrived. He had not understood the changing economic realities or the new, modern, society that he and his wife had both helped to make.

Teta, honoured, respected and loved though she was for her personal qualities, was, because of her economic condition, redundant in the new society. She existed in an empty, undefined space created by the new structure of society, and it was a space that provided little comfort or status for women who had no husband and no property. Teta was dispossessed of the high status traditionally granted to Arab matriarchs precisely by that society which she had helped to form. The new world, of which she had been such a proud founding member, had betrayed her.

Decades after this event, and from the vantage point of her own keenly felt widowhood, Mother was overcome with sadness as she wrote about her mother at this time: 'I wonder how she was able to live on and never grumble, but always with her faith in God, and always loving us, every one of us.'

CHAPTER 17

Schooldays in Beirut

T owards the end of September 1928, Teta's brother Habib, with his daughters Eva and Lily, came to Nazareth from Khartoum on their way to Beirut. It was to be Eva and Lily's second year as boarders at the American School for Girls (ASG) and Mother was to go with them. Uncle Habib, Mother writes in her memoir, was the first person from Teta's family who came to see her after her husband's death: 'I can never forget how sad my poor mother looked then, all in black, with black crepe (they used that for deep mourning then).' Mother herself was fourteen years old, and felt deeply the anguish of the parting:

> I can never forget my misery because I had to leave her and go to Beirut ... I felt I just couldn't do it, and cried my heart out begging not to go ... I knew I wasn't going to be able to go home for Christmas, and that worried me even more. I remember distinctly how I couldn't sleep at all the last few

nights with worry over my Mother. I insisted on wearing black all the time, too, which helped to make me feel still worse and more depressed.

But, she continues, 'Of course, Mama insisted.' For once, Mother regards her grandmother kindly, for Sitti Im Nassib calmed her fears, assuring her that she would look after her daughter. The neighbours, too, promised the reluctant traveller that they would not leave her mother alone for a minute and would spend every evening with her.

At last, the time for Mother's departure came. She clung, sobbing, to her mother until she was finally pulled away, and was driven off with Uncle Habib, Eva and Lily. From this time of parting, of moving on, Mother effectively lost her simple, direct connection to her roots, to her land, to her people. Earlier, when she had gone away to boarding school, it was to the Safad of her warmest memories, with the familiar countryside and her father's many relations. This time, when she left home, she was going much further away. Later, she would move even further away, to Jerusalem, and then to Cairo. From now on, she was to make her connection not to the local and the particular, but to the wider world. In moving around as would be her destiny, in shedding the particularity of her native culture, she was gradually to become more and more 'modern'. And what better place to begin the process of modernization than Beirut?

The American School for Girls was the descendant of the Beirut Female Seminary, which was founded in 1862 as a result of the same upsurge in mission activity following the events of 1860 that had led to the opening of the British Syrian Schools, and the American mission's Sidon Girls School and Tripoli Girls School.

In Mother's day, the school was located on its original premises near her grandfather's church. As a result of the Lebanon war which began in 1975, and which wreaked havoc on the vicinity, it moved from its old premises. Today it is located in the hills just north of Beirut and is called the Beirut Evangelical School for Girls and Boys – Rabiya (not to be confused with the Lebanon Evangelical School for Boys and Girls, the descendant of Teta's school, the British Syrian Training College).

Unlike Teta's, Mother's school records clearly belong to the modern period. The structure of the classes is recognizable from today's standpoint: students progressed from the first to the last class, spent a year in each, and then moved on. The curriculum itself is more modern. Though Bible study is still central – it is the first subject listed on the record sheets – the emphasis has now shifted to more secular subjects. Missionary puritanism was to survive in the social attitudes encouraged by the school and its teachers, rather than in the curriculum.

That Mother was an excellent student is clear from the record. In her first two years at ASG, her average was 93 per cent; in her third and last year, which she remembers in her notes with some disappointment at her lesser performance, her average was 92 per cent. The only comment on her chart is an admiring 'Excellent Student'. The subjects she studied were: Bible, Arabic, English, Economics, History, Science (including, in different years, Physics, Botany and Physiology), Mathematics and French. She took piano lessons and received high marks for Conduct.

In Beirut, not only at the ASG but also later at the American Junior College, Mother was to enjoy stimulating intellectual work, unaccustomed independence and a new physical environment. All of this opened her up to great cultural and mental spaces, towards which she looked back decades later with as much longing as delight. She remained on close terms with her school and college chums until the day she died: I think nothing gave her more pleasure than the lunches and teas they had together, when they sang, danced and laughed, as though all the sorrow of their later years had never happened.

In Safad, Mother had enjoyed and thrived in almost unrestricted freedom under the auspices of the leisurely, poetic and undemanding Miss Mackintosh, in a physical environment that was both comfortingly familiar and very much loved. Now, in Beirut, in this more serious and demanding school, she was to live a far stricter and more austere life. The joy of her many friendships was countered by a thoroughly restrictive set of social and personal values taught by the severe missionaries who were her teachers. This generation of mission teachers were socially quite unlike the founders: many of the women were unmarried and were sent out as professionals:

> As boarders [Mother writes in her journal], we were not allowed out of school at all, except on Saturday afternoon, when the

teacher on duty took us for a walk to Mina al-Hosn, by the sea
… The walks were dull, and there was nothing new to see.

The principal of ASG at the time was Miss Horn, a famous
character in our lives. She was a missionary in the full sense of
the word, and was old-fashioned and very strict. When I asked
her if we could go for a walk one Sunday afternoon, she made
me sit in her office and gave me a few chapters of the Bible
to read! It was a sin to think of taking a walk on Sunday, the
Sabbath!

We were forced to go to church every Sunday morning.
There was the English girls' school, Ahliah (Miss Kessab's
school, it was called) and ours – oh! those long, dull sermons of
Rev. Abdel Karim …

Living conditions at the school were as bleak, if not bleaker than
they had been at Safad:

The bathrooms were quite cold and the lavatories were dirty.
The dormitories were large, cold and uncomfortable … We used
mosquito nets; there were, of course, no carpets anywhere. We
brought all our bedding with us from home, mattress, pillows
and blankets. Each dormitory had at least twenty girls … They
had special bathrooms at ASG with taps and running *cold* water
in them – but no hot water except once a week, when it was
provided for baths.

School food, she complains, like many a boarder before and since,
was 'awful'. The girls were given tiny portions of cheese and *halawa*
for supper, and though lunch was not so bad, 'it was monotonous and
hardly delicious … We felt really hungry most of the time.'

Mother found relief in regular visits, every other Saturday, on
sabt al-ahali (family Saturday), as it was called, to her Uncle Habib's
house in Musseitbeh, where she was warmly received and enjoyed the
companionship of her cousins. She particularly enjoyed the music
sessions, when Uncle Habib would play the piano and the family
would gather around singing old folk songs, including '*alyadi alyadi*'
and '*marmar zamaan*'.

She went home regularly for summer holidays. The first summer, Eva and Lily went with her, and the three of them taught at a summer school set up in Nazareth by a family friend. From the beginning, the destiny of all the mission girls had been closely tied up with teaching: her father had chosen to send her to the ASG with this destiny in mind. Now it seemed that she indeed would become a teacher, like her mother and her aunts before her.

In the months since her father's death, Mother became acutely aware of the family's financial straits, though apparently not of the Great Depression then haunting the world. Her mother was making a supreme effort to keep the family together, and to provide for it.

There is a sad footnote to the episode of kindness and generosity shown by the mourning mother, Mrs Bottoms, who had been part of the celebrations in Nazareth at the opening of the church, and had financed Mother's first year at ASG, trying to keep the memory of her dead daughter alive in another girl, far away:

> A few months after my father died, Mama received a letter from Dr Truett saying that Mrs Bottoms had lost all her money in the American Depression and was almost destitute.

Mother's last year at ASG was marred by anxiety, and she did not do as well as before. Teta had assured her that she would continue, through scrimping and saving, and the sale of her olives, to see her through this last year. Mother had been relieved and happy that she would not have to wait on tables as she had feared at one point, but, weighed down by anxiety, instead of the High Honours she had hoped to receive, she had to be content with simple Honours.

By the end of the academic year, 1930/31, however, things looked up a little. The oil in Rameh had sold especially well and, feeling a little less pressured, Teta accepted her brother Habib's invitation to come to Beirut and attend her daughter's graduation.

After the graduation celebrations, mother and daughter returned to Nazareth. Mother, now seventeen years old, became aware of herself as a marriageable young woman. Her character, beauty, accomplishments and family background made her an object of desire for many a Nazarene mother seeking a bride for her son. As she recalls this episode, she smiles not only at the 'old-fashioned' world of which she had been a part, but also at her own naivety and innocence:

> Quite a few of the Nazareth mothers came to ask my mother if she would let me marry one or the other of their sons. Mama laughed and told me later how stupid they all were and how she insisted that I finish my education first, and then I'd tell her that I promised myself that I would never marry a man from Nazareth.

Mother had already outgrown the town in which she had been born and raised, and was looking elsewhere for her future. During her last year at ASG, a representative of the American Junior College had been to talk to her class and, though she 'wondered whether Mama could manage it', she had been to visit the college and fallen in love with it. Because of Mother's high standing at school, Miss Irwin, then principal of the Junior College, not only offered her a place but also promised to charge her a lower fee. Her mother reassured her that, 'with the reduction Miss Irwin offered, and the sale of oil and olives, and a bit of help from the mission, she'd manage. Oh! How happy I felt that summer in anticipation of my college days.'

The American Junior College for Women was for decades to play an important role in female higher education in the area. From the time of its founding in 1866, the Syrian Protestant College had accepted only male students. In 1905 a nursing school was opened to which women were admitted. At the end of the First World War, the relief efforts of an American Red Cross Commission highlighted for the Protestant missionaries the need for female medical personnel, a need that was not sufficiently met by the nurses graduating from the SPC.

Thus, in 1920, the faculty of the SPC, which had just become the American University of Beirut, voted to allow women to enter its Faculties of Medicine, Pharmacy and Dentistry. Interestingly, however, they voted against allowing female admission into the Faculties of Arts and Sciences, but instead decided to press others among the mission community to open a college especially for women. Pending this event, and on a provisional basis, which in fact was never reversed, the AUB decided to admit women to the School of Arts and Sciences in 1924.

In the meantime, British and American missionaries worked together towards establishing an institution for higher learning for women. From the beginning, and quite predictably, the effort was geared, at least in part, towards adding to the stock of teachers for the mission schools. The American School for Girls had already been expanding its scope. By 1921 it began to plan to add a year beyond its highest secondary class. In the same year a committee was appointed to oversee this expansion, as well as to pursue negotiations with the British Syrian Mission, on a joint venture between the British Syrian Training College, the ASG and the American University of Beirut, to produce the much-needed supply of teachers for the Protestant, English-speaking mission schools.

The final agreement between British and American missionaries was that a new American Junior College be established, but that the training of teachers should remain the sole responsibility of the British Training College on the secondary level at least. The Training College, indeed, remained the principal source of trained teachers for the English-language schools for decades. The American University promised that it would not take in women students for the first two years, leaving them exclusively to the Junior College; in return, it requested that boarding facilities for female university students be provided by the Junior College, which request was eventually granted.

The mission activities in regard to higher education for women were not carried out independently of the wishes or perceived needs of the local population, nor of the political circumstances at the time. The same drive by the local population towards the education and advancement of its daughters, which had fuelled the earlier successes of the mission schools, now fuelled this one. This is made clear even by documents of the mission itself. Local government, in what had become the Republic of Lebanon after the First World War, was now in the hands of the French mandate, which was sublimely indifferent, if not actually hostile, to the needs of the people, and the local initiative towards expanding education was repressed. As in the nineteenth century, therefore, foreigners once again met a deeply felt local need.

That the need for higher education for women was being demanded by the people of the former *bilad al-sham* themselves is affirmed by a

1925 mission survey of their work in the former Ottoman empire, cited
in an unpublished history of the college by Daniel Roberts. 'In the most
advanced of the secondary schools for girls there is a growing demand
for higher education,' the first of several such comments reads. That
this need was emerging from the independent advancement of women
is attested to by the document itself: 'There is general agreement that
the emancipation of women, even Moslems, is proceeding rapidly in
Syria.' The urge towards higher education was 'largely utilitarian', the
survey states; that is, women were interested in seeking professional
advancement rather than 'knowledge for its own sake'.

That the movement of Syrian women – 'even Moslems' – was
tending, through the acquisition of professional rather than non-
utilitarian knowledge, towards social integration is borne out further by
the observations of the missionaries themselves. 'Another motive', they
write, for the desire for higher education 'is the wish to prolong days of
freedom and to postpone restraint and seclusion.' But the missionaries
did not entirely approve of the integration of girls into a man's world:

> Although some parents are willing to allow their daughters to
> attend a man's university, it is doubtful whether this is a wise
> course. The curriculum may in some cases, especially in the
> professional schools, be precisely similar for men and women;
> but the extracurricular life of the students ... will sometimes be
> utterly divergent.

The missionaries perceived the movement towards the emancipation
of women as 'an opportunity to be seized', which, if it is not, the
report warns darkly, 'will be lost'. 'The matter is urgent,' the comment
continues.

What, I could not help wondering, were the writers of these
comments warning their readers of? Might the people themselves have
met their own need, thus becoming independent of the missions?
Might they have embarked in other directions than the educational
dependency that reigns to this day?

During the 1920s there was an extraordinary outburst of feminist
activity in the Arab Mashreq (East). In Egypt, Huda Shaarawi, Safia
Zaghloul and others led women fearlessly into confrontation with

armed British soldiers in demonstrations during the 1919 nationalist revolution against the British led by Saad Zaghloul. Several women were shot dead by the British in these demonstrations. In 1919 the Wafdist Women's Central Committee was founded as a branch of the Wafd nationalist party, and Huda Shaarawi was elected its president. In March 1923 the Egyptian Feminist Union was founded in Cairo. Later that year, along with Nabawiyyah Musa and Seza Nabrawi, Huda Shaarawi attended a meeting of the International Alliance of Women in Rome, and from then on was active in the international women's movement. In her memoirs, Huda Shaarawi makes it clear that one of the issues that fuelled her feminism was the fact that she was denied the education she yearned for as a girl. When Cairo University was founded in 1908 (funded in large part by a grant from an Egyptian princess who wished to see women educated), Shaarawi fought for women's right to attend lectures. Nabawiyyah Musa also fought valiantly for women's right to education. Many women's associations were active throughout the Arab Mashreq at this time. The Palestinian Women's Union was founded in Nablus in 1921, and by 1929 it had joined the Arab Women's Union, founded in Cairo by Huda Shaarawi.

Large numbers of women's societies, some charitable in nature, were founded throughout the region, and women were acquiring administrative experience in funding and running them. Dozens of women's magazines were founded. A host of women writers published novels, essays and poems, and the women's question was widely debated in the Arab world. Literary salons led by women – including the most famous writer of the time, May Ziadeh – flourished in Cairo and Beirut. In Lebanon, Julia Tohmeh Dimishqiyeh wrote articles and editorials in her magazine *al-Mar'a al-Jadida* (The New Woman), which were radical even from today's feminist perspective. A book by Nazira Zeineddin, *al-Soufour w'al-Hijab* (Veillessness and the Veil), caused a sensation when it was published in Beirut in 1928. Anbara Salam became active in national politics at around this time as well. Ibtihaj Kaddoura led the Lebanese movement demanding rights for women.

It is no wonder, then, that missionaries were warning their readers that an educational initiative on their part was a matter of urgency, and 'an opportunity to be seized'. There can be no question that the founding of a women's college was a most important move.

From the beginning, the Junior College was a more professional institution than its ancestors among the girls' mission schools. Unlike the enthusiastic Mrs Bowen-Thompson, armed only with missionary zeal, and unlike the charming and feckless bluestocking, Miss Mackintosh of the Scots College, who liked to sing and act out, in costume, the plays of Shakespeare, the first teachers at the American Junior College were members of a new class of professional academicians. The American women's movement had by now produced a generation of sophisticated female academicians some of whom were eager to travel.

The first principal of the AJC was Frances Irwin. She was born in 1895 and received her BA from the University of Minnesota in 1917, after which she did undertook postgraduate work at the University of Chicago. She arrived in Beirut in 1922 and spent the next three years learning Arabic at the mission language school at Souq al-Gharb, in the mountains south-east of Beirut. In 1925 she took over the AJC.

The first freshman class of the American Junior College embarked on its studies in the classrooms of the ASG in autumn 1924. It consisted of five girls, three of whom earned their diplomas in 1926. Of these three, two went on to become physicians. In autumn 1927 the college moved to a new location and thus became independent of the school. By this time there were three full-time teachers and twenty-one students. Of the three full-timers, Mother speaks lovingly of two, Miss Irwin and especially Miss Winifred Shannon. When Mother knew Miss Shannon, she had just returned from a furlough year in the United States, where she had received a Master's degree in Hygiene and Public Health from Columbia University.

In 1933 the college moved to its present location in Ras Beirut. In 1950 it became a four-year college, chartered by the State University of New York, when it acquired the name, the Beirut College for Women. In 1973 it became co-educational and was re-named the Beirut University College. In 1996, having achieved official recognition as a university, and expanded to include three campuses, it was renamed yet again, and is now the Lebanese American University.

Mother looked back on her one year at the AJC as 'the happiest year of my life'. Her memoirs present an interesting historical picture of the curriculum, as well as of daily life at an American mission college in French mandate Lebanon. She took History, 'which I loved', English

Literature, Arabic, Physiology and, 'unfortunately for me, Chemistry', which was the only course she did not enjoy. Her teachers included Miss Irwin, who taught her History, and Miss Shannon, the Dean, who 'almost ran the college', and who taught her English. Arabic was taught first by Miss Christine Saad, who was 'very clever', but old and ill, and had to leave before the end of the year. She was replaced by Mr Jureidini, from whom Mother 'learned a lot of Arabic' and who admired her essays and her handwriting. A young American, whose name she could not recall, taught Physiology and Hygiene, one of her favourite courses, which included practical lab work done at the AUB outpatient clinic. 'We helped with the sick babies and did a lot of work in first aid and helping the nurses and interns.' The students were given reading assignments in the AUB medical library.

Social life also revolved around AUB. Some of Mother's fellow boarders at the AJC were students of medicine or pharmacy at AUB; one of her roommates, Veronica Beckmijian, was a third-year medical student. Social life was of course very restricted, Mother remembers with some amusement:

> I wish my daughters, or even the younger girls at the college today, could have seen how very strictly we were treated ... Young men were allowed to visit us only a few times a week and we were allowed out only on Saturdays or Sundays and had to write in a book in the office where and with whom we went. Of course, lots went on behind Miss Heitman's [the German housemother] back, but not from me, because I knew very few people other than my uncle's family ... Of course, there were many 'illegal' loves going on, much to Miss Heitman's annoyance. When any men called at the wrong time and asked to take girls out, they called themselves their 'cousins', a joke of course, but she couldn't say anything because cousins were allowed.

Mother's own cousin, Albert, Nora's brother, was a student usher at AUB's West Hall, which is still today the centre of the university's social life. He often brought her tickets for the activities there, especially those of the Arabic Society, when there were plays and 'dancing evenings'. She also went with her brother, Alif, who by then was also a student at the AUB.

Though, comparing it to her daughters' time, Mother thought the rules very strict, she enjoyed a kind of independence she had never known before. 'For the first time,' she writes, 'I went out in the evenings.' For the first time, also, she went to the cinema, and the first two films she ever saw are engraved in her memory: '*Ben Hur* and *Beau Geste* with Gary Cooper and Marlene Dietrich!'

She remembers with pride a paper she wrote on the rise of Hitler and Nazism, the history of Germany, its connection with the rest of Europe and the meaning of the appearance of this new man there, the burning of the Reichstag, and so on. She received an A+ on this paper, which, along with an equally successful paper on *As You Like It*, she preserved until, she notes sadly, they were both lost when her mother closed down her house in Nazareth. From the vantage point of the older woman watching her children achieve academic stature, she writes wistfully: 'How I would have loved my Professor children to have read them!'

The paper on the rise of Hitler reflected her political awareness, which was already comparatively sophisticated because of her Safad friendship with Souad Nassar:

> I do remember in those vaguely troubled days of 1932 that current and world politics interested us a lot, the social status of countries too ... Lebanon was under French mandate. As far as I was concerned, Palestine and its constant revolutions against the British mandate bringing in the Jews etc was constantly on my mind, and we often discussed it with my Lebanese friends who were (except Najla Akrawi) completely unaware, and actually no one really worried that the problem would come along that soon.

At last, Mother's freshman year drew to a close. With Rose Ghorayib, later to become a well-known writer, she won the Scholastic Honors Cup, and she shared with Rose Ghorayib and Mary Karagulla the Torch Award, bestowed for general accomplishments.

When Mother said goodbye to her friends that summer to go home to Nazareth for the holidays, her happiness was completed by her anticipation of a great family event. Her brother Munir was coming back 'to be the man of the family and Mama's helper and the great doctor of the family'. She writes in her memoirs:

> The end of that beautiful year came, but it never occurred to me then that it would be my last in that beautiful place which was (I repeat once more) the best year of my life.

CHAPTER 18

Engagement and Marriage

When Mother returned to Nazareth that summer, the only topic of conversation in the family was her brother Munir's return from his long sojourn abroad. Mother describes Teta's happiness on his arrival:

> The great day arrived. Louis my cousin went to Haifa to meet Munir's boat and bring him home. I'll never forget when Munir arrived. Mama was still wearing jet black. How much she cried! She almost fainted from crying, missing Papa's presence, of course, but at the same time happy to see Munir after seven or eight years' absence. I was stunned at how good-looking he was. He was twenty-six years old then and everyone remarked on his good looks. He hugged and kissed us all, even Halimeh, who cried almost as much as Mama did.

Teta's pride and joy in her accomplished, handsome eldest son made up for the great sorrow she had suffered in the last few years. But for Mother, his return was not an unmixed blessing. Because of the Great Depression then sweeping across the world, and especially the United States, Teta's salary from the mission was gradually diminishing. Now the dwindling resources meant that the family priority shifted from the completion of Mother's education to the advancement of Munir's career. 'Our whole household changed,' she writes. 'Everything now rotated around Munir, the new doctor.' Gradually, it became clear to her that she was not after all going back to college.

It was as the painful realization began to dawn on her that a fateful visit occurred. In her notebook, Mother recounts the event:

> Just then Mrs Marmura ... came from Jerusalem to visit her parents in Nazareth. She was married to Rev. Elias Marmura, the pastor of the Arabic Anglican church in Jerusalem. She came to visit us as she usually did when she came to Nazareth. This time she started to ask Mama many questions about me. How old was I? Was it true that there was someone who wanted to marry me, etc? Mama told me afterwards that was surprised at all these questions and wanted to know her purpose. She told her that a very good friend of hers, Nabiha Said, had begged her to help her find a 'specially nice' girl for her brother whom she loved very much, and who could not seem to find a girl to marry. She praised this man highly and told Mother that she thought of me for him, and if there was no objection she would bring Mrs Said to call on us and see me before she called her brother who lived in Cairo.
>
> I was furious when Mama told me this. Mama laughed and told me not to worry: she had already told Mrs Marmura that I was only eighteen and was going back to college, and I was too bright and clever to accept this kind of arrangement ...
>
> It was a couple of weeks later, as I was going to visit Johara [Mother's school friend], that I met Mrs Marmura and another lady. She introduced her as Mrs Boulos Said, and was surprised that Mama hadn't told me they were coming to visit us! Of course I stayed away, but Mrs Said was really impressed. She thought I

was the right girl for her beloved brother, and thought she never saw anyone as nice as my mother, and she was determined to get her brother to come and see me!

Sure enough, he came, and Mother remembers wistfully: 'It must sound stupid and silly to all of you, reading this [she is addressing her children], but the first Sunday Wadie Said came to call on us, somehow I liked him a lot ...'

Throughout Mother's notes on the period of her engagement, several themes emerge and blend in her memory: her attraction, not only to the person of my father, in spite of the considerable age difference between them, but to the idea of marriage itself. She repeatedly notes how much she liked her suitor, how kind he was, how much he tried to please her, how he overwhelmed her with his generosity, and also how interesting, even fascinating she found him.

But through her notes, too, shines her initial ambivalence. Because of the family's financial straits, and the prosperity of her suitor, she felt she was being pressured, that her education was being cut short and she was being sacrificed. When she wrote to Miss Irwin to say she would not be able to return to college, Miss Irwin wrote back offering her a full scholarship. 'I felt cornered and trapped,' she remembers in her notebook. 'I was so young and innocent. I didn't know what marriage really meant.' 'Yet', she continues, 'I decided to get to know this man. He seemed like a very nice person, and I felt I had no choice.' Her mother, still overwhelmed by sorrow, was not much help: 'Poor Mama – now, in retrospect, I remember how she used to kneel all the time and pray [for guidance].'

The courtship progressed rapidly. Teta, who had in her own way opened up new paths earlier, had in the vulnerability of her widowhood retrenched and become more than ever dependent on the acceptance of society. That acceptance had allowed her to live as she had done, but it also had required a careful respect of local mores, and an acute awareness of which lines must not be crossed. She watched the courtship carefully, making sure that none of the conventions were breached: 'At that time it was the biggest shame in Nazareth for a girl to go out alone with a man, even her own cousin ... Mama wouldn't allow me alone with him at all.' Alif, always her special companion, was now seconded into the role of chaperone.

One of the first things Mother's suitor did was to rent a car and drive her – and Alif, of course – around in it. She was duly impressed: 'No one in Nazareth had a car,' she writes in her memoir, 'and only a few people in Jerusalem.' While the couple were becoming better acquainted, her aunt Emelia set herself the task of investigating the suitor: though he and his family were well known in Jerusalem, she wished to ascertain that there was nothing untoward in his life in Cairo. When she returned to that city after her usual summer visit to Nazareth, she questioned all those who knew him in the Syrian community there, and received a glowing verdict. He was unanimously praised as a man of character, of virtue, 'an honest and decent man if ever there was one'. He possessed exceptional business acumen, and could be expected to be an excellent provider. He had only one flaw: he was not sociable and worked far too hard. Aunt Emelia's report clinched the matter, and all sides approved the marriage.

On 18 September 1932 Mrs Boulos Said, her husband and her brother, accompanied by the Rev. and Mrs Marmura, came to Nazareth from Jerusalem for the formal engagement:

> Mother prepared a very nice dinner: *mahshi, djaj bi riz, kibbeh* and *sfiha*. Of course, they brought flowers and lots of sweets and Wadie brought me a beautiful solitaire, the likes of which no one had seen in Nazareth or Jerusalem. He also bought me a big box with an ivory toilet set and a few other things ... Auntie Emelia had sent me three pieces of beautiful silk – one a burgundy red and two other flowered ones. Our neighbour, who was a dressmaker (an expensive one), made me a beautiful dress and I bought a pair of black satin shoes with my first real high heels.

The engagement sealed, the groom went back to Jerusalem, made his sister and brother-in-law buy a car, and once more drove to Nazareth. With Alif in tow, the engaged couple drove to Haifa, Tiberias and all around northern Palestine. 'Then we went to Jerusalem, where Wadie showed me off to all his friends!' For the first time, in his company, she saw the great sites of Jerusalem, and then he drove her to Ramallah, Bethlehem, 'everywhere!' By now, she was quite taken with him: 'I really enjoyed his company and decided that he was very well informed and had a keen sense of humour.' After he drove her and Alif back to Nazareth, he left for Cairo, to resume his lonely existence for the remaining weeks until the wedding.

My father, Wadie Said, was born in Jerusalem around 1890. The family origins, my father used to boast, lay in the Christian Arab tribe of Beni Ghassan. 'We are', I can hear him say with a twinkle in his eye, 'the princes of Beni Ghassan.' In the middle of the nineteenth century, the family had converted from the Greek Orthodox Church and became Anglicans. There seems also to have been a family connection with the Nazarene tribe of the Khleifis, but I only learned of this quite recently, and do not remember my father mentioning it.

My father's father, Ibrahim, worked with Thomas Cook's in Jerusalem, and guided pilgrims around the Holy City. He knew German, which he must have learned at one of the German mission schools, and when Kaiser Wilhelm came to visit the Holy Places in Palestine, my grandfather showed him around. My father was very proud of this, and on numerous occasions would take out a ribboned medal with the imperial arms emblazoned on it, and show it to us. 'This', he would say, 'was given to my father by the Kaiser.'

The only surviving picture of my great-grandfather Ibrahim shows him seated on a horse, with a rifle on his shoulder. He looks very solemn, as though the Kaiser had just finished decorating him. He is dressed in Arab costume, and his head is covered with a *kaffieh* and *igal*. I do not recognize my father, myself or any of my siblings or cousins in his portrait, except for one thing. From the photos it seems that he had a fair complexion and pale, white skin. Daddy used to pride himself on the whiteness of his skin. I can see him now, only half-joking, raising the cuff of his trousers and pulling down his socks, pointing proudly at the whiteness of his thin ankles.

Ibrahim's wife, Teta Hanneh, after whom I was named, was from the Greek Orthodox Shammas family, though she was married in the Protestant church. There is only one photograph of her, showing her as a dark-skinned woman with long dark hair tied with a *mandeel* behind her neck. Though I cannot tell exactly what she is wearing, she is dressed entirely in black. Even her *mandeel* is black. Perhaps she was in mourning for my grandfather when the picture was taken. She was by no means a beauty, though her face has a kind of tranquil, gentle humour. I rather like her, from her picture. She seems to have been one of those women whose sense of humour and serenity survived her prolific childbearing. She seems like the kind of woman who would have, though perhaps in a vague, absent-minded sort of way, pressed her many grandchildren warmly to her bosom. Surely she would have pressed us, the children of her beloved Wadie, especially warmly. In her face I can trace my father's features and his sister Nabiha's, as well as mine and my cousins'. Most of all, I see the features of my Uncle David, my father's youngest brother, who lived in Brazil. I saw Uncle David only once in my life, when he visited us in Cairo in the early 1950s.

I look especially at Teta Hanneh's hands for identification and recognition. In the photo, one hand, with the thick gold wedding ring, lies in her lap, while the other is laid gracefully on the edge of the carved wooden table, a kind of *étagère*, typical of old Arab furniture, with arches holding up the shelves. This table tells me that my grandmother's house was probably furnished in the old Arab style: it places my father's childhood in a pre-globalized, specifically local world, instead of the wider, cosmopolitan world to which he was to belong. In her hands I recognize my own and my father's: Mother always used to say that my hands were like my father's and his, visibly, were like his mother's. I do not know why I should find it so moving to recognize my hands in the portrait of Teta Hanneh, a Shammas from Jerusalem, my namesake, whom I never knew.

My father had three brothers and two sisters who survived into adulthood, of whom Auntie Nabiha, whom my father loved so deeply, was the one we were to know best. I have only a very vague memory of Uncle Assaad, or Uncle Al as we called him; he had a big lump on his forehead for as long as I knew him. Uncle Al died in Jerusalem in 1946, when a truck went out of control and crushed him on the pavement where he was walking. My father and his brothers went to St George's School in Jerusalem, part of the Anglican mission complex in Palestine;

Nabiha attended St Mary's, also of the Anglican mission. Just before the First World War, with the threat of conscription into the Ottoman army hanging over them, my father and two of his brothers emigrated to the US. That is when his brother David went to Brazil.

When the United States joined the war, my father was drafted into the army and became a US citizen. He had by now taken the name William, which he or the authorities seemed to believe was the closest the English language could come to his Arabic name. In 1920 he received news of his mother's final illness and her deathbed wish to see him one last time. He returned to Jerusalem to bid her farewell, and as she lay dying, she extracted from him the promise that he recounted so many times to us in our childhood: that he would stay and look after what was left of the family in Palestine. Decades later, when Mother complained that her children were far away at university and graduate school, he would chide her: 'Let them be. Let them make their own future. Do not be a selfish, demanding mother who holds her children back for her own satisfaction.' All of us knew that he had always wanted to study law, but had been prevented from doing so by the deathbed promise.

No matter how much he resented it, he remained faithful to this promise. In Jerusalem, he went into business with his first cousin, Boulos Youssef Said, who, by virtue of his marriage to Auntie Nabiha, was his brother-in-law as well. Their business prospered: the Palestine Educational Company sold, in addition to office equipment, English books and records of classical music; much of our family's considerable library, and general experience with books and music, can be traced to my father's occupation. For as long as I can remember, books and records have been an integral part of our family's life.

Eventually, BY and WA, as they used to call each other, decided to expand the business to Egypt, and my father went to Cairo to see to this. He named the business there the Standard Stationery Company, and, remaining faithful to the family tradition, concentrated on the sale of office equipment and stationery. Another branch of the business was started in Alexandria, and his brother Assaad was put in charge of it. Jerusalem remained home, however, and until the war in 1948, trips home were part of his life, as it was of ours. In those days, Cairo and Jerusalem were only separated by a few hours' railway journey.

Mother preserved the letters she exchanged with my father during their engagement. I found them in a small oilskin bag neatly placed among her clothes when I was closing down their house in Beirut following her death, almost sixty years later. I had not known of their existence until then. The letters were written in English between September and December 1932. He wrote from Cairo, she from Nazareth. Also preserved were three envelopes, testimony to a bygone time. They are addressed in English in my father's hand:

> *Miss Hilda Musa.*
> *Nazareth.*
> *Palestine.*

On one of the envelopes, by the word 'Palestine', my father had written the word in Arabic, '*Falastin*'. The 20-millieme Egyptian stamps bear the portrait of King Fouad, wearing a *tarbouche* and sporting his distinctive curled and waxed moustache. It took only two days for the letters to travel from Cairo to Nazareth, with a stop in Haifa. They tell of a time when Palestinian society was being transformed, as the old Ottoman forms disappeared and the modern national system was being set up under the British mandate.

Especially vivid in the accounts is the sense of a new direction in personal habits and relationships. Unlike Shukri Musa, my father had been deeply influenced by his sojourn in the United States. He had experienced American society not on its fringes but at its heart, and had imbibed American political ideas at their most idealistic. He had been brought into contact with the newest in American technology, and it is probably this, more than anything else, that impressed him in that country. Until the end of his days, my father was impatient with old forms, with holding back and with looking back; he was always looking forward, at new ideas, at new and more efficient ways of getting things done.

That this was one of the features that most fascinated his naive, wide-eyed young fiancée as the courtship and engagement progressed is clear from the letters and the notebook. To the end of her days, Mother was to admire this pioneering quality in her husband, his acceptance of and attraction to the new and the modern. She would always be proud that he was among the first to buy the latest machinery available in town. When he had rented a car, to drive her – and of course Alif – around in it, she had been deeply impressed. She writes in her notebook:

> No one in Nazareth had a car, and only a few people in Jerusalem ... Wadie had had a car since he lived in Egypt, he also had a telephone, which very few people in Palestine or Lebanon had.

He always amused and delighted her with his penchant for the new. In a letter dated 15 October 1932, he tells her gleefully:

> There is a yo-yo craze in Alexandria now. I have bought a few and I am sure you will be the first person in Nazareth, if not in Palestine, to play this game.

Later she would write with singular delight of the time early on in their marriage when he bought a record player, and teased her cousin Nora, who had never seen one, or even known of its existence. He placed the machine in the dining-room and closed the door, then played a recording of an operatic aria. Nora could not figure out who could be singing or where the music was coming from; he told her that it was coming direct from La Scala, just for her. Mother laughed and laughed. As she lay dying, she remembered this incident and it warmed her heart.

The Palestinian Anglicans, especially those in Jerusalem, who had been influenced by the church of the British ruling class, were in general far more worldly and less puritanical than their Protestant counterparts in Lebanon, who had been influenced by the stern Americans from New England, or than the Southern Baptists. This worldliness and absence of puritanism, so different from her own upbringing, was, I feel sure, another aspect of the fascination my father held for my mother in those early days of their courtship.

In the letters, I saw a charmed relationship developing between a lonely, good, charismatic, seasoned and protective man of the world and a young, naive, but exceptionally intelligent and perceptive provincial girl. He lives in the great city of Cairo; he has travelled everywhere and seen everything. She, however bright and well-read, is a naive provincial girl, who, though she knows Haifa and Beirut, had never even seen Jerusalem or Bethlehem before he showed them to her. He is totally under the sway of his passion for her, while she looks up to him, shyly but surely, and perhaps above all respectfully. The letters, at first a touch awkward and self-conscious, become more relaxed and are warm, tender, intimate, sometimes funny and sometimes rather sad.

His letters are unrestrainedly passionate. Throughout, he addresses her as 'My Beloved Hilda', 'My own Divine Hilda'. He repeatedly refers to her unforgettable eyes, her beauty, her charm; he always sends her 'thousands and thousands of love and kisses' or 'oceans of love and kisses'; he calls her 'the sweetest girl in the world' and 'my darling shining star'. His very first letter is written as he left Nazareth: 'aboard train from Hilda and Paradise to Cairo and Hope', 28 September 1932. After torrents of words declaring his eternal love, he even describes the countryside through which the train is passing in terms of his feelings for her. The desert reminds him of his loneliness without her. Then he writes:

> Thank God, the scenery now has changed from the desert to the blue Mediterranean. I feel happier as I feel that the sea is near Nazareth, therefore I like it.

The letters follow densely one on another. He writes almost every day, sometimes twice in the same day. She writes a little less frequently, but always responds to his letters. As time passes, her letters become more relaxed and less self-conscious.

In his letters he is always trying to please her, trying to say what he knows is important to her. With the wisdom of his age, he calms her various fears. Her greatest worry always concerns her mother, whose vulnerability and sadness is ever on her mind:

> *2 October*: Poor Mother she is worrying, troubled, and so on. When I see her troubled like this I feel selfish and guilty for having to leave her soon, and yet I realize that I have to leave her sooner or later.

He responds:

Now Hilda, look after her very well, as you always do, so that she will bless us all her life. I know, darling, how hard it will be for her, however such is life.

He always sends her gifts, especially books and records from Jerusalem. His kindness and concern for her are deeply reassuring, his passion flattering, and she is visibly the young woman turning to the older man for fatherly protection and advice. She turns to him also as someone who knows the world; she is its student, and his. In a little postscript to the letter of 2 October, she is concerned about proprieties:

> PS. Wadie, do I need to write 'Private' or 'Personal' on the letters I send you – I don't know whether to do so or not.

Self-consciously, at first, but with growing confidence in him and their deepening relationship, she looks towards him as a father as well as a lover. In a letter dated 18 October she writes of how she is looking forward to seeing him again:

> I have heaps and heaps of things to tell you because you are one of those men to whom a girl can tell things and feel better by doing so – in this respect you are just the man I was looking for, just like Papa.

As the relationship develops, he becomes not just a father figure, but also her model of manliness. When he writes to her that he has, as she requested, given up smoking, but that he is finding this very difficult, she writes back enthusiastically:

> I can imagine how difficult it was for you, but this confirms the fact that you're a man, and a real one too – you don't know how proud I am to be your fiancée.

My father was to remain, until the end of Mother's days, her model of 'a real man', or, as she often said of him simply, 'a man'. As I read these letters I could hear her voice over the years proudly repeating, in reference to him, the lines from *Julius Caesar* that she had studied in school and wanted read at his funeral. Perhaps Teta had told her how, when she met her prospective husband, she had pronounced: 'He is a man.' My father, too, thinks about what it means to be 'a man'. His letter of 21 November is dejected, and even his passionate outpourings have a touch of sadness to them. Things have not been going well at work. At times like these, he writes, he turns for strength to Kipling's poem, 'If', which ends with the resounding claim, 'You'll be a man, my son!'

In general, her letters are quite different in tone from his. They are often coy and playful in a schoolgirlish sort of way. Where his words gush fervently from the heart, hers seem to be, at least in the beginning, more deliberately conventional in their expression of love. Their long-distance courtship is fraught with the dangers of misunderstanding: in his letter of 18 November, he refers in exasperation to what he calls the 'International Correspondence Method' of courtship, which is driving him mad. Aside from their love talk, their letters are full of apologies, declarations of sincerity, corrections of misunderstandings and so on.

Health is a constant, almost obsessive, topic in the letters. The subject is often dealt with in flirtatious banter that disguises a very serious aspect of the courtship: good health was clearly an absolute requirement of marriageability, and of the production of healthy offspring. He urges her to drink milk and eat soft-boiled eggs, knowing that she dislikes both. He, on the other hand, pledges to give up smoking. My father's battle with what he calls 'Mr Nicotine' is a theme that runs through the letters. He writes on 26 September:

> I am bidding goodbye to my best friend, companion and comforter, Mr Nicotine, as tomorrow starts the great day of fasting. He certainly was a great friend, and were it not the fact that I will soon have my beloved to talk to and live with and make happy I should not so willingly give him up.

The next day, 29 September, Mr Nicotine is, not surprisingly, very much on his mind, and the letter opens with the subject: 'Today I started the grand Ramadan of not smoking and it is certainly very difficult.' On 4 October, he is feeling quite triumphant:

I feel entirely a new person. Clearer-thinking, cooler and above all much stronger ... My tennis has improved, and I am playing four days in place of three days a week. I have said goodbye for ever to that beastly cigarette cough.

But this initial triumph is short-lived. On 15 October, after confiding in her about his troubles at work, he writes from Alexandria:

I am very sorry to own up to you that I have cheated in having broken my resolution in not smoking.

The battle with Mr Nicotine continued throughout my father's life. One of the few quarrels I remember between my parents as I grew up concerned his heavy smoking. Eventually, he did give up, but the damage was done, and he died of lung cancer in 1971.

As the letters continue back and forth, Mother's confidence in her fiancé grows. She writes to him about her deep pain over the interruption of her college education. At this stage, the road to scholarship and independence remained open, beckoning, tempting. In early October, she writes of her nostalgia for college and her friends in Beirut:

On Saturday I got some letters from my friends at the college. You know, Mr Said, they made me cry for almost six hours; they were all full of college news and so on. Everybody writing: 'How we miss you when we do this and that and so on,' and one of the teachers told some girls when they were talking about me: 'Never mention Hilda when I am present; it makes me sick to think of it.'

In response, no doubt perceiving danger from this trend of thought, he consoles her but adds a blistering comment directed at her friends:

Please do not cry about any more letters you receive from college, as I am not near you to console you. I can see all your friends crying when you write to them from London, so then you and I will get even with them for making my beloved Hilda cry.

To this she replies on 14 October:

> I got some more letters from the college but I didn't cry this
> time. I acted like a baby the other day.

In November she goes to Beirut with her mother and visits the
college. She writes a letter postmarked 'American Junior College,
Beirut, Syria, 8 November 1932.' Although *le grand Liban* (Greater
Lebanon) had been declared by the French in 1920, with Beirut as its
capital, she is either unaware of it, or, as often happens with imperial
decrees, ignores it as it bears little resemblance to her own experience
of political geography:

> I am actually sitting down on one of the classroom benches in
> AJC attending the Arabic class. I came over at 3.00 p.m. to see
> the girls and I was asked in, so here I am, a schoolgirl once more,
> tho' only for half an hour or so. I forgot for five minutes that I
> am not a schoolgirl but my ring on my right hand reminded me
> that I am Wadie Said's and I smiled to realize that I would never
> give up my Wadie for the Junior College, never.
>   On Monday morning Miss Irwin, the principal, took me to
> her office and began to speak to me, telling me that it isn't late
> as yet to go back to the college and if I changed my mind they
> would have me. She started telling me that Cairo is far and 'You're
> too young to get married, etc.' Both she and Miss Shannon seem
> to have the idea put into their heads that I was forced to get
> married and thus I'm unhappy. I could not find out how or why
> they think things are so, but it is rather funny, isn't it?

On returning to Nazareth, she thinks more about her trip to Beirut
and the whole business of the college. She writes on 17 November:

> The first day I went there – Saturday, everybody was free and
> oh! the shouting and screaming; the girls took me to the living-
> room and everybody started clapping, singing and dancing for
> you and me. Wadie, will it make you stop having your sleepless
> nights (on such silly matters) if I tell you that, although I thought

I loved the Junior College so very much, when I went there and I tried to compare and think which I would rather have, I found out that I would be able to give up all the Junior Colleges and their inhabitants, but not think of giving you up. Miss Shannon was trying to tease me. Once she told me: 'Now, Hilda, let me see how loyal you are to the college: give up your fiancé and come back to us' (of course, for fun), but I laughed and said: 'Thank you, I'd rather be disloyal than give up my fiancé,' so she said: 'The Junior College ought to be very jealous of Mr Said.'

How much of this is diplomatic banter, designed to maintain the sensitive relations with her proud fiancé, and how much of it was authentic emotion, probably she herself could not tell. Indeed, later, looking back in her memoir, she confirms that she took a deliberate decision, even while seeing herself as a will-less little girl, 'poor innocent Hilda'. She remembers her talk with Miss Irwin:

Oh! How tempted I was. I wanted so much to study, to stay at my beloved college; the girls, my friends, all of them, were so happy to see me. But I had gone too far, and somehow I enjoyed being with Wadie. I can't say I was in love, I don't think so, I really didn't know, but somehow I couldn't give up my engagement to Wadie. In Arabic and our tradition, it is my destiny. I wonder!

She writes of a couple of young suitors turning up, who were 'quite good-looking'. But, she continues, 'not for one moment did either of them impress me after being in Wadie's company. I myself noticed that I really looked forward to seeing him and missed him a lot when he went to Egypt!' In this passage, as in many of her letters, I saw a young woman of character and intelligence making a deliberate decision, not a will-less docile girl, as she saw herself decades later. But this road not taken to independence and higher education was to haunt her for the rest of her life: more than a shade of remorse, even a touch of bitterness, and often of self-pity, would creep into her conversation whenever she discussed her youth.

In any case, the decision was made, the road cemented, and there

was to be no turning back. In the meantime, she was to prove a tough
and determined partisan in the quarrel between their families over the
wedding arrangements that dominates the engagement correspondence.
Mother and Teta wanted the wedding to be celebrated in the Baptist
church in Nazareth; the Saids wanted it to take place in Wadie's home
town, Jerusalem, and in his own Anglican Church.

We are told that patriarchy, which is clearly at stake in the quarrel,
is the pillar of the entire social system. Yet in the case of this quarrel, at
least, both the defenders of the system and the attackers on both sides
were women. The most ferocious defenders of the system were Auntie
Nabiha and her bosom friend, Mrs Marmura, the Anglican pastor's
wife. They had position, money and power. Teta and Mother, while
appearing, in their impoverished husbandless and fatherless state, to
be weak and defenceless, led the attack. And yet their attack was based
on loyalty to their husband and father respectively, and, in their eyes at
least, was also a defence of the patriarchy.

As evidenced by the letters, my father, the patriarch himself, is at
first quite indifferent to the whole question: indeed, he is not even
aware of the problem until well after the war between the women
begins. It is the young fiancée who first broaches the topic: Wadie,
it turns out, has been studiously avoiding it. On 2 October she writes:

> Wadie, what about the wedding service, have you thought of
> anything yet? The nearer it draws, the more afraid I feel and the
> more troubled I feel about this matter. I am afraid of trouble
> that might rise up and I hate to have it … What shall we do?

But in response to her boldness, and under the underlined heading
'Wedding Ceremony', he answers her queries with some exasperation:
'What a Chinese Puzzle this is going to be!' Some time later, in his
letter of 10 October, or almost two weeks after the event, he gently
and gingerly tells her of an incident that occurred after he left her in
Nazareth and returned to Ramallah, where his sister and her family
were spending the summer:

> My darling Hilda, I have not written you about what occurred
> when I went to Ramallah after leaving you in Nazareth. You will

recall that I left Nazareth early Monday morning. That same evening Mrs Marmura came to bid me goodbye and of course there was a discussion about you and the wedding. I told them that I had decided to get married at the Baptist Church and you should see that I had thrown a bombshell at my cousin, sister and Marmuras. Suffice it to say that I was almost lynched at that moment, and finally my sister took my side as she said I was free to get married wherever I pleased and she would back me up ... Of course, I did my best with Nabiha to convince them but all to no avail. 'I was a member of the Greek Orthodox Church, but I still got married to Rev. Marmura in his own church,' said the Mrs. 'Your mother was a Greek Orthodox still she married your father in his church,' said BY. 'The Princess of Sweden married the Crown Prince of Belgium in the Roman Catholic Church,' said BY again. (So you see, my darling, you are the Princess of Nazareth and I am the Prince of Cairo.) I tried to cool them down but to no avail.

The letters go on, with tears, threats and storms. In one of his letters, he writes to her that he had been on a visit to Jerusalem: 'I found Nabiha crying. Boulos talked to her and then came and told me that I had broken her heart. Just fancy, darling, how guilty and wretched I felt.' In another, he refers to Mrs Marmura's anger at one of his counter-proposals: 'She almost murdered me,' he writes in despair. The young bride, on the other hand, reports how guilty and wretched she feels for her mother's sake. There is a veiled threat in one of her letters: 'Please understand me and please don't let yourself or me be disappointed because of such a trivial matter after all.'

Protocol and form mean little to my father, and all his arguments are really those of his sister and the pastor's wife on the one hand, and his fiancée and her mother on the other. Yet the form being fought over involved the definition of his position in the family. He seems to have been pushed helplessly about by the women as they fought their ruthless battle over protocol through him. Clearly unnerved by the whole affair, he carries compromise proposals from one of the warring factions to the other, and seems to care nothing for the outcome, only for a peaceful conclusion to the whole crisis.

As I read the letters, I realized that, though to me vastly amusing, there was more to the struggle than the small quarrels of long-dead people. It was an example of the enormous changes taking place in cultural and social values at the time. Barely twelve years since the British mandate had replaced the Ottomans, the old society was dying out and a new system of relationships was replacing it. In the older forms, individuals mattered less than families; in the newer ones, the individual mattered more.

There was certainly something of family competition about the contest. The relative importance and influence of their families would define the relative positions of husband and wife within the smaller unit. The women on both sides were identifying as members of larger units, even of regional units: to a great degree, this was a quarrel not only between families, but also between important, central, powerful Jerusalem on the one hand and provincial Nazareth on the other. It was a re-enactment of the ancient ritual competition between the capital city and the provinces. The competition was also one between the established Anglican Church, on the one hand, and the relatively new Baptist Church on the other.

My father's apparent indifference to the quarrel and its outcome was a function of his having outgrown the institutions to which the women were still attached. He was reacting as an individual. Alone and unattached for such a long time, and influenced as he had been by his lonely sojourn in America and then Egypt, he no longer thought of himself as an inseparable part of a larger family group, though his love for his family, and especially his sister, was legendary in our lives. His position (or absence of one) in the quarrel was crucial, and the defeat of the Jerusalem contingent became inevitable without his support.

The letters go back and forth, and the discussion deepens and thickens with details of the battle; the weapons with which it was fought were tears, rages, coldness and threats. The Jerusalem contingent threatens to boycott the wedding; the Nazareth contingent threatens to break off the engagement. In my favourite letter of all, he writes his fiancée a preliminary surrender, which will be formalized later. By now he is so sick of the whole thing that he says in exasperation:

Suffice it to say that, if necessary, I will even take you to the Mosque of Omar or the Jews' Wailing Wall rather than have little Hilda worried about such small things.

Weeks later, the matter is settled and the Chinese Puzzle solved: she and her mother have won, and he surrenders unequivocally. The terms of his capitulation are absolute: he confesses that not only will he do what she wants, but that all along he had hoped that she would insist on her plan, as in his heart of hearts that is what he had always wanted too!

On 28 October he has some important news. He has received a letter from his sister, who has finally laid down her guns and will give her blessing to the marriage in Nazareth. He summarizes her words as follows:

> I can swear that my aim in life is to see you settled with a nice Christian wife, and I'm sure Hilda is the right girl for you. So no matter where you have your wedding ceremony, it is all secondary to me; the only thing is to see you living in a nice home together.

Having thus achieved the reconciliation so close to his heart, he writes with some relief about the arrangements for the wedding and the wedding trip.

During the wedding preparations, Teta was in a state of confusion and deep distress. Every detail seemed to involve agonizing decisions; every decision seemed to generate gossip. One of the reasons for Teta's distress was her anxiety that, because of her limited means, she might not be able to provide her daughter with a trousseau like those of other brides. She commissioned some embroidered items from the nuns in the convent in Nazareth; she made some things herself, but this was not enough. At last, she was rescued from her dilemma by her sister Emelia, who sent a gift of money for some clothes. Thus mother and daughter, along with an old family friend 'who loved to buy pretty things', embarked on a shopping expedition to Haifa. Reflecting on this in her notebook, Mother writes:

Thinking back over all those years, why didn't I buy more
in Beirut for my wedding than I did in Haifa? It never even
occurred to me not to buy from the new Jewish immigrants
who were actually crowding us out of our country. But we were
not aware. There was no Arab consciousness about the whole
thing.

Throughout her notes, Mother laments the absence of Arab
political consciousness in Palestine. Yet the history of Palestine from
the end of the First World War until 1948 reads as an endless series
of strikes, revolts and uprisings against the British and the Zionists.
Mother herself writes of Najib Nassar, father of her Scots College
friend Souad:

Najib Nassar, owner of the newspaper *al-Carmel* in Haifa, had
been writing for years and warning the Arabs of Palestine to be
careful, their country is being taken away from them sooner or
later, and they are helping the Zionists.

Furthermore, this newspaper, along with its rival, *Falastin*, was
regularly read in their household. In her reflections of her college days,
she had written proudly that she was aware of what was happening in
Palestine.

I was puzzled, as I read her notes, at how to explain this insistent
contradiction in Mother's consciousness, this memory of simultaneous
awareness and non-awareness. Gradually, I began to see a pattern to
the contradiction. Invariably, the memories that provoke in her the
sense of unaware individuals involve shopping sprees in the fashionable
establishments of Haifa, or going to the cinema in Jerusalem. They
concern a certain class of Arabs – not only Palestinians, but Lebanese,
Syrians and Egyptians as well – patronizing the shops of the recently
arrived European Jewish immigrants, or going to their cinemas:

I'll never forget how during the early years of the Second World
War, when we were not getting imports from Europe, everyone
from Egypt, Lebanon and Syria flocked to Palestine to buy from
the Jews, furs, clothes, leather goods, everything!

Mother's 'everyone' and 'everything' ring in my ears as typical of her rhetorical devices, and clearly her statement is wanting in accuracy. Yet she is testifying to an important reality: the birth of an Arab urban, consumer, leisure class, bent on pursuing fashion and comfort, and often quite indifferent to the political and social realities surrounding them. The breaking apart of the old historic Syria, and the British and French mandates over the newly created countries, seem to have produced in these people – many of whom had been educated at mission schools and were influenced by a European culture with which they increasingly identified – a deep sense of alienation, and a kind of wilful oblivion to the reality of their own political situation, over which they felt themselves to have less and less control.

Mother's other memory, that of being politically aware, is always evoked by images of studying, schooldays, newspapers and intellectual activity. This aspect of her consciousness, then, is related to the nascent, but never matured, intellectual in her, and reflects a vision of the intelligentsia. It was reinforced by her fiancé, a man for whom books and 'education' were the basis of life. For my parents, as for so many millions in this part of the world, 'education' was a talisman, a symbol of all that was virtuous and hopeful in human life, including a good society.

But there was another, far simpler, explanation as to why she patronized Stella's. For the Arabs of Palestine, and indeed the rest of the Arab world, the Jews, before the masses of colonizing Europeans arrived, were simply there – they were part of life, part of the environment. It was quite natural for there to have been social intercourse with them. In a letter from Cairo on 1 October 1932, my father writes that he will be playing tennis that afternoon, though it is a weekday and he feels rather guilty about taking time off from work. However: 'Today is the Jewish New Year and the city is almost dead owing to the fact that all Banks and Commercial Institutions are closed.'

As the preparations for the wedding reached their climax, relatives and friends began to arrive in Nazareth for the happy event. The neighbours, 'very kind and helpful as usual', put up some of the guests in the apartment that Auntie Emelia used to stay in on her visits, but, this time, in honour of the wedding, they refused to accept payment for it. The Saids and the Marmuras, now resigned to the arrangements over which they had fought so hard, decided to bury the hatchet and came from Jerusalem. Mother's cousins Eva and Lily arrived with their father from Beirut. Uncle Habib's present to his niece was 10 Palestinian pounds or sterling ('very generous at that time'), with which she later bought a lamp from the fashionable Gattegno's in Cairo. Auntie Emelia sent her some silk brocade from Egypt, and her Aunt Nasra, widow of her beloved Uncle Constantine, gave her one of the gold bracelets that she had always admired.

While most of the guests were put up at the German Hotel in Nazareth, their old family friend Abla Rubeiz and her two children stayed with them. According to Mother's memoir, 'Mama tried to put Abla and her kids up in our sitting room, but Abla screamed that she'd rather stay up all night because there were too many dead people in the room.' It was the fashion at that time to hang photographs on the living-room walls. The more important the people, the larger the size of the pictures. 'There were my two sets of grandparents (four dead people),' Mother continues, 'my father and Uncle Constantine; my mother's dead brother, Khali Rashid, etc.' Abla categorically refused to share the living-room with all those dead people, though Mother does not say where she did stay.

Nora came from Jerusalem. It was she who introduced Mother to depilation, the custom of pulling hair off arms and legs with a caramelized paste of melted sugar, which was either introduced by Turkish ladies to the aristocratic circles in Egypt or was an ancient custom from Pharaonic Egypt. Nora had learned of this custom in Egypt; it was then entirely foreign to the women of Lebanon, though it was not unknown in Palestine. Today it is painfully familiar to every woman and girl in the area, as it was to me and my sisters when we were growing up and Nehmido used to practise her art on us. Mother writes:

> Nora took charge of me. She said I had too much hair and, seeing that she was an expert, she cooked some caramelized sugar and fixed it like a glue to spread on my thighs, arms, legs, etc. and pull all the hair out. I was shocked and utterly refused after the first *lazqa* [application]. Nora was furious.

Another visitor from Cairo restrained Nora's enthusiasm by informing her that 'at the best public houses in Egypt' they had ceased to pull out all a woman's hair. By now the bride was in tears: 'I just sat and cried and cried.' But finally, she submitted to Nora's ministrations. Halimeh contributed happily to the proceedings by helping to press all the dresses, underwear, nightgowns and linens that were being packed up as the trousseau. She used a coal iron, about which Mother muses: 'Today they are only used as flower stands or door stops.'

At last the wedding day arrived. Before going to church, the bride, wearing her long white dress and veil bought from fashionable Stella's in Haifa, went through the cobblestone streets to her Aunt Nasra's house, to show off her outfit to her cousin, Musa, who was recovering from typhoid fever and could not come to the church. 'He was thrilled, of course, and so was Aunt Nasra, poor woman.'

A final chapter of the wedding controversy was written on the wedding day itself. The wedding was to be conducted by Mother's cousin Louis, her father's successor as pastor. His American wife, Velora, was in charge of the wedding music, including the organ processional and the choir:

> Jokingly, Velora told me (at least I thought it was a joke) that in America the marriage service does not include the word 'obey' for the woman, so I told her 'Why don't we do the same thing here?' and that was that. In the meantime Boulos Said, an elder of the Anglican Church and a very serious man, asked to speak to the pastor who was going to marry us ... Louis told him it was the same service as the Anglican one, and showed him his book! Oh! the great shock to the Saids, even to me and my mother, when Louis deliberately omitted the word 'obey' from the marriage service. I felt Wadie go pale and stiff, also shocked!

Aside from this 'great shock', all went well. Mother's wedding was most emphatically not a traditional Galilee wedding, but she had also moved away from her mother's puritanical simplicity. She writes in her journal:

It seems I made a beautiful bride, and Wadie really looked
very handsome. Of course the church was full, and Munir
walked down the aisle with me. Rev. Marmura and Rev. Assaad
Mansour, the Nazareth Anglican pastor, both helped Louis in
giving the final blessing, and that at least assured the Saids that
this was an official and recognized service!

The bride entered the church to the strains of the wedding march
played by Velora on the organ Rev. Shukri had worked so hard to
obtain. Her white gown, that famous gown bought from Stella's in
Haifa, had a long train; she was attended by bridesmaids, and Aunt
Nabiha's young twin sons, Robert and Albert, were dressed up as
flower boys. One of the groom's second cousins, Youssef Beydas, who
had just finished school and was at the time working at the Palestine
Educational Company, was best man. A choir sang, and the traditional
boxes of candy distributed to the wedding guests came from Cairo:

> The bon-bon boxes we gave away were the talk of Nazareth for
> a long while. They'd never seen anything like them, of course.
> They were from Cairo. Even the candy was large and much
> better than the usual Nazareth ones!

After the ceremony, the wedding party proceeded to the German
Hotel, where the bride was to change into her travelling dress. She
could not go home, 'as it is a bad omen for the bride to go back to her
parents' house to change'. And then came the time to bid her mother
goodbye:

> Poor Mother, she cried so much after the service and during it
> that I wouldn't let go of her, and I insisted that she come with me
> to the hotel. Of course, then everyone else came, my brothers,
> cousins, etc. I noticed the look of disapproval on the faces of
> Boulos and Nabiha, but at that point I was so scared, lonely,
> homesick, etc that I didn't care. I cried so much that I fainted
> completely and Munir quickly got me brandy and medicine to
> rouse me, but it was soon over, and I told everyone goodbye and
> went with my new husband and his family to Jerusalem.

Mother also marked her final separation from the traditions of her people in another way. It had fallen to the bride to see to the text of the invitation cards. She had written them out herself, and they were printed in Cairo. Her brother Munir, who was by now establishing his reputation as an up-and-coming physician, had teased her mercilessly, wounding her feelings. 'I did the best I could,' she writes defensively in her journal, 'and not many brides wrote their own wedding invitations!' In one of her last letters to her fiancé she had added a strange request. Would it be possible, she writes, to add to the wedding invitations a printed request to show the card at the door of the church?

> Nazareth people are very disorderly and noisy [she explains], and you being a stranger, people from all parts of Nazareth will flock to see the wedding, and then the church will not hold everyone or else the people invited will not have good seats.

The very notion of wedding invitations, of some people from the community being welcomed while others are barred from entrance, is alien to the old customs. My parents' wedding was of a new sort – no longer a communal affair in which everyone participated, but a private, personal and individual celebration to which people were invited by engraved cards. The path of new manners and lifestyle painstakingly carved out by Teta was now a highway, and Mother was firmly set on it. Mother herself was excruciatingly aware of this change, though she may not have recognized its significance.

CHAPTER 19

Modern Bride, Housewife, Mother

A long and leisurely honeymoon followed the wedding. Those were the days, after all, when brides and grooms scarcely knew one another, in which brides had to be initiated into what Mother delicately referred to as 'knowing about life', and in which long holidays were not unusual. From Nazareth the couple went to Jerusalem, where, finding no rooms at their first choice, the King David Hotel, they spent a day or two at 'the next best', the New Royal Hotel. In Jerusalem, Auntie Nabiha gave a luncheon in honour of the newly-weds. Among the guests were cousins, relations, business associates and friends of the family. Mother especially remembered the presence of her husband's two maternal uncles, Michel and Issa Shammas, both over a hundred years old: 'Both ate very heartily and then sat down, read the paper without glasses and dozed off.' My father was always proud of his eyesight, and of the fact that he only needed glasses for reading, and that when he was relatively old.

Mother comments sympathetically on the labour this luncheon cost her new sister-in-law. She insists:

I'm not going to forget to write about it … I still remember how big that party was and with very little help from outside, she did it all alone … I was told she had stayed up all night cooking!

After Jerusalem, the couple drove to Jaffa, where they boarded the Dollar Line steamer *Theodore Roosevelt* and sailed to Alexandria, the first stop on a long Mediterranean cruise. Alexandria was a far larger city than any Mother had seen so far, and she remembers her wonderment at 'the beautiful streets of Alexandria.' From Alexandria they sailed to Italy, and then to France. From Marseilles, they took the train to Paris.

On the honeymoon, her husband was her guide, her teacher and her coach. In Paris, he took her to the Opera, where *Thaïs* was playing. He took her to the Casino de Paris, the Lido and the Folies Bergères, where they saw Josephine Baker. 'I was shocked,' she writes, 'and surprised at the almost naked girls dancing.' They toured the city with Thomas Cook's, seeing all the sights. He took her to the best restaurants, but, she remembers: 'I can't say that I enjoyed the food as much as I would have today or later. My palate was only used to our own cuisine.' He took her to the Paris boutiques and bought her clothes, including 'two beautiful overcoats with fur collars and lovely evening and day clothes'.

From Paris they went to England, where 'I had a most beautiful time. I was so thrilled to see all the places I had studied about all my life.' They often went to the theatre, where they saw, among other plays, some of Shakespeare's, which thrilled her. They made trips to Stratford, Oxford and Cambridge. In those days, of course, evening clothes were *de rigueur* at the theatre, so my father took her to the best shops, where he bought her suits and evening dresses. Again, this time in the company of his business acquaintances, they were 'wined and dined' at the best London restaurants.

After London, they made their way to the Côte d'Azur, where they stayed in Nice, whose elegance and beauty overwhelmed her, so that 'my eyes popped.' From Nice they finally went to Toulouse, from where they caught the boat back to Egypt. She was seasick on the way:

Oh! How happy I was to be in Port Said, and I wanted badly to
eat some Arabic bread! I think I enjoyed that meal in Port Said
of *foul m'dammas* and *tahini* salad with Egyptian bread more
than any meal I had ever had.

They toured Port Said, where he bought her 'a beautiful hat from the
famous Simon Arts', patronized especially by British travellers on their
way to and from India.

And then at last from Port Said, my parents made their way to
Cairo. Their arrival ended the honeymoon journey, and their married
life began in earnest. Mother's reflection on the honeymoon was that
her husband had enormously enjoyed not only showing her the sights of
the great cities they had visited, but also buying her fashionable clothes
in Paris and London, teaching her the ways of the world, introducing
her to the great hotels and restaurants. And most important of all,
she remembers his kindness, his sensitivity and his understanding of
her 'fear, innocence and naivety'. Never, she remembers fondly, did
he force his attentions on her; never did he begrudge her her privacy.
She had been utterly swept off her feet by the honeymoon experience.
In her notebook, she writes wistfully to another generation: 'I don't
think any of my children or grandchildren can understand my thrill
and excitement.' For she had been, she writes over and over again, a
naive, innocent girl, who 'knew nothing about life'.

For the next fifteen years, until the 1948 Palestine war, my parents,
with their growing family, were to balance their lives between Cairo
and Jerusalem. Though my father claimed not to be terribly fond of
his ancestral city, Jerusalem was the anchor of their historical existence,
the pivot around which their lives revolved. My father always regarded
his stay in Egypt as temporary; as it turned out, it lasted for more
than thirty-five years. They went to Jerusalem two or three times a
year; sometimes they stayed for months, sometimes for a whole year,
sometimes only for a few weeks. Even for Mother, Jerusalem became
home; it was there that she saw Teta and her brothers, especially after
1936, when they no longer kept a home in Nazareth.

Later, Mother grew into Cairo; eventually, she mastered it. But
when she first arrived, she was awed by the size and splendour of the

great city. Compared to Jerusalem, Beirut, and especially Nazareth, she found Cairo and her apartment in Sharia al-Falaki, in the Bab al-Louk quarter, dazzlingly modern. Like everyone of their acquaintance they had a telephone. City gas ran her oven. They had a 'huge' bathroom, which included a shower and a bath-tub, and plenty of hot, running water. In addition, Boulos and Nabiha had given them a piano as a wedding present, 'and I was thrilled.'

At first she had little to do. Abdou, a manservant retained from my father's bachelor days, did the shopping, the cooking and the cleaning. Spared the burden of housework, Mother visited all the sights during her first months in Egypt. The Pyramids of Giza, the Sphinx, the Step Pyramid in Saqqara, Old Cairo, including the great mosques and the Citadel, the Coptic quarters, the museums, the *souqs* – she saw them all. As usual, her husband was her guide, coming home early from work to take her out. When they were not touring, they would just go for a drive along the banks of the Nile, or up and down the great lit-up streets of Cairo.

Mother had few companions at first, other than their next-door neighbours, the Kettanehs, her Aunt Emelia, and her Uncle Nassib and his daughters. Before his marriage, my father had had little to do with Cairene society; though he was well known in the business community, his solitary nature had prevented him from making many personal friends. He had always read a great deal, and enjoyed listening to his growing collection of records of Western classical music; he played tennis several times a week with a couple of steady companions. When he wanted company, he had turned to a few of his fellow Jerusalemites, especially his neighbours, the Kettanehs, an elderly couple who would eventually take his bride under their wing.

From the beginning of my parents' married days in Egypt, Auntie Melia, who was at the height of her career at the American School for Girls, came to see them very often. She usually stayed for supper, insisting that this meal should consist of soup, which her niece had much trouble learning to make to her satisfaction. She drank coffee only if it was made precisely as she directed. At the end of the evening, my parents would drive her back to the college. Occasionally, she would bring with her for the evening meal one or two of her fellow Lebanese teachers, never one of the Americans. Eventually, she guided my parents in the ways of that most interesting segment of Egyptian society, the Syrian community, on whose fringes my father had lived before his marriage.

As mentioned previously, the Syrian expatriates in Egypt were known as the *shawwam*, those from *bilad al-sham*, or historic Syria, including Lebanon and Palestine. Most of the original community were Greek Catholics from Aleppo who had come to Egypt in the nineteenth century. Some of them had taken refuge in foreign embassies during periods of persecution or danger, such as the great sectarian wars of 1860, and from there had been escorted to safety in Egypt. Others had come from the provincial cities looking for wealth and advancement in the great metropolises of Egypt. To their numbers were added graduates of the Syrian Protestant College in Beirut, who became best known as founders of some of the most important newspapers, magazines and publishing houses in Egypt.

The *shawwam* had a distinct character and way of life, based largely on the nature of their situation in their ancestral lands, where they had often been the middlemen between two cultures. From their homes in the Syrian cities of the Ottoman empire they had engaged in commerce and trade with Europe. They were travellers who were familiar with two worlds, and they developed a taste and culture based on that unique synthesis. The clothes they wore, the language they spoke, the food they ate, the way they decorated their homes, all this spoke of their particular experience.

Now in the mid-twentieth century many of the *shawwam* were still writers, journalist and intellectuals. Others were engaged in the business community, or as industrialists. It was these people who were eventually to shape my parents' social lives, and though their particular background and circumstances – principally their Protestant values and the Palestinian experience – differentiated them in many ways from the others, it was with the *shawwam* that my parents became principally identified, and shared their lives and tastes. They also mixed with non-Syrian Egyptians, however, and, to a lesser extent, with the foreign community.

Emelia Badr was an intimate member of the *shawwam* community, though her experience extended beyond it. Many of the well-off Syrian families sent their girls to her school, where they were watched over by her, guided in their studies and their character building. She eventually introduced Mother to her friends in the community, and taught her how to conduct herself with them. Occasionally, Emelia took the young bride on her visits to the homes of some of the wealthy Egyptians, including, Mother mentions tantalizingly in her journal and without further elaboration, Huda Shaarawi. Mother had never seen anything like the homes of the Egyptian rich, and writes that 'their homes and lives were fantastic'. But she was too intelligent, and had had too moral an upbringing, not to notice the social realities of Egypt:

> It broke my heart to see the miserably poor little boys and girls with torn clothes shivering in winter and running around the streets collecting cigarette stubs (*sbars*, they called them). Of course, there were poor people in both Nazareth and Beirut, but I had never seen the poverty and the hovels of Egypt.

Once the excitement of her new life had died down a little, Mother entered a period of voluntary seclusion as she undertook her own domestic training. Her upbringing at the hands of her mother, as well as her mission schooling, made this phase of her life inevitable. The manservant Abdou had become increasingly surly and difficult as his position in the household was gradually eroded by the presence of a mistress in the house. In spite of her timidity in her dealings with him, he began to regard her as a usurper, and treated her as such. As time passed, she became increasingly annoyed with him, and disgusted with his less than perfect housekeeping. She was once horrified to see cockroaches in the kitchen. But, though she already had a strong personality, she was very young and did not have sufficient experience to know how to deal with a recalcitrant servant.

The competition between them eventually led to his making a fatal mistake: he complained to the person he regarded as his only legitimate boss, the man of the house. Foolishly, he threatened to quit if she did not leave him to do his work without interference. Needless to say, he was promptly fired and the young bride was now installed as the unchallenged ruler of the household. Much to her aunt Emelia's horror, Mother refused after this to have a servant at all, insisting on learning housekeeping by herself, 'from scratch', with only some books enthusiastically supplied her by her supportive husband. Gradually, Mother became a skilled housekeeper and she kept a spotlessly clean and tidy house, applying the stringent standards of hygiene she had learned from her own mother. She learned the art of cookery and put into practice those laws of hospitality that she had also inherited from her mother. At first, she had few guests to honour and impress; later her circle was to widen considerably.

As the years passed, there were to be great differences between her domestic life and her mother's, which spoke not only of the inevitable changes between one generation and another, one city and another, but also of the changes in social structures, taste and decorum brought about by political developments.

When Mother had dismissed Abdou, and deliberately taken over the housework, she had done so to practise and master the domestic lessons she had been taught, and to take control of her own environment. I believe this act can be considered political in nature; in this secure corner of the world which was her own private home, and around which she gradually constructed protective barricades, she was to create an independent province over which she reigned supreme. Gradually, as time passed and her family grew, she did indeed hire servants, but she always prided herself on participating in and directing her own household and on looking after her own children, on being her husband's proud and equally hard-working 'second half'.

Her early act of control was as original and unconventional as it was spontaneous and unstudied. Later, as she matured and took her place in society, she was marked out as different. Hardly anyone of her class and status in Egypt did their own housework or looked after their own children. When she took her toddlers to the public gardens near which we lived, she found herself in the company of nannies and foreigners. She says this proudly in her journal, and she said it to me proudly over the years, seeing in this an aspect of her own modernity, her refusal to delegate her precious children to nannies and servants, as the Egyptian upper classes routinely did. Her aunt Emelia was scandalized by her behaviour, and tried to persuade her to put aside her foolishness, and live the life that others in her circle did, but she insisted on her own way. In those Cairo years, Mother was to become immured in a domestic sphere that became, as time passed, increasingly sophisticated and complex, and more absorbing and isolating for being so.

After the surly Abdou, she hired a young woman named Hamida, who came in regularly to help with the laundry. In those days, the laundry was boiled in a big bowl, a *dist*, the whites soaked with the *zahra*, or washing blue; everything was then hand-scrubbed in other big copper basins, wrung out and hung out to dry. The laundry and the copper bowls and basins had to be carried to the roof, and then, dried and smelling of the sun, the clean clothes would be brought down to be ironed. It was only as her third confinement approached that Mother was finally persuaded to hire a sleep-in maid who could baby-sit while she was at the hospital.

Like her mother before her, Mother thought of housework not as drudgery, but as a mark of distinction. Cleanliness, order, hygiene, mothercare, and perhaps above all good financial management, all this spoke to her of modernity, of something of which she was inordinately proud, of something that marked her out and made her shine, like her college education.

Teta, though she expressed herself differently from the community in which she lived, had never been isolated from that community. Even her maids, especially 'our beloved Halimeh', were intimately integrated with the family. Halimeh was scarcely a maid at all, more a kind of lesser aunt to the children. What social difference existed between her and her employers seems to have been secondary to their relationship. Though she was illiterate, and there was a large cultural gap between her and Teta, it was nothing like the gulf that would form between Mother and her helpers.

When Mother finally took on servants, they generally came from among the Egyptian, and later the Syrian, rural poor. The class difference was absolute and without nuances, and though such figures as Ahmed and Hassan, my parents' *suffragi* and cook, or Aziz the driver, form a major part of our childhood memories, and we looked on them with great fondness, there was no possibility of enjoying with them the kind of relationship that Mother and her brothers had enjoyed with Halimeh.

In Teta's time, hospitality and kinship were expressed simply. Furniture was almost entirely utilitarian, and ornaments were rare and unimportant. Mother's household was much more absorbing and complex. Curtains and upholstery were elaborate, and required infinitely more time and attention than the ones Teta had used; the velvets and brocades that covered sofas and armchairs could not simply be washed as Teta had washed her cotton covers; nor could they be beaten, like the *kilims* that covered many of the sofas and cushions in Teta's time. Mother's silver ornaments and dishes had to be polished; her fine Regency-style mahogany tables and chairs had to be waxed and polished. Teta had known nothing of the *chinoiseries* and *japoneries*, cabinets, screens, pictures, porcelain bowls and plates that eventually graced Mother's apartment and that were typical of the *shawwam* touch. The Bohemian crystal chandeliers, the collections of antique jewel-coloured opaline vases, compote jars, tea cups and other domestic ware, richly decorated with enamel and gold leaf, originally designed for practical use by the Turkish court and aristocracy, but now relegated to a purely decorative function – all these had to be sought out, collected, properly displayed and cared for. The exquisite embroideries from Bukhara, Samarkand, Uzbekistan and other exotic places had to be learned about, identified, framed and hung. Mother was eventually to become adept at the auction houses, where she learned to buy paintings, and Persian miniatures in their red velvet and gilded wood frames.

One of my father's old friends and tennis partners was a jeweller named Isaac Goldenberg. When each of the children was born, Isaac helped my father choose a diamond ring for Mother. Eventually she learned the secrets of antique jewellery, and the best quality of gems for new designs. Teta's knowledge of jewellery, though sophisticated for her time, did not extend to the heights that Mother had learned to negotiate. Like everything else, jewellery had been simpler in Teta's time, and learning about it was simpler too.

In Teta's time, food was served in simple earthenware dishes, and there was not much interest in presentation. Teta must surely have been deeply puzzled when Mother, in the 1950s, sent her cook to the famous Cairo restaurant, Groppi's, to learn how to carve and serve turkey and legs of lamb, how to place them in the silver serving dish, adding paper frills to their trussed-up legs, how to dot chopped parsley becomingly around the arrangement, and how to sort out the exact place on the dish for the silver carving knife and serving fork.

Though housework in Teta's time was difficult and time-consuming, it was certainly less isolating. As her children's memories prove, there was great pleasure, almost a festivity, in some of the necessary work, and it was a communal, not an individual activity. In Mother's mature household, the rest of the family had nothing to do with the proceedings in the kitchen or the laundry room that she oversaw with the servants. Though we were delighted consumers of the good things emerging from the inner sanctum, there were no festivities associated with them. The festive occasions, indeed, were exclusively those involving the old, communal ceremonies, such as the ritual making of *ka'k* and *ma'moul* at Easter, when the women would gather around the table to make these delicacies, gossiping and exchanging wisdom as they did so.

Always among the first in town to have the latest domestic appliances, we were the first family in Dhour al-Schweir to own an electric refrigerator, replacing the old orange icebox that used to cool the food with a big slab of ice delivered by the ice man two or three times a week. Mother was one of the first in her circle to own an automatic washing machine.

But the new machinery created its own demands. When she acquired an American ice-cream maker, Mother started to make ice-cream at home. Indeed, her friends and ours began to clamour for her ice-cream, and Saturday afternoons were always devoted to the ice-cream tasting, for she now began experimenting with different flavours, fruit and colours. She used regularly to bake American-style cakes, cookies and cup cakes using her American cookbook, mixers and baking equipment. She used to make doughnuts once a week, frying the batter in boiling oil, and then sprinkling the little circles with powdered sugar. The waffle-maker demanded waffles; the waffles demanded a recipe book, special syrup and a special serving dish – in general, the appliances generated as much labour as they saved. Mother's kitchen eventually became a private, closed-off, place, not a communal, open one.

This was the kitchen I was to inherit, that place of women's work and women's isolation against which modern women have been rebelling, clamouring for a more modern situation, not understanding that it was precisely modernity that put us there in the first place.

But all of this was to come later, much later. Now Mother was a young bride far away from home, and she missed her mother and brothers. In early June 1933, just a few months after they had settled in Cairo, my parents embarked on the first of their many journeys to Jerusalem. In her journal, Mother is at pains to describe it in detail, as it recalls a bygone, pre-war era:

> Finally we took the train at 6 p.m. and sleepers from Cairo Station. It travelled for almost three hours to Qantara, the Palestinian border. We got off and our passports and luggage were looked at first by the Egyptian and then by the British mandate officers. Then we crossed from one side to the other and took the train once more to Palestine. It was quite a tiring trip, but we had wagons-lits sleepers so it wasn't too bad. I can't remember whether on those early approximately thirty trips we got off at Lydda and drove to Jerusalem, or the Boulos Saids met us. The train stopped in Lydda, then went on to Haifa, the last stop.

Mother's happiness at the forthcoming reunion with her mother and brothers was marred by the fact that she had not yet conceived: she would frequently be reminded of this failure by inquisitive friends and relations at home in Palestine. 'Both in Jerusalem and Nazareth everyone asked why I wasn't expecting a baby. "*Shou, ma fi shi?*"' (What, is there nothing?) But my father, ever her protector, put a stop to at least some of the friendly harassment: 'Wadie stopped Nabiha's curiosity and Mrs Marmura's, by telling them it's our business only.'

By November of that first year, she was pregnant, however, and there was rejoicing not only in their own home, but in the wider family as well. Everywhere in the world, pregnancy and childbirth had always been women's business, and midwives still occupied the prime place at the lying-in of Mother's contemporaries and friends in Palestine. In the provinces and in the countryside women went into labour and gave birth with only other females in attendance. The men of the family would gather elsewhere, in the coffee-house or in the home of a friend or relation, to await the news of the birth. In the villages of Mount Lebanon, if a woman was having a difficult labour, the husband would be required to assist her symbolically. His *tarbouche* would be placed on her head, his *abah* on her shoulders; often, if her labour was particularly difficult, he would be asked to climb on to the roof of the house and, standing above the spot where she was lying, roll the great rolling stone, the *mahdala*, normally used for thickening and flattening the earth on the roofs, back and forth, back and forth.

In the towns, women also delivered at home. Midwives with varying degrees of skill attended. By Mother's generation, women gave birth lying on a bed: not long before that, a birthing chair was used. Teta delivered all her babies on such a chair. She told my cousin Lulu that her midwife, whose name was Nofa, used to bring her chair with her and rub her belly with warm oil during her labour. Mother's contemporary and fellow Nazarene, Asma Hishmeh, remembers seeing her mother's midwife bring in the chair for the delivery of her youngest brother. In Nazareth, Asma recalled, the best-known midwife, probably the same Nofa, was a Lebanese woman, well trained and licensed – 'a Protestant', I was told, as though that were a licence in itself.

A story told by Princess Musbah Haidar about her own birth in Istanbul in 1908 struck me as symbolic of the changes in childbirth customs. The princess was the daughter of the deposed Sharif of Mecca, and the circle in which they moved in Istanbul included the Sultan and the highest members of his court. Thus the characters in the story, which takes place in the princely household, include eunuchs and slaves, and bear no resemblance to the members of the Syrian middle-class commoners about whom I am writing. Nevertheless I found much significance in the story.

The Sharif's English wife, the Princess Fatima, attended by her midwife, was having a difficult labour. The proceedings were being watched over by 'Big Dadeh', the Sharif's old nurse. Though this woman was a Circassian slave, she was the supreme authority among the other slaves and servants in the household. The princess's labour was so difficult that the Sharif decided to flout tradition and send for a trained physician. When she heard that a male doctor had been sent for, the old slave woman expressed her horror at the thought of such an intrusion, and when Dr Omar Pasha Novotny arrived, she refused to permit him entrance into this most female of female sanctuaries. Instead, she gave instructions that the door of the room where the princess lay in labour should on no account be opened, and that a broom should be placed near it to ward off the evil eye.

The doctor stood outside, banging on the door for a long time, aware of his awkward situation as a male intruder into the female sanctuary, but also aware of the dangers faced by the princess. Eventually the midwife, fearing for the life of the woman she was tending and recognizing her own inability to handle the situation, opened the door and let him in, despite the continuing protests of Big Dadeh. The doctor's efforts saved both mother and child, but the success of the operation was attributed by Big Dadeh not to the skills of modern medicine but to the charms of the broom standing faithfully at the door.

No doubt this story can be read as a denunciation of the ignorance and superstition of the old women, and the arrival of scientifically sound medical practices. But it can also be seen as a heroic, though futile, last stand of women holding the fort of their own business against the invasion of the modern, male-dominated medical establishment.

From the beginning of her first pregnancy, Mother was cut off from childbearing traditions, and from other women, especially her mother. Her nearest female relation was her maiden aunt, who knew nothing of childbirth. The story of the birth of Mother's first child is as much the story of the modernizing world as Princess Fatima's, but, unlike the latter's, it was a disaster.

Even the preparations for the birth were 'modern'. Instead of making her own infant's clothes, of being taught by her mother what would be required, she and her husband turned to the great shops of London, spurning even the grand boutiques of Cairo:

> We were so excited that before I had finished the first month, we got catalogues from England for layettes. There were beautiful baby shops in Cairo, of course, but no! we wanted to have better things. The place in London was called 'Treasure Cot'. I'll never forget the beautiful pink, blue and white clothes, with dainty lace and ribbons. We even got baby toys!

As soon as he heard the joyful tidings, Boulos Said sent word from Jerusalem insisting that the birth take place there, in the ancestral city, but my father would not hear of this. He wanted nothing but the best for his young wife, and the best was the most modern lying-in hospital in Cairo. After some research, he concluded that Papayounou Hospital, in Dokki, which was run by a Greek gynaecologist, Dr Joanides, who was also 'the best', was the right place for the birth.

Mother's excitement at the prospective birth was no different from that of most young women's: 'I was too excited and thrilled to do anything else besides thinking and planning – fixing rooms, cots, etc.' Her only unfulfilled desire at this time was to have her mother with her. Teta was now struggling to keep her family together and, with the small salary she was being paid, trying especially to keep her house. At the time, the Egyptian authorities did not easily give visas to Palestinians, and Teta was unable to come to Cairo to be with her daughter.

And so, cut off from the natural inheritance of women, the young woman entered her last days of pregnancy:

> Finally the day came, and at about 11 a.m. on 18 September 1934, I had the first strong pain and phoned Wadie. He came home immediately and took me and my bag to the hospital. We had no one, Mama was unable to come, and Auntie Emelia was no help.

When they arrived at the hospital, they discovered that Dr Joanides was absent: his mother had died and he had gone to Athens to attend her funeral. My mother was attended by his substitute, an Austrian doctor, who, she later discovered, was drunk that day. In spite of the protests of the head nurse, 'a very sweet German' woman, he gave her one injection after another to speed up the delivery, and finally the baby was born dead.

Needless to say, the new parents were devastated by this experience, and by the doctor's prediction that my mother could not have other children without further treatment:

> God only knows how miserable I was. What an experience! I'll never forget Wadie's kindness and his concern for me. He wouldn't leave me at all that night. He sat on the chair holding my hand until I slept.

As she lay in the hospital recuperating, Auntie Melia and Uncle Nassib came daily to visit her, as did her elderly neighbours, the Kettanehs. But it was her mother that she wanted, her mother that she yearned to see. A few days after the birth, Teta arrived at last. She stayed with her daughter all day, only leaving the hospital at night, when my father would come to pick her up after work:

> Even now, after forty-seven years, I cannot forget that experience, and it always stands vividly in my mind. Mother was most comforting. She told me, 'I hope I'll be alive when you don't want any more children, and yet they come!'

That this dead first-born was a son seems to have deepened the wound. Mother never admitted any such bias in the many times I heard her tell this story, but in her journal she wrote: 'But I only had one other boy afterwards.' She continued:

> It was always Wadie's sore spot, though he never mentioned it, that he only had one son. Though no one loved his daughters more than he did, he kept on hoping he'd have one more son!

After the birth, and apparently as a result of the drunken doctor's ministrations, Mother developed a high fever. Gradually, however, she recovered her health, and not long afterwards she became pregnant again. This time, there were decidedly to be no modern hospitals, no foreign doctors. 'Both Wadie and I decided: no more fancy doctors, hospitals, etc. We'll go to Palestine to Boulos' house and have the baby there.' In June, they went to Jerusalem. Mother, who was four months pregnant, stayed there until after the delivery in November. They lived with Auntie Nabiha and her husband Boulos, who had moved into a new house in the Talbieh quarter of Jerusalem. My father took over the principal responsibility for the Palestine Educational Company from his cousin, who could now enjoy a badly needed holiday.

At last, Mother's day arrived. The second floor of the house had just been completed, and the Boulos Saids were moving into it. Mother was helping, carrying things up and down the stairs. 'Suddenly', she remembers, 'I felt a twinge of sharp pain in my back.' Her first reaction was once again to call for her mother: 'I just felt I wanted her there.' In the midst of a great deal of commotion – Auntie Nabiha's large family were all there – she was taken to bed, and the Jewish midwife who had attended all of Auntie Nabiha's births was called in:

> It was about 1.30 p.m. on 1 November, and it was a very beautiful and mild sunny afternoon. The pains came very fast now and Mme Bear was chanting some Hebrew chants and saying in Arabic all the time:
> *Ya sayyidna Nouh*
> *khalis rouh min rouh*
> [Oh, our lord Noah, save one soul from the other].

The birth was a communal occasion and was accompanied by all the warmth of a large family gathering. 'Boulos's tears were running down his cheeks, and the twins Albert and Robert, six years at the time, were peeping in from the windows and were happy to have a baby boy cousin.' Teta had arrived to attend her daughter. Mother's brothers, Alif, Rayik and Emil, were at the time living in Jerusalem and Ramallah, and throughout the period following the birth, they regularly came to visit their mother and sister, and were always asked to lunch or supper.

The new baby was named Edward:

> Don't ask me why [Mother writes querulously in her journal]. We both liked the name. There was so much talk about Edward, Prince of Wales, and we chose that name, though Edward as a man later hated it and would have preferred an Arabic name.

They called in 'the great child specialist', Dr Grunfelder, a German Jew, to attend the baby. 'I followed what he told me to the letter,' Mother remembered proudly, 'and carried it on to the four younger ones later.' The first thing Dr Grunfelder did was to undo the tight swaddling that Teta and Auntie Nabiha had prescribed. The baby was unusually thin, and the doctor was told that, apparently in an attempt to remain slim, as befitted the modern woman she saw herself to be, the mother had dieted during her pregnancy. 'Of course, I told him all my past experience and he was very sympathetic, a really kind and pleasant old man.'

They stayed in Jerusalem for several weeks after the birth. They seem to have lingered deliberately, reluctant to leave, savouring the sweetness of the experience, the security of being constantly surrounded by family and friends, the pleasure of sharing their happiness with their community. But at last they had to get on with their lives, and they returned to Cairo after Christmas.

My parents' return to Jerusalem for the birth of their second child was their way of trying to undo the damage caused by Cairo's 'fancy doctors and fancy hospitals'. The old-fashioned midwife, chanting mysteriously in Hebrew and Arabic, the swaddling bands tightly wound around the infant's stomach, the festivities, the family celebrations, all this made them feel restored, re-warmed and ready to go on.

But in the end there is no turning back, and modernity was utterly and inexorably upon them. As surely as Big Dadeh's broomstick had given way to Dr Novotny's ministrations, so Teta's swaddling cloths, the old midwives, the old chants, and the delivery at home, surrounded by family, would give way to the sterile delivery rooms, hospitals, doctors and licensed nurses of our time. My parents' next baby, my sister Rosemarie, was born a few years later in a small, modern, 'very clean' maternity hospital in Cairo. Mother was attended by a Greek physician, Dr Vlakhos, who 'was very clever, and took very good care of me.' Even the naming of the new baby was derived from modern sources:

> We had just seen a beautiful film a week before, and the heroine (Jeanette MacDonald) was called Rose Marie, so we decided to call our baby, when it is born, if it is a girl, Rosemarie.

Though Auntie Melia showed her unhappiness openly at the birth of a daughter for her niece, the new parents were delighted.

When Mother was pregnant with Rosemarie, my parents had moved from the Bab al-Louk quarter of Cairo to the more exclusive Zamalek, a quiet, residential, tree-lined neighbourhood, full of gardens and embassies. They took a larger, more luxurious flat, and exchanged some of the old furniture which predated their marriage for newer, finer pieces. They joined the exclusive Maadi Sporting Club, where for years they would enjoy the luscious lawns, the tennis and the swimming. After Rosemarie's birth, Mother remembers peacefully, 'We felt a family now, two kids, Wadie and myself.' And, she writes, 'I was content.' She was now fulfilling that notion of womanhood that had been her inheritance from her mother. She had become a skilled housewife, she had two healthy children, and she was the 'helpmeet' to her husband that Mrs Bowen-Thompson had said all women should be.

But her mind was not at rest. Memories of the destruction of her mother's happiness began to haunt her. In her memoir she does not mention – perhaps she had forgotten the connection – that this period of her secure domesticity was the one in which Teta finally lost her home and her independence. What if, Mother remembers worrying, something happened to her husband?

Reports of the educational progress of her cousins, Eva and Lily, regularly brought to her by Auntie Melia, added to her unease. Having completed her two years at the AJC, Eva had moved on to the American University of Beirut, where she had earned a BA. Later she would earn an MA and teach at the university. Lily was finishing a business course and was working as a secretary. Auntie Melia was 'always telling' the young mother about them. No wonder that Mother, looking back at this period, saw that, in spite of her general contentment, she had felt a deep malaise: 'Those were the times I would wish my life were different, that I had finished my education and was able to work or do something with my life …'

CHAPTER 20

Beyond the Memoir

With her account of the year in which my sister Rosemarie was born, Mother ended her notebook. She could no longer bear to look back, and the war in Lebanon, which was the background to her writing, was closing in on her more with every passing day. She ended her memoirs with an anecdote surrounding the 1936 revolution in Palestine 'that I must tell you'. Perhaps this little story, and the memory of all the anguish the question of Palestine would bring was too much; writing about it may have been the straw that broke the camel's back, making any further memories of this time unbearable.

The family business in Jerusalem, like all the others, had closed its doors for some months beginning in 1936 when, during the Palestinian revolt against the growing Zionist threat and the British occupation, a general strike was called. Boulos Said and family had come to Cairo and rented a flat in *midan al antikhana*. 'Of course,' Mother writes,

'both Boulos and Nabiha felt like fish out of water, and were miserable.'
When they returned home after the strike ended, Boulos wrote saying
that a piece of land adjoining the family house in Jerusalem had just
been put on the market, and he suggested that my parents buy it, to
which proposal they happily assented:

> Just imagine [writes Mother] that at that time Boulos Said was
> sure that Jerusalem was our final home, and we were all going
> to live there for the rest of our lives, in spite of what was going
> on in Palestine.

The 1936–39 revolt was to bring about Teta's final social demise.
By 1935, and at least partly because of the American Depression, her
salary from the mission had been entirely cut off and her association
with her church had ended. Earlier, in 1933, she had borrowed money
against the sale of the next year's olives to pay Rayik's fees at the Friends'
School in Ramallah, to which she had sent him after he finished the
local primary school. The following year she sent Emil to the same
school. 'I don't know how she managed,' he writes in his memoir. 'She
must have borrowed more,' he muses, and she must have 'saved to her
bare bones'.

For some time after her retirement, Teta supported herself and
her younger sons (her older sons were working and were financially
independent) from the sale of olives and olive oil from their own trees,
and the sale of goats that her husband had bought just before he died,
which bargain he had mentioned in his letter to Munir. She was able to
keep her home, and her place in it, until the 1936 revolution. By the
time the strike ended, however, she had lost whatever income she had,
and with it whatever independence. She had to close down her house,
and from this time until the end of her long life she had no home of
her own. She became entirely dependent on her children, living first
with one and then another.

The Second World War erupted, and soon British, German, French,
and Italian armies confronted one another at different stages and in
different combinations in Egypt, Palestine and Lebanon. Internally,

Egypt was simmering with strife: anti-royalist feeling was growing, as was active resistance to the British occupation. In Lebanon, French forces loyal to the Vichy government were threatened by the Free French army under the command of General de Gaulle, and the British forces with whom they were allied.

Surrounded by anxiety, uncertainty and danger, the family moved to Jerusalem as usual in the summer of 1940, and I was born there in September. Though both my younger sisters, Joyce and Grace, were born in Cairo, Jerusalem continued to be the family centre until the disastrous war of 1948, when the creation of the state of Israel sent hundreds of thousands of Arab Palestinians into exile.

After 1948, Teta's social decline accelerated and became irreversible. Like most Palestinians, she was now totally dispossessed. She had already lost her home and property; now she lost her place in the world and in society. She lost not only her present, but also her past and her future. She lost the status in the family that she had spent a lifetime of hard work earning. Her last defence, the world of her children, had been blown up, and she had to watch helplessly as they scattered. The political geography of the world in which she had lived had been radically altered twice. This time, after 1948, the change cut her out altogether. There was no longer any place in it for her.

Once the finality of the loss became clear, there had to be a search for new identity papers. Uncle Munir, who settled in Ramallah where he established a medical practice, was given Jordanian papers, and as the eldest son of the family, eventually acquired the same for his mother. Teta was indignant that she, whose father and mother were natives of Mount Lebanon, was unable to acquire Lebanese papers or to help her sons acquire them. Mother, too, was angry until the day of her death that she had lost for ever her Palestinian passport, confiscated by the British authorities in Palestine when she married. She often indignantly recounted to us how the British official told her upon her marriage: 'Your Palestinian passport will now go to a Jewish woman.' For many years, when we travelled as a family, we would line up in two separate queues at airports, train stations and harbours: my father and all five of us children, armed with our American passports, in one, where we were dealt with politely and respectfully; and Mother, alone with her *laissez-passer*, which allowed her to travel through without a national identity, in another, harassed, questioned, bothered.

The new states that had been created following the collapse of the Ottoman empire were singularly unsympathetic to individuals who happened to be in the wrong place at the wrong time. Lines were drawn by the British and French, sometimes through villages, and individuals became citizens of Palestine or Lebanon or Syria or Transjordan by chance. The political and geographic logic of the new borders had nothing to do with the logic that preceded them.

For women, the price of the European incursion was even more unjust. The notion of female citizenship, as understood by the British and French in 1920, was imposed on constitutions and public institutions, and this legacy of 'modernity' survives to this day: nationality is still passed only patrilineally, and a woman may not pass on her nationality to her children. One of the demands of the women's movement, of which I would like to think I am an active member, is a change in this law. In several Arab countries, including Lebanon and Egypt, however, the question is directly tied up with Palestine: fear that Palestinians would have easy access to Lebanese citizenship if Lebanese women were given the right to pass nationality to their husbands and children, is the principal reason for the law not being changed. For the same reason, I am sorry to say, this demand is not being pressed very hard by the Lebanese women's movement.

Things were rather different in the 1950s. The Lebanese authorities, under President Camille Chamoun, were eager to increase the number of Christians in the country, and so made it possible for many Christian Palestinians to acquire Lebanese citizenship. My uncles Emil, Rayik and Alif acquired theirs by re-establishing their links with their cousins, the Bishutis, who had settled in Beirut generations earlier. Throughout historic Syria, branches of the same family had settled in what had since the First World War become Lebanon, Syria and Palestine, and family relationships were easily traced. By establishing this connection, my uncles reverted to the family surname taken by that branch of the family and became known as 'Bishuti', while Mother, Uncle Munir and Teta retained the surname 'Musa'. Thus did history once again stamp itself on our names, and thus was established a linguistic separation already physically achieved by war and politics. Eventually, Mother did acquire Lebanese citizenship, and though she died in America, it was as a Lebanese that she was buried.

Teta spent much of her time after 1948 with us in Cairo and Dhour al-Schweir, but her primary residence was with Uncle Munir and his family in Ramallah. In August 1957 the wedding took place in Ramallah of his daughter, my cousin Lulu, and I was her bridesmaid. The West Bank and Old, or East, Jerusalem were then Jordanian territory, and therefore still accessible to us. I spent a couple of weeks there, saw Teta in a different environment from the one I was used to seeing her in, partook of the legendary *mousakhan* chicken that Aunt Latifeh, Uncle Munir's wife, was famous for, and then joined in the rituals of the Greek Orthodox wedding ceremony, with Lulu, her bridegroom Elias and I each wearing a floral crown and walking around the altar three times. Elias whispered to the priest to hurry the lengthy ceremony along, as Lulu and I pretended not to hear, trying to maintain a straight face and trying not to laugh at his irreverence.

The most important part of the trip for me, however, was seeing Old Jerusalem, walking its streets and visiting its shrines. I remember standing on the Mount of Olives, in the Garden of Gethsemane, looking across at the ancient walls, the golden dome of the Dome of the Rock mosque with al-Aqsa nearby, and feeling the sanctity of the place. Then walking to Haram al-Sharif and the Church of the Holy Sepulchre, and the other churches and mosques. My only other visit to Jerusalem was for another cousin's wedding which I attended with my father and brother: Robert, Auntie Nabiha's youngest son, married in 1966. This was the first time my father had been to Jerusalem since 1948, and I shall never forget his face as we surveyed the whole city, now so changed, from the top of the YMCA building near the Mandelbaum Gate, separating the two parts of the divided city. Of course, the Jerusalem that I remembered from my childhood was inaccessible to me, and could only be viewed from a distance.

After the 1967 war, following the Israeli occupation of the West Bank and the rest of Jerusalem, Uncle Munir and his family moved to Amman. The last years of Teta's life were mostly spent in the house of her youngest son, Emil, in Beirut.

WOMEN TOGETHER:
MOTHER AND ME

Mother holding Edward, Jerusalem, 1935.

Jean holding Saree, Washington D.C., 1964.

CHAPTER 21

Beirut Revisited

Though my parents remained in Egypt throughout the period of the 1952 revolution and the Suez crisis, they were forced to leave by the ensuing social revolution. The government of Gamal Abdel Nasser began to implement its revolutionary goals with land-reform laws, and then went on to expropriate and sometimes nationalize the businesses and industries that had been hitherto run almost exclusively by foreigners, many of whose homes were confiscated as well. Although my father's business was not yet nationalized, it was prudent to liquidate it and leave before it was.

By the early 1960s, almost all of my parents' friends of the Syrian community had left Cairo. Of these, the majority settled in Beirut. Some, however, having witnessed the loss of Palestine, the Iraqi revolution of 1958, the 1958 disturbances in Lebanon that pre-shadowed the long civil war that was to come later, and the Egyptian revolution, felt that the Arab world would be unstable for decades to come, and decided to eschew it altogether, ending up in the United States, Canada, Europe and even East Asia. Following the summer of 1961, when my father suffered the grave illness described earlier in this book, and after my wedding in February 1962, the family returned to Cairo to close down the house, liquidate the business and make the final move to Beirut.

When my parents moved to Beirut in 1962, the city was in the midst of its spiral towards the economic and cultural boom that reached a peak in the early '70s. The Palestine war of 1948 had brought hundreds of thousands of destitute Palestinian refugees to Lebanon, but it had also brought Palestinian businessmen, bankers, lawyers, writers, teachers, civil servants, artists and poets. Prosperous Iraqis, Syrians and Egyptians – including thousands of *Shawwam* – settled in Beirut following the revolutions in their respective countries in the 1950s. In addition, because of the intellectual freedom and cultural diversity it offered, Beirut had attracted dissidents and revolutionaries from as far away as Afghanistan and Sudan and the Arab Maghreb. Freedom of financial transactions and banking secrecy, as well as an efficient and open infrastructure, made Beirut a financial and business centre for the entire region. A pleasant climate, spectacular scenery, important archaeological sites, educational freedom and diversity, as well as a plethora of cafes, cinemas, restaurants, nightclubs, hotels, skiing and summer resorts, beaches, golf courses and yacht clubs, made Beirut attractive to tourists. A large and prosperous foreign community chose to live and send their children to school here even while perhaps doing business elsewhere in the region. Because of its openness and relative freedom, Beirut was also an important centre of information and journalism.

As the other major cities of the area were more subject to revolutionary fervour and discipline, often socialist in nature, or ferociously conservative ways of life, Beirut increasingly came to mean freedom, on both a serious and a more frivolous level, and pleasure – at least, to the middle and wealthier classes.

My parents, I think, rather liked being in Beirut, though they greatly missed Cairo. They enjoyed the closer presence of family and friends made possible by the smaller size of Beirut relative to Cairo. Mother caught up with her old school friends, and the cousins who had been so important to her as a child. Two of her brothers, Alif and Emil, were living in Beirut, as well as other members of the family. Several of the Cairenes who moved at the same time as they, together with my father's nephews who moved to Beirut after the 1967 war, gave them a very large social circle, one that was probably more informal, more relaxed, than the one in Cairo.

My father was never the same after his long and debilitating illness and following the move from Cairo. Physically weakened, he spent less and less time at the new Standard Stationery Company he had founded in Beirut with Lebanese partners. Partly because of his physical condition, and partly due to the alien business environment and the often unscrupulous practices which he could not understand and no longer had the energy to deal with, his means were much reduced. The move from Cairo had already reduced the family income considerably. Still, my parents were comfortable enough, and able to enjoy their lives without too much anxiety.

Every afternoon, my father played bridge or *tawleh* (backgammon). He went for walks and drives, and took Mother out to dinner and lunch at some of the great Beirut restaurants. They especially loved to dine on the terrace of the Hotel St Georges, situated on St George's bay, at the Lucullus, at Temporel Sur Mer, and the restaurant on the roof of the Bristol Hotel. They also loved the many mountain cafes and restaurants by the side of brooks and waterfalls, where they ate *kabab* and grilled chicken with garlic sauce.

He still loved to spend the summers in Dhour al-Schweir, where he forgot his troubles and where picnics, backgammon and bridge remained his favourite pastimes. Mother always claimed to hate the eternal shortages of water and electricity, which made her housekeeping there so difficult. But in her heart of hearts, I believe she enjoyed Dhour al-Schweir more than she would admit, and when, after his death, she gave up these summer visits, part of her went numb and died with him.

My parents particularly enjoyed one of the most extraordinary aspects of life in Lebanon during this period from the 1950s to the outbreak of the Lebanese war in 1975: the spectacular annual international arts festival at Baalbek, in the Bekaa valley. Held every summer in the sublime open-air setting of the Graeco-Roman ruins, which were magnificently lit for the occasion, the festival boasted evening performances by some of the world's greatest artists. Classical soloists such as Claudio Arrau, Arturo Benedetti Michelangeli, Jean-Pierre Rampal, Elisabeth Schwarzkopf and many others played there; as did the great orchestras, the Berlin Philharmonic, the State Symphony Orchestra of the USSR and the New York Philharmonic; conductors such as Herbert von Karajan, Karl Munchinger, Charles Munch, and many others; chamber groups including among others the Amadeus Quartet, the Chamber Orchestras of Prague, Moscow and Stuttgart, and the Santa Cecilia of Rome. Margot Fonteyn, Rudolf Nureyev and the Royal Ballet danced on the steps of the ancient temples, as did the Alvin Ailey group, the Ballet du XXe Siècle of Maurice Béjart and many other great companies; the Paris Opera performed Gluck's *Orphée*; Shakespeare, Corneille, Racine, Césaire, Schaffer, O'Neill and Anouilh were performed by the London and Bristol Old Vics, the Comédie Française and others; jazz artists such as Ella Fitzgerald, Oscar Peterson, Miles Davis, Dizzy Gillespie, as well as the Modern Jazz Quartet played at the festival. The folk ballet companies from Mexico and the Philippines, among others, danced here as well. Even the Amherst Glee Club sang here.

Arabic music was also well represented at the festival. Among the most popular performances, invariably sold out the moment they were announced, were those by Um Kulthoum, the Egyptian diva, for which enormously expensive black-market tickets were sold months ahead of time; and the *Nuits Libanaises,* which included elaborately staged folk dancing, and operettas starring such Lebanese musical luminaries as Sabah, Nasri Shamseddine, Wadi al-Safi and, above all, the incomparable Fairouz. The Lebanese and Arab theatre found in Baalbek a welcome and magnificent venue for experiments in theatrical form and language.

The festival was typical of Beirut at this time – for although far away from the capital, it reflected the city's spirit, rather than that of the impoverished farming communities in whose midst the dancing and the music took place. There was a kind of extraordinary audacity and arrogance about the festival, a wonderful ability to unselfconsciously aim at the highest stars, utterly rejecting the second rate, together with a sublime indifference to the outside world and its problems. It was not surprising, though it may have been sad, that civil war was brewing while the great artists were playing in Baalbek, and while Beirut hostesses gave magnificent parties in honour of the visitors.

Indeed, the *grandes dames* of Beirut had a conspicuous presence that was part of the atmosphere of the festival. Not only did they serve as hostesses to the artists, throwing fabled parties in their honour, but their clothes, jewels, coiffures and general manner, rarely if ever understated, became as much part of the setting at the performances as the columns and altars of the ancient temples. During the evening performances, and in their desire to innovate, the elegant women at the festival took to wearing *kaftans* and *abayas* from the national tradition, but glamourized to make the class distinctions quite clear: these *abayas* and *kaftans* were of velvet or silk, with lavish gold and silver embroidery. Suddenly national costume, banished from fashionable circles for generations, made a dramatic comeback for the wealthy urban classes – the rural and urban poor had never stopped wearing it.

Along with the richly embroidered velvet *abayas* there turned up designer cotton *galabiyas* to wear comfortably at home, woollen *abayas* to wear in the mountain house on chilly evenings. The Western political stance in support of Israel, especially after the 1967 war, had led to an angry reaction which manifested itself not only politically but also in a new, defensive interest in the cultural heritage. A new fascination with traditional designs, costumes and household objects was linked to a growing rejection of the Western world – and its clothes – which had so betrayed the Arabs, and to a renewed and defensive interest in roots, in the past and in the Arab cultural heritage.

This revival led to the opening of new shops designing and making dresses, cushions, carpets, tablecloths and other objects in traditional fabrics and designs. Brass and copper came back too, and suddenly it became fashionable once more to use brass coffee-pots, from which one's ancestors used to pour coffee, as doorstops or decorations, and old brass braziers as planters. Old shops in the crowded Basta quarter in downtown Beirut were patronized by people searching for the same lamps, tables, rocking chairs and chests that their mothers and grandmothers had thrown away a generation before.

Though Mother bought or commissioned many *abayas* for my sisters and me, she herself never went in for them or for the designer *galabiyas*. I think she felt no nostalgia for a lost past; hers was with her, part of her life and memory, though I did not know it then.

Nor did she ever go in for the brasses and inlaid tables of the Basta. Mother brought with her from Cairo all her furniture and *objets d'art*. She recreated in Beirut her Cairo home, and thus participated, though unintentionally, in the transformation of domestic fashion. Most middle-class Beirut homes were, at the time that Mother arrived, decorated quite simply, Persian carpets being their major adornment. Except in the households of the richest and most sophisticated people, clumsy imitations of bulky late Victorian and art deco European furniture had over the decades replaced the old Arab interiors.

Thus, when Mother brought the English Regency-style dining set, the French-style sofas and chairs, the grand piano, the Turkish silver and Bohemian crystal, the Japanese Satsuma porcelain, the Bukhara embroideries and the Chinese screens, she helped to create a new sense of style. This existed side by side with that renewed interest in old patterns and designs, which in any case were used principally for ornamentation. She and the other migrating Cairenes had not intended to make this contribution to Beirut life, yet they were none the less extremely aware of having done so.

Mother's one concession to the revival of traditional designs was her use of cushions embroidered in the colours and patterns specific to each region of Palestine. The designs that peasant women had for ages embroidered on their dresses, which were functional and were worn every day, were now taken up in exile and transferred to cushions, tablecloths and other decorative objects. The idea was to save the patterns, not to allow them to die out. Palestinian history and culture was being denied and invalidated by Israeli propaganda, and here in this entirely female sphere was a practical way of reaffirming their existence. Social workers and volunteer designers in Mother's circle, many of them her personal friends, supervised the production and sale of the cushions in Beirut, also intended to help women in the Palestinian refugee camps become productive economically. She commissioned a tablecloth for me, in the most famous of the designs, the black and red embroidery of Ramallah.

Once settled in Beirut, Mother tried to reorganize her life, and to reclaim it from pure domesticity. The move itself, as well as my father's dramatic illness at around the same time, was a kind of *memento mori* for her. Her children were now grown up, and most of us were away.

In 1963 she registered at the Beirut College for Women, formerly the American Junior College where she had spent that blissfully happy year. There she attended courses, from which she preserved detailed and enthusiastic notes. One course was in Humanities. Detailed and excellent notes in her elegant and distinctive script are on Aristotle's *Poetics* and *Politics*, *The Agamemnon*, Euripides and Plato. Mother carefully copied into her notebook the questions of a long examination: 'Compare and contrast the tragic theme of civil war in Corcyra (Thucydides: the Peloponnesian War) with the tragic theme of "Civil War" in the House of Atreus.' After Christmas the course continued. They read Catullus and Horace, and then St Augustine; *The Song of Roland*; Anglo-Saxon poetry, including *The Seafarer*; they read *The Romance of the Rose* and Dante. She attended a course in Contemporary Literature, which included works by Joyce and Hemingway. They also read Yeats, Pound, Eliot and Shaw. Her notes on Contemporary Literature peter out, and suddenly in December the first notes appear for the History of Lebanon. Her notes on Lebanon are detailed and enthusiastic, although sometimes, in her zeal to write everything down, they lapse into uncharacteristic illegibility.

After this: nothing. She soon gave up this attempt to go back to school. A hint as to the reason appears on the very last page of the notebook:

Plan menu for Rosie
Buy macaroni and gruyère
Give blouse to dressmaker
Buy [eye drops]
A shopping list also appears:
macaroni, meat, vegetables (peas, beans, carrots), salad, lettuce, tom.

The enormous effort required of Mother to pull herself out of her domestic routine, to start a new life, and above all to take herself and her task seriously, was probably not supported by her circle, or at least not enough to help her make this enormous effort. I remember her telling me once that some of her friends teased her: 'Hilda is going back to school with her white hair!' And 'Hilda is going to school to be taught by her daughters!' Two of my sisters, Rosemarie and Joyce, were now teaching at the college, one music and the other English. I was still living in the United States, as was Grace, who was studying at Duke University. Edward was embarking on his illustrious academic career.

Mother's attempt to redeem this part of her life was doomed. She could not do it; she had not the strength to fish herself out of the waters in which she had swum for more than thirty years; she was too deeply committed to the form of family she had created, and which had consumed her. I do not know what my father's position was as regards her studies: I cannot imagine that he would have stood in her way, and yet that touch of jealousy of the college, and his fear of losing her to it, expressed in his letters during their engagement may well have survived in his unconscious.

Defeated, Mother turned away from the open road which beckoned. She rejected the adventures and dangers involved. She turned back to the security of the comfortable domestic life she knew. From this moment, the seeds were sown of a deep resentment, which would in her final years, fed by the surrounding bitterness of Beirut's never-ending war, occasionally blossom forth like one of those terrible flowers that bloom in the forest once a year.

Occasionally, she was given a respite from the empty nest. When I gave birth to my first son, Saree, in 1964, she came to Washington a few weeks early, bearing a trousseau of blankets, caps and socks knitted by her and Teta, to preside over the birth, and to instruct me, in the age-old tradition, on his care. She gave him his first bath, cooed over him when he cried, calmed my nerves, taught me what to feed him, how to change his nappies, how to burp him. She taught me some of the songs she had herself sung to her own babies. She wrote letters announcing the birth, and received the congratulatory phone calls. She cooked the celebratory *mughli*, the sweet rice pudding flavoured with caraway, cinnamon and aniseed, and served it to those who called on us. Eventually, however, she had to return home and resume her own life.

Mother, who had so prided herself on her modernity, was as defeated by it as her own mother had been before her. Having devoted her life to the kind of housewifery which was the harbinger of the modern age, to the kind of home and to the nuclear family which she had so deliberately and carefully constructed, she was now the victim of all these things. The old family form, in which the aging matriarch was allowed such a powerful place, was denied her as much as it had been denied her mother. The cosmopolitanism of her children, which she had been instrumental in teaching them and encouraging; the higher education which they pursued at her and her husband's behest – of which she was so proud, even while she fought it for taking them away from her – all this in the end contributed to her loneliness and pain.

When Mother died in 1990, towards the end of the Lebanon war, I was the only one of my siblings living in Beirut, and it was left to me to close down her house. As I did so, I discovered much about her that I did not know, so many things that spoke of her life and her memories. Going through her closets and her papers was like exploring a river flowing deep into a jungle, a search into her psyche after her death. This is when I found the oilskin bag containing the letters she and my father had exchanged during their engagement, almost sixty years earlier, as well as a letter she wrote to him on their twenty-fifth wedding anniversary. But I was to make an even more startling discovery.

In one of the cupboards I found a cardboard box containing stacks of blue notebooks, which at first, in my exhaustion, I was tempted to throw away without further ado. Just to be sure, however, I opened one and glanced through it. I opened another, and then another. To my astonishment, I found that the notebooks contained carbon copies of letters Mother had written from 1966 right up to 1983. The letters, some of them barely legible because of the fading ink, fill up almost twenty-five thick notebooks, and read as an extraordinary record not only of those years, but of her life and concerns over the decades. They chronicle the life and times of a middle-aged, middle-class Arab urban woman during a period of enormous political upheaval.

I had known that Mother kept carbon copies of her letters; I had indeed occasionally been commissioned to buy her a new notebook when the old one was filled up. I had even expressed amusement at this habit. But it was not until after her death that I saw all the copy-books together, and realized with a shock that she had kept a systematic record of herself and her life. Why? I kept asking myself. What does it mean that she did this extraordinary thing? A handful of the letters concerned business matters, for which carbon copies made sense: there were a couple with instructions to a banker or a lawyer, others to foreign embassies requesting a visa. A few letters were addressed to old friends and relatives. The vast bulk, however, were addressed to myself, my brother and my sisters.

The letters are full of reminders of long-forgotten items of family and public history. When Mother moved to Beirut, she was in her late forties. Her children were almost all grown-up. For the first few years of these letters, I was in the United States, newly married at first, and then, as the years passed, I had one, two and then three children. Then I moved to Beirut. When the first letters were written, my brother Edward was at graduate school. Later he was teaching at university and taking the first steps towards fame. Later still, he was to become a paterfamilias, and then became politically involved. Mother worried about him constantly, though she took enormous pride in his accomplishments.

Rosemarie was at home, teaching at university, and then in London, studying for her PhD. Then she was back at home, teaching and then again travelling. Then she married and settled in Beirut, while still travelling constantly. Then, when the war in Lebanon was in its second year, she moved to England with her husband. Joyce was here, teaching; then she married and moved to Switzerland. Grace starts out, when the letters begin, at Duke University; then she comes home, then goes to the US again for postgraduate work at the University of Maryland, then she returns and teaches for a long time; then, during the war, she leaves permanently. My father recuperates from his terrible illness, and for a few years his precarious health improves. Then he gets sick again, and finally dies. Teta figures in the early letters, then she too becomes ill and dies.

Political and social events are recorded; cultural life continues, including the centennial celebrations of the American University of Beirut, the Baalbek festival, lectures, concerts and plays. The 1967 war takes place; resulting in a new set of displacements of various people in Mother's life, especially her brother Munir and his family. The death of Gamal Abdel Nasser in 1970 and the ensuing riots in Beirut; the 1973 war; the continuing unrest in Beirut, finally bursting into open warfare in the spring of 1975; the comings and goings of all and sundry, as well as her growing personal anguish – all of this is described and chronicled in her letters.

The letters are full of support, advice, congratulations, commiseration, love, scolding, gossip, information and news of the comings and goings of friends and relations. She writes of the weather, and of the dishes she has served at luncheons, teas and dinners. She writes with the skill of the born narrator that she was, her letters as lively, interesting and full of character as herself. Even when she repeats an item of news – which she regularly does as she writes the same news to five absent children and occasionally to a relative or friend – varies the telling for each reader.

She gives advice and offers admonitions on a variety of subjects. She regularly reports where and with whom she dined, and with whom she took tea. Her letters provide a record of the social manners of the Beirutis, with their famous insouciance, seen through a sensitive, intelligent, moral glass.

Thus, from a long distance, Mother tried to maintain or re-establish family relationships long after the nest had emptied. She remained just as much mother, mother-in-law and grandmother as if she had been physically present. In this way, she tried to defeat history, and time, and change. And to some extent she succeeded in doing so. There was no difference in our relationship when she was present or when we were far away and settled in our own lives.

In October 1968 she wrote me a series of letters on the very premature birth of my second son, Ussama, who weighed in at a little more than two pounds. As I read them over, I remembered the anguish I had suffered and the real comfort her letters had brought me. She wrote not just about the baby, but about goings-on in Beirut, creating a mixture of comfort, encouragement and entertainment:

> *21 October 1968* [two days after the birth]
> My darling child,
>   … We happened to have been all home … Dad and I were still arguing on whether you're having a girl or a boy, and I said it is sure to be a girl … At that moment the cable came. Let me say to start with, *al-hamdillah 'ala 'l-salameh* [Thank God

for your safety]. I called Samir and he told me all the news possible on the phone. According to Nada [Samir's sister], a lot of Makdisis are born ahead of time. We are all hoping and praying that the little one will live, ... but in case *la samah allah* [God forbid] he doesn't live, please, sweetheart, don't be too unhappy. Remember only that if he doesn't live he's a weak child and life would have been difficult for him ... I'm going to write you every other day so I'll keep in touch.

And then, she tries to cheer me up with the usual subject matter of her letters:

You must have read of the presidential crisis? It looks better now, but no one knows for how long. The Ms are here from Cairo, and E had a small dinner for them. LF is expecting another baby, but not until late April or early May. F is going on a business trip to New York in early November. X is in London, otherwise everyone is fine. You and Samir have a big laugh over this: NK (married to Dr S) gave a huge cocktail party for 400 people! The occasion: the opening of their roof [penthouse]! It seems they bought fabulous things for decorating the roof, from Paris! Aren't people just crazy! ... SK in the meantime got engaged officially to RD. AK lost her excellent maid, who left her suddenly stealing a lot of things for her and the baby.

24 October 1968
Everyone who has heard keeps on phoning to find out all the news about the baby. Of course 'all Beirut' knows by now and everyone seems to know of someone who is a premature baby. Mrs LS told me that twenty-three years ago when her son was born, another little boy was born. He was 600 grams and six and a half months and they used to come and get a few drops of breast milk from her every day for him. Today, he is her son's classmate and an engineer too. EA and I were invited to M this morning for morning coffee. E had her second boy born on 21 October instead of 10 January. Dr Nachman [a prominent paediatrician] took care of him at AUB. He stayed in the

incubator for two and half months! By the way, you prepared so many girls' names, what did you name the little fellow?

10 November
On Wednesday I had thirty 'girls' for lunch in honour of Mrs Hamadi from Flint. I made *kibbeh*, roast, *maqlouba* of eggplants, pigeon and a cold fish, and for dessert *kenaffe* and *mughli*, telling everyone this is for the new baby. Everybody ate it and said *Inshallah yislam* [May he be blessed].

Xmas 1968
Our call to you was not so good this time, but it was nice hearing you, just to tell you *mabrouk* [congratulations] for Ussama's homecoming. Uncle Anis [Samir's father] invited us all to eat *mughli*, all his friends and relations too, and it was excellent. He also read us the poem [written in honour of Ussama's birth] – really good for a man of any age, but wonderful for his.

In spite of her long-distance mothering, and as though recognizing the futility of her own efforts, the deep malaise of her situation creeps throughout the letters. Again and again she refers to repeated, valiant, but always failed, attempts to get her own life in order, to find a meaning for it outside the domesticity that was no longer satisfying her. During the 1960s and early 1970s, her letters are full of references to potential driving lessons: 'I am going to start driving lessons next week,' she writes, week after week. Eventually, references to these driving lessons peter out: Mother never did learn to drive. She tried to become interested in social work. She writes on 7 November 1968:

I am starting next week on my social work. I've been asked to do flower arrangements for the hospital. I'm also offering my house two afternoons a week for the church to play bridge and collect money. I'm also helping one afternoon and one morning a week at the YWCA. I'm trying to keep busy anyway, and it's better than chatting away and talking nonsense.

A week later she writes of her efforts to keep abreast of cultural

events: 'Yesterday I went to the BCW to attend the opening lecture
of a series on "The Novel in the Post War Era".' She even tried to find
work, but only half-heartedly, knowing that neither she nor the society
in which she lived were ready for a middle-aged woman of comfortable
means who had been a housewife for so many years, to suddenly move
into the labour force.

But her letters were not all concerned with strictly personal
matters: they chronicle historical events as well. Beginning with the
Intra Bank affair, often cited as an early sign of the coming civil war in
Lebanon, Mother relates the public aspect of these events with a certain
indifference concentrating on those things which affect people of her
acquaintance. The owner of the Intra Bank, for instance, was Youssef
Beydas, that old friend and relation who had been my father's best man
at their wedding. Thus her account of the collapse of the bank is fed by
her interest in his personal fate.

Gradually, however, and especially during and after the catastrophic
1967 Arab–Israeli war, and perhaps under pressure from her absent
children pressing her for details of the political situation, she becomes
more self-conscious and committed a witness; she becomes, indeed, a
systematic chronicler of public events. As time passes, she intervenes in
the narrative, and interprets it. This function of chronicler reawakened
the political interest in her. By the time the Lebanese war began in
1975, she had once again become involved – at least as a narrator – in
the public life around her.

Perhaps the most interesting aspect of her letters for outsiders is that
they show that the memory preserved by most Beirutis of the 1960s
and early 1970s as a 'golden era', a time of great stability, prosperity and
carefree happiness, is deceptive. Her letters chronicle a continuous and
ominous unrest which belies the rosy picture that post-war nostalgia
has painted of pre-war Lebanon.

21 March 1967
Last night Nadim and Pauline, Uncle Anis and Nida and
Freddy all came to spend the evening here. While talking, there
was a big explosion and we found that some dynamite sticks
had exploded near the John F. Kennedy [the American Cultural
Center] library in Abdel Aziz St.

February 1968 [after a trip to Cairo]
As usual, a Lebanese passport had to be checked and rechecked and rechecked! After about forty-five minutes' wait they gave it to me, and I was able to get to customs.

12 January 1969
The attack on the airport [by Israeli forces that destroyed the fleet of the Lebanese national carrier, Middle East Airlines, on the ground] left everyone speechless ... Celebrations for New Year went on as usual. Now and for the past week, all universities and now schools are on strike, and now a hunger strike; there's no government yet, and people are all worried in case of an Israeli attack on the South.

18 October 1969
Zelpha Chamoun [wife of the former president of Lebanon] came to see Renee [Renée Dirlik, Mother's close friend from Cairo, who was visiting her in Beirut] and left us all very morbid. She is very pessimistic about Lebanon, and is very worried about civil war here and a *madbaha* [bloodbath] – everyone is pessimistic about the political situation these days, both from outside and inside Lebanon.

26 October 1969
We're under curfew again, only this time it's really serious, and people are very scared.

28 October 1969
It has been a hectic and worrisome few days. The curfew is almost over, from 3 a.m. to 8 p.m. [*sic*] but today a lot of dynamite was thrown all around Ras Beirut, near the Strand and Colisee Cinemas, near the Marble Tower, under a CD [*corps diplomatique*] car near Aoun House. People are worried and scared, and so don't leave their home too often. It reminds us all of the troubled days in Egypt before the revolution.

But Beirut's renowned energy continued unabated:

24 February 1970

Last night Joyce and I went to AUB and heard the Munich Chamber Orchestra in a fantastic programme of Mozart, Beethoven and Haydn – it was very crowded. Myrna and her fiancé were there, and she asked about you. The night before, they had the Warsaw Symphony Orchestra at the Casino ... We three attended a beautiful performance of Barbara Jefford and John Turner in *The Labours of Love* taken from different British dramas and we really enjoyed it immensely. Now [Roger] Assaf and Nidal al-Ashkar are in a play called *Carte Blanche* at the Phoenicia as a political satire, and we plan to see it, providing it stays. They are now having a world surgical conference here, even [Christian] Barnard and his bride are here.

The death at the end of September 1970 of Gamal Abdel Nasser, who personified the dream of Arab unity and was by far the most charismatic leader in recent Arab history, sent shock waves around the Arab world. Mother's letter describing the reaction in Beirut is typically mixed in with domestic details:

5 October 1970

On Monday evening, Youssef and Aida were playing bridge at our house [in Dhour al-Schweir] and we were so engrossed we forgot ... to hear the 10 o'clock news from London. At 10:15 Shadia called and told us and we couldn't believe it ... It was madness in Beirut, people actually went crazy ... There were fires everywhere, broken glass, random shooting. In those three days of mourning, one hundred and fifty people were injured and twenty or thirty killed (according to the papers). Poor Joyce [who was in Beirut] had no food at home; we had cleaned the fridge and were planning to stock it on Tuesday. No shops or bakeries etc were open ... The government wouldn't put its foot down till after the funeral. It's a shame, his death was so sad, and they spoilt it here by all this silly commotion. This is why the new president, though he's scheduled to go to the funeral decided to stay. On Friday, everything was calm and we all came down.

In the summer of 1970, the family gathered for the last time in Dhour al-Schweir. Mother's letters show how close we came to missing this reunion: not only I, but all the others as well. Each of us was busy and had complicated plans, but Mother kept on smoothing out one problem after another until, by sheer force of her will, the reunion came about. It was as though some deep family instinct had warned us that we should all come, that our time together was coming to a close.

A sinister note had already begun to creep into Mother's letters in 1969. 'We are fine, but Dad had a cough and a cold.' Again: 'Dad has had a cough.' And again: 'Dad has had another cold and cough, but he is fine now.' On 29 March 1969 my father himself had written a letter, one of two or three by him carefully carboned and preserved among hers. In it is an implicit confession that his old enemy, Mr Nicotine, was still getting the better of him, and he writes: 'Upon receipt of this letter I wish you would buy from a drug store two boxes of ... [illegible] against smoking.'

Although Samir and I were still living in Washington at this time, my youngest son, Karim, was born in Beirut on 23 August. Having discovered how much pain the first few months of Ussama's life had brought us, his premature birth having caused severe illness and stress, my parents had insisted that I spend the last months of this pregnancy with them, so that I could be taken care of.

When the new baby was a few weeks old, my husband and I and our brood returned to Washington. My parents came with us to the airport but were not allowed inside. Beirut airport was in a state of maximum alert, and closed to the public except those travelling: only a few days earlier Palestinian guerrillas had hijacked their first planes and blown them up. In Amman, the heavy fighting between the Jordanian army and the Palestinian forces was at its height. My cousin Robert Said had sent his wife Rima and their young children from Amman to stay with my parents. Black September, as it came to be called, ended with the defeat of the Palestinian forces in Jordan. The PLO moved to Lebanon, where they regrouped: the scene was being set for the war that erupted in 1975. As we entered the airport building, we turned to wave a final goodbye to my parents. That was the last time I saw my father.

By the end of 1970, the subject of my father's health had been cropping up with menacing regularity in Mother's letters, and soon there was no escape from the knowledge that had been with us for some time: Mr Nicotine had won the lifelong battle. My father had lung cancer, and the doctors gave him six months to live.

Mother was a model of fortitude and gallantry. Reading her letters, one gets the impression that all the years of her moral education, all her work in trying to create the perfect family and to be the perfect wife, culminate in this time. It is as though her entire life had been a rehearsal for this trial, which demanded of her not only that she be courageous but that she create courage in the rest of us, that she should comfort not only her dying husband, but her children as well.

Her letters contain an almost clinical account of the last phase of his illness, with graphic descriptions of symptoms and doctors' reports. But they are also a record of a kind of absolute devotion which we may have lost for ever: we 'modern' women may be too taken up with ourselves, too busy, too distracted, to be able to do what Mother did, lighting the way for her dying husband.

She had written him a letter on the occasion of their twenty-fifth wedding anniversary; it is dated, in his hand, 24 December 1957. I found it among her papers when she died. That he had written the date on it suggests the pleasure and satisfaction the letter gave him. She wrote it as an accompaniment to a gift and addresses it 'to the best husband in the world', who was, she continues:

> a partner, a friend, a husband and a father who has fully graced every single one of these four words. No children could have a better and more understanding man for a Dad. So warm and loving, and so full of cheer ... No wife could have had such wonderful company ... It seems like yesterday when twenty-five years ago on that Xmas Eve in Nazareth I became Mrs William Said. Today I'm more than proud to carry that name, and with it not only my love but deep respect made stronger, admiration made greater, by the trials, troubles and tribulations so magnificently and bravely faced.

In four, closely written pages, the letter was a proud acknowledgement not only of the success of the marriage itself, but of the roles each partner had adopted and played.

At the end of January, my father slipped into a coma. When they called to tell me, I was overwhelmed with panic. I felt I was dangling by a thread over a bottomless pit of indescribable dangers. My protector was going. Though his influence on my life had faded in the last years – for in his eyes, I think, he had stepped away from me, having handed over the role of protector and provider to my husband (whereas Mother's influence had grown: she was, after all, guiding me in my role as wife and mother) – I had always thought of him as my guardian, someone who would with his kindness and generosity look after me for ever.

Collecting myself, I left the United States for Beirut with my brother, leaving the children behind with my husband and friends. When Edward and I arrived at Beirut airport the following evening, we could see Grace and Uncle Emil waiting for us beyond customs. Grace was wearing black and Uncle Emil looked grim. We knew at a glance that we were too late, and that our father had died while we were on our way.

Among the most painful memories of my life is the memory of that evening. I remember arriving at the door of my parents' house and hearing the hushed murmur of voices from inside. I stood at the door as Uncle Emil and the others waited for me to pass through it before them. I could not move, and more than anything I wanted not to go through that door. I wanted my beloved father not to be dead.

I felt I could not face Mother. I was afraid of what she might look like, as though I was expecting to find a new person, someone I did not know and would not recognize. So central had been his existence to hers, and hers to his, that it seemed inconceivable that one should live without the other. 'What shall I say to her?' I asked, in a panic. Standing there, I knew I was crossing not only the threshold of my mother's house, but a new stage in the life of the family, and in my life as well.

At last, I entered. The living-room was full of people gathered, as is customary, to offer their condolences. The women were all dressed in black; the men were wearing ties and jackets. They were speaking in hushed tones. At first I could not pick Mother out from all the women, but soon I focused on her sitting, between my sisters, on a sofa in the middle of the room. A deep silence fell over the assembly as Edward and I entered, and I was vaguely conscious of people whispering and weeping as we embraced first Mother and then our sisters. Then we took our places with the others, and all of us sat together, receiving the condolences. Mother had not fallen apart, as I had half expected her to have done; she was not sobbing wildly, nor was she in a state of collapse, as I had feared. She was composed and quiet, intensely aware, I think, of the importance of the moment and of the necessity to maintain a dignified presence among the community that now surrounded her.

The conventions of communal mourning provide a well-rehearsed ritual to fill up the immense empty space that follows death. In those terrible hours, having something to do, something which one has done dozens of times before for other mourners, following a set pattern of standing, shaking hands, embracing, whispering the right words and then sitting down again, sitting with one's community of relatives, neighbours, friends and acquaintances, is sedating, comforting, quieting. Some of the old accompaniments of communal mourning – the ritual wailing, the beating of heaving breasts, the laying out of the dead person in the house, such as those Mother described upon the death of her own father – these are no longer appropriate in an urban setting, but what is left is the community, and the people gathering to sit quietly together, pausing in the contemplation of death.

And mourning is the function of women. Later, men's tasks would take over again, the legal paperwork, the transfer of property, the official notices. But death itself, and mourning, is women's work. Mother had always been a dutiful mourner. She had taken the role of condoling visitor very seriously. I had frequently heard her tell me the duties of a neighbour, of the family, of the passing acquaintance, at times like these. Never, she used to say, never should the smell of cooking penetrate the atmosphere of a house in mourning. Therefore it is the duty of neighbours and close friends to provide the food for the duration of the condolence period. Especially on the day of the funeral, but also throughout the period of condolence, all the family, brothers, sisters, cousins, aunts, uncles and in-laws, are expected to share the family luncheon, and the quality and quantity of the food offered must be worthy of the deceased. Over the years, I had often helped her take

food to a mourning friend's house: it was, as I see it now, as surely part
of my female apprenticeship as any aspect of my upbringing. Now she
sat, fully aware that it was her turn to receive, as she had so often given,
the comfort or at least the respectful notice of her mourning.

Some time later that evening, Teta appeared. She had not yet
fallen into her dementia, but she had been ill, and had not seen
Mother since my father's death. She faltered into the room, walking
uncertainly with the aid of a walking-stick, looking tinier and
frailer than ever. She looked around the room, searching for her
daughter among all the women. As soon as Mother saw her, she
rose and walked to meet her in the middle of the room. I got up
to greet Teta at the same moment, and thus overheard the private
exchange between them. Before they embraced, I heard Mother,
looking directly and intently at her own mother, say, in a clear and
distinct voice: 'No crying. Remember what we said. No crying.' And
Teta, visibly making a great effort to hold back her tears, nodded
obediently. They embraced, and then, having also embraced the
rest of us, Teta too took her place among the mourners.

I have often wondered about that moment. When had Mother and
Teta promised each other not to cry? Was it as Daddy lay dying? Or
was it decades earlier, following that fateful day in August 1928? Had
they jointly resolved never to cry again as they had cried then, never to
allow themselves to be as wounded as they had been then? I never asked
the question – it would have been an invasion of their privacy. But
now, as I write, I hear a voice echoing through the years: 'Be strong. Do
not whine. Be strong.'

Daddy's funeral was held the next day at All Saints, the Palestinian
Anglican Church of Beirut. This small but pretty church, located on
the coast, on St George's Bay, where the old dragon had been slain, was
the spiritual home of the Palestinian Anglican community which had
settled in Beirut after 1948.

We buried Daddy at first in his beloved Dhour al-Schweir, but
some years later, unable to acquire a permanent plot in the cemetery,
we had to remove his remains to Beirut. Even in death, there was to be
no rest for him. There was no way to take him to Jerusalem, where he
would have lain at rest in the family plot by the side of his parents, his
brothers who had died there, and his old friend and cousin, Boulos.

Auntie Nabiha had been to visit it after the 1967 war, and she had told us how it had been desecrated after the Israelis took all of Jerusalem.

For the next few months, Mother wrote no letters at all. Like so many women in her situation, after things had settled down and she had recovered some of her equilibrium, she went on a long journey, travelling from one of her children to another. When at last she takes up her pen again, she writes to her sister-in-law, Nabiha:

> I'm so constantly thinking of Wadie that sometimes I think I'm losing my mind. I miss him more and more every day, and tho' my children are all trying to make me as happy as possible, and tho' I'm terribly busy, sometimes I wonder if I can go on living without him, but, like everyone else, I suppose I will.

Mother was never to recover from her loss. It was a loss not only of her husband's person, but also of her situation in life. She had constructed herself as wife and mother, as caretaker and nurturer, as nurse and housekeeper. Now she could be none of these things, except occasionally, when one of her children was ill, or for one reason or another, needed her in that capacity. The core of her existence had been taken away, leaving a deep and terrible emptiness that she was never able to fill, in spite of all her efforts.

CHAPTER 22

More Letters and War

After her travels following the death of my father, Mother gradually returned to try and reconstruct her life in Beirut. Her letters at this time gallantly resume something of their former tone, and she takes up the account of trips to Baalbek, concerts, plays, teas and lunches. But no matter how hard she tries, her letters are tinged with a deep sadness.

In 1972, the year Samir and I and our children moved back to Beirut, Edward and his family spent a year there as well; Rosemarie and Grace were there too, working. Only one of us was now away, Joyce, who was living in Switzerland with her Swiss husband. Most of Mother's letters in this period are addressed to her.

This was a time when Mother enjoyed a happy interlude, a normal matriarchal life, a recapitulation of the old role of widowed matriarch surrounded by her children: looking after grandchildren; doting and being doted upon; sometimes cooking for the family and sometimes being entertained by daughters and daughter-in-laws who had perfected recipes she had taught them; going with daughters, son, sons-in-law and daughters-in-law on condolence visits and picnics, to the cinema and to weddings; sharing the social duties and child-rearing responsibilities of a new generation. Having completed her work as child-rearer, she now shared the pleasures of helping her children bring up their own children. The Arabic proverb that she quoted repeatedly at this time was 'No one is dearer than one's child to the heart, except one's child's child.'

From this time until her death, Mother established a close and important relationship with my children. She was a shelter for them, an extension; her home was an extra place in the world for them. When Samir and I quarrelled with them over homework not done, baths not taken, spinach not eaten, teeth not brushed, unsavoury language used – or any of the childish transgressions that we felt duty-bound to correct and punish – they would find protection and shelter with her. Once Saree, a twelve-year-old rebel, ran away, and having searched for him everywhere I found him at last in her kitchen, being treated to waffles which he was helping her make. Much to his delight she scolded me for being hard on him, and when I took him home at last, he was at peace with me, and I with him.

She was also a model of courtesy and generosity for my boys. She taught them regularly, not only the religious education that had been her mother's task in the lives of her children, but also how they should conduct themselves in order to become 'men'. She taught them grandness of spirit, courage and a kind of deep and unfailing affection. They have not forgotten these lessons, many of them learned before they were conscious of their importance. Although they deeply loved their other surviving grandparent, Samir's father, Anis Makdisi, he was a more remote figure in their lives, and they enjoyed nothing like the intimate relationship with him that they had with her. And he died sooner, in 1977, when they were younger, so they did not have the benefit of engaging with him as adults. Mother was their certain and secure connection with the past, as her mother had been mine.

Aside from the many times during the week that she dropped in to see them, every Saturday, almost without fail, we had lunch at her house: almost every Saturday in the summer, she would make us the *mouloukhia* that she had perfected long ago. At other times she would organize culinary treats for each of the boys. 'This is for Saree – his favourite food.' 'This is for Ussama – I know he loves it.' 'This is for Karim, I can't wait to see his face when he sees it.' Mother had always been a wonderful cook, and I have often thought that only people like Mother, who love life, can be good cooks; and that to be a good cook, one has also to be generous and fearless. Adding that touch more of spice, garlic, lemon juice or butter, which makes the difference between a good dish and a superb one, requires an adventurous spirit, real courage, true generosity.

Even now, in her widowhood, there was always plenty of food at table, prepared not only for us, but also for any unexpected guests whom we might bring along, or who might just happen by, and whom she always welcomed enthusiastically. Only another housewife could know what planning, patience and labour was involved in being always prepared for guests, and later Mother wrote grimly that she did not think her children had appreciated her hard work, her hospitality or her contribution to their lives. I think she was right. As time passed, she became increasingly bitter about the fact that the labour to which she had devoted her life, and which was the only yardstick of success in her generation, came to be regarded by the subsequent one as superfluous, banal, unimportant.

She always found comfort, however, in the company of her many close friends and contemporaries. Mother made friends easily, and kept them for decades: friendships of the sort Mother had are perhaps dying out in the world. For Mother and her old school-chums, friendship had nothing to do with interests, with benefits and advantages, not even with common ideas and shared notions, only with sentiment and familiarity: they seemed genuinely to love each other, to accept each other in spite of all the differences, adventures and tragedies that life had imposed on each of them separately. They seemed to cling to that moment in each of their lives when they were full of promise, and disappointment had not yet marred their girlish beauty.

When Mother invited her old stchoolfriends to lunch, which she often did, especially in those winter days of her widowhood, she would be elevated, somehow, more intense than ever, more alive, more laughing, more sparkling. There was something schoolgirlish about these reunions, a great deal of laughter, singing and sometimes even clapping of hands as they gathered around and occasionally burst into an impromptu dance. Invariably Mother would have prepared too much food, and putting away the leftovers would be a major part of the day's labour.

Even with her own children and grandchildren she would press hospitality on them, saying: 'How about a little more?' or 'Have some more of this: I made it especially for you.' '*Al-akl 'ala ad al-mahaba*' (Eating is the measure of your love), she used to coax her guests laughingly. If they did not eat more she would say coyly: 'It must be that you did not like my food,' and they, of course, would intensify their compliments on her cooking, which compliments she would graciously receive.

Mother's letters to Joyce, that happy year of 1972–73, are full of gossip, family news and domestic subjects. 'We had a wave of stomach flus,' she writes in one letter. In another: 'It is very cold and has been raining for some time.' There is happy news of the grandchildren:

> The four little ones are darlings … Yesterday they all had lunch here, and you should see the mess! Wadie [Edward's young son, named after his grandfather] is just as big a rascal as [Jean's] three – he doesn't stop one minute, and climbs all over his play pen, his bed, etc.

Only once in this period does she note a political event: the shooting down of a Libyan civilian aircraft by the Israelis in February 1973. Among the passengers were some Lebanese from prominent families who were well known to the community:

> *24 February 1974*
> You must have heard about the Libyan plane, such a tragedy and those five young Lebanese – it's really sad, but no one doing anything about it either. Everyone here is terribly upset and worried, but as usual nothing happens ever.

The correspondence is peppered with news of Teta's decline:

Teta is fine physically, I'm going to take her to Alif's to spend the day soon, but mentally, she's deteriorating a great deal ...

Teta is losing her memory daily and gradually, it's quite sad watching her deterioration, though sometimes she's more lucid than others ...

Her sister, Aunt Najla, died in Carbondale but we didn't tell her; there was no point to it at all.

In May 1973, just two months before Teta, Auntie Nabiha died of intestinal cancer in Amman. Mother was crushed. They had become the best of friends, and after Daddy died, Auntie Nabiha had often come to stay with Mother in Beirut. Mother's relationship with Auntie Nabiha had gone through several stages. At first, as a young bride and mother, she had been scared of her older sister-in-law, awed by the vast domestic and maternal experience she had, by the solemn look on her face and the force of her personality. A wordless struggle was waged between the two women over the prime loyalty of the man who united them: the furore over the wedding exerted its influence for some time after. Looking back in her memoir to the early days of her marriage, Mother wrote fondly of the subtle put-downs directed at her by Auntie Nabiha. My sister Rosemarie was, writes Mother in her notebook, an exceptionally beautiful infant. But when anyone remarked on the baby's beauty in her presence, Auntie Nabiha would immediately respond: '*Tamam mitl abouha*' (Exactly like her father!). Later, however, they had become good friends, and when my father died, their relationship was cemented by the sorrow that united them.

In the autumn of 1973, Edward and his family left to resume their life in the United States. Mother's letters to her absent children continue with the usual mixture of gossip, family news and politics. The October 1973 Arab–Israeli war does not elicit much enthusiasm from her, and there are only one or two references to it in the dozens of letters following it.

The next spring, however, her letters are full of news of the student strikes at the universities, which presaged the outbreak of the civil war in Lebanon by a few months:

15 April 1974
The students at BUC [Beirut University College] have again occupied Sage Hall and forbidden [college officials] to enter.

26 April
At last the army broke through to AUB [American University of Beirut] and kicked the strikers out, but no one knows when and if AUB will open this year.

1 May
The strike is over and the AUB opens at last this coming Tuesday … It seems tho' that it is not really over, and every day we hear all sorts of rumours. The IC [International College] is having trouble also.

8 May
The AUB opened yesterday, but there was too much fighting, so they closed once more; no one seems to know exactly what is happening and why or rather who's what.

17 May
The weather so far is superb. Yesterday the air-raid alarm sounded and the Israelis threw a lot of bombs around Beirut, in the refugee camps – the rascals!

In March 1975 Mother took a trip to visit Edward in New York, and Joyce in Geneva. She returned to Beirut on 13 April 1975, the fateful day which marked the beginning of the civil war in Lebanon that was to last for almost sixteen years. A bus full of Palestinians had been ambushed in the predominantly Christian suburb of 'Ain al-Rumanneh, and all its passengers killed. Earlier, a drive-by shooting in the same suburb had caused the death of a bodyguard of one of the principal Christian politicians. These incidents sparked the first of many series of armed clashes between the Christian militias and the PLO. Later, of course, the situation became infinitely more complex and involved many other factions and even countries, regional and international.

Neither Mother nor anyone else had any idea of the gravity of the situation, nor did anyone dream that the war – we did not even call it a war at first – would go on for anything like as long as it did. Still, in her description of the first day, there is a mixture of disdain and uncertainty as, in her inimitable style, she describes the events and the official radio stations' attempts to disguise the ominous reality:

April 24 1975
Of course, you've heard and read all about the chaos and foolishness here last week and realize that even if I'd written you'd never have received it. I'm not sending any letters by mail – there are ten tons of mail lying down filling the post office and they say they may burn them ... It was one week of shooting, explosions, fear and rumours, and no one – almost not one person – on the streets the whole week.

There is a touch of irony when she describes the insouciance of the official state radio: the government was split down the middle, and the media officials, unclear as to what stand they should take, chose to avoid the subject altogether, sometimes to comic effect:

The first two days, only people who heard the BBC and Israel knew about it, so many many people were killed by stray bullets and great explosions – our TV and radio were constantly talking about the president's gall-bladder operation.

From here on, her letters offer a blow-by-blow account of the progress not so much of the war itself, but of living conditions and her own inner feelings. Although Mother was extraordinarily brave during the war, she became increasingly depressed by its side-effects, especially the absence of electricity, which imposed long, lonely evenings, in the dark. Her apartment was on the fifth floor, and as time passed, the elevator became increasingly erratic, which meant that she was able to go out less and less frequently. Her elderly neighbour, Souad Richani, who lived on the second floor, was her only evening companion for several years. Her loneliness was alleviated at first by the telephone, but as it too became unreliable, her world of easy society, of old friendships, seemed to be gradually closing down.

23 October 1981

We get water from the C's and Jean's. I do my laundry at Jean's and try to play bridge most of the time so as not to listen to stupid words about the war ... Still, I can't see where I can live otherwise. I hate to become a bitter and unhappy depressed woman, which I'm slowly turning into, so maybe an occasional trip is what I need to get away from it all.

21 December 1981

I am sorry to be always a pessimist, but Beirut these days is a very bad place to be in, all sorts of explosions every place.

In the summer of 1982, during the terrible Israeli invasion of Lebanon, she wrote no letters, but kept her head. Like most others in West Beirut, resisting the Israeli siege in those frightful months kept her morale high, and her resolve was great. 'Do not whine; do not be weak; be strong': if ever there was a time to put those words into practice it was now, and she did just that.

At the end of that year, a new and final phase of her life began. On 1 January 1983, she writes to my brother and sisters (I was with her in Beirut):

I am very sorry, but I'll have to give you some bad news this time – a couple of weeks ago, I felt a lump in my left breast.

After this, Mother writes only sporadically. She underwent a modified radical mastectomy a couple of weeks later at the American University Hospital. Later, Grace and I took turns accompanying her to her radiotherapy sessions. Finally she was pronounced fit to travel and she went on a long journey to visit, once again, all her absent children. She returned a few weeks later. By the summer of 1983, Grace, the only one of my siblings who had remained this long, left Beirut too: I was the only one of Mother's five children left.

The service infrastructure, which had held up sporadically for the first few years of the war, had broken down almost entirely after the onslaught of the Israeli bombings. Electricity, telephones and water supplies were almost non-existent. Mother writes in December 1983:

I cannot possibly describe my loneliness, especially that now they're being so nasty in cutting the electricity a great deal. There is no shooting, but everyone is saying that … is being bribed so the businessmen who are getting the generators can sell them before the electricity is restored for good. There is no government and all the rich people have huge generators and to hell with the rest … At least I can play bridge with my friends.

But life still carried on, after a fashion:

There were two choir concerts last week; they came after explosions being planted in four churches, and everyone was scared stiff. But in spite of everything, the chapel was packed.

My arthritic neck is much better now, and it makes me much more comfortable, of course. Thank God, I feel fine these days, if only the electricity was not cut off in the evening – it gets dark at 4.30 and there is no TV …

Now a very Merry Xmas to all of you, and the best of New Years.

18 January 1984
It was such a shock, Kerr's murder [Malcolm Kerr, the American president of AUB, was shot and killed in his office on campus on 17 January]. It is getting to be terrible living here; there is no pleasure whatsoever – especially with the lack of electricity. I have been trying for a month to get a generator but seem unable to. It is so complicated to run and I'm waiting for Naim the hairdresser to get himself one and he'll get me one with him. The stairs don't bother me too much – it's good exercise – but the darkness at night does. The only redeeming grace is the warm weather; we had very little rain so far.

Shortly after this letter, on 6 February 1984, Beirut exploded into the most violent, chaotic and dangerous phase of the war, which was to last, in varying degrees of intensity, until the final disarming of the militias in 1991, more than a year after Mother died. Semi-permanent barricades were set up between the two halves of the city, across which a vicious sectarian conflict was fought. In addition, on each side of the barricades, street fights broke out between allied militias or their factions. These were the darkest days of the long war.

Mother did indeed buy a generator, which she placed on her kitchen balcony, always aware of the dangers inherent in this benzine-burning machine. Her old letter-writing habits had by now collapsed. There are no more letters until December of 1984, and after that she writes only sporadically. In the interval, she had become increasingly depressed, lonely and irritable. The tone of the remaining letters is completely different from the earlier ones. They are full of references to her being 'over-touchy' and 'very sensitive' and to her 'old age'. Although the old gallantry never entirely disappears, and she constantly makes the effort to reassert it, to pull herself together and to give the old kind of news, it is far outweighed by the depressing circumstances that she recounts. Beirut's infectious *joie de vivre* had turned into a never-ending cycle of violence and gloom, and there was little to report that did not increase her depression.

It was in these terrible days that Mother's normally elegant appearance came to seem extraordinary by the mere fact that she kept up her efforts at what she called 'looking nice'. Her hair had gone grey early. As time passed it had become whiter and whiter; eventually she added a delicate tint of blue. She had high cheekbones and full lips, large brown eyes set wide apart, and a distinctive high arch to her brows. Like her mother, she had an excellent complexion, and her pink skin gave her a naturally healthy, though never florid, look. She had a great love of clothes, and in her last years chose colours to set off her invariably well-groomed hair to best advantage – various shades of violet, blue and pink. She never wore drab colours, and rarely light pastels: they suited neither her complexion nor her character.

I believe it was her colour and the way she walked in her old age that made people turn and look again as she passed. When she was young, she walked, as mothers of large families tend to do, briskly, in a perpetual hurry. As she grew older, however, she was slowed down not only by the passage of time and weak knees, and by the necessity of carefully negotiating the war-damaged pavements of Beirut, but by a habit she had developed of becoming abstracted as she walked, as though she were not quite aware of her surroundings. Somehow her slow pace, combined with her abstraction and her beauty, gave her a regal air and attracted the attention of passers-by. As she walked down the street, heads invariably turned. I often stood on my balcony and watched her slowly approach my house: there was something poetic and really quite extraordinary about her looks as she walked down the street.

And in the context of the war, her appearance created a powerful reaction in others. Someone once said to me: 'I watch to see your mother, with all her beauty and elegance, picking her way through the ruins, the rubbish-littered streets! I actually look out for her, and every time I see her, I am astounded by the sight.'

I think Mother's elegance was seen as a refusal to give way to the depression that everyone (and she most of all) felt during the war. It somehow created a sense of repair where there had been nothing but desolation. People saw it as restorative, a statement, a form of resistance, an affirmation of life. It lifted their spirits and made them feel good.

This was her contribution towards endurance during the war, the lifeline she was willing to put out for everyone, her own single, incontrovertible contribution, her own statement of affirmation in the midst of the war's massive denial. In spite of all the bitterness and anger she felt in her last years for what history had done to her, there was always this elegance and beauty with which she expressed a lingering hope for the future. There was too much of love of life in her to be killed by this, the last of the many wars and displacements she had endured. Her extraordinary appearance had nothing to do with spending money or with expensive taste: it had to do with what she had always seen as female self-respect. For her there had never been an excuse, even among those professional women she had admired and a little envied, for being *muhargala* (sloppy).

But at last the war was too much even for her. On 11 December 1984, she writes:

> I've decided to leave Beirut. I've been without electricity for fourteen hours and I'm very cold. I can't run the heaters on the generator and I only have one Butagaz heater, I couldn't go anywhere to buy a second one, and the phones never work … The bombings are starting very badly now on the East side, and they're just starting to retaliate.

Her very last preserved letter from Beirut is dated 18 February 1985:

> Unfortunately the electricity is still being rationed, and I don't leave my house unless the elevator is working, which of course is very uncomfortable and lonely and boring, but there's nothing I can do about it ... So many people are leaving the country for good and life is really depressing ... I am closed in from 5.30 p.m. and even tho' I try to read I can't do that all the time. Because of electricity I don't go too far away from the house, so I don't have to climb the stairs. Yesterday I saw Karim and Ussama for the first time in two weeks, imagine! Once in a while I spend the night at Jean's, but it's uncomfortable for me to change my sleeping habits for one night. Jean passes by me every now and then, but she works full time at BUC ... I can't tell you how expensive life has become, really unbelievable!

Memory, of course, plays tricks on all of us. I do not remember that I 'passed by her every now and then': I remember a rigorous daily exercise of passing by to see her, and making sure that my sons saw her as well. I remember her spending every weekend at my house during these difficult times, and never going anywhere on Sunday without her. I remember driving her home in dangerous times; I remember going with her on visits when she asked me; I remember helping her provide food when one of her friends was in mourning. I remember taking her shopping, helping her arrange her bridge games, taking her out to lunch and tea when conditions permitted. I remember, with my husband and children, trying hard to allay her pain.

My memory of doing these things provides me with some small solace, but her words cut deep into my heart. Are we daughters ever free of guilt? In Mother's letters, I felt my own and my siblings' lack of awareness of the depth of her inner pain as she struggled, especially in her last years, to cope with her world as it had devolved into a maelstrom of war and discomfort, and as she tried to cope with the terror of the possible recurrence of her cancer. I felt her vulnerability as I traced the breakdown of that protective shield of matriarchal power and strength that she had built up around herself when she was young and strong. I see it clearly now (as I did not while she was alive) cracking, and then falling away altogether.

If for Mother, who was in her final years, the war was a knell tolling the end of her life in this part of the world, for me it was a quite different experience. Each of us had different strategies for dealing with the war. I dealt with it by writing about it. During those hectic years of mothering, teaching at the college and keeping house, I had retreated more and more from the political world. We became almost completely divorced from each other, the world and I.

In the early days of the war, I felt like an unattached piece of flotsam floating on a sea whose waters were taking me back and forth, as they had throughout my life. In anger at the world of politics which excluded me – and at myself for having allowed myself to be excluded – I reached out to attach myself, to stop myself from floating about and being tossed back and forth, from being carried by decisions and circumstances which seemed to have nothing whatever to do with me. My first task was to try and understand the conflicts that had erupted so violently around me, and to establish my connection with them. Otherwise, my life would remain unconnected with reality and I would float away completely.

In the summer of 1975, just a few weeks after the first bouts of the war, I began writing about it. In those early days, as I have already remarked, we did not call what was happening a war: we had no idea it would become one. We tried at first to deny the importance of the 'disturbances', 'events', 'clashes' and 'incidents' even while they threatened us physically. When I began, I wrote about my life, as I saw it, in fragmented glimpses into a fragmented reality. As the fabric of the political and social world about me began to fall apart, its various strands became visible, as one by one they were exposed in the shreds. I took a needle to the cloth, picking up one thread at a time, trying to find the corresponding thread in my life. I knitted them together on the page, in ink, with words. My aim was entirely personal, and my writing was entirely private, secret even. Eventually, from the private narrative, the space widened. My horizons expanded and I was no longer writing only about my life.

In the beginning, writing about the war reattached me to the political world, but soon the war itself brought crashing down the domestic barricades built up around me by my upbringing and social situation. The war was a school for women. We were taught our own strength as nothing had ever taught us before. Decisions had to be taken, under direct physical threat, with no recourse to any sort of authority outside our own intelligence and instincts. Often these decisions were domestic in nature; leadership roles were reversed and the men were relegated to assisting in the carrying out of women's instructions. Class roles were abolished, too, as in the shelter neither class or gender roles remained functional.

With Mother's words, 'Be strong,' echoing to me throughout the years of the war, I felt it was a personal and vital challenge not to show fear or the slightest weakness, not to shed a tear, not to waver in my husband's and my resolve to see the thing through. The nature of the war gave women an unaccustomed strength. Of the thousands of people kidnapped at barricades, to be held hostage or even murdered on the spot, only a few were women. The respect for women, especially mothers, that was left over from the previous age of normal, civilized social intercourse, kept the young men who were conducting the war in a bondage they could not break, no matter how heavily armed they were or how frail their potential victims. This attitude towards women broke down only after the most ferocious battles, when the victors entered the territory of their enemies. At those times, they demonstrated their triumph by deliberately overcoming their own restraints towards women. That is when the rapes and massacres took place, and when the humanity of victors and vanquished alike was denied.

In more normal times, however, the attitude towards women kept us relatively safe and we were therefore more likely to take risks. I used to drive with my husband and sons if they had to go somewhere during the weeks of fighting, feeling that I was their protector in the face of the men at the roadblocks. The presence of a matriarchal figure – no matter how young or old, a mother is a mother – put a strange restraint on their hostility, and often they could not bring themselves to do, or even to say, anything disrespectful, let alone violent.

If there had been something of the ivory tower in the private schools and universities before the war, it broke down completely during the conflict. Class barriers were smashed, as more and more people from the suppressed regions and classes of the country were admitted. These students, many of whom were members of armed militias, asked questions that made even the most seasoned teachers question the material they had unthinkingly taught for years. This was a refreshing intellectual experience. Though the same remnants of social custom allowed male professors the respect and deference due from the young, women teachers and administrators were even more protected from threat and other forms of pressure. I became quite used to addressing those in power, those with the guns, those with force. I began at last to deal directly with the world in which I lived, to be part of it, to interact with it on its terms.

Strangely enough, in so many ways, the war set women free. It freed us from all the constrictions of daily convention. It freed us from the restrictions imposed by the state and from the unjust laws that gave women a lower status than men in political and economic affairs. It freed us from the class barricades that had separated people from each other. As the state broke down, rank and privilege broke down too, and were often turned on their heads. It was each individual for him- or herself, and may the best man – or woman – win, survive, manage, carry on. The individual, entangled for generations in the webs of bureaucracy and legal institutions, was released, blown out into the howling winds and churning waters of anarchy.

For me, it was not just the war, not just teaching in such unusual circumstances, not just bringing up my children in the midst of all the dangers, but writing about all this, articulating it, which was my passport out of the isolation of middle-class domestic life.

CHAPTER 23

Gentle Into the Night

I n 1986 Mother went to America, to live with Grace, her youngest child. Eventually, Joyce, now divorced, joined them there with her son, Marwan. In February 1990 I received a call from Edward in the US: 'Come quickly if you want to see Mother. She is declining very rapidly.' I left for Washington the next day. It was the middle of the semester, and two of my colleagues kindly took over my classes for me. When I arrived, Mother was better than I expected, still mobile, still vocal, still able to walk and move from bed to bath to dining-room, although with less and less strength. Her first words to me were: 'See how ugly I have become.' She was not at all ugly, though her face was mildly distorted by a paralysis on the right side, her eyelid was drooping and her mouth was twisted to one side in a permanent grimace.

Her elegance persisted, however, and as my sisters and I helped her get dressed every morning, she would not tolerate any sloppiness: before the laborious process began, we had to show her which blouse, which sweater, which skirt or dress, which shoes, even which pair of stockings, we planned to help her into. Sitting on the edge of the bed, leaning on her walker, she would review the suggestions, pronouncing her verdict in no uncertain terms, imperiously and sometimes impatiently rejecting this combination or assenting to that. Occasionally we even received a gracious compliment on our taste.

One day she could no longer walk, no longer give the right commands to her legs to move her even so much as a step. We carried her back to bed and she never got up again. From this point it was almost four months until she died. I stayed with her for two of those months. Perhaps in my entire life, I will never again know such a shatteringly painful and yet extraordinary time. I felt privileged, in a strange sort of way. It was a time when I felt more at peace with her than ever before. We had shared the maternal domestic life which she had taught me, though I had sometimes resented the lesson. In the last years, we had shared the daily terrors of the war in Lebanon and she had shared my anxiety about the safety of my husband and children. We had shared shelters, and the dwindling resources, the food and water, the electricity and telephone lines. We had shared the agonies and doubts, and the despair of the situation. Sometimes we had taken out our rage and anxiety on each other. But now, the time had come for healing, comforting, leave-taking.

Mother was always, together with my own family, the dearest person to my heart. I had modelled my life on hers and followed closely in her footsteps, sharing her life and beliefs. She adored my children, and they adored her. It was fitting that I should be by her side, just as it was fitting that all her children should be. Each of them had a special connection with her, as I had mine; each had a special understanding of and with her. All of them came to be by her side.

She knew she was lucky: she once said to Grace that God had been good to her, to allow her to have her children at her bedside, looking after her, as she lay dying. That was typical of Mother, that she should at the end redeem everything, even her dying, with a touch of graciousness, a grand gesture of words, an acknowledgement of good fortune. She had always maintained her faith, though she was never one to impose or even announce her beliefs. She read her *Daily Light* every night of her life and went to church every Sunday for as long as she could. Even towards the end, she would recite the Lord's Prayer and the Twenty-First Psalm.

One day, the hospice called to ask if she would like a pastor to visit her. I leapt at the offer, and Mother approved. The Anglican pastor who came was a middle-aged woman with a kind and gentle appearance, but unfortunately she talked to Mother in a patronizing tone, mistaking illness for senility. 'How are you, dear?' she asked gently, and then talked to Mother about her prospective 'long journey'. Mother was by then too weak to offer any but passive resistance, and so a few minutes into the visit, she appeared to fall asleep, putting paid to the interview. The pastor made several efforts after that to communicate, but each time she came Mother promptly fell asleep, remaining in that state until the woman withdrew. Eventually she got the message, which neither Grace nor I had the courage to put explicitly. One day Mother had a visit from her old Beirut pastor, Rev. Fouad Bahnan, who sat and prayed by her side. The comfort his visit provided her was visible, because he said all the prayers in Arabic. That is how Mother had learned to pray, and how she knew to pray.

I stayed with her almost to the end. The time had come for me to leave, and we both knew it. I took some notes during the weeks I stayed, jotting down thoughts, impressions and images as she lay there helpless, but still, in a strange and overwhelming sort of way, utterly herself.

Saree walks into the room on tiptoe. He does not want to wake her up, but he wants to see her, to look at her face again. Suddenly she opens her eyes and sees him. Her face lights up with the most extraordinary joy. It is not just a broad smile which, coming on so suddenly, has entirely transformed her face; it contains a hint of surprise, as though she could never get over the astonishing wonders and beauties of the world. He and I are on the verge of tears: we cannot reciprocate that lighting up. What we see in her makes us sad. I look at his face and see in it, as through her eyes, his old childhood beauty, he the first, adored grandchild.

Ussama is my middle son, the child who cost me so much pain at his birth and in his infancy. That was when Mother was such a great comfort, writing across the oceans, 'Don't worry, we are praying for the little one.' She made *mughli* for him while he still lay in the incubator, willing him from across the world to live. When he comes to see her, now a young man at university, he stands by her bed, holds her hand and says softly, 'Hi, Teta, *keefik?*' (How are you?), trying to make the words ordinary, not knowing what else to say or how else to express his love. And in response, her face lights up in that extraordinary way and she squeezes the hand he has put in hers.

Her face lights up too when Karim comes to see her, Karim my youngest; of all her grandchildren, he is the one who has lived the longest with her and is the closest to her. They have a secret relationship together; on the outside sometimes gruff and teasing, but there is something deeper, an endless love. She often used to scold him for making a mess, for not doing the errand she had asked of him, for any of a thousand small childish transgressions, but then she would whisper, '*Ism Allah alay*' (God's name is on him) and smile adoringly, and prepare his favourite food. He too used to spoil her, bringing her a rose every now and then, and showing her that in spite of everything, she was the grand lady of his life, *sitt al-sittat*.

It moves me to see my sons with her. Sometimes, when they were young, they used to tease her; sometimes she got angry with them if they broke or spilled something in her house when they were children. But now they are not children, they are men; and knowing her, being connected to her, has been good for them. She is a world that no longer exists, a world of kindness and family and cooking and washing up and singing – yes, and scolding as well, and being irritable. But always the connection is acceptance, and unquestioning, bottomless love and loyalty. It is good for them that they have known her; their lives are richer for this knowledge and they are better men. Will they be 'men'? 'Men' as she used the word? I hope so. I think so.

Her other grandchildren visit her bedside as well. Wadie, Edward's son, named after my father but so closely resembling his own; Najla, the only girl in this new generation, who did not know then that she had inherited her acting talent from her grandmother; Marwan, the little Swiss boy, only recently arrived in America – the three of them regularly appear at their grandmother's bedside to pay homage and receive her blessing.

There is something ancient and epic about all this, this ritual leave-taking, this ritual shedding of tears, this evocation of heroic images at the deathbed.

I sometimes stroke her face. I can feel the bones now, unmitigated bone, unmitigated, merciless skull. There is nothing repulsive about it, though, and she seems more beautiful than ever. She seems to like it when I stroke her face, pushing her hair gently back, as one does with a child. Many times, she looks at me, and I at her. We sit, staring at each other, sometimes for an hour at a time, without exchanging a single word. Sometimes I hold her hand as we sit like that, until she pulls it away or moves it to another position. I am not sure she knows who I am – but then I am not sure I know who she is, or who I am.

As I washed her the other day, she called me 'Mama'. In Arabic, we do that: we mothers call our children 'Mama', just like we call our mothers. But something leads me to believe that she really thinks I am her mother. When I was a child she often used to tell me that I resembled Teta. Since the other day she has called me 'Mama' many times. There is no way of knowing whether she thinks she is addressing her mother or her daughter. At first I found this perplexing, urgent: I wanted to know; I desperately felt I must try to find out. But now I feel it doesn't matter. We are all each other's daughters and each other's mothers. We have all lovingly washed each other's helpless bodies.

All of the people she was (perhaps all of the people I was too) are gradually being flattened out into one person, dying. The incredible wealth of her existence, the complexity, the colour and action of her life, all of it is being flattened, like a complex, convoluted sculpture being hammered out into a simple, straight, flat line. The things I disliked in her, the things that made me angry, that wounded me, that made me proud or happy, made me laugh or cry – all of them are going, melting into this agony of dying. There is only the primordial relationship, and dying.

There is no domination by me, the strong one, over her, the sick one, or the old domination by her of me. I have the strength but not the desire to impose my will on her: on the contrary, I wish more than ever before in my life to know what her wish is so that I can carry it out. Perhaps it is the first time that I have wished to do this: perhaps I have spent most of my life trying *not* to do her will, trying to escape it, trying to separate mine from hers. Now I wish to give her peace, to comfort her and give her love. We have arrived at a strange equality, a peaceful coexistence of old and young, dying and living, sick and well. It is like a seesaw suspended at the moment of its equilibrium, no longer dipping this way or that.

Every now and then she looks at us, her children gathered around the deathbed, and says urgently: 'Take me home. Take me home.' We have interpreted her plea to mean that she thinks she is in the hospital, because of the hospital bed that she refused to tolerate when she was strong enough, so we say to her: 'You are at home,' but she says again: 'Take me home.'

Over the years, I tried so hard to keep her home for her in Beirut, to make sure that it was always there for her. I used sometimes to feel like the goddess Shiva, preserving her apartment from the maelstrom so that she could come home to it, willing her house to remain intact as one terrible episode after another of the war passed. Mostly I had to protect it from the waves of refugees who came, during every new episode, from somewhere else – desperate, displaced people, looking for refuge and taking it wherever they could. I also had to protect it from unscrupulous people, pretending to be refugees, who were scouring neighbourhoods for empty flats, looking for an opportunity to move in and demand compensation for moving out. There were also many ordinary robbers, for whom this was a golden time of opportunity.

And I succeeded: her apartment remained intact, although it was of no use to her. I wanted her to die in her own home, at home, but there was always the war. 'I opened my eyes to war,' she complained to me so many times. Now she is no longer in a position to complain, but I want to scream my refusal at this on her behalf: that she is dying far away from home, that she will be buried in alien soil, she who spent so much of her life moving from one place to another.

Part of the grief, one of the things that hurts so much, is the realization that I must now reinterpret everything anew. So many of my views, needs, desires, obsessions and fears, so many of my attitudes, are either inherited from her or the result of my struggle with her. Now I will have to look at them again, alone, without her.

One day, she talked a great deal, feverishly, without much intelligibility, and most of her chatter was in French. I am torn between laughter and tears, and finally I call Grace at work and tell her: 'She's speaking French today.' Grace comes home earlier than usual and we stand together, laughing and crying at the same time, as Mother talks breathlessly on in French. Her French was correct, and I sometimes used to remark that she spoke it with what I took to be an Italian accent, reflecting the cultural and demographic mix of Egypt, where she had used it. She had learned French in Nazareth that summer of 1928, when her parents were preparing her to go to school in Beirut and the career as a teacher that they had planned for her. She was fourteen. But then her father died. She had used French when she penetrated fashionable society in Cairo, but I think she never really felt at home either in French or in that fashionable society – or liked either much.

Now she mostly talks in Arabic. It is as if she has forgotten her English, yet as soon as the nurse addresses her in English, she answers in that language. Her Arabic is usually the Egyptian dialect; the Lebanese accent of the last thirty years has apparently worn off. This business of language is important, I feel: languages peel off her like petals off a dying rose. I am afraid that as the languages recede and change, we will reach the inner core, where language no longer exists. And then perhaps we will lose touch with her altogether.

Sometimes, when we speak to her, we have to suppress the impulse to raise our voices. We feel a desperate need to get through, to penetrate the thickening wall between us, and so we are tempted to raise our voices higher and higher, until we are almost shouting, as one does at someone who is deaf. But she is not deaf, and we realize that gentle sounds are more important than accurate exchanges of useless information.

Often, she is too weak to talk audibly, so she whispers. On those occasions, even when I can make out the words, I do not always understand what she is saying. I have to come very close to her lips, sometimes putting my ear to them or, bringing my face very near hers, trying to lip-read, trying desperately to understand what she wants so urgently to communicate. Gradually I come to understand that it is not important: there is a kind of closeness, a kind of elementary confidentiality, in this form of communication, in which words and their meaning are the least significant factors. What counts is that closeness, physical as well as moral: her need to tell me, and my need to hear.

One morning she was startled by my appearance. She was staring intently at a spot on the ceiling when I came in and stood by her, and suddenly she saw me and was startled. I could see her jump a little at seeing me. She clutched my hand and pointed at the ceiling, and babbled of some incomprehensible, untransmittable terror. Her heart was pounding, I could see it leaping against her ribcage, now visible in her thin body, and there was a new strength in her hand as it clutched mine. I tried to calm her, tried to soothe her, and felt my tears overwhelming me as I could do nothing to lessen her terror. Finally, not knowing what else to do, I just stroked her face and sang a song I used to sing to my children when they were frightened during the war. She is my mother, and I am hers. Eventually she calmed down and her heart stopped pounding, but I think it had nothing to do with me or my silly little song: it was just a crisis that passed.

Her thirst is unquenchable. Her need for ice and ice-cold water. Sores on her mouth, lips and tongue. Dark-blue veins, almost black or charcoal grey, on the good arm; the other, yellow and still visibly swollen, though so thin.

One day, Aida, daughter of her beloved cousin Nora, came to visit. When she arrived, we went and looked in on Mother, who lay staring at the ceiling. 'Mother, Aida is here,' I announced, knowing that the news would please her. Aida stood by her and stroked Mother's hand, holding back her tears: 'Hello, Auntie Hilda', she said over and over again. But there was no response. Several times during the long day we repeated this effort, tiptoeing into her room and indicating to her that Aida was there. Aida would hold her hand and say gently: 'Hello, Auntie Hilda'. But not a word or a look registered the slightest recognition. Aida whispered to me when she first went in: 'She looks so beautiful and peaceful', but then she remembered her own mother and wept.

That night a new nurse came in, long after Aida had left. Mother seemed to be asleep. As soon as the nurse moved her arm to measure her blood pressure, Mother opened her eyes and said to her, as though continuing a conversation begun a few minutes earlier: 'Her mother was a very beautiful woman. She was not only my cousin, but my very good friend. I loved her a lot.' Nora's death years before had caused her great sadness.

That night was one of the happiest I ever had with Mother. She did not sleep all night, but chatted about Nora and school and the old days. Sometimes she seemed to be addressing Nora, at others she seemed to think Daddy was in the room with her, and they were talking to each other, laughing with Nora, of whom Daddy was also very fond. There was no pain in all this; these encounters with the ghosts of the past were just happy memories. It was very low-keyed and relaxed, not Mother's usual high-intensity enjoyment. She was not talking to me in particular: I was a receptacle for these happy memories, and only once in a while did she look at me or say anything that required a response. She was just remembering her happiness out loud.

I felt none of the usual weariness of a sleepless night, none of that restless and desperate looking at the watch, hoping to hasten daybreak. On the contrary, I wished the night would never end. I sat by her silently, just listening and watching her in amazement, lapping up the warmth, feeling the respite from the pain of her illness and even from the anxieties and self-doubt of her old age. Even when I could not understand what she was saying, when her voice faded away, or when she spoke so rapidly that her speech was incoherent, I did not feel I had to strain to understand her words, as I did on other occasions. I felt utterly relaxed and happy, enjoying her relaxation and happiness.

That night I had a glimpse of what Mother must have been like before I knew her, or even after I knew her, but when she was still strong – before the war, before she became anxious and nervous. I saw her as a young woman, self-confident, strong, cheerful, ebullient, full of hope and trust, laughing with Nora, exchanging girlish confidences. I saw her as a bride, showing off her new home and her new husband to a favourite cousin come to visit, the new couple teasing Nora, all of them laughing at the joke. At last she fell asleep, and the magic ended.

I had to leave her before the end. The war in Lebanon was still raging, and I had to return to my husband, and to my students. There was a terrible lucidity in our farewell. I sat by her side all morning. At last I said to her: 'I love you, Mother,' but I called her 'Mama' not 'Mother', and I addressed her in Arabic. And then, feeling the need for the ancient ritual blessing, I asked her: 'Do you love me?' '*Awi, awi*' (Very much, very much), she answered fervently in Arabic, in the Egyptian dialect. I sat, stroking her face, pushing her hair gently back.

Then suddenly she said unpleasantly: 'Leave me alone.' Her harshness did not wound me, as it would have done before. So much had passed between us in these long weeks that the old sparring no longer existed, and the old wounds had healed. I understand: she is hurt by my leaving, she does not want me to go, but, impatiently, she wants us to get on with it.

I cannot believe I will never see her again, even as I look back to get a last look at her, lying, so tiny and frail, under her blankets, her face turned away from me.

Mother died on 28 June 1990. My four siblings phoned from Washington to tell me. I knew as soon as the phone rang, before I answered it, that she had died. And yet her death came as a huge and horrible shock, as though I had not known for so many months that it was just a question of time, as though I had not prayed for the end to come quickly, to put a stop to the suffering and the humiliation. I felt as if I had just been born, and as if the umbilical cord attaching me to her had just been cut. I felt like howling with the violent, wrenching, bottomless terror of being alone in the world. All that held me, that attached me to life, had passed away, had gone.

I did not go to her funeral in Washington, feeling instead that I had a duty to give her many friends in Beirut a chance to mourn for her. A memorial service was held in Beirut, timed to coincide with her funeral in Washington. 'Only your mother,' Samir said to me, with a touch of sad humour, 'could manage to have two funerals.' They had been the best of friends, and in her last years in Beirut, she had come to rely on him for the kind of support that only a man could give. She had been for him a second mother, and he for her a second son.

She was buried in Washington D.C. She should have been buried in Beirut, where she belongs, or in Nazareth, her home town. All the separations which have haunted our lives have been cemented in this final bitterness, the separation of Mother from her land, from the earth on which she lived, from the sounds and smells and textures which had surrounded her and which, in spite of everything, she loved.

Until the last, if only she could have known it, she dominated the lives of her children and grandchildren. The power of her personality and the enormous effort she had dedicated to the family had paid off. Though we were all far-away and scattered, she had remained the pivot around which we all turned.

CHAPTER 24

Balance

My finished book about the war came in the mail one day, a few weeks after Mother died. My husband and sons like to laugh as they remember the panic with which, most unreasonably, I greeted it. Perhaps my panic was heightened by the fact that I had been so recently cut off from the reassuring security of Mother's presence.

I had signed the contract for the book as we sat one night, all the neighbours, or at least all those who had not already left the country, my husband, my children and I, on the second floor of the building in which we lived. It was a night of bombing; at one point artillery shells landed around us every few minutes. Then it quietened down a little, and we came up from the basement shelter where we normally sat out nights like that, to take refuge on the second floor, which, while we hoped it was still safe, was certainly more comfortable. I signed the papers and then gave them to my neighbour, who was leaving in an hour or two. 'Please mail them when you get to London,' I said. 'Sure:

no problem,' he replied. But I was certain he would forget to take them, or that they would get lost in the post, or even that I would not survive that night, or the next one.

But in the end the book survived and so did I. My secret work was no longer secret. My personal detachment from the world had ended. I felt exposed, fully and totally exposed. The *hijab* was ripped off my face and there I stood, an articulate, independent being, speaking for myself, in my own name. Now I could no longer hide behind my husband or my brother, deferentially allowing them to speak for me while I retreated behind a curtain of domestic activities that shielded me from the responsibility of speaking for myself. I had broken ranks and I knew there was no going back, that I had won the independence I had claimed to yearn for. I was terrified, but henceforth I had to act as an independent being.

The war ended a few months later. The state and all its institutions reasserted themselves, and women once again retreated behind the domestic lines and into the old forms. The old conventions returned and the freedom brought by anarchic conditions was lost.

I had more occasion to think about my role in society as time passed. In May 1992 my husband became Lebanese Minister of Economy and Trade. As he dealt with the enormous economic problems left over from the war, becoming absorbed in them, I continued to live my own life as teacher, writer, wife and mother. My sons, brought up during the war, had now grown up: the two eldest were engaged in postgraduate work in the United States, the youngest had just graduated from university. Later, a new government took over, and my husband was appointed Deputy President of the American University of Beirut. As time passed, our sons took up posts as university professors. I have hung framed photocopies of the three doctoral diplomas behind my desk: I feel that in some remote and magical way I earned them too.

My three sons are married, and now, through them, I feel I have three daughters as well. If globalization is an abstract concept to many people, to our family it is a concrete reality, a continuation of the paths opened up by Teta and her generation. All three of their weddings were international affairs, with friends and relations literally coming from around the world to attend.

Saree's wife, Christina, is the daughter of Lebanese–Palestinian parents, but she was born in the United States and brought up in Canada. Christina and Saree met when she came to Beirut to visit her late maternal grandparents, our friends and neighbours. Joe, her mother's father, was born and raised in Chile, to which his father had emigrated around the time my father went to the US. Ussama's wife, Elora, is from Bangladesh. They met while they were both studying for their doctorates at Princeton. The daughter of diplomats, Elora grew up in the world at large, travelling from one country to another, experiencing different cultures from within. Karim's wife, Hala, is the granddaughter of old friends of my parents, but Hala grew up in the United Kingdom. Her paternal grandmother is Anglo-Irish; her maternal grandmother was Palestinian, like me.

My three daughters-in-law all had professional experience before their marriages, and continued their careers afterwards. All three are now mothers, making me a Teta in my own right. I am in awe of their intelligence and wisdom in handling their lives. Perhaps my generation did pave the way for a change in attitudes, allowing the younger women a better chance. But I warn them not to fall into the traps of my generation, the traps that caused me so much pain.

The enormous effort required by my life as a mother has been the most important and draining aspect of my life, though it enriched me even as it wore me out. Mother often quoted Auntie Nabiha's words: '*Ma byikbar jeel ma byihrum jeel*' (No generation grows up without wearing out a generation). When I look at my sons today, I feel enormous pride not only in their accomplishments, but also in their goodness and strength of character. I recognize, above all, that their achievements are their own, and that they alone must be given full credit for what they have accomplished. I recognize that a large element of luck accompanies parenting, and yet I take pride in the fact that I had something to do with my sons' success.

Yet I cannot pretend, as others have done, that mothering was an unmitigated delight. I often felt trapped, bogged down, bored. Sometimes I felt angry, even furious, that my life had always to be secondary to theirs, that decisions had always to be made in their interests and that my interests were always secondary. At those times I used to feel like a tree that was slowly and inexorably being strangled by an ivy which was climbing its trunk, covering its branches, blocking out its sun, choking its air, smothering it.

Sometimes I would be frantic with impatience at having to spend so much time watching sandboxes and slides, when I would rather have been reading a book or playing the piano or going, alone, for a walk by the sea, developing my thoughts without interruption. I especially remember my irritation at the interminable proceedings at bedtime. As the years passed, these proceedings became more and more exhausting. Increasingly, I wondered what I might have achieved had I not had to do what I had to do.

I remember the paper cups thrown into the toilet, and the consequent flood that I had to clean up. The water splashed in a game, but wetting my hair, which I had just done up, and my glasses, so that I could not see. Laughing, but feeling the fatigue wearing me down. The struggles. The boys, returning from hours of football practice, smelling of muddy sweat, caked with dirt and then resisting the bath.

I remember supper-time so clearly, and the 'I hate this!' and 'Yukh! It's disgusting! I won't eat it,' followed by the obligatory response: 'Yes, you will. It's good for you.' And then the ultimate threat: 'You will sit here until you do. Even if it means sitting here all night.' At those times, I would ask myself in despair what preternatural force had made me set up these hopeless confrontations. I remember the fights, my sons' use of unacceptable language, and what seemed at the time the impossible task of teaching them manners.

I think of the excruciating pain, the crushing oppression of the daily routine. My husband did not feel that it was any of his business to help handle the domestic burden, and if the truth be told, neither did I, though I complained endlessly to him of his indifference to household duties.

But in the end, I am glad that I did what I did. I did not achieve professionally what I might have done, that is true, but I acquired something else instead, something of enormous value. My sons, grown men now, husbands and fathers, often heard my complaints and, as they grew older, sympathized with my situation. I have not had a chance to show or tell them the other side of the coin, that aspect of my life that today I value beyond anything.

I remember my little boys when they fell down and came, crying, into my arms for comfort. I remember when they fell asleep in my arms, and I would hold and rock them, marvelling at their beauty. I used to think then, for each one in his turn, that there could be no more beautiful creature under the sun. I used to think too with astonishment at the depth of feeling I was experiencing.

After bath-time, when they would at last be sweet-smelling and quiet, when they would permit my embrace, permit me to feel their sweetness instead of their prickly recalcitrance, came story-time when we read together those wonderful books. I remember especially a family favourite, *Frederick the Mouse* by Leo Lionni. Frederick was a round, purplish-grey mouse. While all his family and tribe were frantically busy in the summer months collecting grain and nuts to store for the long winter ahead, Frederick would sit in the sun, staring at the flowers and the sky. They would scold him and say: 'Frederick, you're lazy.' But then winter came, and all the mice sat in their burrow, and after they had consumed their stores of nuts and grain, they shivered in freezing isolation. Then Frederick began to speak. He told them of the summer sky, he warmed them with images of the sun, and he filled their bleak winter space with the colours of the flowers. Then one of the mice looked at Frederick and said: 'But Frederick, you are a poet.' And Frederick smiled and said: 'I know it.' When I read this and other books to them, the children used to wait patiently for the punchline, and when it came, they would all recite in loud voices with me: '"But Frederick, you are a poet," and Frederick smiled, and said: "I know it."'

I remember Saree, who could never sit still, careening down the street when he was four or five, totally absorbed in his imagination. Now, with his arms outstretched and weaving through the pedestrians, veering first to the right and then to the left, he is a jet plane, the scream of the jet coming from deep in his diaphragm. Now, on his tricycle, his siren blowing deafeningly, his arms waving away the imagined cars in his path as he careens along, cycling madly, and then heroically he arrives, brakes screeching, at the scene: he is a fire engine and its crew. Now he gallops down the street, a racehorse winning the Grand National.

Ussama, who had caused me such anguish as an infant, became

when he was ten or eleven a versatile BBC football commentator, imitating precisely the tone and pitch of the professionals. I would hear him in the bath-tub: like some childish deity, he was all things at once, commentator, goal-keeper, attacker and defender, his voice rising in pitch as the excitement mounted: 'And now Ussama Makdisi gets the ball and takes it past the defence – Ussama Makdisi tackles him, but no – he kicks it into the goal and – no – [his voice now at the height of pitch and volume] superb save by Ussama Makdisi!'

Karim was to become the champion footballer, collector of medals and cups; but he was always the youngest, the cuddly one, who regularly begged visitors for chocolates, and who enjoyed sitting very close to guests, looking up at them, fascinated. Once, our friend Jamal said in conversation: 'I have a musical ear,' and Karim, sitting very close to him and looking up, promptly parodied: 'And I have a musical nose!'

I remember the awkwardness of the growing and metamorphosing body, with its stages of puppy fat, the down on the lips, the pimples, the sweat pouring from the most unlikely places. The thirteen-, fourteen-year-old hands, not knowing their own strength, unintentionally break almost everything they touch, the jars they are asked to open, the plates they are asked to carry, the bottles they are asked to pour from. Like the sorcerer's apprentice, those growing muscles, tended, catered-to for so long, take on a life of their own and become powerful reminders of the passage of time and the approaching strength of the incipient man. I remember the hopelessness and despair of the teenagers; the silly and often crude jokes; the cackles of laughter coming from breaking voices; the endless arguments and small rebellions; and suddenly, in the midst of all this, the pleasure of a gratuitous hug, or a red rose wrapped in foil and offered with embarrassment, which comes just when one thinks one can't stand any more arguments or pimples, or smelly feet.

And I often think of those feet, at first so incredibly tiny, and then becoming huge in teenage days. Often at this stage, and no matter how many times I exhorted their owner to proper manners, they would be spread out on the table like inelegant sculptures, the toes twitching, curling, flexing. The tennis shoes, kicked carelessly off, lie smelly on the floor to trip up the unobservant passer-by. Yet those big, clumsy, smelly teenage feet show the same exquisite vulnerability as the tiny ones they had been so many years before.

When I remember feeling sometimes that I wanted to leave, to walk away from the messy house, the infinite piles of laundry, the uneaten spinach, the endless quarrels, and save myself, to run for my life, when I think of all this now, I cannot feel it quite as I did then. If I could communicate with my younger self, I would tell her that all that frustration was part of a greater achievement – having good sons – and that it would all be worth the struggle. I doubt that my younger self would have believed me, though. She would not have heeded – or understood.

I have watched my children become men, and I have felt enormous relief, and calm acceptance, as they did so. I have seen the undone homework, tossed aside as 'boring' or even lied about, turn gradually into elegant essays; the interminable arguments and quarrels of childhood turn gradually into cultivated and honourable debate; the childish fibs and evasions turn into an acute and daring honesty; the violent fraternal fist-fights and obscenities yelled out in the raucous voices of teenage frenzy, all this gradually turn into deep fraternal love and mutual loyalty; the frustrated and tearful protests against parental authority turn into a manly enmity to inhuman political and military establishments, and into a defence of the poor and the dispossessed; the childhood protests against parental unfairness turn into brave demands for justice in the world. I have seen stubbornness turn into steadfastness, terror into bravery, hesitancy into self-confidence, crudeness into refinement, painful shyness into eloquence, selfishness into generosity and open-heartedness, awkwardness into manly beauty, and impetuosity into wisdom. I have seen another generation take its place in the struggle for justice in the world.

I have watched my sons, this new generation of men, share in the domestic labours, and in the child-rearing, of their families. I have watched them encourage their wives on to the fulfilment of their dreams. I have seen all this and I am proud. Of them. And of myself and of my husband, Samir. And if I did more of the deadly work than Samir, because that is what society dictated, then I must claim more than he. Those regrets, those protests, the cries of unfairness, those tears of anger, have not gone away entirely: it would be a lie to say they have. I still think with some regret of what I might have accomplished.

One day, a few years ago, I was lunching with my friend Najla, who, though she is a feminist, was holding forth, as so many people in the Arab world do, against the Western feminist movement. 'They want us to deny our maternal role,' she fumed. 'They want us to feel guilty about every minute we spend as mothers. I refuse to deny the value of my maternal role. It is the most precious thing in my life.'

I was rather shocked by her words. I wondered if I had been unduly influenced by the rhetoric of the feminist movement, and if I had indeed all along failed to value my life as a mother, so busy had I been regretting my failure to achieve the professional advancement that had inevitably been sacrificed. Was professional advancement really more important than maternal satisfaction? Why? Was it, on the other hand, true, as Najla was proclaiming, that maternal satisfaction was more important than professional? Why? Would it ever be truly possible to balance the two? I found myself, thirty or forty years later, arguing the woman's issue all over again, as though the same arguments had not been made and remade a thousand times before.

Today, my daughters-in-law are not free of the same questions: it is no more clear to them than it was to me where the line should be drawn, and they have to sort it out with their husbands, pushing it forward here and pulling it back there. I wonder if my little grandchildren will be asking the same questions when they grow up.

Postlude

This book began steeped in a felt reality, as a direct inquiry into my mother's, my grandmother's and my own womanhood. I was a young mother when I began to think about this project; I am now a Teta to a new generation.

As I read and worked, I arrived at a complex re-reading of the condition of women, not a simplifying one. It was as though I had viewed the lives of my ancestresses through a prism, whose many sides were composed of my life, my thoughts, my view of history and feminism. This prism, instead of clarifying the light, analysed it, showing me the various hues of its composition. The illusion of the whiteness and oneness of the light has been lost for ever to me: instead I see always in front of me a rainbow of hues, changing, changeable, beautiful, elusive.

As I look at the future and contemplate the life of my sons, their wives and their children, I see it through the different lights cast on me and the various shades of identity of which I am composed. A thousand forks lie in the road ahead. Some of the choices about which direction to take will have to be made carefully, deliberately, slowly. Other choices will be made for us by historical forces over which we have no control. Some of these, like the many storms that have passed over us and overwhelmed us in the past, may overwhelm us in an instant.

Over the largest fork in the road ahead, however, like a gigantic neon sign on a highway, lighting the alternative directions from far away, flashes the dichotomy: 'traditional' and 'modern'. So pervasive is the discussion of this set of alternatives, so ubiquitous is it in all debates over women's issues, and particularly Arab women's issues, that its truth seems inevitable and absolute.

It is my growing conviction, however, that this dichotomy is not only misleading and confusing, if not downright false, but that it is also, and above all, divisive. It is, I am convinced, a red herring, flashing at us, making us chase down a road leading nowhere, missing, as we frantically sprint in the wrong direction, more subtle and truer directions. This choice between 'traditional' and 'modern' is posed in such language, and is illustrated with such imagery, as to create a web of sticky threads in which we are all trapped and from which escape into a freer future becomes almost impossible.

I first became aware of this trap when, as I wrote about Mother, I found that I had written the words: 'She lived the traditional role of mother and wife.' No sooner was the ink dry on the paper than I paused, feeling the sticky threads on my cheek. What, I asked myself, was the 'tradition' to which I had mechanically referred, just as I and everyone I knew had referred to it thousands of times before? What were its definitions? Whose tradition was it? How did I know that such a tradition existed? On what evidence was I basing my use of this heavy word, which brought with it such a long trail of meanings and connotations?

And then, from the murky waters of the history into which I had plunged, emerged the image of my great-grandmother, Sitti Im Shukri, the famous horsewoman, whose existence and way of life I only discovered as I worked on this book. She lived her whole life in Galilee; she knew neither English missionaries, nor Turkish emissaries – surely she is the one I must call 'traditional'? But she rode her horse through Galilee, her hair flying, her clothes in disarray, her legs straddled on either side of the horse's back, and she had enormous power over her son and his family – this is certainly not the picture of 'traditional' that we have been led to see.

How many of what we have been used to calling 'traditional' domestic activities were exclusively the realm of women? The description in both Mother's and her brothers' memoirs of the annual making of the *burghul*, for instance, shows clearly that this activity was a family event. Everyone was involved: father, mother, servants and children. Similarly, shopping, travelling, tending the children and bathing them were all activities in which my grandfather shared.

What was 'tradition', then? I asked myself. What does it mean to be 'traditional'? I am not at all sure. The word 'tradition' is used much more than it is explained. There has simply not been enough scholarship, enough clearly thought-out discussion over this mysterious quantity as it relates to the Arab world for us to be able to answer this question clearly.

But surely, the kind of housekeeping and mothering I was involved in has nothing to do with 'tradition', and much more to do with being 'modern'. The kind of life I and others of my class have led is linked with the 'modern' nation-state and with 'modern' capitalist society, with modern schooling and education, and with the modern bourgeois household. And so what is the meaning of the other half of the dichotomy, the 'modern', in the context of women's history?

During the early flowering of the Western women's movement in the late 1960s and early 1970s, women experienced a new pleasure in female association – going out to lunch and dinner together, without the imposing and restricting presence of their husbands. This was a hard-earned 'modern' liberty. Women had to fight for access to clubs, restaurants and bars where previously they had been denied access, or at least where no 'respectable' woman would have been seen without male protection. Professional women defiantly started to use their maiden names at work, renouncing the borrowed definition of their married names. Women demanded and, after a long struggle, won the right to financial independence and responsibility, the right to borrow from the bank, to buy a house, to earn financial credit.

But in the 'traditions' of the Arab world, the association of women was a way of life. If there were some places which were forbidden to women, there were others which were forbidden to men. In the Arab-Muslim tradition women always kept their maiden names; Muslim *sharia* always allowed women to own property and run their own financial affairs. It was the 'modern' nation-state, modelled on the Western institution, which demanded the registration of unified family names, restricted the independent economic activity of women, and legislated their secondary status.

Ironically, some Arab women, careless of these nuances, see freedom in the Western model and seek to imitate those women who are demanding the very rights that these others are losing in their search for 'modernity'. These women, who are often ignorant of the burden of Western women (whom they see cloaked in stereotypes as misleading as those that mask the reality of Arab women in Western eyes), pursue, in their own version of dress, language and behaviour, a phantom freedom in a phantom modernity. Others reject the basic concepts of feminism because they think that these belong to Western modernity, and therefore to imperialism, and that they undermine Arab culture. Indeed, 'modernization' is often taken to mean 'Westernization', as though Arabs have no claim to their own modernity, or as though modernization were a process totally alien to them and imposed by others, and therefore invalid, foreign, of mischievous intent.

These concepts of 'traditional' and 'modern' are false, divisive and misleading. We must find new and more meaningful definitions. Rather than concentrating our efforts on choices that are red herrings, it is our full humanity in our full rights of citizenship that we should be pursuing.

Teta and Mother took what they understood to be modernity by the horns and led it through the corridors of their own homes and neighbourhoods, through their memories and the customs of their people. And that same vision of modernity led them, partly by their own volition, and partly by circumstances over which they had no control, away from the customs and the costumes of their past into an increasingly isolating domestic life. And in the path they followed, they became separated from the women who did not share their particular form of modernity, women from other classes, women who had had a different cultural background.

In order to close the gap that opened in my grandmother's day, I have tried, since the end of the war in Lebanon to learn a new way of being that does not recognize the physical boundaries of home as a moral or social limit. I have tried to undo some of the isolating aspects of the modern social and economic system which began in my grandmother's time, even while remaining faithful to some of my grandmother's and mother's domestic teachings, and to my own personal education and experience. I have tried not merely to collect tasks, piling them one on top of the other until I faint from the labour, but to synthesize them rationally, picking and choosing, recognizing my own priorities.

Without renouncing that vision of home and family in which I have found sustenance, and without which the world would be a harder, crueller, colder place, I have tried to reconnect with the world from which I have been separated by the social and political realities of women's history, and with the political realities around me.

It is a world of war, of death, of prisons in which unspeakable things happen, a world of smoke and horrors that has little respect for me and those like me in the urban cosmopolitan professional classes, with our finicky refinements, our aversion to violence, our need for art and beauty, and fine words and emotions. Somehow we will have to find ways to bend that world to our will, to force it into a shape that is less appalling, less inhuman.

The experiences of my mother and grandmother, as well as my own, persuade me that it is the task of the women of my generation and the next to reinterpret our place in the world, but not by turning our backs on, or by returning blindly to, a past of our own invention. We must renegotiate the nooks and crannies of our own history, understand our past, ground ourselves firmly in it, and then move consciously towards a modernity of our own deliberate making. Only then will we be able to lay full claim not only to the future ahead, but also to the present and the past.

Acknowledgments

This book would not have been possible without the assistance and encouragement of many people who, over the course of the years, helped me in its production either by providing me with information, guiding me to sources, taking the time to answer questions and solve problems or reading and commenting on the text in its various manifestations. I hope I will be forgiven if I have forgotten to mention anyone to whom I owe thanks; any such omission would be due to absent-mindedness rather than ingratitude.

The chapter on Teta's early family history owes a great deal to the help of George Sabra, who was unstintingly generous with his time and knowledge. He introduced me to the subject and shared with me his archival research in monastery and mission records, as well as his knowledge of genealogy and dates – all of which he later put down in his unpublished paper 'The Badr Story'. He also read an early version of my manuscript and corrected many of my mistakes and prejudices.

My uncles Alif and Emil Bishuti kindly wrote down their memories for me, and then responded to other questions that arose over the years as I worked. They, too, provided me with interesting background material on their family. Their cousins Lily and Albert Badralso answered some of my questions about events lost in the mists of time. They lent me the memorial issue of *Cartouche*, the American College for Girls magazine, dedicated to Auntie Melia – from which I was able to understand much about her and her contribution to the college. The late Wadad Badr talked to me about Auntie Melia as well, and gave me access to old family pictures. My cousins Lulu, Shukri and Marwan Musa shared with me many of their childhood memories of Teta, and Marwan allowed me access to letters that our grandfather wrote just before his death in 1928.

Mikhail Sawaya guided me around the area of Schweire and showed me churches, monasteries and side roads, filling me in on much local lore and mythology. His help was invaluable in giving me a feel of the area.

Youssef Khoury kindly set me on the right course in my search for missionary material on my great-grandfather. I owe great thanks to the library staff at the Lebanese American University (formerly Beirut University College) and especially to Aida Naaman and Aida Hajjar, for their infinite patience and kindness in guiding me to sources and then allowing me their free use. The library staff at the Near East School of Theology, especially Mary Soghomonian, was also extremely helpful in guiding me through the old missionary journals. Ellen Kunyuki Brown, archivist at Baylor University, kindly sent me material on the Baptist seminaries and the local history of Texas at the time my grandfather Shukri Musa lived there, including the stories of some of the men with whom he worked.

Colin White, principal of the Lebanese Evangelical School for Boys and Girls, was kind enough to search for, locate and then make available to me my grandmother's school records, on which most of Chapter 11 ('A Nineteenth-Century Syrian Schoolgirl') is based. I owe him a great debt of thanks, for without that old book of records whatever insight I might have garnered into my grandmother's nineteenth-century mission formation would have been missing. Daad Jabara, then Registrar at Beirut University College, kindly found and gave me access to Mother's records when she was a student at the American Junior College. Anselmo Deeb kindly sent me a photocopy of Mother's school records when she was a student at the American School for Girls.

From a lengthy interview with Dr. Hisham Nashabi I learned about nineteenth-century Muslim educational history and methods, and especially about the early history of the Makassed Institutions. Miss Fatima Hamza of Ramses College in Cairo (formerly the American College for Girls), a former student of Auntie Melia, kindly spent a morning guiding me around the school, speaking to me about my aunt, emphasizing Auntie Melia's role as upholder of 'eastern culture', and drawing my attention to the connections between her and the women's movement in Egypt. Mrs Salma Mirshak Slim also gave me some valuable insights, early on in my work, into the *Shawwam* of Egypt.

I spent many happy hours interviewing Asma Hishmeh, Huda Butros, Shafika Nasrallah, the late Rafika Mikati, Salma Makdisi, Saada Bishuti and other women – too many to mention here – on their early memories of childhood, schools and their own female relations. The late Kamal Kaawar spoke to me at length on Nazareth and some of its customs and memories.

I would like to thank Noor Majdalani Hakim for providing me with valuable knowledge on the ways and costumes of the past, which greatly assisted me in writing the chapter on Hums. She was then kind enough to read and comment on the chapter, as did Yahya Hakim. Nada Sehnaoui also kindly read this chapter and offered valuable comments and corrections. Malek Sherif introduced me to me the memoirs of the Sherifa Musbah Haydar, an invaluable source for some of the material on childbirth.

Karen Braziller, Ann Askwith, Joan Ibish Leavitt, Najla Hamadeh, Nuhad Makdisi and Aida Hadawi Karaoglan all read and commented on early versions of the book, as did Marianne Marroum, whose insightful and detailed comments were especially helpful. To all of them, my thanks. My sister Joyce Said provided invaluable advice on the writing, and often had to put up with my petulant defensiveness. She was always right in her judgment, however.

I would like to thank my editor Heather Reyes for guiding me in the restructuring of this book. Her advice and enthusiastic support were invaluable. Penny Warburton was a model not only of good advice but also of badly needed patience and calm, as was Mitch Albert. The Saqi office staff in Beirut, especially Dina Halawi Dally and Soukna al-Sayyed Ali, were unfailingly courteous and helpful. Thanks especially to Mai Ghoussoub and André Gaspard for their support and their confidence in this work.

Many thanks to Alane Mason for her wonderful insights in preparing the American edition of this book, and Vanessa Levine-Smith for all her help and hard work.

I owe a special debt of gratitude to Swain Wood who, from a great distance and with the unstinting generosity of his time, helped me bring this book to light.

For my sons Saree, Ussama and Karim, I have not words of thanks enough. I know that they have had to put up with a great deal of nervousness and uncertainty in the years since work on this book began. Their encouragement and confidence in my project, and their knowledge and intelligence, were my greatest asset. Saree always guided me intellectually and theoretically, and helped me solve some of the more difficult problems I encountered; Ussama shared with me his vast knowledge of missions, missionaries and nineteenth-century history; Karim, last but never least, clearly showed me the goal I had to strive towards when I was bucking around, lost in the storm. Elora, Christina and Hala not only read parts or all of the manuscript, but bravely put up with the numerous *crises de nerfs* that accompanied this endless production. I wish all mothers-in-law could have the joy of such daughters.

Samir, of course, was always there for me, providing the strength that I lacked. Without his endless sustenance and bottomless support this book would never have seen the light of day.

My late brother Edward and my sisters Rosemarie, Joyce and Grace, to whom this book is dedicated, have been my companions since the first, and are to me like fingers of my own hand. My consciousness was shaped with and through them.

Selected Bibliography

Over the years that this book was in progress. I read dozens of books and attended many lectures and academic conferences, especially on nineteenth-century Ottoman Syria, the background of much of the early history of my family. It is impossible to list all of these, so I shall confine myself to mentioning the texts or lectures that have had a direct impact on the writing of this book – especially those from which I directly quote or from which I derived specific information reflected in the text.

In addition, I relied to a large extent on unpublished documents, including family memoirs and letters.

Of the general histories, the one I most relied on was Albert Hourani's *A History of the Arab Peoples* (London: Faber and Faber, 1991). It was also to Albert Hourani that I turned for nineteenth-century Arab intellectual history, included in his *Arabic Thought in the Liberal Age, 1798–1939* (Cambridge: Cambridge University Press, 1993), as well as for *The Lebanese in the World: A Century of Emigration*, with Nadim Shehadeh (London: St. Martin's Press, 1992).

Kamal Salibi's classic *A Modern History of Lebanon* (London: Weidenfeld and Nicholson, 1965), and *A House of Many Mansions* (London: IB Tauris, 1988) were important in guiding me through the history of nineteenth-century Lebanon, and specifically the mission movement in it. A B L Tibawi's classic *American Interests in Syria, 1800–1901: A Study of Educational, Literary, and Religious Work* (Oxford: Clarendon Press,

400 Selected Bibliography

1966) and *British Interests in Palestine 1800–1901: A Study of Religious and Educational Enterprise* (Oxford: Oxford University Press, 1961) were important to my understanding of the mission complex.

Ussama Makdisi's book *The Culture of Sectarianism: Community, History, and Violence in Nineteenth Century Ottoman Lebanon* (Berkeley: University of California Press, 2000) was invaluable. Also in that context, Leila Tarazi Fawaz's *Merchants and Migrants in Nineteenth Century Beirut* (Cambridge: Harvard University Press, 1983) and Marwan Buheiry's 'The Rise of the City of Beirut' in *The Formation and Perception of the Modern Arab World: Studies by Marwan T Buheiry*, Lawrence I Conrad, ed. (Princeton: The Darwin Press, 1989) were most helpful. Leila Ahmed's *Women and Gender in Islam: Historical Roots of a Modern Debate* (New Haven: Yale University Press, 1992) was especially interesting in its discussion of nineteenth-century Egypt.

Of the many American missionary sources that I turned to I shall mention only those I directly used in my book. These include the journals *The Missionary Review of the World* and *The Missionary Herald* over the decades covered in my book; *The Reminiscences of Daniel Bliss, Edited and Supplemented by His Eldest Son* (New York: Fleming H Revell Co., 1920); the two volumes of Henry Harris Jessup's *Fifty-Three Years in Syria* (New York: Fleming H Revell Co., 1910); Arthur Judson Brown's *The Why and How of Foreign Missions*, Revised Edition (New York: The Board of Foreign Missions and the Women's Board of Foreign Missions, 1921).

The primary source of information on Mrs Bowen Thompson and the British Syrian schools was *Daughters of Syria: A Narrative of Efforts by the Late Mrs Bowen Thompson for the Evangelization of the Syrian Females*, ed. Rev. H B Tristram, MA, LLD, FRS, Master of Greatham Hospital and Hon. Canon of Durham. (London: Seeley, Jackson and Halliday, 1872). The book includes the biographical sketch of Mrs Bowen Thompson by her sister Suzette Smith, as well as letters and other pieces written by its subject. Another extremely important source was *The Missing Link Magazine, or Bible Work at Home and Abroad*, volumes I through IV, 1865–70, which include letters from Mrs Bowen Thompson, her obituary and much interesting information on 'the Bible Women'.

Other sources include Frances E Scott's *Dare and Persevere: the story of one hundred years of evangelism in Syria and Lebanon, from 1860 to 1960* (sic: no capitals) (London: Lebanon Evangelical Mission, 1960), and *The Autobiography of Theophilus Waldemeier* (London: The Friends Bookshop, 1925).The biography of Jane Digby to which I refer in Chapter 10 is *A Scandalous Life: the Biography of Jane Digby el Mezrab* by Mary S Lovell (London: Fourth Estate, 1995). Pat Jalland's *Women, Marriage and Politics*

1860–1914 (Oxford: Clarendon Press, 1986), and Mary Lyndon Shanley's *Feminism, Marriage and the Law in Victorian England* (Princeton: Princeton University Press, 1989) were particularly helpful on English law governing women. Mary Poovey's *Uneven Developments: The Ideological Work of Gender in Mid-Victorian England* (Chicago: University of Chicago Press, 1988), Sarah M Evans's *Born for Liberty: A History of Women in America* (Free Press Paperbacks, 1997) and Catherine Clinton's *The Other Civil War: American Women in the Nineteenth Century*, revised edition (New York: Hill and Wang, 1999) also taught me a great deal.

Of the local sources related to the missions, Anis Khoury al-Makdisi's memoirs *ma' alzamaan*, ed. Youssef Khoury and Youssef Ibish (Beirut, n.d.) and Abraham Rihbany's *A Far Journey* (Boston: Houghton Mifflin, 1914) were most useful. On educational matters, I used A B L Tibawi's *Islamic Education* (London: Luzac and Co. Ltd., 1972) and especially his fascinating book *Arabic Education in British Mandate Palestine: A Study of Three Decades of British Administration* (London: Luzac and Co., 1956). The Makassed Islamic and Philanthropic Association in Beirut's First Annual Report was translated into English and entitled *The True Dawn* (Beirut: Thamarat al-Funun Press, 1297 AH [1880 AD]). My account of the history of the AJC is based largely on Daniel Roberts' unpublished 'The Beirut College for Women: A Short History', written in Beirut in 1958.

The chapter entitled 'Alternative Paths' was based largely on the above-mentioned books and journals as well as, more specifically, the memoirs of Huda Shaarawi (d. August, 1947), *muthakarat ra'idat almar'a al-arabiya alhaditha huda shaarawi* (Cairo: Dar al-Hilal, 1981) and Anbara Salam al-Khalidy's *jawlat fi althikrayat bayn lubnan wa filistin* (Beirut: Dar an-Nahar Lilnashr, 1978). Julia Tohmeh Dimechkieh's journal *al-mar'a al-jadida* (The New Woman), published between 1922–6, as well as Nazira Zein al-Din's *al-sufur wa'l hijab,* originally published in Beirut in 1929 (Damascus: al-Mada Press, 1998) were among the many Arab feminist works written before and during the 1920s that I read. Hala Dimechkieh 's study *julia tu'meh dimashqiyyi,* 1883–1954 (MA thesis: American University of Beirut, 1998) was particularly useful in setting out the parameters of her subject's life, times and works.

My own work and that of others, in the papers presented at a conference on Arab women in the 1920s held in Beirut in 2001, was also important for the formation of many of the ideas that lie behind my book. (See the conference papers as published in *al-nisa' al-'arabiyat fi al-'ishrinat: hudouran wa hawiyya* (Beirut: Tajamu' al-Bahithat Allubnaniyat, 2002). References to clothes, architecture, customs, and manners (particularly in the chapter on Hums) were culled from the general histories and especially from the many illustrated books and pictures – including photographs, paintings, etchings, etc – of nineteenth-century Syria, as well as my own observations of present-day rural and urban areas, and from many discussions with older people, especially those in remote areas where ancient habits live on.

More specific references are derived mostly from the following sources:

A series of letters sent by the French Jesuit priest, Père François Badour, from Beirut to his colleague in France, Père Louis Allard, from 1852–55, in *Une histoire du Liban a travers les archives des jesuites, 1846–1862*, Sami Khuri, s.j. ed. (Beirut: Dar al-Machreq, 1991, pp. 347–68);

Anis Frayha, *al-qaryya allubnaniyya: hadara fi tariq al zawwal* (The Lebanese Village: A Civilization on the Road to Oblivion) (Tripoli: Jroos Press, 1957);

Shelagh Weir, *Palestinian Costume* (London: The British Museum Press, 1989);

Vittoria Alliata, *Le case del paradiso* (Milan: Arnoldo Mondadori, 1983);

Mary Eliza Rogers, *Domestic Life in Palestine*, first published in 1862, (London: Kegan Paul International, 1989);

Nada Sehnaoui, *L'occidentilasition de la vie quotidienne à Beyrouth, 1860–1914* (Beyrouth: Editions Dar an-Nahar, 2002);

Mémoire de soie: Costumes et parures de Palestine et de Jordanie: Catalogue de la collection Widad Kamel Kawar presentee à l'Institut du Monde Arabe, Paris. (Paris: Institut du Monde Arabe, 1988);

Friedrich Ragette, *Architecture in Lebanon: The Lebanese House During the 18th and 19th Centuries* (Delmar, New York: Caravan Books, 1980);

Michel Fani, *Liban: L'Atelier photographique de Ghazir 1880–1914* (Beyrouth, Editions de l'Escalier, 1995);

L'Atelier de Beyrouth: Liban 1848–1914 (Beyrouth, Editions de l'Escalier, 1996);

Brigid Keenan, *Damascus: Hidden Treasures of the Old City* (London: Thames and Hudson, 2000).

About World War I, and specifically Palestine, the following books by Bayan Nuwayhed al-Hout were most useful: *filstin, al-qadiya, al-shaab, al-hadara* (Beirut: Mu'assassat al-Dirassat al-Filistaniyah, 1981) and *al-qiyadat w'al-mo'assassa al-siyassiya fi filistin, 1917–1948* (Beirut: Dar al-

Istiqlal Lildirasat wal Nashr,1991); likewise, Elise G Young's *Keepers of the History: Women and the Israeli-Palestinian Conflict* (New York: Teachers College Press, Columbia University, 1992) was especially helpful about the British mandate authority's attitude towards women's education. Of course, all Edward W Said's work on Palestine forms an important part of the background.

A lecture by Professor Nicolas Ziadeh on his memories of World War I and its aftermath in Palestine at a conference in the German Orient Institute in Beirut, March, 2001, was most useful in providing details of everyday life. Also especially useful for my purposes in this book was the International Conference on Arab Provincial Capitals in the Late Ottoman Empire, organized by the Beirut Orient Institute in cooperation with the Center for Behavioral Research at the American University of Beirut in April and May, 1999. The paper given by Friederike Stolleis entitled 'Women and Public Space in Late Ottoman Damascus' was most important.

Women's memories of the events in Palestine leading up to the 1948 war in general, and of Jerusalem specifically, are included especially in Hala Sakakini's *Jerusalem and I: A Personal Record*, 2nd printing (Jordan: Economic Press Co., 1990), and Serene Husseini Shahid's *Jerusalem Memories* (Beirut: Naufal Press, 2000). More general are the memoirs of Fadwa Touqan, *al-rihlat al-asaab: sira thatia* (Amman: Dar al-Shourouq Lil Nashr Wa al-Tawzee', 1988) and Fadwa Touqan's *rihlat jabaliyya, rihla saaba: sira thatiyyah*, 3rd printing (Amman: Dar al-Shourouq Lil Nashr Wa al-Tawzee' 1993).

The following women's memoirs were also useful: Wadad Makdisi Cortas's *thikrayat: 1917–1977* (Beirut: Mu'assat al-Abhath al-'Arabiyyat, 1982) and Sharifa Musbah Haidar's memoir *Arabesques* (London: Hutchinson and Co., 1944), from which I quoted the wonderful story of the princess's birth in Istanbul and the part played by the old Circassian slave with her broomstick. Much of the information on childbirth came from the various interviews mentioned in my acknowledgments at the front of this book.

Unpublished Sources

George Sabra, 'The Badr Story', Beirut, 2002.

Untitled memoirs written by my mother and her two surviving brothers, Alif and Emil Bishuti.

The last letters written by my grandfather Shukri Musa to his son, Munir

Musa, when the latter was studying medicine in the United States, 1928.

Letters exchanged between my parents during their engagement, Autumn 1932.

My grandmother's and mother's school records from the Syrian Training College, the American School for Girls, and the American Junior College, respectively.

Pamphlets of the American Girls' College, Cairo, including one on the founding of the school (now Ramses College) and a memorial issue of the school magazine, *Cartouche*, dedicated to Auntie Melia, Emelia Badr (1954)

Daniel Roberts's *The Beirut College for Women: A Short History*, written in Beirut in 1958.

Letters written by my mother from Beirut between 1966 and 1983 and addressed mostly to her children.

Interviews with Asma Hishmeh, Huda Butros, Shafika Nasrallah, the late Rafika Mikati, Salma Makdisi, Saada Bishuti, Kamal Kaawar and others.